THE OXFORD AUTHORS

JOHN CLARE

EDITED BY
ERIC ROBINSON
AND
DAVID POWELL

Oxford   New York
OXFORD UNIVERSITY PRESS
1984

Oxford University Press, Walton Street, Oxford OX2 6DP

London Glasgow New York Toronto
Delhi Bombay Calcutta Madras Karachi
Kuala Lumpur Singapore Hong Kong Tokyo
Nairobi Dar es Salaam Cape Town
Melbourne Auckland

and associated companies in
Beirut Berlin Ibadan Mexico City Nicosia

Oxford is a trade mark of Oxford University Press

British Library Cataloguing in Publication Data

Clare, John, 1793–1864
John Clare.—(The Oxford authors)
I. Title   II. Robinson, Eric, 1924–
III. Powell, David
828'.709   PR4453.C6
ISBN 0–19–254191–9
ISBN 0–19–281395–1 Pbk

Library of Congress Cataloging in Publication Data

Clare, John, 1793–1864.
John Clare.
(The Oxford authors)
Bibliography: p.
Includes index.
I. Robinson, Eric, 1924–   . II. Powell, David,
librarian. III. Title.
PR4453.C6A6 1984   821'.7   83–13382
ISBN 0–19–254191–9
ISBN 0–19–281395–1 (pbk.)

Set by Eta Services (Typesetters) Ltd.
Printed in Great Britain
by Thomson Litho Ltd,
East Kilbride, Scotland

THE OXFORD AUTHORS

General Editor: Frank Kermode

JOHN CLARE (1793–1864), an agricultural labourer, rose to fame as the Northamptonshire Peasant Poet in 1820 with the publication of his *Poems Descriptive of Rural Life and Scenery*. Despite the success of this work and the subsequent publication of three more volumes of verse, he fell into want and neglect. Suffering from mental illness he entered an asylum in Epping Forest as a voluntary patient. Four years later he walked away from this place to his home at Northborough, but in 1841 he was committed to Northampton General Lunatic Asylum, where he ended his days.

Throughout most of his life he wrote voluminously—remarkable observations of the natural life of the Soke of Peterborough, love songs and lyrical poems of the greatest delicacy, ribald satire and ballads. He was also one of the earliest and best recorders of English folk-traditions.

ERIC ROBINSON is Professor of History at the University of Massachusetts, Boston. Since publishing Clare's *The Shepherd's Calendar* with Geoffrey Summerfield in 1964, he has edited *John Clare's Birds* (1982), *John Clare's Autobiographical Writings* (1983) and other selections of Clare's writings. He and his associate editor, David Powell, are at work on the Oxford English Texts *Clare* (*The Later Poems of John Clare*, Vols. I and II, 1984).

DAVID POWELL is Senior Librarian at Nene College, Northampton. He has written the Northampton Public Library catalogue of Clare manuscripts and edited a selection of Clare's poems entitled *The Wood is Sweet*.

CONTENTS

Introduction   XV

Chronology   xxvii

Note on the Text   xxx

POETRY

Poems of the Helpston Period, c.1812 1831

Helpstone   1
The Setting Sun   6
Evening ('Now grey ey'd hazy eve's begun')   6
The Gipsies Evening Blaze   9
Epigram   9
To a Rose Bud in Humble Life   10
A Scene   11
To a Winter Scene   11
The Harvest Morning   12
[Summer Evening]   14
A Maiden-haid   18
The Lamentations of Round-Oak Waters   18
Noon ('All how silent and how still,')   24
What is Life?   26
[Summer]   27
Proposals for Building a Cottage   27
[A Copse in Winter]   28
Ballad ('Winter winds cold and blea')   29
Langley Bush   30
Evening Bells   31
The Woodman ('The beating snow clad bell wi sounding
    dead')   32
Childish Recollections   38
Ballad ('I love thee sweet mary but love thee in fear')   40
Recollections after an Evening Walk   41
To my Cottage   43
Second Adress to the Rose Bud in Humble Life   43
Written in November   44
[On Taste]   45

Poems of the Helpston Period (*cont*):

[Summer Morning]   45
[Joys of Youth]   46
Song ('Swamps of wild rush beds and sloughs squashy
    traces')   46
Song ('And wheres there a scene more delightfully seeming')   47
Song ('One gloomy eve I roamd about')   47
The Gipseys Camp   48
from The Village Minstrel   49
Reccolections after a Ramble   52
My Mary   59
Helpston Green   62
The Meeting   64
[Noon]   65
To the Winds   65
[Patty]   66
Rural Morning   66
Rural Evening   70
Rustic Fishing   74
Sunday Walks   76
The Fate of Genius   80
Winter ('From huddling nights embrace how chill')   83
Ballad ('Where the dark ivy the thorn tree is mounting')   91
To the Rural Muse ('Simple enchantress, wreathd in
    summer blooms')   92
The Last of March   93
Winter ('The small wind wispers thro the leafless hedge')   96
To a Fallen Elm   96
from The Parish   98
Sudden Shower   102
Home Pictures in May   102
The Wheat Ripening   103
Careless Rambles   103
To the Rural Muse ('Muse of the Fields oft have I said
    farewell')   104
[Bloomfield I]   108
[Bloomfield II]   108
[Woodland Thoughts]   109
Impulses of Spring   109
The Old Willow   113
from Childhood ('The past it is a magic word')   113

Sport in the Meadows   120
Wild Bees   121
Songs Eternity   122
Summer Images   124
November ('Sybil of months and worshiper of winds') 130
The Lady Flye   130
Autumn ('Autumn comes laden with her ripened load') 131
Nutting   131
The Woodman ('Now evening comes and from the new laid
   hedge')   132
Hay Making   132
The Cottager   133
The Shepherd's Calendar: June   135
The Shepherd's Calendar: November   139
The Heath   145
[Winter in the Fens]   146
[The Lament of Swordy Well]   147
The Progress of Ryhme   153
Autumn ('Syren of sullen moods and fading hues')   161
The Eternity of Nature   165
The Mores   167
Pleasant Places   169
Shadows of Taste   170
St Martins Eve   174
To P * * * *   180
Emmonsales Heath   181
The Summer Shower   183
Love and Memory   187
Insects   189
Sabbath Bells   190
Peggy Band   191
An Idle Hour   193
The Flood   193
Labours Leisure   194
Mist in the Meadows   195
Signs of Winter   195
Angling   196
Winter Fields   198
Winter Evening   199
Snow Storm   199
[Showers]   200

Poems of the Helpston Period (cont):
The Meadow Grass	200
The Pasture	203

Bird Poems
To the Snipe	205
Birds Nests ('How fresh the air the birds how busy now')	207
Sand Martin	208
On Seeing Two Swallows Late in October	208
The Fern Owls Nest	209
The March Nightingale	210
The Thrushes Nest	210
The Wren	211
The Happy Bird	211
Emmonsails Heath in Winter	212
The Firetails Nest	212
The Wrynecks Nest	213
The Nightingales Nest	213
The Sky Lark	215
The Sky Lark Leaving Her Nest	216
The Ravens Nest	218
The Moorehens Nest	219
Sedge Birds Nest	221
[Crows in Spring]	222
The Robins Nest	223
The Autumn Robin	225
The Pettichaps Nest	229
The Yellowhammers Nest	230
The Yellow Wagtails Nest	231
Partridge Coveys	232
The Blackcap	232
Hedge Sparrow	233
The Landrail	233
The Reed Bird	235
The Woodlarks Nest	235
Field Cricket	236
['And often from the rustling sound']	237
[The Fens]	238
['And yonder by the circling stack']	241
['High overhead that silent throne']	241
[Autumn Evening]	241

[Birds in Alarm]   242
['In the hedge I pass a little nest']   242

Animal Poems
Hares at Play   244
[The Marten]   244
[The Fox]   245
[The Badger]   246
[The Hedgehog]   248
[The Vixen]   248

Poems of the Northborough Period, 1832–1837
The Flitting   250
Decay A Ballad   256
Remembrances   258
['Ive ran the furlongs to thy door']   261
['The hoar frost lodges on every tree']   262
[The Mouse's Nest]   263
[Sheep in Winter]   263
['The seeding done the fields are still at morn']   263
[Wild Bees' Nest]   264
[Storm in the Fens]   264
[The Fen]   265
[Autumn Morning]   266
[November]   266
[Autumn Birds]   267
[Farmer's Boy]   267
['With hook tucked neath his arm that now and then']   267
[The Squirrel's Nest]   268
[Quail's Nest]   268
[Morris Dancers]   269
['A hugh old tree all wasted to a shell']   269
[Stone Pit]   270
[Wild Duck's Nest]   270
['The schoolboys in the morning soon as drest']   271
[The Green Woodpecker's Nest]   271
[Woodpecker's Nest]   272
[The Puddock's Nest]   272
[The Groundlark]   273
[Turkeys]   273
[Rook's Nest]   274

Poems of the Northborough Period (cont):

['The old pond full of flags and fenced around']   275
[Dyke Side]   275
[The Partridge]   276
[The Crane's Nest]   276
[The Nuthatch]   276
[The Partridge's Nest]   277

Poems written in Epping Forest and Northampton Asylum,
1837–1864

The Water Lilies   278
The Gipsy Camp   278
Child Harold   279
Don Juan A Poem   318
['Tis martinmass from rig to rig']   326
['Lord hear my prayer when trouble glooms']   327
Spring ('The sweet spring now is come'ng')   328
Song Last Day   330
['The red bagged bee on never weary wing']   331
['Summer is on the earth and in the sky']   331
Song ('The bird cherrys white in the dews o' the morning')   332
['The thunder mutters louder and more loud']   333
['Look through the naked bramble and black thorn']   334
['I love the little pond to mark at spring']   334
Spring ('Pale sun beams gleam')   334
['The wind blows happily on every thing']   335
['God looks on nature with a glorious eye']   336
['I'll come to thee at even tide']   336
['Spring comes and it is may—white as are sheets']   337
Song ('O Love is so decieving')   338
Love's Pains   338
Haymaking   339
Song: O wert thou in the storm   340
Mary   341
To Mary   342
A Vision   343
The Droneing Bee   343
To the Lark   344
Sonnet ('Enough of misery keeps my heart alive')   345
A Lament   346
Song ('A seaboy on the giddy mast')   347

CONTENTS   xi

Song ('The daiseys golden eye')   347
Autumn ('The autumn day it fades away,')   348
Sonnet ('The flag top quivers in the breeze,')   349
Out of Door Pleasures   349
An Invite to Eternity   351
Sonnet ('The silver mist more lowly swims')   352
Morning   352
Wild Flowers   353
The Invitation   354
Sonnet: The Nightingale   355
Spring ('How beautiful is Spring! the sun gleams gold,') 356
Ballad ('We'll walk among the tedded hay,')   357
Evening ('It is the silent hour when they who roam,') 358
Stanzas   359
'I Am'   361
Sonnet: 'I Am'   361
Sleep of Spring   362
Song ('Love lives beyond')   363
Some Days Before the Spring   364
The Blackbird   365
My Early Home was This   366
Hesperus   367
The Round Oak   367
Twilight   368
Song ('I fly from all I prize the most')   370
Larks and Spring   371
The Autumn Wind   372
Song ('I would not be a wither'd leaf')   374
The Winters Spring   374
Sonnet: Wood Anemonie   375
Sonnet: The Crow   376
Silent Love   376
Loves Story   377
['I love thee nature with a boundless love']   378
['How hot the sun rushes']   379
Song ('Tis evening the sky is one broad dim of gray') 380
Song ('The rain is come in misty showers')   381
Sonnet ('How beautiful the white thorn shews its leaves') 382
Autumn ('I love the fitfull gusts that shakes')   382
Evening ('How beautiful the eve comes in')   383
Song ('The autumns come again')   385

Poems written in Epping Forest and Northampton Asylum (cont):

Recolections of Home	386
Boys and Spring	387
The Bean Field	388
Spring Wind	388
['There is a charm in Solitude that cheers']	390
The Shepherd Boy	390
['Swift goes the sooty swallow o'er the heath']	391
Clock a Clay	391
The Wind	392
Song ('I went my Sunday mornings rounds')	393
Childhood ('O dear to us ever the scenes of our childhood')	394
['O could I be as I have been']	396
Clifford Hill	397
First Love	398
The Humble Bee	399
Little Trotty Wagtail	401
The Swallow	401
The Gardeners Bonny Daughter	402
The Red Robin	403
The Ladybird	404
The Corn Craiks Rispy Song	404
Autumn ('The thistle down's flying Though the winds are all still')	405
The Peartree Lane	405
The Crow Sat on the Willow	406
In Green Grassy Places	408
The Peasant Poet	408
Lines on 'Cowper'	409
['The Even comes and the Crow flies low']	410
['Know God is every where']	410
Song ('I hid my love when young while I')	411
Song ('I wish I was where I would be')	411
Song ('She tied up her few things')	412
Song ('I peeled bits o straws and I got switches too')	413
['The dew drops on every blade of grass']	413
The Winters Come	414
Birds: Why are ye Silent?	415
The Yellowhammer	417
Primroses	417
Meet Me in the Green Glen	418

Perplexities 419
Spring ('In every step we tread appears fresh spring') 419
The Rawk o'the Autumn 421
Woman had we Never Met 421
Written in Prison 422
The Maple Tree 423
The Chiming Bells 423
Mary Helen from the Hill 424
Born upon an Angels Breast 425
Flow on Winding River 426
Fragment 427
To John Clare 427
Birds Nests ('Tis Spring warm glows the South') 427

PROSE

[Autobiographical Passages] 429
[Journey out of Essex] 432
[The Farmer and the Vicar] 438
[Apology for the Poor] 445
['If the nessesitys of the poor'] 447
['Every farmer is growing into an orator'] 448
['I never meddle with politics'] 448
['I say what good has been yet done'] 449
['long speeches'] 449
['These out of place patriots'] 449
['. . . I fear these tory radicals'] 450
[The Poor Man *Versus* the Rich Man] 450
[Nature Notes] 452
[Letter to Messrs Taylor and Hessey, I] 453
['I went to take my walk to day'] 455
[Letter to Messrs Taylor and Hessey, II] 457
['It has been often asserted that young frogs'] 459
['Blackbirds and Thrushes'] 460
['Swallows'] 460
['The country people here distinguish'] 460
['When Woodpeckers are making or boring'] 461
['When the young of the Nightingale'] 461
['I have often been amused with the manners'] 462
[Signs of Spring] 463
[More Signs of Spring] 465
[Letter to Messrs Taylor and Hessey, III] 467

Prose (cont):
　['The little Robin']   469
　[Letter to Messrs Taylor and Hessey, IV]   471
　['I took a walk']   474
　[Hunting Pooty Shells]   477
　[Taste]   479
　[Grammar]   481
　[Life Peerages]   482
　[Knowledge]   482
　[Letter to William Hone]   483

Notes   488

Further Reading   505

Glossary   506

Index of Titles and First Lines   517

INTRODUCTION

CLARE'S place in the tradition of English literature cannot be established by simple chronology or solely by reference to the leading writers of his age, though he was born just one year later than Shelley and lived until a year before Yeats was born. Since Clare continued to write from his adolescence until a few years before his death, he belongs chronologically to the age of Blake, Bloomfield, Scott, Crabbe, Coleridge, Byron, Shelley, Keats, and Wordsworth, but his poetical heritage derives, in his early poems, most firmly from James Thomson, Isaac Watts, and William Cowper, and in his maturity from that great body of English and Scottish folk-song which, because of its constant recreation and its intermingling both with the literary ballad and with Victorian vaudeville, can have no particular age or date ascribed to it. In his choice of models he was often eclectic, either harking back to Marvell and Davenant in the seventeenth century or sounding sometimes like a rustic Byron, or, occasionally, dropping into the accents of a tavern balladeer. Yet, in all his writing, he achieves a voice that is unmistakably his own. A song by Clare, published under an assumed name in a Victorian miscellany, cannot be confused with any other writer's work; and, in looking at many pieces which because of their subject-matter, place of publication, or anonymity of authorship might conceivably be Clare's, one seldom hesitates for more than a few seconds before setting them aside. As with all writers of the first rank, Clare's is a unique voice.

He was born in 1793 in the village of Helpston, then in Northamptonshire, to a thresher, Parker Clare, and his illiterate wife, Ann, who came from the neighbouring village of Castor. His twin sister died soon after her birth and may have been buried surreptitiously at night. The village was small and poor, little more than a single, dirty street of cottages, though it boasted taverns and a church. Much of its life was lived under the patronage of the Fitzwilliam family which resided at its great house, Milton, near by, and for Helpston the twin centres of all commerce and civilization were Stamford and Peterborough. To the north-east, far beyond the villager's perspective, Boston Stump towered above the wind-swept and often flooded Fens; even further away, to the south, at the end of the high road, along which sometimes passed great droves of Scottish cattle, destined to feed the hungry masses of Cockneys, was that great

focus of sin and splendour, the city of London. A man travelled as far
as his own feet or a farm-wagon could take him, confident that
however early he rose he would be asleep in his own bed not long after
sunset. At the horizon's edge the world ended. A great traveller might
have visited London: a great scholar might have been educated at
Cambridge, only a few miles across the marshes. But everything
necessary for survival was near at hand: fields to plough, and
commons for pasture, dykes and ponds in which to fish or shoot
wildfowl, and village fairs for young and old to take part in an
occasional junketing.

Religion was handed down by the village parson or the itinerant
Methodist preacher, and justice was dispensed, often contemptuously,
by the local magistrate. Medicine was the province of the elderly
goodwife or the travelling quack. Books were few and education was
got at the knee of some old dame or under the stern eye of the village
schoolmaster, during the dull parts of the agricultural year. People's
amusement was made by them and not for them. The festivals,
religious and pagan, were assiduously kept, the morris-dancers fooled
and sang in the street and their cavortings were not yet totally
divorced from the fertility rituals of prehistoric times; birth,
copulation, and death were all surrounded by their ceremonial; and
people swapped yarns or sang songs to preserve their common values
and to adorn their short and weary lives. Helpston was undoubtedly
off the highway and behind the times, and John Clare thanked God
for it:

> Me not the noise of brawling pleasures cheer
> In nightly revels or in city streets
> But joys which sooth and not distract mine ear
> That one at leisure meets
> In the green woods and meadows summer shorn
> Or fields where bee flye greets
> Ones ear with mellow horn
>
> ('Summer Images')

Yet all was not well. If the village was small, it was also small-
minded. It resented the early success of a boy whom it had judged to
be little more than a simpleton and used gossip to destroy his
equanimity: he drank too much, he wenched too much, he consorted
with gypsies, and perhaps he was a poacher, but above all he was
getting 'above his station', particularly after the publication of *Poems
Descriptive of Rural Life and Scenery* in 1820. As he said:

> I hate the very name of troublous man
> Who did and does me all the harm he can

and

> Goosey goosey gander
> Where would you wander
> Up the fen and down the fen
> To cackle and to slander

His breach with his childhood sweetheart, Mary Joyce, was probably the result of her father's snobbery, his subsequent marriage to Martha Turner was hastened by her pregnancy; and before visiting London he bought himself a new *green* suit. If he was not being criticized by his neighbours, he was receiving the unwelcome visits of ignorant sightseers or being summoned from his work in the fields to wait upon the presumptuous wife of a high-handed magistrate. His hob-nailed boots rattled on the polished wooden floors of the local 'big house', but no farmer would give him a steady job. He was both part and not part of his native village, though he never, to the end of his days, forgot one of his neighbours and brought undying fame to them all.

Moreover, customs and habits, even in that small village, were changing. The parson no longer lived in a cottage little better than that owned by his parishioners but moved into a big rectory, consorted with the gentry, and rode to hounds. Farmers gave up their pewter and drinking horns to eat off Wedgwood's Queensware and drink from glasses. Valentine's Day and May Day rituals were considered vulgar and were preached against by middle-class Evangelicalism which would deny every countryman both his ale and his wench. The commercial spirit was stronger than ever before and was symbolized, above all, by—Enclosure. Clare's nostalgic picture of good fellowship and harvest revelry in his essay on Farmer Thrifty and the Vicar may have some exaggeration in it, but his observations of rural tyranny in 'The Parish' were first-hand and undeniable. He witnessed the fluctuations of agricultural prosperity in the post-Napoleonic years, the increasing severity of the poorhouses (even before the Poor Law Amendment Act), and the dubious advantages for the rural poor of the Corn Laws. He saw reductions in the malt tax go into the brewer's pocket rather than down the poor man's gullet and he observed the tithe commuted into a larger farm for the parson. But, more than that, he saw venerable trees cut down, whole coppices destroyed, and the streams diverted from their natural courses. The commons were fenced off and 'No Trespassing' notices posted, old women were forbidden to gather sticks from the hedges, and labourers were transported for taking a hare for the pot. A man could not even whistle a tune or rest under a tree without being taken for a poacher. No longer could a man labour in the day and be sure of sleeping with his wife at night, for he might be away from home, planting hedges round the enclosures and making his bed in the fields. Clare sees the poor man beset on all sides by dishonesty and deceit:

> Churchwardens Constables and Overseers
> Makes up the round of Commons and of Peers
> With learning just enough to sign a name
> And skill sufficient parish rates to frame
> And cunning deep enough the poor to cheat . . .
>
> ('The Parish')

Thus, Clare's poetry, though composed in an isolated village, reflects the changing temper of the times much more accurately than Wordsworth's ever did, because Clare felt enclosure in his bones. Moreover, Clare's sympathies were always with the outcast and the persecuted—the gypsy, the poacher, Robin Hood and his outlaws, the runaway apprentice, the old woman taken for a witch, the pauper with his household goods branded, the fox or the hare pursued by the hounds, the wild duck shot by the hunter, the badger savaged by dogs, the sparrow pelted by boys, the negro begging in the streets of London, or the poet thrown in the madhouse. Whatever lives, for Clare lives equally. It was Mary Joyce's compassion for weak and defenceless things that earned Clare's love and preserved her in his memory.

Clare's subject-matter in his earliest poems reflects these concerns. Some of the poems are sentimental—'On a Lost Greyhound', 'The Fate of Amy', and 'The Village Funeral'—as well as being expressed in an idiom that was already dated when they were written, so that we have not given space to them here. Not a great deal is lost, however, because later poems like 'The Badger', 'The Marten', and 'The Cottager' treat similar themes with much greater boldness and assurance. When Clare learns how to let the occasion speak for itself instead of preaching about it, his poems gain in strength. Some of his first poems, like 'Helpstone' and 'The Lamentations of Round-Oak Waters', however, reveal how from the first he realized that his strength was in expressing his own experience in his own setting.

Though much of their idiom derives from Thomson, Cowper, and
Goldsmith, yet the experience of these poems is Clare's and only Clare
could have expressed it for us. It is not surprising therefore that
Clare's first volume went into four editions and that he received so
much acclaim by the critics, even though his Evangelical patron, Lord
Radstock, was put out by Clare's occasional vulgarity and by his
criticism of his betters. The poet's promise is unmistakable in 'The
Harvest Morning', 'Noon', 'What is Life?', and several other poems.
There is a sharpness of observation and freshness of feeling that
introduce a new note into English poetry.

Unfortunately for Clare, he was typecast from the first. His
publisher, John Taylor, had earlier been involved with the successful
publication of Robert Bloomfield, another rural poet, and was
convinced that he had now acquired a Robert Bloomfield of his very
own. At the same time, in the face of a dwindling public for poetry and
a growing market for works of instruction, practical and spiritual,
Taylor was anxious to respond to the growing taste for sentiment and
philosophical musing. As Mr Chilcott has written:

In several obvious ways, Taylor's position as a publisher often revealed
similar objectives to the Reviews. Like them, he was concerned to establish a
firm relationship between writers and the reading public. Like them too, he
looked towards 'the public mind' to discover its interests and general
movement.[1]

Clare was therefore subjected to a good deal of advice from Taylor, as
well as from his patrons, Lord Radstock and Mrs Emmerson, just
at a time when he was struggling to find his own voice and to free
himself from the idiom of the past and the expectations of the present.
Nevertheless, despite advice from Taylor to 'raise his views' and
'speak of the Appearances of Nature each Month more philo-
sophically' and from Mrs Emmerson to prove himself 'capable of
higher subjects than talking of Birds and flowers', Clare increasingly
went his own way, testing his poetry on the ears of his parents and his
tried friends, handling the subjects about which they and he felt
deeply, and drawing strength from his local idiom.

A study of his sonnets, for example, except for a short period when
he pandered to the editors of the annuals, the *Keepsakes*, the
Friendship's Offerings, etc., shows him moving fairly steadily away

[1] T. Chilcott, *A Publisher and his Circle: The life and work of John Taylor, Keats's
publisher* (1972), 78.

from conventional sonnets 'On Death' or 'To an Hour-Glass' to immediate evocations of Nature, such as 'Sudden Shower' or 'Home Pictures in May', to triumph ultimately in the certainty of 'Mist in the Meadows' or 'Winter Evening'. It cannot be said that Clare never falters. His output was immense and he had his backslidings, but an increasingly personal and characteristic voice emerges in *The Shepherd's Calendar* (1827), *The Rural Muse* (1835), and, of course, in *The Midsummer Cushion*, which was not published until 1979 by Anne Tibble and R. K. R. Thornton. The collected poems of John Clare which the present editors have in preparation will show that growth in maturity even more clearly. The scope of Clare's poetry also grew with the years. Far from being confined to lyrics and songs, though these always represented some of his best work, he attempted odes such as 'Summer Images' and 'To the Snipe', satire in 'The Parish', prose letters on natural history, somewhat in the mode of White of Selborne, georgics in the descriptive poems of *The Shepherd's Calendar*, and many superb poems about birds growing out of his precise knowledge of Northamptonshire birds and their habitat.[2] After the onset of severe mental illness in 1837, he made his last protracted effort to write a long poem of Spenserian stanzas, intermixed with songs, which would depict his long struggle for self-realization. Though flawed, 'Child Harold' is by no means a failure.

During the early years of his fame Clare made the acquaintance of several men of letters. At John Taylor's he met, among others, Hazlitt, Coleridge, Lamb, Reynolds, Cary (the translator of Dante), and De Quincey. Such reactions to Clare by these men as remain on the record do not suggest condescension to a *parvenu* but the appreciation of fellow-writers. The comments about Clare by Keats and about Keats by Clare, though critical both ways, show no disrespect on either part but are the observations by one professional writer of another. Clare's criticisms of his contemporaries, as well as of Chaucer, Pope, Cowper, and several earlier writers, show an ability to make reflective estimates unaffected by literary fashions. He appreciated Pope when Pope was in disfavour, read Donne when Donne was largely out of fashion, loved Thomson and Cowper, who happen to be out of favour today (though undeservedly), and deferred to no man in his admiration of Byron and of Burns. More than that, he loved the ancient ballads and the folk-songs of his native heaths, preserving words and music whenever he was able. His contributions

---

[2] See E. Robinson and R. S. Fitter, *John Clare's Birds* (Oxford, 1982).

to ornithology, his observations of insects, flowers, and animals, his recording of customs, music, and dialect, as well as his political and social observations, show him to have been a man of rare insight and (dare one say it?) broad education.

It is with this word 'education' that one comes to the nub of the problem of Clare's literary reputation. Though the preoccupation with his insanity and with his moving life-story has done much to divert attention from his true achievement, reflecting our modern avidity for the sensational, perhaps more harm has been done by the blinkers imposed by modern critics' own education, which has produced in them a reverence for standardized English and a condescension to dialect forms. In much of his work Clare's grammar is the grammar of his speech. Subjects and verbs do not always agree in number; punctuation, after a very early period when he crammed in commas, semi-colons, and periods wherever he could find space, is often missing; spelling is eccentric (and a pitfall to his editors); his vocabulary contains dialect words or slang expressions of the time; and, most disgraceful of all to the state-educated, he is unrepentant. Clare's is not a language in which to write philosophy and his prose is sometimes clumsy when he discusses philosophical or religious ideas, but it is vigorous, full of sensuous imagery, and packed with humour when he describes the people and scenes he knows:

. . . the Vicar was somtimes disposed to be merry and would ramp with the servant wenches in hay time about the Cocks and rarely missed kissing them beneath the missletoe at Christmass which he considered as a nessesary preface to good luck thro the year for like his old neighbour he was a stickler for old customs . . .

Clare's language is not, however, embedded in a provincial ice-age: it grows, adapts, and changes not only with the economic and cultural changes of Helpston but also with the personal growth of the author. No detailed study of Clare's language has yet been undertaken, though it would surely be a rewarding task.[3] John Barrell's examination of the grammatical structure of Clare's poetic language has already proved to be a key to Clare's individuality and to his ability to evoke a *locality*.[4] W. K. Richmond, who also wrote illuminatingly

---

[3] An important start has been made, however, by Barbara M. Strang, 'John Clare's Language', Appendix I to *The Rural Muse: Poems by John Clare, A second edition of Clare's volume of 1835*, ed. R. Thornton (Ashington, 1982).

[4] J. Barrell, *The Idea of Landscape and the Sense of Place 1730–1840: An Approach to the Poetry of John Clare* (Cambridge, 1972), 127–8 *et passim*.

about Clare, reminds us of the communal element in Old English poems:

We should, of course, read them for their own bald vigour, but more can be gained by what we read *into* them, learning by inference something of that greater, popular literature now dissipated in air. That universal singing has long ago been stilled, all its alliterative ecstasies silenced, its emphatic rhythms forgotten (—or at least not consciously remembered). Folk-memory retained some part of it and it will appear later how, in a gradually diminishing way, it survived in the hearts of the peasantry, lingering on until the last years of the nineteenth century.[5]

At its best, Clare's language cannot be divorced from his sense of place, from his part in a tradition, from his *growing* awareness of who he is. That is why to adhere faithfully to his own way of writing is not, as some have suggested, to condescend to him but to respect him, except, paradoxically, that to retain all his redundant punctuation when he was first trying to conform to the educated world or to preserve the proprieties thrust upon him by his publishers and patrons is to misrepresent his intentions, better reflected in his manuscripts.

English life changed more rapidly, even in the countryside, during Clare's lifetime (1793–1864) than at any previous period. At first sight Clare's countryside would appear to have been little affected by the Industrial Revolution. Yet when we think of the enclosure of Clare's village it is clear that changes were taking place, even though the changes were not the devastating ones suggested by left-wing historians. Barrell's argument that Clare is not writing about the effects of enclosure because, in the first place, he is operating within a literary tradition and, secondly, because 'the real subject of *The Parish* is the increasing gap between the large farmers—converting themselves into a middle class, into professional men, literate, preferring plate to pewter—and the agricultural labourers',[6] is simplistic. Enclosure, agricultural prosperity for some and not for others to a comparable extent, social mobility, changing attitudes towards the poor are all part of a complex which Clare experienced and which he did not have to read about. Of course Clare, because he is not a historian, analyses the situation as he sees it and the way in which he sees it is also affected by a literary tradition of rural protest. Like other men writing from within a historical situation, he is not

[5] W. K. Richmond, *Poetry and the People* (1947), 13–14.
[6] Barrell, op. cit. 197.

always consistent, or, at least, he changes his emphasis from time to time. At one time he is informing a middle-class friend of the presence of dubious strangers in his neighbourhood, at another he is demonstrating in a poem his sense of solidarity with Swing rioters; at one moment he is an enthusiast for the Ranters, at another he is denouncing their hypocrisy; at one instant he sounds like a perfect rural Tory, at another he is outraged by the presumption of his social superiors. Yet to deny that much of his poetry reflects upon the social conditions of his time or is valuable source-material for historical study is an extraordinary perversion. The surprising thing is that he seems to have been so little read by social and economic historians. It must be recalled that his is one of the very few voices of the rural poor of his age that may still be heard. From him we can learn what it felt like to be part of the 'awkward squad' in the volunteer army raised against Napoleon, to be oppressed by vicars who were also magistrates, to be told by one's social superiors how one should think and feel, to have one's country rambles blocked by 'No Trespass' signs or to be suspected by gamekeepers, to run away in fear from one's employer and sleep in the fields between jobs. If this is not the stuff of history, what is it?

The starkness of Clare's experience in the early 1830s led to some of the poet's best writing in a series of sonnets and lyrics arising from his flitting to Northborough, where he had been offered a cottage by Lord Fitzwilliam. Critics have marvelled at the sense of devastation felt by Clare in this removal only three or four miles away from his birthplace. Yet even today there is a significant difference of atmosphere between the two places. One can see that the Northborough cottage did not have the same sense of belonging to its village as did the old place next to the Blue Bell tavern. Northborough's rambling rectory, unlike the vicar's cottage in Helpston, was a symbol of nineteenth-century pretension and Clare's new house was closer than his old cottage to the main road between Market Deeping and Peterborough. Clare was further in distance and in status from his old neighbours as he tried to make his way as a smallholder. The changes must have been severe. In the event the experience led to a series of carefully etched vignettes of rural life and rural isolation in which the poet constantly appears as the onlooker, the stranger, the outsider. There is nothing to spare in these poems. The lines are mostly end-stopped, snapshots of a way of life. The tension in these verses is so severe that the string of Clare's life seems about to break; but the result is a series of tiny masterpieces represented here by the poems on pages 250–77. It seems as if Clare is struggling to retain his sanity by writing down each image as it floats into his mind. If only we could give you here the actual scraps of paper, old letters, and sales bills on which he wrote, with their actual texture, but to see them you must visit the museum at Peterborough.

Finally came the breakdown and Clare's admission into Dr Matthew Allen's asylum at High Beach in Epping Forest, a place, as far as we can see, of enlightened humane treatment, though Clare suggests otherwise in his 'Don Juan'. The nature of Clare's illness has never been satisfactorily established. There seem to have been epileptiform incidents in his early life, experiences during his visits to London which suggest a shaky hold upon reality, confusion about his relationship to Mary Joyce, nightmares, some bouts of heavy drinking, and the suggestion, by Clare himself, that he might have been venereally infected. The account of Clare's escape from High Beach is a strange mixture of dream-world, literary reminiscence, and realistic reporting. There are the first recorded signs that Clare is not sure of his own identity. Is he Robinson Crusoe, Gulliver, Queen Victoria's father, or just a battered piece of flotsam? Clare himself is not sure. The two major undertakings of this period are 'Child Harold' and 'Don Juan', names which suggest still another *persona* for Clare, and both poems—but particularly the former—are concerned with Clare's struggle to know who he is.

That in the midst of this breakdown Clare should have been able to write a long poem of the quality of 'Child Harold' is surely an amazing tribute to his determination:

> Fame blazed upon me like a comets glare
> Fame waned and left me like a fallen star
> Because I told the evil what they are
> And truth and falshood never wished to mar
> My Life hath been a wreck—and I've gone far
> For peace and truth—and hope—for home and rest
> —Like Edens gates—fate throws a constant bar—
> Thoughts may o'ertake the sunset in the west
> —Man meets no home within a womans breast

That it ultimately fails to achieve unity reflects Clare's own failure to realize his personal unity. It remains, however, a major effort at self-realization.

The asylum poems, through J. L. Cherry's *Life and Remains of John Clare* (1873) to G. Grigson's *Poems of John Clare's Madness* (1949), have attracted, at least in selection, more than their fair share of attention, not only because of the pathetic circumstances in which they were written but also perhaps because it seemed easier to editors to establish a text for them. In many instances it is not possible to go beyond the transcriptions made by W. F. Knight and others at the asylum. We have included a fairly large selection of them here because several of them have a special intensity not met with elsewhere in Clare's poetry—some of them, such as 'I Am', are familiar and well loved—and because there is a greater variety in them than is always appreciated. Yet there is a sense in which Clare's poetic development was retarded during his asylum years. For example, an undue number of the poems written in imitation Scots dialect do not rise above sentimentality, though it may be that Clare thought of them as songs set to music, so that we are lacking a dimension that may have been in the poet's mind. Nevertheless, there is an impetus born of growth and development in the poetry up to and including 'Child Harold' which seems to have been lost in much of the later poetry. While there are exceptionally fine poems here and there, the general level of inspiration seems lower than in the poems of *The Shepherd's Calendar* period or even those of the Northborough years. Though Clare was given much freedom while he was at Northampton and was allowed to wander along the banks of the River Nene, yet he could be instantly restricted to the asylum if his behaviour did not accord with his doctor's standards of decorum. He was, in fact, a prisoner. He had no home to which he could return and no opportunity to make an independent living. Victorian taste had largely turned against poetry and to the novel. It turned in general not to simplicity but to the exotic and the highly decorated. A high degree of finish and a craving for ornamentation seem to have been demanded both in the fine and the practical arts, while in such poetry as was published—Scott, Tennyson, and Browning—the dramatic sense was highly developed. Clare's quiet voice from the English countryside went unheard. At Clare's death in 1864 Joseph Whitaker was contemplating an edition of his collected poems and Frederick Martin was commissioned to write his biography, but *Whitaker's Almanac* and the *Statesman's Year Book* seemed to be more profitable enterprises than Clare's poetry.

Though there has always been some editor or critic to cherish Clare, it is in the twentieth century that he has come into his own. What would have pleased Clare, however, is not the approval of academics, but the love of his writing shared by so many ordinary readers who have read his poetry and prose for simple pleasure. To that pleasure we hope that this volume will add.

Acknowledgements

Scholars are helpless without librarians—and so we want to thank all the librarians and archivists who worked with us. Authors are often at the mercy of their publishers—ours were very merciful to us. Editors are often obliged to travel widely in search of their materials. They come to appreciate the hospitality and understanding of their friends. Eric Robinson wishes to thank Bruce Bailey, Ian and Donnie Bowman, Sara and Jim Currie, Isabelle and George Deacon, Margie and Basil Mitchell, Anthea and Robert Morton Saner, and Edward Storey. For helpful conversation he also wishes to thank Margaret Grainger and Mark Storey.

David Powell wishes to thank the British Academy and its Small Grants Research Fund in the Humanities, the Leverhulme Trust, and the East Midlands Arts for financial assistance during the preparation of this work. He is also grateful for the help of his wife Margaret, who as always put up with a lot of disruption, and to Mrs Irene Butcher, who willingly typed a large part of the manuscript.

We wish to thank The Carl and Lily Pforzheimer Foundation, Inc. and The Carl H. Pforzheimer Library for permission to print *To the Winds, Autumn* ('Syren of sullen moods and fading hues'), *The Eternity of Nature, The Mores, The Flitting* and four prose pieces, [*Life Peerages*], [*The Poor Man* Versus *the Rich Man*], [*Grammar*], and [*Letter to William Hone*]; The Pierpont Morgan Library for *Rural Morning, Rural Evening, Rustic Fishing, Sunday Walks, The Fate of Genius, Winter* ('From huddling nights embrace how chill'); the Henry W. and Albert A. Berg Collection, The New York Public Library, Astor, Lenox and Tilden Foundations for *Song* ('A seaboy on the giddy mast'), *Song* ('The daiseys golden eye'), *Song* ('The autumns come again').

CHRONOLOGY

1792   Shelley born.

1793   John Clare born at Helpston, 13 July. His twin sister dies.

1794   Blake's *Songs of Experience*. Erasmus Darwin's *Zoönomia*.

1795   Keats born. Speenhamland system of poor relief introduced.

1796   Death of Burns.

1797   Bewick's *History of British Birds*.

1798   Battle of the Nile. *Lyrical Ballads*.

1799   Religious Tract Society founded.

1800   Bloomfield's *The Farmer's Boy*. Death of Cowper. *Preface to Lyrical Ballads*.

1802   Scott's *Minstrelsy of the Scottish Border*. Bloomfield's *Rural Tales*.

1803   Hayley's *Life of Cowper*.

1804   Napoleon proclaimed Emperor.

1805   Clare befriends Mary Joyce at school in Glinton. Cary's translation of Dante's *Inferno*. Battle of Trafalgar (21 October).

1805–9 Clare worked as an agricultural labourer.

1806   Roscoe's *The Butterfly's Ball and Grasshopper's Feast*. Byron's *Fugitive Pieces*.

1807   Kirke White's *Remains*.

1808   Byron sails for the Mediterranean.

1809   Battle of Corunna. Enclosure Act for Helpston. Clare renews friendship with Mary Joyce.

1810   Crabbe's *The Borough*.

1810–13 Clare works at different jobs—a gardener at Burghley House, a militia recruit, a gang-labourer, a harvester.

1811   Luddite Riots. Bloomfield's *The Banks of Wye*.

1812   Byron's *Childe Harold* (I and II).

1813   Coleridge's *Remorse*.

1814   Cary completes his translation of Dante's *Divina Commedia*.

1814–18 Clare works at Helpston, Bridge Casterton, and Pickworth. Courts first Elizabeth Newbon and later Martha ('Patty') Turner. Issues in 1817 a proposal for publishing by subscription which catches the attention of Edward Drury, John Taylor's cousin.

1815   Waterloo. Napoleon exiled to St Helena. Byron's *Hebrew Melodies*.

1816   Shelley's *Alastor*.

1817   Keats's *Poems* published by Taylor and Hessey, who were to become Clare's publishers.

1818   Keats's *Endymion* published by Taylor and Hessey.

1819   Clare meets Taylor, who agrees to publish his poems.

1820   Publication of *Poems Descriptive of Rural Life and Scenery*. Marries 'Patty'. Clare visits London for the first time.

1821   *Poems Descriptive*, fourth edition. *The Village Minstrel and other Poems*. Taylor acquires the *London Magazine*. Death of Keats.

1822   Death of Shelley.

1822–4 Clare meets prominent literary figures during his visits to London. Writes 'The Parish'. Increasing anxiety and illness.

1823   Death of Octavius Gilchrist. Elizabeth Kent's *Flora Domestica*.

1824   Death of Byron. First number of Alaric Watt's *Literary Souvenir*. Taylor withdraws from the *London Magazine*.

1825   Taylor and Hessey dissolve their partnership. Cunningham's *Songs of Scotland, Ancient and Modern*. Death of Lord Radstock.

1825–6 Clare writes imitations of older poets. Prolific output.

1826   Hone's *Every-Day Book*.

1827   Publication of *The Shepherd's Calendar, with Village Stories and Other Poems* (written in 1824—by 1829 only 400 copies sold).

1828   Lockhart's *Life of Burns*. Clare visits London for relief of depression. Writes 'Pleasures of Spring'. Does field-work until 1831.

1829   Hogg's *The Shepherd's Calendar*. Tennyson's *Timbuctoo*.

1830   Publication of Dr Matthew Allen's *Cases of Insanity*. Moore's *Life of Byron*. Captain Swing Riots. Clare writes 'Hue and Cry'.

1831   Ebenezer Elliott's *Corn Law Rhymes*.

1832   Reform Act. Moves to Northborough to a cottage provided by Earl Fitzwilliam. Clare writes 'The Flitting'.

1833–4 Clare, planning to publish *The Midsummer Cushion*, meets endless delays.

1834   Poor Law Amendment Act.

1835   Publication of *The Rural Muse*, which is sympathetically received and sells reasonably well.

1836   Suffers lapses of memory and delusions.

1837   Publication of Dr Matthew Allen's *Classification of the Insane*. Clare enters High Beach as a voluntary patient. Accession of Queen Victoria.

1838–41 Clare treated by Dr Allen and improves physically but not mentally.

1841   Writes 'Child Harold' and 'Don Juan'. Escapes from Allen's (July),
        walks home to Northborough, and is removed to Northampton
        Asylum (December).

1842–64 Clare spends his remaining years in Northampton Asylum.

1845   W. F. Knight appointed House Steward, Northampton Asylum.

1849   Death of Thomas Inskip and of Peter De Wint.

1850   W. F. Knight leaves Northampton for Birmingham.

1864   Clare dies at Northampton, 20 May, aged 70. Taylor dies 5 July.

1865   W. B. Yeats born. Martin's *Life of John Clare* published.

NOTE ON THE TEXT

IN this edition we have departed as sparingly as possible from our copy-text. Words and letters in square brackets, including titles, are not in the copy-text, but have been supplied by us or in a few cases are taken from earlier printed texts. Occasionally we have preferred another autograph reading to our copy-text. Where Clare has written a word or words twice we have omitted one, and we have similarly corrected occasional punctuation irregularities. In transcribing titles we have followed normal practice in using initial capitals where Clare sometimes uses lower case.

The degree sign (°) indicates a note at the end of the book.

We have not preserved Clare's ampersands. We have corrected Clare's occasional slip of the pen and a few of the more puzzling spelling irregularities. We have, however, retained all Clare's characteristic spelling. One soon gets used to *hugh* for 'huge', *sutty* for 'sooty', *hurd* for 'hoard', *haloo* for 'halo', etc., and even when a word with a different meaning is involved, e.g. *ryhme* for 'rime', *loose* for 'lose', *were* for 'where', the context always makes Clare's meaning clear. However, we advise the reader, if in doubt, to turn to the Glossary. We also give a special warning about Clare's habit of omitting the apostrophe in such phrases as 'I'm', 'we'll', 'they'll', 'can't', 'I'd'. Again one soon gets used to this practice. It was decided to preserve the original spelling because, as the Introduction makes clear (pp. xxi–xxii), Clare is a special case.

Prose passages have been left unpunctuated, but, to assist the reader, a gap is left between sentences.

We have followed the same principles when working on copy-texts not in Clare's hand, in particular the Knight transcripts. We have not, however, put the titles in square brackets, although they may not be Clare's.

Our full editorial apparatus is reserved for our edition of Clare's poetry in the Oxford English Texts series which is currently in preparation.

POEMS OF THE HELPSTON PERIOD

c.1812–1831

Helpstone°

Hail humble Helpstone where thy valies spread
And thy mean village lifts its lowly head
Unknown to grandeur and unknown to fame
No minstrel boasting to advance thy name
Unletterd spot unheard in poets song
Where bustling labour drives the hours along
Where dawning genius never met the day
Where useless ign'rance slumbers life away
Unknown nor heeded where low genius trys
Above the vulgar and the vain to rise   10
Whose low opinions rising thoughts subdue
Whose railing envy damps each humble view
Oh where can friendships cheering smiles abode
To guide young wanderers on a doubtful road
The trembling hand to lead, the steps to guide
And each vain wish (as reason proves) to chide—
Mysterious fate who can on thee depend
Thou opes the hour but hides its doubtful end
In fancys view the joys have long appear'd
Where the glad heart by laughing plenty's cheer'd   20
And fancys eyes as oft as vainly fill
At first but doubtful and as doubtful still

So little birds in winters frost and snow
Doom'd (like to me) wants keener frost to know
Searching for food and 'better life' in vain
(Each hopeful track the yielding snows retain)
First on the ground each fairy dream pursue
Tho sought in vain—yet bent on higher view
Still chirp and hope and wipe each glossy bill
Nor undiscourag'd nor disheartn'd still   30
Hop on the snow cloth'd bough and chirp again
Heedless of naked shade and f[r]ozen plain

With fruitles[s] hopes each little bosom warms
Springs budding promise—summers plentious charms
A universal hope the whole prevades
And chirping plaudits fill the chilling shades
Till warm'd at once the vain deluded flies
And twitatwit their visions as they rise
Visions like mine that vanish as they flye
In each keen blast that fills the higher skye   40
Who find like me along their weary way
Each prospect lessen and each hope decay
And like to me these victims of the blast
(Each foolish fruitless wish resign'd at last)
Are glad to seek the place from whence they went
And put up with distress and be content—

Hail scenes obscure so near and dear to me
The church the brook the cottage and the tree
Still shall obscurity rehearse the song
And hum your beauties as I stroll along   50
Dear native spot which length of time endears
The sweet retreat of twenty lingering years
And oh those years of infancy the scene
Those dear delights where once they all have been
Those golden days long vanish'd from the plain
Those sports those pastimes now belovd in vain
When happy youth in pleasures circle ran
Nor thought what pains awaited future man
No other thought employing or employ'd
But how to add to happiness enjoy'd   60
Each morning wak'd with hopes before unknown
And eve possesing made each wish their own
The day gone bye left no pursuit undone
Nor one vain wish save that they went too soon
Each sport each pastime ready at their call
As soon as wanted they posses'd em all
These joys all known in happy infancy
And all I ever knew were spent on thee
And who but loves to view where these were past
And who that views but loves them to the last   70
Feels his heart warm to view his native place
A fondness still those past delights to trace

The vanish'd green to mourn the spot to see
Where flourish'd many a bush and many a tree
Where once the brook for now the brook is gone
Oer pebbles dimpling sweet went whimpering on
Oft on whose oaken plank I've wondering stood
(That led a pathway o'er its gentle flood)
To see the beetles their wild mazes run
With jetty jackets glittering in the sun   80
So apt and ready at their reels they seem
So true the dance is figur'd on the stream
Such justness such correctness they impart
They seem as ready as if taught by art
In those past days for then I lov'd the shade
How oft I've sighd at alterations made
To see the woodmans cruel axe employ'd
A tree beheaded or a bush destroy'd
Nay e'en a post old standard or a stone
Moss'd o'er by age and branded as her own   90
Would in my mind a strong attachment gain
A fond desire that there they might remain
And all old favourites fond taste approves
Griev'd me at heart to witness their remove[s]

Thou far fled pasture long evanish'd scene
Where nature's freedom spread the flowry green
Where golden kingcups open'd in to view
Where silver dazies charm'd the 'raptur'd view
And tottering hid amidst those brighter gems
Where silver grasses bent their tiny stems   100
Where the pale lilac mean and lowly grew
Courting in vain each gazer's heedless view
While cowslaps sweetest flowers upon the plain
Seemingly bow'd to shun the hand in vain
Where lowing oxen roamd to feed at large
And bleating there the shepherd's woolly charge
Whose constant calls thy echoing vallies cheer'd
Thy scenes adornd and rural life endeard
No calls of hunger Pity's feelings wound
Twas wanton Plenty rais'd the joyful sound   110
Thy grass in plenty gave the wish'd supply
Ere sultry suns had wak'd the troubling fly

Then blest retiring by thy bounty fed
They sought thy shades and found an easy bed

But now alas those scenes exist no more
The pride of life with thee (like mine) is oer
Thy pleasing spots to which fond memory clings
Sweet cooling shades and soft refreshing springs
And though fate's pleas'd to lay their beauties by
In a dark corner of obscurity   120
As fair and sweet they blo[o]m'd thy plains among
As blooms those Edens by the poets sung
Now all laid waste by desolations hand
Whose cursed weapon levels half the land
Oh who could see my dear green willows fall
What feeling heart but dropt a tear for all
Accursed wealth o'er bounding human laws
Of every evil thou remainst the cause
Victims of want those wretches such as me
Too truly lay their wretchedness to thee   130
Thou art the bar that keeps from being fed
And thine our loss of labour and of bread
Thou art the cause that levels every tree
And woods bow down to clear a way for thee

Sweet rest and peace ye dear departed charms
Which once industry cherish'd in her arms
When Peace and Plenty known but now to few
Were known to all and labour had his due
When mirth and toil companions thro' the day
Made labour light and pass'd the hours away   140
When nature made the fields so dear to me
Thin scattering many a bush and many a tree
Where the wood minstrels sweetly join'd among
And cheer'd my needy toilings with a song

Ye perishd spots adieu ye ruin'd scenes
Ye well-known pastures oft frequented greens
Though now no more—fond memory's pleasing pains
Within her breast your every scene retains
Scarce did a bush spread its romantic bower
To shield the lazy shepherd from the shower   150

Scarce did a tree befriend the chattering pye
By lifting up its head so proud and high
(Whose nest stuck on the topmost bough sublime
Mocking the efforts of each boy to climb
Oft as they've fill'd my vain desiring eye
As oft in vain my skill essay'd to try)
Nor bush nor tree within thy vallies grew
When a mischevious boy but what I knew
No not a secret spot did then remain
Through out each spreading wood and winding plain   160
But in those days my presence once possest
The snail horn searching of the mossy nest

Oh happy Eden of those golden years
Which mem'ry cherishes and use endears
Thou dear beloved spot may it be thine
To add a comfort to my life's decline
When this vain world and I have nearly done
And Time's drain'd glass has little left to run
When all the hopes that charm'd me once are oer
To warm my soul in extacy no more   170
By dissapointments prov'd a foolish cheat
Each ending bitter and beginning sweet
When weary age the grave a i[e]scue seeks
And prints its image on my wrinkl'd cheeks
Those charms of youth that I again may see
May it be mine to meet my end in thee
And as reward for all my troubles past
Find one hope true to die at home at last

So when the traveller uncertain roams
On lost roads leading every where but home   180
Each vain desire that leaves his heart in pain
Each fruitless hope to cherish it in vain
Each hated track so slowly left behind
Makes for the home which night denies to find
And every wish that leaves the aching breast
Flies to the spot where all its wishes rest

The Setting Sun

This scene how beautious to the musing mind
That now swift slides from my enchanting view
The Sun sweet setting yon far hills behind
In other worlds his Visits to renew
What spangling glories all around him shine
What nameless colours cloudles[s] and serene
(A heavnly prospect brightest in decline)
Attend his exit from this lovly scene—
—So sets the christians sun in glories clear
So shines his soul at his departure here   10
No clouding doubts nor misty fears arise
To dim hopes golden rays of being forgiven
His sun sweet setting in the clearest skyes
In safe assurance wings the soul to heaven—

Evening

Now grey ey'd hazy eve's begun
    To shed her balmy dew—
Insects no longer fear the sun
    But come in open view

Now buzzing with unwelcome din
    The heedles[s] beetle bangs
Agen the cowboys dinner tin
    That oer his shoulder hangs

And on he keeps in heedless pat
    Till quite enrag'd the boy   10
Pulls off his weather-beaten hat
    Resolving to destroy

Yet thoughtless that he wrongs the Clown
    By blows he'll not be driven
But buzzes on till batter'd down
    For unmeant Injury given

Now from each hedgerow fearless peeps
   The slowly pacing snails
Betraying their meandering creeps
   In silver slimy trails   20

The dew worms too in couples start
   But leave their holes in fear
For in a moment they will part
   If aught approaches near

The owls mope out and scouting bats
   Begin their giddy rounds
While countless swarms of dancing gnats
   Each water pudge surrounds

And 'side yon pool as smooth as glass
   Reflecting every cloud   30
Securely hid among the grass
   The Crickets chirup loud—

That rural call—'Cum-mulls cum-mulls'
   From distant pasture grounds
All noises now to silence lulls
   In soft and ushering sounds

While Echo's weak from hill to hill
   Their dying sounds deplore
That wimper faint and fainter still
   Till they are heard no more   40

The breezes once so cool and brief
   At eves aproach all dy'd
None's left to make the aspin leaf
   Twirl up its hoary side

But breezes all are usless now
   The hazy dun that spreds
Her moist'ning dew on every bough
   Sufficient coolness sheds

The flowers reviving—from the ground
  Perk up again and peep   50
While many different tribes around
  Are shutting up to sleep

O lovliest time O sweetest hours
  The musing soul can find
Now meditations thinking powers
  At freedom fills the mind

Now let me hid in culterd plain
  Pursue my evening walk
Where each way beats the nodding grain
  Aside the narrow bau'k   60

While fairy visions intervene
  Creating dread suprise
From distant objects dimly seen
  That catch the doubtful eyes

And Fairy's now (no doubt) unseen
  In silent revel sups
With dew drop bumpers toast their queen
  From crowflowers golden cups

The plough man moiling all the day
  To addle needy pelf   70
Now homward plods and on his way
  Thus argues to himself

'Now I am left the fallow Clods
  I'm happy and I'm free
Then can I think there's ony odds
  Between a King and me?

'Why if there is the best I'se sure
  (That I confess wi' pride)
Tho kings ar' rich as I am poor
  'T'will fall to nathans side'   80

Thus Nat conceits as on he goes
  To seek his natal cot
Such fancies gives his soul repose
  And smooths his rugged lot

So welcome Evening since thy hours
  Brings happiness to all
And may nought cause thy soothing powers
  Contrary ways to fall

The Gipsies Evening Blaze

To me, how wildly pleasing is that scene
  Which does present in evenings dusky hour
A group of gipsies, center'd on the green
  In some warm nook, where Boreas has no power
Where sudden starts the quivering blaze behind
  Short shrubby bushes nibbl'd by the sheep
  That mostly on these short-sward pastures keep—
Now lost now shines now bending with the wind
And now the swarthy sybil kneels reclin'd
  With proggling stick she still renews the blaze   10
  Forcing bright sparks to twinkle from the flaze
When this I view the all attentive mind
  Will oft exclaim so strong the scene prevades
  'Grant me this life thou spirit of the shades!'

Epigram

For fools that would wish to seem learned and wise
  This Receipt a wise man did bequeath
'Let 'em have the free use of their ears and their Eyes
  'But their Tongue'—says he 'Tye to their teeth'

To a Rose Bud in Humble Life

Sweet uncultivated blossom
Reard in springs refreshing dews
Dear to every gazers bosom
Fair to every eye that views
Opening bud whose youth can charm us
Thine be many a happy hour
Spreading rose whos beauty warms us
Flourish long my lovley flower

Tho pride looks disdainful on thee
Scorning scenes so mean as thine   10
Altho fortune frowns upon thee
Lovley blossom ne'er repine
Health unbought is ever wi' thee
—What their wealth can never gain
Innoscence her garments gie thee
Such as fashion apes in vain

Far be every evil from thee
Bud to blight or bloom decay
Still unborn the wretch to wrong thee
First beguile and then betray   20
—Who so destitute of feeling
Would such Innoscence beguile?
Who so base to be a villian
Would thy spotless sweets defile?—

When fit time and season grants thee
Leave to leave thy parent tree
May some happy hand transplant thee
To a station suiting thee
On some lovers worthy bosom
Mayest thou thy sweets resign   30
And may each unfolding blossom
Open charms as sweet as thine

Till that time may joys unceasing
Thy bards every wish fulfill
When thats come may joys increasing
Make thee blest and happier still

—Flourish fair thou artless Jessy
Pride of each admiring swain
Envy of despairing lasses
Queen of Walkherds lonly plain   40

A Scene

The landscapes stretching view that opens wide
With dribbling brooks and rivers wider floods
And hills and vales and darksome lowering woods
With grains of varied hues and grasses pied
The low brown cottage in the shelter'd nook
The steeple peeping just above the trees
Whose dangling leaves keep rustling in the breeze
—And thoughtful shepherd bending oer his hook
And maidens stript haymaking too apear
And hodge a wistling at his fallow plough   10
And herdsman hallooing to intruding cow
All these with hundreds more far off and near
Approach my sight—and please to such excess
That Language fails the pleasure to express

To a Winter Scene

Hail scenes of Desolation and despair
Keen Winters over bearing sport and scorn
Torn by his Rage in ruins as you are
To me more pleasing then a summers morn
Your shatter'd scenes appear—despoild and bare
Stript of your clothing naked and forlorn
—Yes Winters havoc wretched as you shine
Dismal to others as your fate may seem
Your fate is pleasing to this heart of mine
Your wildest horrors I the most esteem.—   10
The ice-bound floods that still with rigour freeze
The snow clothd valley and the naked tree
These sympathising scenes my heart can please
Distress is theirs—and they resemble me

The Harvest Morning

Cocks wake the early morn wi' many a Crow
Loud ticking village clock has counted four
The labouring rustic hears his restless foe
And weary bones and pains complaining sore
Hobbles to fetch his horses from the moor
Some busy 'gin to team the loaded corn
Which night throng'd round the barns becrouded door
Such plentious scenes the farmers yards adorn
Such busy bustling toils now mark the harvest morn

The birdboy's pealing horn is loudly blow'd   10
The waggons jostle on wi' rattling sound
And hogs and geese now throng the dusty road
Grunting and gabbling in contension round
The barley ears that litter on the ground—
What printing traces mark the waggons way
What busy bustling wakens echo round
How drives the suns warm beams the mist away
How labour sweats and toils and dreads the sultry day

His scythe the mower oer his shoulder leans
And wetting jars wi' sharp and tinkling sound   20
Then sweeps again 'mong corn and crackling beans
And swath by swath flops lengthening oer the ground
While 'neath some friendly heap snug shelterd round
From spoiling sun lies hid their hearts delight
And hearty soaks oft hand the bottle round
Their toils pursuing with redoubl'd might
Refreshments cordial hail—
Great praise to him be due that brought thy birth to light

Upon the waggon now with eager bound
The lusty picker wirls the rustling sheaves   30
Or ponderous resting creaking fork aground
Boastful at once whole shocks o' barley heaves
The loading boy revengefull inly greaves
To find his unmatch'd strength and power decay
Tormenting horns his garments inter weaves
Smarting and sweating 'neath the sultry day
Wi' muttering curses stung he mauls the heaps away

A Motley group the Clearing field surounds
Sons of Humanity O neer deny
The humble gleaner entrance in your grounds   40
Winters sad cold and poverty is nigh
O grudge not providence her scant suply
You'll never miss it from your ample store—
Who gives denial harden'd hungry hound
May never blessings crow'd his hated door
But he shall never lack that giveth to the poor

Ah lovley Ema mingling wi' the rest
Thy beauties blooming in low life unseen
Thy rosey cheeks thy sweetly swelling breast
But ill it suits thee in the stubs to glean   50
O poverty! how basely you demean
The imprison'd worth your rigid fates confine
Not fancied charms of an arcadian queen
So sweet as Emas real beauties shine
Had fortune blest sweet girl this lot had neer been thine

The suns increasing heat now mounted high
Refreshment must recruit exausted power
The waggon stops the busy tools thrown bye
And 'neath a shock's enjoy'd the beavering hour
The bashful maid—sweet healths engaging flower   60
Lingering behind—oer rake still blushing bends
And when to take the horn fond swains implore
With feign'd excuses its dislike pretends
So pass the beavering hours—So harvest morning ends

O rural life what charms thy meaness hide
What sweet descriptions bards disdain to sing
What Loves what Graces on thy plains abide
O could I soar me on the muses wing
What riffel'd charms should my researches bring
Pleas'd would I wander where these charms reside   70
Of rural sports and beauties would I sing
Those beauties wealth which you but vain deride
Beauties of richest bloom superior to your pride

[*Summer Evening*]°

The sinken sun is takin leave
And sweetly gilds the edge of eve
While purple [clouds] of deepening dye
Huddling hang the western skye
Crows crowd quaking over head
Hastening to the woods to bed
Cooing sits the lonly dove
Calling home her abscent love
Kirchip Kirchip mong the wheat
Partridge distant partridge greet   10
Beckening call to those that roam
Guiding the squandering covey home
Swallows check their rambling flight
And twittering on the chimney light
Round the pond the martins flirt
Their snowy breasts bedawbd in dirt
While the mason neath the slates
Each morter bearing bird awaits
Untaught by art each labouring spouse
Curious daubs his hanging house   20
Bats flit by in hood and cowl
Thro the barn hole pops the owl
From the hedge the beetles boom
Heedless buz and drousy hum
Haunting every bushy place
Flopping in the labourers face
Now the snail has made his ring
And the moth with snowy wing
Fluttering plays from bent [to bent]
Bending down with dews besprent   30
Then on resting branches hing
Stren[g]th to ferry oer the spring
From the haycocks moistend heaps
Frogs now take their Vaunting leaps
And along the shaven mead
Quickly travelling the[y] proceed
[Flying] from their speckled sides
Dewdrops bounce as grass divides

[Now the blue fog creeps along,
And the bird's forgot his song:]   40
Flowrets sleeps within their hoods
Daisys button into buds
From soiling dew the butter cup
Shuts his golden jewels up
And the Rose and woodbine they
Wait again the smiles of day
Neath the willows wavy boughs
Nelly singing milks her cows
While the streamlet bubling bye
Joins in murmuring melody   50
Now the hedger hides his bill
And with his faggot climbs the hill
Driver Giles wi rumbling joll
And blind ball jostles home the roll
Whilom Ralph for doll to wait
Lolls him oer the pasture gate
Swains to fold their sheep begin
Dogs bark loud to drive em in
Ploughmen from their furrowy seams
Loose the weary fainting team[s]   60
Ball wi cirging lashes weald
Still so slow to drive afield
Eager blundering from the plough
Wants no wip to drive him now
At the stable door he stands
Looking round for friendly hands
To loose the door its fastening pin
Ungear him now and let him in
Round the Yard a thousand ways
The beest in expectation gaze   70
Tugging at the loads of hay
As passing fotherers hugs away
And hogs wi grumbling deafening noise
Bother round the server boys
And all around a motly troop
Anxious claim their suppering up
From the rest a blest release
Gabbling goes the fighting geese
Waddling homward to their bed

In their warm straw litterd shed   80
Nighted by unseen delay
Poking hens tha[t] loose their way
Crafty cats now sit to watch
Sparrows fighting on the thatch
Dogs lick their lips and wag their tails
When doll brings in the milking pails
With stroaks and pats their welcomd in
And they with looking thanks begin
She dips the milk pail brimming oer
And hides the dish behind the door   90
Prone to mischief boys are met
Gen the heaves the ladders set
Sly they climb and softly tread
To catch the sparrow on his bed
And kill em O in cruel pride
Knocking gen the ladderside
Cursd barbarions pass me by
Come not turks my cottage nigh
Sure my sparrows are my own
Let ye then my birds alone   100
Sparrows come from foes severe
Fearless come yere welcome here
My heart yearns for fates like thine
A sparrows lifes as sweet as mine
To my cottage then resort
Much I love your chirping note
Wi my own hands to form a nest
Ill gi ye shelter peace and rest
Trifling are the deed[s] ye do
Grait the pains ye undergo   110
Cruel man woud Justice serve
Their crueltys as they deserve
And justest punishment pursue
And do as they to others do
Ye mourning chirpers fluttering here
They woud no doubt be less severe
Foolhardy clown neer grudg[e] the wheat
Which hunger forces them to eat
Your blinded eyes worst foes to you
Neer see the good which sparrows do   120

Did not the sparrows watching round
Pick up the inscet from your grounds
Did not they tend your rising grain
You then might sow—to reap in vain
Thus providence when understood
Her end and aim is doing good
Sends nothing here without its use
Which Ign'rance loads with its abuse
Thus fools despise the blessing sent
And mocks the givers good intent   130
O god let me the best pursue
As Id have other[s] do to me
Let me the same to others do
And learn at least Humanity
Dark and darker glooms the sky
Sleep gins close the labourers eye
Dobson on his greensward seat
Where neighbours often neighbour meet
Of c[r]aps to talk and work in hand
And battle News from foreign land   140
His last wift hes puffing out
And Judie putting to the rout
Who gossiping takes great delight
To shool her nitting out at night
Jingling newsing bout the town
Spite o dobs disliking frown
Chattering at her neighbours door
The summons warns her to give oer
[Prepar'd to start, she soodles home,
Her knitting twirling o'er her thumb,   150
As, loth to leave, afraid to stay,
She bawls her story all the way:
The tale so fraught with 'ticing charms,
Her apron folded o'er her arms,
She leaves the unfinished tale, in pain,
To end as evening comes again;
And in the cottage gangs with dread,
To meet old Dobson's timely frown,
Who grumbling sits, prepar'd for bed,
While she stands chelping bout the town.]   160
Night winds now on sutty wings

In the cotters chimney sings
Sweet I raise my drowsy head
Thoughtful stretching on my bed
Listning to their ushering charms
That shakes the Elm trees mossy arms
Till soft Slumbers stronger creep
Then rockd by winds I fall to sleep

A Maiden-haid

A maiden head the virgins trouble
Is well compared to a bubble
On a navigable river
—Soon as touch'd 'tis gone for ever

The Lamentations of Round-Oak Waters°

Oppress'd wi' grief a double share
    Where Round oak waters flow
I one day took a sitting there
    Recounting many a woe
My naked seat without a shade
    Did cold and blealy shine
Which fate was more agreable made
    As sympathising mine

The wind between the north and East
    Blow'd very chill and cold   10
Or coldly blow'd to me at least
    My cloa'hs were thin and old
The grass all dropping wet wi dew
    Low bent their tiney spears
The lowly daise' bended too
    More lowly wi my tears

(For when my wretched state appears
  Hurt friendless poor and starv'd
I never can withold my tears
  To think how I am sarv'd   20
To think how money'd men delight
  More cutting then the storm
To make a sport and prove their might
  O' me a fellow worm)

With arms reclin'd upon my knee
  In mellancholly form
I bow'd my head to misery
  And yielded to the storm
And there I fancied uncontrould
  My sorrows as they flew   30
Unnotic'd as the waters rowl'd
  Where all unnoticed too

But soon I found I was deciev'd
  For waken'd by my Woes
The naked stream of shade bereav'd
  In grievous murmurs rose

'Ah luckless youth to sorrow born
  Shun'd Son of Poverty
The worlds made gamely sport and scorn
  And grinning infamy   40
Unequall'd tho thy sorrows seem
  And great indeed they are
O hear my sorrows for my stream
  You'll find an equal there

'I am the genius of the brook
  And like to thee I moan
By Naiads and by all forsook
  Unheeded and alone
Distress and sorrow quickly proves
  The friend sincere and true   50
Soon as our happines removes
  Pretenders bids adieu

'Here I have been for many a year
    And how My brook has been
How pleasures lately flourish'd here
    Thy self has often seen
The willows waving wi' the wind
    And here and there a thorn
Did please thy Mellancholly mind
    And did My banks adorn   60

'And here the shepherd with his sheep
    And with his lovley maid
Together where these waters creep
    In loitering dalliance play'd
And here the Cowboy lov'd to sit
    And plate his rushy thongs
And dabble in the fancied pit
    And chase the Minnow throngs

'And when thou didst thy horses tend
    Or drive the ploughmans team   70
Thy mind did natturally bend
    Towards my pleasing stream
And different pleasures fill'd thy breast
    And different thy employ
And different feelings thou possest
    From any other Boy

'The sports which they so dearley lov'd
    Thou could's't not bear to see
And joys which they as joys approv'd
    Ne'er seem'd as joys to thee   80
The joy was thine couldst thou but steal
    From all their Gambols rude
In some lone thicket to consceal
    Thyself in Sollitude

'There didst thou joy and love to sit
    The briars and brakes among
To exercise thy infant wit
    In fancied tale or song

And there the inscect and the flower
  Would Court thy curious eye   90
To muse in wonder on that power
  Which dwells above the sky

'But now alas my charms are done
  For shepherds and for thee
The Cowboy with his Green is gone
  And every Bush and tree
Dire nakedness oer all prevails
  Yon fallows bare and brown
Is all beset wi' post and rails
  And turned upside down   100

'The gentley curving darksom bawks
  That stript the Cornfields o'er
And prov'd the Shepherds daily walks
  Now prove his walks no more
The plough has had them under hand
  And over turnd 'em all
And now along the elting Land
  Poor swains are forc'd to maul

'And where yon furlong meets the lawn
  To Ploughmen Oh! how sweet   110
When they had their long furrow drawn
  Its Eddings to their feet
To rest 'em while they clan'd their plough
  And light their Loaded Shoe
But ah—there's ne'er an Edding now
  For neither them nor you

'The bawks and Eddings are no more
  The pastures too are gone
The greens the Meadows and the moors
  Are all cut up and done   120
There's scarce a greensward spot remains
  And scarce a single tree
All naked are thy native plains
  And yet they're dear to thee

'But O! my brook my injur'd brook
    'T''is that I most deplore
To think how once it us'd to look
    How it must look no more
And hap'ly fate thy wanderings bent
    To sorrow here wi' me   130
For to none else could I lament
    And mourn to none but thee

'Thou art the whole of musing swains
    That's now resideing here
Tho one ere while did grace my plains
    And he to thee was dear
Ah—dear he was—for now I see
    His Name grieves thee at heart
Thy silence speaks that Misery
    Which Language cant impart   140

'O T—l T—l dear should thou°
    To this fond Mourner be
By being so much troubl'd now
    From just a Nameing thee
Nay I as well as he am griev'd
    For oh I hop'd of thee
That hadst thou stay'd as I believd
    Thou wouldst have griev'd for me

'But ah he's gone the first o' swains
    And left us both to moan   150
And thou art all that now remains
    With feelings like his own
So while the thoughtles[s] passes by
    Of sence and feelings void
Thine be the Fancy painting Eye
    On by'gone scenes employ'd

'Look backward on the days of yore
    Upon my injur'd brook
In fancy con its Beauties o'er
    How it had us'd to look   160

O then what trees my banks did crown
   What Willows flourishd here
Hard as the ax that Cut them down
   The senceless wretches were

'But sweating slaves I do not blame
   Those slaves by wealth decreed
No I should hurt their harmless name
   To brand 'em wi' the deed
Altho their aching hands did wield
   The axe that gave the blow   170
Yet 't'was not them that own'd the field
   Nor plan'd its overthrow

'No no the foes that hurt my field
   Hurts these poor moilers too
And thy own bosom knows and feels
   Enough to prove it true
And o poor souls they may complain
   But their complainings all
The injur'd worms that turn again
   But turn again to fall   180

'Their foes and mine are lawless foes
   And L–ws thems—s they hold
Which clipt-wing'd Justice cant oppose
   But forced [and] yields to G—d
These are the f—s of mine and me
   These all our Ru–n plan'd
Alltho they never felld a tree
   Or took a tool in hand

'Ah cruel foes with plenty blest
   So ankering after more   190
To lay the greens and pastures waste
   Which proffited before
Poor greedy souls—what would they have
   Beyond their plenty given?
Will riches keep 'em from the grave?
   Or buy them rest in heaven?'

Noon

All how silent and how still,
Nothing heard but yonder mill;
While the dazzled eye surveys
All around a liquid blaze;
And amid the scorching gleams,
If we earnest look it seems
As if crooked bits of glass
Seem'd repeatedly to pass.
O! for a puffing breeze to blow,
But breezes all are strangers now.   10
Not a twig is seen to shake,
Nor the smallest bent to quake;
From the river's muddy side,
Not a curve is seen to glide;
And no longer on the stream,
Watching lies the silver bream,
Forcing from repeated springs,
'Verges in successive rings'.°
Bees are faint and cease to hum,
Birds are overpow'r'd and dumb;   20
And no more love's oaten strains,
Sweetly through the air complains;
Rural voices all are mute;
Tuneless lies the pipe and flute;
Shepherds with their panting sheep,
In the swaliest corner creep;
And from the tormenting heat,
All are wishing to retreat;
Huddled up in grass and flow'rs,
Mowers wait for cooler hours;   30
And the cow-boy seeks the sedge,
Ramping in the woodland hedge,
While his cattle o'er the vales,
Scamper with uplifted tails;
Others not so wild and mad,
That can better bear the gad,
Underneath the hedge-row lunge,
Or, if nigh, in waters plunge;

O to see how flow'rs are took!
How it grieves me when I look:— 40
Ragged-robbins once so pink
Now are turn'd as black as ink,
And their leaves being scorch'd so much
Even crumble at the touch.
Drowking lies the meadow-sweet
Flopping down beneath one's feet;
While to all the flow'rs that blow,
If in open air they grow,
Th'injurious deed alike is done
By the hot relentless sun. 50
E'en the dew is parched up
From the teazle's jointed cup.—
O poor birds where must ye fly,
Now your water-pots are dry?
If ye stay upon the heath
Ye'll be chok'd and clamm'd to death,
Therefore leave the shadeless goss,
Seek the spring-head lin'd with moss

There your little feet may stand,
Safely printing on the sand; 60
While in full possession, where
Purling eddies ripple clear,
You with ease and plenty blest,
Sip the coolest and the best;
Then away and wet your throats,
Cheer me with your warbling notes;
'Twill hot Noon the more revive:
While I wander to contrive
For myself a place as good,
In the middle of a wood; 70
There, aside some mossy bank,
Where the grass in bunches rank
Lift it's down on spindles high,
Shall be where I'll choose to lie;
Fearless of the things that creep,
There I'll think and there I'll sleep;
Caring not to stir at all,
Till the dew begins to fall.

What is Life?

And what is Life? An hour-glass on the run
A mist retreating from the morning sun
  A busy bustling still repeated dream
Its length? A moment's pause, a moment's thought
  And happiness? A bubble on the stream
That in the act of siezing shrinks to nought

Vain hopes—what are they? Puffing gales of morn
That of its charms divests the dewy lawn
  And robs each flowret of its gem and dies
A cobweb hiding disappointments thorn   10
  Which stings more keenly thro' the thin disguise

And thou, O trouble? Nothing can suppose,
And sure the Power of Wisdom only knows,
  What need requireth thee.
So free and lib'ral as thy bounty flows,
  Some necessary cause must surely be.

And what is death? Is still the cause unfound
The dark mysterious name of horrid sound
  A long and ling'ring sleep the weary crave—
And peace—where can its happiness abound?   20
  No where at all but Heaven and the grave

Then what is Life? When stript of its disguise
  A thing to be desir'd it cannot be
Since every thing that meets our foolish eyes
  Gives proof sufficient of its vanity
'Tis but a trial all must undergo
  To teach unthankful mortals how to prize
That happiness vain man's denied to know
  Until he's call'd to claim it in the skies

[Summer]°

How sweet when weary dropping on a bank
Turning a look around on things that be
Een feather headed grasses spindling rank
A trembling to the breeze one loves to see
And yellow buttercups where many a bee
Comes buzzing to its head and bows it down
And the great dragon flye wi gauzy wings
In gilded coat of purple green or brown
That on broad leaves of hazel basking clings
Fond of the sunny day—and other things   10
Past counting pleases one while thus I lye
But still reflective pains are not forgot
Summer somtime shall bless this spot when I
Hapt in the cold dark grave can heed it not

Proposals for Building a Cottage

Beside a runnel build my shed
Wi' stubbles coverd oer
Let broad oaks oer its chimley spread
And grass plats grace the door

The door may open wi a string
So that it closes tight
And locks too woud be wanted things
To keep out thieves at night

A little garden not too fine
Inclosed wi painted pails   10
And wood bines round the cot to twine
Pind to the wall wi nails

Let hazels grow and spindling sedge
Bent bowering over head
Dig old mans beard from woodland hedge
To twine a summer shade

Beside the threshold sods provide
And build a summer seat
Plant sweet briar bushes by its side
And flowers that smelleth sweet   20

I love the sparrows ways to watch
Upon the cotters sheds
So here and there pull out the thatch
As they may hid[e] their heads

And as the sweeping swallows stop
Their flights along the green
Leave holes within the chimney top
To paste their nest between

Stick shelves and cupboards round the hut
In all the holes and nooks   30
Nor in the corner fail to put
A cubboard for the books

Along the floor some sand Ill sift
To make it fit to live in
And then Ill thank ye for the gift
As somthing worth the giving

[*A Copse in Winter*]

Shades tho yere leafless save the bramble spear
Whose weather beaten leaves of purple stain
In hardy stubbornness cling all the year
To their old thorns till spring buds new again
Shades still I love ye better then the plain
For here I find the earliest flowers that blow
While on the bare blea bank does yet remain
Old winters traces little heaps of snow
Beneath your ashen roots primroses grow
From dead grass tufts and matted moss once more   10
Sweet beds of vi'lets dare again be seen
In their deep purple pride and sweet displayd
The crow flowers creeping from the naked green
Adds early beautys to thy sheltering shade

Ballad

Winter winds cold and blea
Chilly blows oer the lea
Wander not out to me
   Jenny so fair
Wait in thy cottage free
   I will be there

Wait in thy cushiond chair
Wi thy white bosom bare
Kisses are sweetest there
   Leave it for me   10
F[r]ee from the chilly air
   I will meet thee

How sweet can courting prove
How can I kiss my love
Muffld i' hat and glove
   From the chill air
Quaking beneath the grove
   What love is there

Lay by thy woolen vest
Rap no cloak oer thy breast   20
There my hand oft hath prest
   Pin nothing there
There my head drops to rest
   Leave its bed bare

Curl thy sweet auburn [h]air
Keep thy sweet bosom bare
Kisses are sweetest there
   Love leave it free
Be the night foul or fair
   Ill be wi thee   30

When thy friends go to sleep
Down from thy chamber creep
Fall the snow ere so deep
   Chill be the air

Love will his promise keep
I will be there

When the latch gis a tink
Who it is ye may think
Wi no feard fancys shrink
    Undo the door   40
Or at the window blink
    Then yell be sure

Shut from the chilly air
To thee Ill hitch my chair
Snudgd on thy bosom bare
    Lost in thy charms
O how Ill revel there
    Rapt in thy arms

Langley Bush°

O Langley bush the shepherds sacred shade
Thy hollow trunk oft gaind a look from me
Full many a journey oer the heath ive made
For such like curious things I love to see
What truth the story of the swain alows
That tells of honours which thy young days knew
Of 'langley court' being kept beneath thy boughs°
I cannot tell—thus much I know is true
That thou art reverencd even the rude clan
Of lawless gipseys drove from stage to stage   10
Pilfering the hedges of the husband man
Leave thee as sacred in thy withering age
Both swains and gipseys seem to love thy name
Thy spots a favourite wi the smutty crew
And soon thou must depend on gipsey fame
Thy mulldering trunk is nearly rotten thro
My last doubts murmuring on the zephers swell
My last looks linger on thy boughs wi pain
To thy declining age I bid farwell
Like old companions neer to meet again   20

Evening Bells

Sweet the merry bells ring round
On even zephers dying swells
The sweetest chord the harp can sound
Sounds not so sweet as evening bells
   O merry chiming bells

Swinging falls and melting rise
On viewless echo how it swells
Tis but the music of the skies
Can breath so sweet as evening bells
   O merry chiming bells   10

Faint and fainter how they fall
Humming thro the lonly dells
No sounds to charm this earthly ball
Can charm so sweet as evening bells
   O merry chiming bells

Zephers breathing once again
Once again the zephers swells
Still I lye upon the plain
Entrancd to hear the evening bells
   O merry chiming bells   20

While the runnel curdles clear
Once again the zepher swells
Sweeter still the strains appear
O evening bells o evening bells
   How sweet is evening bells

The Woodman

The beating snow clad bell wi sounding dead
Hath clanked four—the woodmans wakd agen
And as he leaves his comfortable bed
Dithers to view the ryhmey featherd pane
And shrugs and wishes—but its all in vain
The beds warm comforts he must now forgo
His family that oft till eight hath lain
Wi out his labours wage coud not do so
And glad to make them blest he shoffles thro the snow

The early winters morns as dark as pitch   10
The warey wife keeps tinder every night
Wi flint and steal and many a sturdy twitch
Sits up in bed to strike her man a light
And as the candle shows the rapturous sight
Aside his wife his rosey sleeping boy
He smacks his lips wi exquisite delight
Wi all a fathers feelings fathers joy
Then bids his wife good bye and hies to his employ

His br[e]akfast water porridge humble food
A barley crust he in his wallet flings   20
Wi this he toils and labours i' the wood
And chops his faggot twists his band and sings
As happily as princes and as kings
Wi all their luxury—and blest is he
Can but the little which his labour brings
Make both ends meet and from long debts keep free
And keep as neat and clean his creasing family

Far oer the dreary fields the woodland lies
Rough is the journey which he daily goes
The wooley clouds that hang the frowning skies   30
Keep winnowing down their drifting sleet and snows
And thro his doublet keen the north wind blows
While hard as iron the cemented ground
As smooth as glass the glibbed pool is froze
His nailed boots wi clenching tread rebound
And dithering echo starts and mocks the clamping sound

The woods how gloomy in a winters morn
The crows and ravens even cease to croak
The little birds sit chittering on the thorn
The pies scarce chatter when the[y] leave the oak   40
Startld from slumber by the woodmans stroke
The milk maids songs is drownd in gloomy care
And while the village chimleys curl their smoke
She milks and blows and hastens to be there
And nature all seems sad and dying in despair

The squirking rabbit scarcly leaves her hole
But rolls in torpid slumbers all the day
The fox is loath to gin a long patrole
And scouts the woods content wi meaner prey
The hare so frisking timid once and gay   50
Hind the dead thistle hurkles from the view
No[r] scarcely scard tho in the travellers way
Tho waffling curs and shepherd dogs pursue
So winters riggid power affects all nature through

What different changes winters frowns supplies
The clown no more a loitering hour beguiles
Nor gauping tracks the clouds along the skyes
As when buds blossom and the warm sun smiles
When la[w]rence wages bids on hills and stiles
Banks stiles and flowers and skyes no longer charm   60
Deep snow and ice each summer seat defiles
Wi hasty blundering step and folded arm
He glad the stable seeks his frost nipt nose to warm

The shepherd seeks no more his spreading oak
Nor on the sloping pond head lyes at lare
The arbour he once wattld up is broke
And left unworthy of his future care
The ragged plundering stickers have bin there
And bottld it away—he passes bye
His summer dwelling desolate and bare   70
And neer so much as turns a 'serning eye
But gladly seeks his fire and leaves the 'clement skye

The scenes all clothd in snow from morn till night
The woodmans loath his chilly tools to sieze
The crows unroosting as he comes in sight
Shake down the feathery burthen from the trees
To look at things around hes fit to freeze
Scard from her pearch the fluttering pheasant flies
His coat and hat wi ryhme is turned white
He quakes looks round and pats his hands and sighs   80
And wishes to him self that the warm sun woud rise

And be the winter cutting as it will
Let north winds winnow fit to nip one through
In the deep woods hard fate demands him still
To stand the bitterest blasts that ever blew
Where trees instead of leaves and pearly dew
In ryhme and snow and Iscicles abound
The proverb 'use is second natures' true
It must be so or how coud he be found
To weather out the blast and daily stand his ground   90

And yet tho fortune frowns upon the poor
And dooms their life to slavish hard employ
Tho wealth forever gainst em shuts her door
And strives their fainting wishes to destroy
Yet still poor souls they have a glimpse of joy
A sugard charm still sweets the sours of fate
His sparing bliss when met does never cloy
While over much does paul the idly great
As rich and sumptious foods does surfeitings create

Good luck it is his providential wealth   100
That hardy labour and the freshning air
Shoud 'crease his strength and keep entire his health
And neer let illness on his soul despair
Wi wife and childern pending on his care
What woud he do a livlihood to gain
The parish moneys but a pining fare
Such scant benevolence he does disdain
Who grudges what they give and mocks the poor mans pain

But if unwell from toil hes forcd to stop
He quickly then repairs to medcines aid   110
Tho not to nauciates of the druggists shop
Or cant advice of docters mystic trade
But to such drugs as daily are displayd
Een round his walks and cottage door profuse
'Self heal' and 'agrimony' which has made
Full many an huswife wonderous cures produce
These he in summer seeks and hurds up for his use

The robin tamest of the featherd race
Soon as he hears the woodmans sounding chops
Wi ruddy bosom and a simple face   120
Around his old companions feet he hops
And there for hours in pleasd attention stops
The woodmans heart is tender and humane
And at his meals he many a crumble drops
Thanks to thy generous feelings gentle swain
And what thy pity gives shall not be gave in vain

The woodman pleased views the closing day
To see the sun drop down behind the wood
Sinking in clouds deep blue or misty grey
Round as a football and as red as blood   130
The pleasing prospect does his heart much good
Tho tis not his such beautys to admire
He hastes to fill his bags wi billet wood
Well pleasd from the chill prospect to retire
To seek his corner chair and warm snug cottage fire

And soon the dusky even hovers round
And the white frost gins crizzle pond and brook
The little family are squinting round
And from the door dart many a wistful look
The suppers ready stewing on the hook   140
And every foot that clampers down the street
Is for the coming fathers step mistook
And joyd are they when he their eyes does meet
Bent neath his load snow clad as whites a sheet

I think I see him seated in his chair
Taking the bellows up the fire to blow
I think I hear him joke and chatter there
Telling his childern news they wish to know
Wi leather leggings on that stopt the snow
His broad brimd hat uncoothly shapen round   150
Nor woud he Ill be bound woud it were so
Gi two pence for the chance did it abound
At that same hour to be the king of england crownd

Soons suppers down the thrifty wife seeks out
Her little jobs of family conserns
Chiding her childern rabbling about
Says theyll 'stroy more then what their father earns
And their torn clohs she bodges up and darns
For desent women cannot bear the sight
Of dirty houses and of ragged ba[i]rns   160
Tis their employment and their chief delight
To keep their cots and childern neat and tight

The woodman smokes the brats in mirth and glee
And artless prattle evens hours beguile
While loves last pledge runs scrambling up his knee
The nightly comfort from his weary toil
His chuff cheeks dimpling in a fondling smile
He claims his kiss and says his scraps of prayer
Begging his daddys pretty song the while
Playing wis jacket buttons and his hair   170
And thus in wed locks joys the labourer drowns his care

Nor can one miss the bliss from labour freed
Which poor men meeteth on a Sunday morn
Fixt in a chair some godly book to read
Or wandering round to view the crops and corn
In best cloaths fitted out and beard new shorn
Dropping adown in some warm shelterd dell
Wi six days labour weak and weary worn
Listning around each distant chiming bell
That on the softening air melodiously doth swell   180

His pipe pufft out he edges in his chair
And stirs the embers up his hands to warm
And with his singing book he does repair
To humming oer an anthem hymn or psalm
Nor does he think a ballad any harm
But often carrols oer his cottage hearth
'Bold robin hood' the 'Shipwreck' or the 'storm'°
O where we find this social joy and mirth
There we may truly say a heaven exists on earth

The clock when eight warns all for bed prepare   190
The childern still an extra minute crave
And sawn and stammer longer oer their prayers
And they such tempting fond excuses have
The 'dulging father oft the boon has gave
And sung again the younkers to delight
While every hard earnd farden glad to save
The carfull wife puts out the candle light
And oer the fire the song and tale makes sweet the winters
    night

And as most lab'rers knowingly pretend
By certain signs to judge the weather right   200
As oft from 'noahs ark' great floods desend
And 'burred moons' fortell great storms at night
In such like things the wood man took delight
And cre he went to bed woud always ken
Wether the sky was gloomd or stars shone bright
Then went to comforts arms till morn and then
As cheery as the sunrise beams resumd his toils agen

And cre he slept he always breathd a prayer
'I thank thee lord what thou to day didst give
Sufficient strength to toil I bless thy care   210
And thank thee still for what I may recieve
And o almighty god while I still live
My eyes if opend on the last days sun
Prepare thou me this wicked world to leave
And fit my passage ere my race is run
Tis all I beg o lord thy heavenly will be done'

Holland to thee this humble ballads sent°
Thee who for poor mans well fare oft hath prayd
Whose tongue did neer belye its good intent
Preacher as well in practice as in trade   220
Alas too often moneys business made
O may the wretch thats still on darkness living
The bibles comforts hear by thee displayd
And many a woodmans family forgiven
Have cause for blessing thee that led their way for heaven

Childish Recollections°

Each scene of youth to mes a pleasing toy
Which memory like a lover doats upon
And mixt wi them I am again a boy
And tears and sighs regret the things thats gone

Ah wi enthusiast excesses wild
The scenes of childhood meet my moistning eye
And wi the very weakness of a child
I feel the raptures of delights gone bye

And if Im childish wi such trifling things
If littleness it shows and vain and weak   10
When such like foolishness in memory spring[s]
Vain as it is I cannot help but speak

And still I fancy as around I stroll
Each boyish scene to mark the sport and game
Theres others living wi a self like soul
That thinks and loves such trifles just the same

An old familiar spot I witness here
Wi young companions were we oft have met
Tho since we playd tis bleachd wi many a year
The sports as warmly thrills my bosom yet   20

Here winds the dyke were oft we jumpt across
Tis just as if it were but yesternight
There hangs the gate we calld our wooden horse
Were we in swee swaw ridings took delight

And every thing shines round me just as then
Mole hills and trees and bushes speckling wild
That freshens all those pastimes up agen
O griveous day that changd me from a child

To seek the play thing and the pleasing toy
'The painted pootey shell and summer flowers   30
How blest was I when I was here a boy
What joys were mine in these delightfull hours

On this same bank I bound my poseys up
And culld the sweetest blossoms one by one
The cowslips still entices me to stoop
But all the feelings they inspird are gone

Tho in the midst of each endeard delight
Where still the cowslaps to the breezes bow
Tho all my childish scenes are in my sight
Sad manhood marks me an intruder now   40

Here runs the brook which I have damd and stopt
Wi choaking sods and water weeds and stones
And watchd wi joy till bursting off it plopt
In rushing gushes of wild murmering groans

Here stands the tree wi clasping ivy bound
Which oft Ive clumb to see the chaps at plough
And checkerd fields for many a furlong round
Rockd by the winds upon its topmost bough

Ah on this bank how blest I once have felt
When here I sat and mutterd namless songs   50
And wi the shepherd boy and netterd knelt
Upon yon rush beds plaiting whips and thongs

Fond memory warms as here with gravel shells
I pild my fancied cots and walled rings
And scoopt wi wooden knife my little wells
And filld em up wi water from the springs

Ah memory sighs now hope my heart beguiles
To build as yet snug cots to cheer despair
While fate at distance mocks wi grining smiles
And calls my structures castles in the air   60

Now een the thistles quaking in the wind
The very rushes nodding oer the green
Hold each expressive language to my mind
That like old mayteys tell of what has been

O 'sweet of sweets' from infancy that flow
When can we witness bliss so sweet as then
Might I but have my choice of joy below
I'd only ask to be a boy agen

Life owns no joy so pleasant as the past
That banishd pleasure rapt in memorys womb   70
It leaves a flavour sweet to every taste
Like the sweet substance of the honey comb

Ballad

I love thee sweet mary but love thee in fear
Were I but the morning breeze healthy and airy
As thou goest a walking Id breathe in thy ear
And wisper and sigh how I love thee my mary

I wish but to touch thee but wish it in vain
Was thou but a streamlet a winding so clearly
And I little globules of soft dropping rain
How fond woud I press thy white bosom my mary

I woud steal a kiss but I dare not presume
Was thou but a rose in thy garden sweet fairy　　　10
And I a bold bee for to rifle its bloom
A whole summers day woud I kiss thee my mary

I long to be wi thee but cannot tell how
Was thou but the eldern that grows by thy dairy
And I the blest woodbine to twine on the bough
Id embrace thee and stick to thee ever my mary

Recollections after an Evening Walk

Just as the even bell rung we set out
To wander the fields and the meadows about
And the first thing we markt that was lovly to view
Was the sun hung on nothing and bidding adieu
He seemd like a ball of pure gold in the west
In a cloud like a mountain blue dropping to rest
The clouds all around him were tingd wi his rays
And the trees at a distance seemd all on a blaze
Till lower and lower and sunk from our sight
And blue mist came creeping wi silence and night　　10
The woodman then ceasd wi his hatchet to hack
And bent a way home wi his kid on his back
The mower too lapt up his scythe from our sight
And put on his jacket and bid us good night
The thresher once lumping we heard him no more
He left his barn dust and had shut up his door
The shepherd had told all his sheep in his pen
And hummed his song to his cottage agen
But the sweetest of all seeming music to me
Was the song of the clumbsy brown beetle and bee　　20
The one was a hastning away to his hive
The other was just from his sleeping alive
And our hats he kept knocking as if hed no eyes
And when batterd down he was puzzld to rise
The little gay moth too was lovly to view
A dancing wis liley white wings in the dew

He wiskd oer the water pudge flirting and airy
And perchd on the down headed grass like a fairy
And there came the snail from his shell peeping out
As fear full and cautious as thieves on the rout   30
The sly jumping frog too had venturd to tramp
And the glow worm had just gun to light up his lamp
The sip of the dew the worm pep[t] from his den
But dreading our footsteps soon vanishd agen
And numbers of creatures apeard in our sight
That live in the silence and sweetness of night
Climbing up the tall grasses or scaling the bough
But these were all namless unoticd till now
And then we wound round neath the brooks willow row
And lookt at the clouds that kept passing below   40
The moons image too in the brook we coud seet
As if twas the tother world under our feet
And we listnd well pleasd at the guggles and groans
The water made passing the pebbles and stones
And then we turnd up by the rut rifted lane
And sought for our cot and the village again
For night gatherd round and shut all from the eye
And a black sutty cloud crept all over the sky
The wet bush we past soon as touchd it woud drop
And the grass neath our feet was as wet as a mop   50
And as to the town we aproachd very fast
The bat even popt in our face as he past
And the crickets sung loud as we went by the house
And by the barn side we saw many a mouse
Quirking round for the kernels that litterd about
As shook from the straw which the thresher hurld out
And then we came up to our cottage once more
And shut out the night dew and lockt up the door
The dog barkd a welcome well pleasd at our sight
And the owl oer our cot flew and woopt a good night   60

To my Cottage

Thou lowly cot where first my breath I drew
Past joys endear thee childhoods past delight
Where each young summer pictures on my view
And dearer still the happy winter night
When the storm pelted down wi all his might
And roard and bellowd in the chimney top
And patterd vehement gainst the window light
And oer the threshold from the eaves did drop
How blest Ive listnd on my corner stool
Heard the storm rage and hugd my happy spot   10
While the fond parent wound her wirring spool
And spard a sigh for the poor wanderers lot
In thee sweet hut I all these joys did prove
And these endear thee wi eternal love

Second Adress to the Rose Bud in Humble Life

Wild delight of fairest feature
Beautys topmost crowning gem
Negligence of carless nature
Left to deck a lowly stem
Left to every vice assailing
Vulgar tongues delight to tell
Left to blights so oft prevailing
Dangerd sweet I wish thee well

Far be every evil from thee
Bud to blight or bloom decay   10
Still unborn the wretch to wrong thee
First beguile and then betray
Who so destitute of feeling
Woud thy innoscence beguile
Who so base to be a villian
Woud thy spotless sweets defile

Far may every sensless looby
Leave thy unprotected tree
As the swine admires the ruby
So the clown woud value thee   20
Soul of feeling warmly beating
Warmth that can of love impart
Shoudst thou such a one be meeting
Be thou gratfull to his heart

Far be fates reverse to morrows
Bidding hopes to day decline
All lifes sweets without its sorrows
May they tender charm be thine
May the sun that opes thy blossom
Gilding sweet thy blushy flower   30
Set in smiles upon thy bosom
Neer to know a swaily hour

Long may live my artless beauty
Long thy sweetness I may tell
Tis thy poets humble duty
Thus to see and wish thee well
Tis thy poets latest blessing
When fates hazard race is run
That thy life no pains expressing
End as sweet as it begun   40

Written in November

Autumn I love thy latter end to view
In cold novembers day so bleak and bare
When like lifes dwindld thread worn nearly thro
Wi lingering pottering pace and head bleachd bare
Thou like an old man bids the world adieu
I love thee well and often when a child
Have roamd the bare brown heath a flower to find
And in the moss clad vale and wood bank wild
Have cropt the little bell flowers paley blue
That trembling peept the sheltering bush behind   10

When winnowing north winds cold and blealy blew
How have I joyd wi dithering hands to find
Each fading flower and still how sweet the blast
Woud bleak novembers hour Restore the joy thats past

[*On Taste*]

Taste is from heaven
A inspiration nature cant bestow
Tho natures beautys where a taste is given
Warms the ideas of the soul to flow
With that enchanting 'thusiastic glow
That throbs the bosom when the curious eye
Glances on beautious things that give delight
Objects of earth or air or sea or sky
That bring the very senses in the sight
To relish what it sees—but all is night   10
To the gross clown—natures unfolded book
As on he blunders never strikes his eye
Pages of lanscape tree and flower and brook
Like bare blank leaves he turns unheeded bye

[*Summer Morning*]

I love to peep out on a summers morn
Just as the scouting rabbit seeks her shed
And the coy hare squirts nestling in the corn
Frit at the bowd ear tottering oer her head
And blundering pheasants that from covert spring
Their short sleep broke by early trampling feet
Making one sturtle wi their rustling wings
As thro the boughs they seek more safe retreat
The little flower begemd around wi drops
That shine at sunrise like to burnishd gold   10
So sweet to view the milk maid often stops
And wonders much such spangles to behold
The hedger too admires em deck the thorn
And thinks he sees no beauties like the morn

[*Joys of Youth*]

How pleasing simplest recollections seem
Now summer comes it warms me to look back
In the sweet happiness of youths wild track
Varied and fleeting as a summer dream
Here have I pausd upon the sweeping rack
That specks like wool flocks thro the purple skye
Here have I carless stooped down to catch
The meadow flower that entertaind my eye
And as the butterflye went wirring bye
How anxious for its settling did I watch   10
And oft long purples on the waters brink
Have tempted me to wade in spite of fate
To pluck the flowers—oh to look back and think
—What pleasing pains such simple joys create

Song

Swamps of wild rush beds and sloughs squashy traces
Grounds of rough fallows wi thistle and weed
Flats and low vallies of king cups and daiseys
Sweetest of subjects are ye for my reed
Ye commons left free in the rude rags of nature
Ye brown heaths be cloathed in furze as ye be
My wild eye in rapture adores e'ery feature
Yere as dear as this heart in my bosom to me

O native endearments I woud not forsake ye
I woud not forsake ye for sweetest of scenes   10
For sweetest of gardens that nature coud make me
I woud not forsake ye dear vallies and greens
Tho nature neer dropt thee a cloud resting mountain
Nor water falls tumble their music to thee
Had nature denyd thee a bush tree or fountain
Thou still woud bin lovd as an eden by me

And long my dear vallies long long may ye flourish
Tho rush beds and thistles make most of your pride
May showers never fail the greens daiseys to nourish
Nor suns dry the fountain that rills by its side   20
Yer skies may be gloomy and misty yer mornings
Yer flat swampy vallies unholsome may be
Still refuse of nature wi out her adorning[s]
Yere as dear as this heart in my bosom to me

Song

And wheres there a scene more delightfully seeming
To eyes like to mine that is blinded wi love
Then yon setting sun on the steeple point gleaming
And blue mist deep tinging the edge of the grove
Nigh comes the hour that is anxiously waited
Sweet the sensations that glows in the mind
When blisses of love are by fancy elated
As I steal in silence my mary to find

Mary thy worth and thy goodness Ive tryd it
And if a beauty more fairer may be   10
If the bare world owns a blessing beside it
Who will and welcome may take it for me
Hopes flye to thee and there finish their travels
Wishes look on thee and there they are crownd
All that I hope for thy beauty unravels
All that I wish on thy bosom is found

Song

One gloomy eve I roamd about
Neath oxeys hazel bowers°
While timid hares were daring out
To crop the dewy flowers
And soothing was the scene to me
Right placid was my soul
My breast was calm as summers sea
When waves forget to roll

But short was evens placid smile
My startld soul to charm   10
When nelly lightly skipt the stile
Wi milk pail on her arm
One carless look on me she flung
As bright as parting day
And like a hawk from covert sprung
Id pounce my peace away

The Gipseys Camp

How oft on Sundays when Id time to tramp
My rambles led me to a gipseys camp
Where the real effegies of midnight hags
Wi tawney smoaked flesh and tatterd rags
Uncooth brimd hat and weather beaten cloak
Neath the wild shelter of a notty oak
Along the greensward uniformly pricks
Her pliant bending hazels arching sticks
While round topt bush or briar entangld hedge
Where neath broad flag leaves spring or ramping sedge   10
Keep off the bothering bustle of the wind
And give the best retreat they hope to find
How oft Ive bent me oer their fire and smoak
To hear their gibberish tale so quaintly spoke
While the old sybil forcd her boding clack
Twin imps the mean while bawling at her back
Oft on my hand her magic coins bin struck
And hoping chink she talkd of morts of luck
And still as boyish hopes did erst agree
Mingld wi fears to drop the fortunes fee   20
I never faild to gain the honours sought
And Lord and Squire was purchasd wi a groat
But as mans unbelieving taste came round
She furious stampt her shooless foot aground
Wipd by her sut black hair wi clenching fist
While thro her yellow teeth the spittle hist
Swearing by all her lucky powers of fate
That like as foot boys on her actions wait

That fortunes scale shoud to my sorrow turn
And I onc day the rash neglect shoud mourn 30
That good to bad shoud change and I shoud be
Lost to this world and all eternity
That poor as Job I shoud remain unblest
Alas for fourpence how my dye is cast
Of neer a hurded farding be possest
And when alls done be shovd to hell at last

from *The Village Minstrel*°

In autumn time how oft hes stood to mark
What tumults tween the hogs and geese arose
Down the corn litterd street and the rude bark
Of jealous watch dog on his masters clo'hs
Ben rousd by quawkings of the swopping crows
And every tinkle in that busy toil
In sultry field and dusty lane that flows
He gleand his corn and lovd to list the while
For lubins self was mixt to share of autumns spoil

And when old women overpowrd by heat 10
Tuckt up their tails and sickend at the toil
Seeking beneath the thorn the mole hill seat
To tell their tales and catch their breath awhile
Their gabbling talk did lubins cares beguile
And some woud tell their tales and some woud sing
And many a dame to make the children smile
Woud tell of many a funny laughing thing
While merrily the snuff box charm went pinching round the
    ring

Here lubin listn'd wi a struck supprise
When hickerthrifts great strength has met his ear 20
How he killd jiants as they were but flies
And lifted trees as one woud lift a spear
And not much bigger then his fellows where
He knew no troubles waggoners have known
Of getting stalld and such dissasters drear
Up hed chuck sacks as one woud hurl a stone
And draw whole loads of grain unaided and alone

And goodys sympathy woud fetch the tear
From each young listner seated by her side
When cruel barbary allen they did hear°   30
The haughty stubborness of female pride
To that fond youth who broke his heart and dyd
And jack the jiant killers tales shed say
Which still the same enchanting power supplyd
The stagnant tear amazment wipd away
And jacks exploits were felt for many an after day

These were such tales as lubin did delight
But shoud the muse narate wi goodys pains
And tell of all she told from morn till night
Fays ghosts and jiants woud her songs detain   40
And be at days return resumd again
Wi cinderella she has charmd awhile
Then Thumbs dissasters gen a moments pain
That true thought legends woud each soul beguile
As superstition willd to raise the tear or smile

And as the load joggd hom ward down the lane
When welcome night shut out the toiling day
His followings markt the simple hearted swain
Joying to listen on his homward way
As rests warm rapture rousd the rustics lay   50
The thread bare ballad from each quavering tongue
As 'peggy bond' or the 'sweet month of may'°
As how he joyd to hear each 'good old song'
That on nights pausing ear did echo loud and strong

The muse might sing too for he well did know
The freaks and plays that harvest home doth end
How the last load is crownd wi boughs and how
Wi floating ribbons diznd at their end
The swains and maids wi fork and rake attend
And how the childern on the load delight   60
Wi shouts of harvest home their throats to rend
And how the dames peep out to mark the sight
And all the feats that crown the harvest supper night

He knew all well a young familiar there
And often lookd on all for he him sen
Mixt wi the sun tand group the feast to share
As years rolld round him wi the change agen
And brought the masters equals wi their men
Who pusht the beer about and smoakd and drank
Wi freedoms plenty never shown till then   70
Nor labourers dard but now so free and frank
To laugh and joke and play so many an harmless prank

Much has he laughd each rude rude act to see
The long neckt sheet clad crane to poke about
Spoiling each smokers pipe and cunningly
Tho blindfold seen to pick each bald head out
And put each bashful maiden to the rout
The 'fircy parrot' too a laughing scene
Where two maids on a sheet invite the lout
Thrown oer a watertub to sit between   80
And as he drops they rise and let him swearing in

The 'dusty miller' playing many a rig
And the 'scotch pedlars' wi their jokes and fun
The 'booted hogs' drove over 'lunnon brig'
Boys who had mischief in the harvest done
As loads oerturnd and foul on posts had run
And brandy burning ghosts most deadly blue
That each old woman did wi terror shun
These wi the rest did lubin yearly view
And joind his mirth and fears wi the low vulgar crew   90

To close the ranting night the masters health
Went round in bumping horns to every swain
Who wisht him best of crops to 'crease his wealth
And's merry sport when harvest came again
And all i' chorus rallyd out amain
And soons the song (a tugging pull) begun
Each ere its end the brimming horn must drain
Or have it filld again—there lay the fun
Till hodge went drunk to bed and morts of things wer done

Reccolections after a Ramble

The rosey day was sweet and young
The clod brown lark that haild the morn
Had just her summer anthem sung
And trembling dropped in the corn
The dew raisd flower was perk and proud
The butterflye around it playd
The skyes blue clear save wooly cloud
That passt the sun without a shade

On the pismires castle hill
While the burnet buttons quakd   10
While beside the stone pavd rill
Cowslap bunches nodding shakd
Bees in every peep did try
Great had been the honey shower
Soon their load was on their thigh
Yellow dust as fine as flour

Brazen magpies full of clack
Fond of insolence and sport
Chattering on the donkeys back
Percht and pulld his shaggy coat   20
Odd crows settld on the pad
Dames from milking trotting home
Said no sign was half so bad
And shakd their heads at ills to come

While cows restless from the ground
Plungd into the stream and drank
And the rings went wirling round
Till they toucht the flaggy bank
On the arches wall I knelt
Curious as I often did   30
To see what the sculpture spelt
But the moss its letters hid

Labour sought the water cool
And stretching took a hearty sup
The fish were playing in the pool
And turnd their milk white bellys up
Cloths laid down behind a bush
Wading close beside the pad
Deeply did the maiden blush
As she passd each naked lad   40

Some with lines the fish to catch
Querking boys let loose from school
Others side the hedgrow watch
Where the linnet took the wool
Tending hodge had slept too fast
While his things had strayd abroad
Swift the freed horse gallopd past
Pattering down the stoney road

The gipsey tune was loud and strong
As round the camp they dancd a gig   50
And much I lovd the brown girls song
While listing on the wooden brig
The shepherd he was on his rounds
The dog stopt short to lap the stream
And gingling in the fallow grounds
The ploughman urgd his reaking team

Often did I stop to gaze
On each spot once dear to me
Known mong those rememberd days
Of banishd happy infancy   60
Often did I view the shade
Where once a nest my eyes did fill
And often markd the place I playd
At 'roley poley' down the hill

In the woods deep shade did stand
As I passd the sticking troop
And goody begd a helping hand
To heave her rotten faggot up

The riding gate sharp gerking round
Followd fast my heels again   70
While echo mocks the clapping sound
And 'clap clap' sung the woods amain

The wood is sweet I love it well
In spending there my leisure hours
To look the snail its painted shell
And search about for curious flowers
Or neath the hazels leafy thatch
On a stulp or mossy ground
Little squirrels gambols watch
Oak trees dancing round and round   80

Green was the shade—I love the woods
When autumns wind is mourning loud
To see the leaves float on the floods
Dead within their yellow shroud
The wood was then in glory spread
I love the browning bough to see
That litters autumns dying bed
Her latest sigh is dear to me

Neath a spreading shady oak
For awhile to muse I lay   90
From its grains a bough I broke
To fan the teasing flies away
Then I sought the woodland side
Cool the breeze my face did meet
And the sun the shade did hide
Tho twas hot it seemed sweet

And as while I clum the hill
Many a distant charm I found
Pausing on the lagging mill
That scarcly movd its sails around   100
Hanging oer a gate or stile
Till my curious eye did tire
Leasure was employd awhile
Counting many a peeping spire

While the hot sun gun to wain
Cooling glooms fast deep[n]ing still
And freshning greeness spread the plain
As black clouds crept the southern hill
Labour sought a sheltering place
Neath some thick wood woven bower   110
While odd rain drops dampt his face
Heralds of the coming shower

Where the oak plank crosst the stream
Which the early rising lass
Climbs each morn wi gathering cream
Crookd pads tracking thro the grass
There where willows hing their boughs
Briars and black thorns formd a bower
Stunted thick from sheep and cows
There I stood to shun the shower   120

Sweet it was to feel the breeze
Blowing cool without the sun
Bumming gad flies ceasd to teaze
All was glad the shower to shun
Sweet it was to mark the flower
Rain drops glistning on its head
Perking up beneath the bower
As if rising from the dead

And full sweet it was to look
How clouds misted oer the hill   130
Rain drops how they dimpt the brook
Falling fast and faster still
While the gudgeons sturting bye
Cringd neath water grasses shade
Startling as each nimble eye
Saw the rings the dropples made

And upon the dripping ground
As the shower had ceasd again
As the eye was wandering round
Trifling troubles causd a pain   140

Overtaken in the shower
Bumble bees I wanderd bye
Clinging to the drowking flower
Left without the power to flye

And full often drowning wet
Scampering beetles racd away
Safer shelter glad to get
Drownded out from whence they lay
While the moth for nights reprief
Waited safe and snug withall   150
Neath the plantains bowery leaf
Where there neer a drop coud fall

Then the clouds did wear again
And full sweet it was to view
Sunbeams trembling long in vain
Now they gun to glimmer thro'
And as labour strength regains
From ales booning bounty given
So revivd the freshning plains
From the smiling showers of heaven   160

Sweet the birds did chant their songs
Blackbird linnet lark and thrush
Music from a many tongues
Melted from each dripping bush
Deafnd echo on the plain
As the sunbeams broke the cloud
Scarce coud help repeat the strain
Natures anthem flowd so loud

What a freshning feeling came
As the suns smile gleamd again   170
Sultry summer w'n't the same
Such a mildness swept the plain
Breezes such as one woud seek
Trembld thro the bramble bower
Fanning sweet the burning cheek
Cooling infants of the shower

Inscets of misterious birth
Sudden struck my wondering sight
Doubtless brought by moister forth
Hid in notts of spittle white   180
Backs of leaves the burthen bears
Where the sunbeams cannot stray
'Wood sears' calld that wet declares
So the knowing shepherds say

As the cart rutt rippl'd down
With the burthen of the rain
Boys came drabbling from the town
Glad to meet their sports again
Stopping up the mimic rills
Till it forced its frothy bound   190
Then the keck made water mills
In the current wiskerd round

Once again did memory pain
Oer the life she once had led
Once did manhood wish again
Childish joys had never fled
Coud I lay these woes aside
Which I long have murmurd oer
'Mix a boy wi boys' she sighd
Fate shoud neer be teazd no more   200

Hot the sun in summer warms
Quick the roads dry oer the plain
Girls wi baskets on their arms
Soon renewd their sports again
Oer the green they sought their play
Where the cowslip bunshes grew
Quick the rush bent fannd away
As they dancd and bounded thro'

Some went searching by the wood
Peeping neath the weaving thorn   210
Where the pouchd lip'd cuckoo bud
From its snug retreat was torn

Where the ragged robbin grew
With its pipd stem streakd wi jet
And the crow flowers golden hue
Carless plenty easier met

Some wi many an anxious pain
Childish wishes did pursue
From the pond head gazd in vain
On the flag flowers yellow hue   220
Smiling in its safety there
Sleeping oer its shadowd blow
While the floods triumphing care
Crimpld round its root below

Then I stood to pause again
Retrospection sighd and smild
Musing 'tween a joy and pain
How I acted when a child
When by clearing brooks Ive bin
When the painted sky was given   230
Thinking if I tumbld in
I shoud fall direct to heaven

Many an hour had comd and gone
Sin the town last met my eye
Where huge baskets mauling on
Maids hung out their cloths to dry
Granny there was on the bench
Cooly sitting in the swail
Stopping oft a love sick wench
To pinch her snuff and hear her tale   240

Be the journey ere so mean
Passing by a cot or tree
In the rout theres somthing seen
Which the curious love to see
In each ramble tastes warm souls
More of wisdoms self can view
Then blind ignorance beholds
All lifes seven stages through

Rurallity I dearly love thee
Simple as thy numbers run   250
Epics song may soar above thee
Still thy sweetness yields to none
Cots to sing and woods and vales
Tho its all thy reed can do
These with nature shall prevail
When epics war harps broke in two

My Mary°

Who lives where Beggars rarley speed?
And leads a humdrum life indeed
As none beside herself would lead
    My Mary

Who lives where noises never cease?
And what wi' hogs and ducks and geese
Can never have a minutes peace
    My Mary

Who nearly battl'd to her chin
Bangs down the yard thro thick and thin?   10
Nor picks a road nor cares a pin
    My Mary

Who (save in sunday bib and tuck)
Goes daily (waddling like a duck)
Oer head and ears in grease and muck
    My Mary

Unus'd to pattins or to clogs
Who takes the swill to serve the hogs?
And steals the milk for cats and dogs
    My Mary   20

Who frost and Snow as hard as nails
Stands out o' doors and never fails
To wash up things and scour the pails
    My Mary

Who bussles night and day in short
At all catch jobs of every sort
And gains her mistress' favor for't
    My Mary

And who is oft repaid wi praise?
In doing what her mistress says   30
And yielding to her wimmy ways
    My Mary

For theres none apter I believe
At 'creeping up a Mistress' sleve'
Then this low kindred stump of Eve
    My Mary

Who when the baby's all besh–t
To please its mamma kisses it?
And vows no Rose on earths so sweet
    My Mary   40

But when her Mistress is'n't nigh
Who swears and wishes it would die
And pinches it to make it cry
    My Mary

Oh rank deceit! what soul could think—
But gently there revealing ink
—At faults of thine this friend must wink
    My Mary

Who (not without a 'spark o' pride'
Tho strong as Grunters bristly hide)   50
Does keep her hair in papers ty'd?
    My Mary

And mimicking the Gentry's way
Who strives to speak as fine as they?
And minds but every word they say
    My Mary

And who (tho's well bid blind to see
As her to tell ye A from B)
Thinks herself none o' low degree?
    My Mary 60

Who prates and runs oer silly stuff?
And 'mong the boys makes sport enough
—So ugly, silly droll and ruff
    My Mary

Ugly! Muse fo' shame o' thee
What faults art thou a going to see?
In one thats lotted out to be
    My Mary

But heedless sayings meaneth nought
Done Innoscent without a thought 70
We humbly ask thy pardon for't
    My Mary

Who low in Stature thick and fat
Turns brown from going without a hat?
Tho not a pin the worse for that
    My Mary

Who's laugh'd at too by every whelp
For failings which they cannot help?
But silly fools will laugh and chelp
    My Mary 80

For tho in stature mighty small
And near as thick as thou art tall
That hand made thee that made us all
    My Mary

And tho thy nose hooks down too much
And prophecies thy chin to touch
I'm not so nice to look at such
    My Mary

No no about thy nose and chin
Its hooking out or bending in   90
I never heed nor care a pin
  My Mary

And tho thy skin is brown and ruff
And form'd by nature hard and tuff
All suiteth me! so thats enough
  My Mary

Helpston Green°

Ye injur'd fields ere while so gay
When natures hand display'd
Long waving rows of Willows gray
And clumps of Hawthorn shade
But now alas your awthorn bowers
All desolate we see
The tyrants hand their shade devours
And cuts down every tree

Not tree's alone have felt their force
Whole Woods beneath them bow'd   10
They stopt the winding runlets course
And flowrey pastures plough'd
To shrub nor tree throughout thy fields
They no compasion show
The uplifted ax no mercy yields
But strikes a fatal blow

When ere I muse along the plain
And mark where once they grew
Rememberance wakes her busy train
And brings past scenes to view   20
The well known brook the favorite tree
In fancys eye appear
And next that pleasant green I see
That green for ever dear

Oer its green hill's I've often stray'd
In Childhoods happy hour
Oft sought the nest along the shade
And gather'd many a flower
With fellow play mates often joind
In fresher sports to plan   30
But now encreasing years have coind
This play mate into man

The greens gone too ah lovly scene
No more the king cup gay
Shall shine in yellow oer the green
And add a golden ray
Nor more the herdsmans early call
Shall bring the cows to feed
Nor more the milk maids awkard brawl
Bright echo in the mead   40

Both milkmaids shouts and herdsmans call
Have vanish'd with the green
The king kups yellow shades and all
Shall never more be seen
For all the cropping that does grow
Will so efface the scene
That after times will hardly know
It ever was a green

Farwell delightful spot farwell
Since every efforts vain   50
All I can do is still to tell
Of thy delightful plain
But that proves short—increasing years
That did my youth presage
When every new years day appears
Will mellow into age

When age resumes the faultering tongue
Alas theres nought can save
Take one more step then all along
We drop into the grave   60

Reflection pierces deadly keen
While I the morral scan
As are the changes of the green
So is the life of man

The Meeting°

Here we meet too soon to part
Here will abscence raise a smart
Here Ill press thee to my heart
  Where nones a place above thee
Here to say I love thee well
Had but words the power to spell
Had but language strength to tell
  I wou'd say how I love thee

Here the rose that decks thy door
Here the thorn that spreads thy bower   10
Here the willow on the moor
  The birds that rest above thee
Had they thoughts and eyes to see
Sense and looks like thee and me
Quickly woud they prove to thee
  How dotingly I love thee

And by the night skys purple ether
And by the evens sweetest weather
That oft has blest us both together
  The moon that shines above thee   20
And shows thy beauty face so blooming
And by pale ages winter coming
The charms and casual'ties of woman
  I will for ever love thee

[*Noon*]

The mid day hour of twelve the clock counts oer
A sultry stillness lulls the air asleep
The very buzz of flye is heard no more
Nor one faint wrinkle oer the waters creep
Like one large sheet of glass the pool does shine
Reflecting in its face the burnt sun beam
The very fish their sturting play decline
Seeking the willow shadows side the stream
And where the awthorn branches oer the pool
The little bird forsaking song and nest   10
Flutters on dripping twigs his limbs to cool
And splashes in the stream his burning breast
O free from thunder for a sudden shower
To cherish nature in this noon day hour

To the Winds

Hail gentle winds I love your murmuring sounds
The willows charm me wavering too and fro
And oft I stretch me on the dasied ground
To see you crimp the wrinkling flood below
Delighted more as brisker gusts succeed
And give the landscape round a sweeter grace
Sweeping in shaded waves the rip'ning mead
Puffing their rifl'd fragrance in my face
Pictures of nature ye are doubly dear
Her childern dearly loves your wispering charms   10
Ah ye have murmurd sweet to many an ear
That now lies dormant in deaths Icey arms
And at this moment many a weed ye wave
That hide the bard in his forgotten Grave

[*Patty*]

Ye swampy falls of pasture ground,
    And rushy spreading greens;
Ye rising swells in brambles bound,
    And freedom's wilder'd scenes;
I've trod ye oft, and love ye dear,
    And kind was fate to let me;
On you I found my all, for here
    'Twas first my Patty met me.

Flow on, thou gently plashing stream,
    O'er weed-beds wild and rank;   10
Delighted I've enjoy'd my dream
    Upon thy mossy bank:
Bemoistening many a weedy stem,
    I've watch'd thee wind so clearly;
And on thy bank I found the gem
    That makes me love thee dearly.

Thou wilderness, so rudely gay;
    Oft as I seek thy plain,
Oft as I wend my steps away,
    And meet my joys again,   20
And brush the weaving branches by
    Of briars and thorns so matty;
So oft reflection warms a sigh,—
    Here first I met my Patty.

Rural Morning°

Soon as the twilight thro the distant mist
In silver hemmings skirts the purple east
Ere yet the sun unveils his smiles to view
And drys the mornings chilly robes of dew
Young hodge the horse boy with a soodling gait
Slow climbs the stile or opes the creaky gate
With willow switch and halter by his side

Prepard for dobbin whom he means to ride
The only tune he knows still whistling oer
And humming scraps his father sung before
As 'wantley dragon' and the 'magic rose'°
The whole of music which his village knows
That wild remembrance in each little town
From mouth to mouth thro ages handles down
Onward he jolls nor can the minstrel throngs
Entice him once to listen to their songs
Nor marks he once a blossom on his way
A sensless lump of animated clay
With weather beaten hat of rusty brown
Stranger to brinks and often times a crown
With slop frock suiting to the ploughmans taste
Its greezy skirtings twisted round his waiste
And hardnd hiloes clenchd with nails around
Clamping defiance oer the stoney ground
The deadly foes of many a blossomd sprout
That luckless happens in each mornings rout
In hobbling speed he roams the pasture round
Till hunted dobbin and the rest are found
Where some from frequent meddlings of his whip
Well knows their foe and often trys to slip
While dobbin tam'd by age and labour stands
To meet all trouble from his brutish hands
And patient leads to gate or knowley brake
The teazing burthen of his foe to take
Who soon as mounted with his switching weals
Puts Dobs best swiftness in his heavy heels
The toltering bustle of a blundering trot
Which whips and cudgels neer increasd a jot
Tho better speed was urged from the clown
And thus he snorts and jossles to the town
And now when toil and summers in its prime
In every vill at mornings earliest time
To early risers many a hodge is seen
And many a dob's heard clattering oer the green
Now straying beams from days unclosing eye
In copper colour patches flush the sky
And from nights prison strugglingly encroach
To bring the summons of warm days approach

10

20

30

40

Till slowly mounting oer the ridge of clouds
That yet half shows his face and half enshrouds   50
Th' unfetterd sun takes his unbounded reign
And wakes all life to noise and toil again
And while his opening mellows oer the scenes
Of wood and field the many mingling greens
Industrys bustling din once more devours
The soothing peace of mornings early hours
The grunt of hogs freed from their nightly dens
And constant cacklings of new laying hens
And ducks and geese that clamorous joys repeat
The splashing comforts of the pond to meet   60
And chirping sparrows dropping from the eaves
For offal curnels that the poultry leaves
Oft signal calls of danger chittering high
At skulking cats and dogs approaching nigh
And lowing steers that hollow echoes wake
Around the yard their nightly fast to brake
As from each barn the lumping flail rebounds
In mingling consert with the rural sounds
While oer the distant fields more fainter creep
The murmuring bleetings of unfolding sheep   70
And ploughmens callings that more hoarse proceed
Where tuff industry urges labours speed
And bellowing cows that wait with udders full
The welcome haloo of the maids 'cum mull'
And rumbling waggons deafen now again
Rousing the dust along the narrow lane
And cracking whips and shepherds hooting crys
From wood land echoes urging sharp replys
Hodge in his waggon marks the wonderous tongue
And talks with echoe as he drives along   80
Still cracks his whip bawls every horses name
And echo still as ready bawls the same
The puzzling mysterey he woud vainly cheat
And fein woud utter what it cant repeat
Till speedless trials proves the doubted elf
As skilld in noise and sounds as hodge himself
And quite convinc'd with the proofs it gives
The boy drives on and fancys eccho lives
As some wood fiend that fright benighted men

The troubling spirit of a robbers den   90
And now the blossom of the village view
With airy hat of straw and apron blue
And short sleevd gown that half to guess reveals
By fine turnd arms what beauty it conceals
Whose cheeks health flushes with as sweet a red
As that which strip[e]s the woodbine oer her head
Deeply she blushes on her morning pad
To prove the fondness of some passing lad
Who with a smile that thrills her soul to view
Holds the gate open till she passes through   100
While turning nodds beck thanks for kindness done
And looks—if looks coud speak proclaims her won
With well scourd buckets on proceeds the maid
And drives her cows to milk beneath the shade
Were scarce a sunbeam to molest her steals
Sweet as the thyme that blossoms were she kneels
And there oft scarcs the cooing amorous dove
With her own favourd melodys of love
Snugly retird in yet dew laden bowers
The sweetest specimen of rural flowers   110
Proving red glowing in the morning wind
The powers of health and nature when combind
Last on the road the cow boy carless swings
Leading tamd cattle in their tending strings
With shining tin to keep his dinner warm
Swung at his back or tuckd beneath his arm
Whose sun burnt skin and cheeks chuffd out with fat
Are dy'd as rusty as his napless hat
And others driving loose their herds at will
Are now heard howping up the pasture hill   120
Peeld sticks they bear of hazel or of ash
The rib markd hides of restless cows to thrash
In sloven garb appears each bawling boy
As fit and suiting to their rude employ
Their shoes worn down by many blundering treads
Oft shows the tennants needing safer sheds
And tatterd cloaths that scarcely screen the back
Which pasture hedges daily put to rack
The pithy bunch of unripe nuts to seek
And crabs sun-reddend with a tempting cheek   130

And daubd about as if besmeard with blood
Staind with the berries of the brambly wood
That stud the straggling briars as black as jet
Which when their cattle lare they run to get
Or smaller kinds as if beglossd with dew
Shining dim powderd with a downy blue
That on weak tendrils lowly creeping grow
Where choakd in flags and sedges wandering slow
The brook purls simmering its declining tide
Down the crookd boundings of the pasture side   140
There they to hunt the luscious fruit delight
And dabbling keep within their charges sight
Oft catching prickly struttles on their rout
And miller thumbs and gudgeons driving out
Hid side the archd brig under many a stone
That from its wall rude passing clowns have thrown
And while in peace cows eat and chew their cuds
Moozing cool shelterd neath the skirting woods
To double uses they the hours convert
And turn the toils of labour into sport   150
Till morns long streaking shadows loose their tails
And cooling winds swoon into f[l]uttering gales
And searching sunbeams warm and sultry creep
Warming the teazing inscets from their sleep
And dreaded gadflyes with their drowsey hum
On the burnt wings of mid-day zephers come
Urging each lown to leave his sports in fear
To stop the gadding cows from sturting bye
Droning unwelcome tidings on his ear
That the sweet peace of rural morns gone bye   160

Rural Evening

The sun now sinks behind the woodland green
And twittering spangles glow the leaves between
So bright and dazzling in the eye it plays
As if noons heats had kindld to a blaze
But soon it dims in red and heavier hues
And shows wild fancy cheated in her views

A mist like moister rises from the ground
And deeper blueness stains the distant round
The eye each moment as it gazes oer
Still loosing objects which it markd before 10
The woods at distance changing like to clouds
And spire points croodling under evenings shrouds
Till forms of things and hues of leaf and flower
In deeper shadows as by majic power
With light and all in scarce percievd decay
Puts on mild evenings sober garb of grey
While in the sleepy gloom that blackens round
Dies many a lulling hum of rural sound
From cottage door farm yard and dusty lane
Were home the cart horse tolters with the swain 20
And padded holm were village boys resort
And bawl enrapturd oer their evening sport
Till night awakens superstitious drcad
And drives them prisoners to a restless bed
Thrice happy eve of days no more to me
Who ever thought such change belongd to thee
When like to boys whom now thy gloom surounds
I chasd the stag or playd at fox and hounds
Or wanderd down the lane with many a mate
To play at swee swaw on the pasture gate 30
Or on the threshold of some cottage sat
To watch the flittings of the shrieking bat
Who seemly pleasd to mock our treacherous view
Woud even swop and touch us as he flew
And vainly still our hopes to entertain
Woud stunt his rout and circle us again
Till wearied out wi many a coaxing call
Which boyish superstition loves to brawl
His shill song shrieking he betook to flight
And left us puzzld in short sighted night 40
Those days have fled me as from them they steal
And Ive felt losses they must shortly feel
For sure such ends makes every bosom sore
To think of pleasures they must meet no more
Now from the pasture milking maidens come
With each a swain to bear the burthen home
Who often coax them on their pleasant way

To soodle longer out in loves delay
While on a molhill or a resting stile
The simple rustics tries their arts the while   50
With glegging smiles and hopes and fears between
A snatching kiss to open what they mean
And all the utmost that their tongues can do
The honyd words which nature learns to woo
The wild flowers sweets of language 'Love' and 'dear'
With warmest utterings meets each maidens ear
Who as by magic smit she knows not why
From the warm look that waits a wishd reply
Droops fearfull down in loves delightfull swoon
As slinks the blossom from the suns of noon   60
While sighs half smotherd from the throbbing breast
And broken words sweet trembling oer the rest
And cheeks in blushes burning turnd aside
Betrays the plainer what she strives to hide
The amrous swain sees thro the feignd disguise
And proves the fondness she at first denies
And with all passions love and truth can move
Urges more strong the simpering maid to love
More freely using toying ways to win
Tokens that echo from the soul within   70
Her soft hand nipping that with ardour burns
And timid gentlyier presses its returns
And stealing pins with innoscent deciet
To loose the 'kerchief from its envyd seat
And unawares her bonnet to untye
Her dark brown ringlets wiping gently bye
To steal a kiss in seemly feignd disguise
As love yields kinder taken by supprise
While she near conquerd less resentment move[s]
And owns at last mid tears and sighs she loves   80
With sweetest feelings that this world bestows
Now each to each their inmost souls disclose
Vow to be true and to be truly taen
Repeat their loves and vow it oer again
And pause at loss of language to exclaim
Those purest pleasures yet with out a name
And while in highest extacy of bliss
The shepherd holds her yielding hand in his

He turns to heaven to witness what he feels
And silent shows what want of words consceals 90
And ere the parting moments hussles nigh
And night in deeper dye his curtain dips
Till next days evening glads the anxious eye
He swears his truth and seals it on her lips
At evens hour the truce of toil tis sweet
The sons of labour at their ease to meet
On piled bench beside the cottage door
Made up of mud and stones and sodded oer
Were rustic taste at leisure trimly weaves
The rose and straggling woodbines to the eaves 100
And on the crouded spot that pails enclose
The white and scarlet daisey rears in rows
And trailing peas in bunches training neat
Perfuming even with a luscious sweet
And sun flowers planting for their gilded show
That scale the windows lattice ere they blow
And sweet to 'habitants within the sheds
Peep thro the diamond pane their golden heads
Or black smiths shop were ploughs and harrows lye
Well known to every child that passes bye 110
By shining share[s] that litter on the floor
And branded letters burnt upon the door
And hard burnt cinders flung as usless bye
That year by year in some spare corner lye
Were meddling boys their ready weapons meet
To pelt each other up and down the street
Or aught that pleases each mischievous eye
As harmless hogs and bullocks passing bye
Or squatting martins neath the eves at rest
That oft are wakd to mourn a ruind nest 120
And sparrows now that love their nests to leave
In dust to flutter at the cool of eve
For such like scenes the gossip leaves her home
And sons of labour light their pipes and come
To talk of wages wether high or low
And mumbld news that still as secrets go
As gossips knowledge of awaited births
Expected marriages and dreaded deaths
And heedless seen to all the rest may say

The beckoning lover nodds the maids away   130
And at a distance many an hour employs
In jealous wisperings oer their amorous joys
As childern round their teazing sports prolong
To twirl the top or bounce the hoop along
Or shout across the street their one catch all
Or progg the hous'd bee from the cotters wall
While at the parish cottage walld wi dirt
Were all the cumber grounds of life resort
From the low door that bows two props between
Some feeble tottering dame surveys the scene   140
By them reminded of the long lost day
When she her self was young and went to play
And turning to the painfull scenes agen
The mournfull changes she has met since then
Her aching heart the contrast moves so keen
Een sighs a wish that life had never been
And vainly sinning while she strives to pray
Half smotherd discontent pursues its way
In wispering providence how blest shed been
If lifes last troubles shed escapd unseen   150
If ere want sneakd for grudgd support from pride
Shed only shard of childhoods joys and dyd
And as to talk some passing neighbours stand
And shoves their box within her tottering hand
She turns from echos of her younger years
And nips the portion of her snuff wi tears

Rustic Fishing

On sunday mornings freed from hard employ
How oft I mark the young mischevous boy
With anxious haste his poles and lines provide
For make shifts oft crookd pins to threadings ty'd
And delve his knife with wishes ever warm
In rotten dunghills for the grub and worm
The harmless treachery of his hooks to bait
Tracking the dewy grass wi many a mate
To seek the brook that down the meadows glide
Where the grey willow shadows by its side   10

Were flag and reed in wild disorder spread
And bending bulrush bows its taper head
And just above the surface of the floods
Where water lileys mount their snowy buds
On whose broad swimming leaves of glossy green
The shining dragon flye is often seen
And hanging thorns whose roots washd bare appear
That shields the morehens nest from year to year
While crowding osiers mingling wild among
Prove snug asylums to her brood when young   20
Who when suppris'd by foes approaching near
Plunge neath the weeping boughs and dissapear
There far from terrors that the parson brings
Or church bell hearing when the summons rings
Half hid in meadow sweet and kecks high flowers
In lonly sports they spend the sunday hours
Tho ill supplyd for fishing seems the brook
That breaks the mead in many a stinted crook
Oft choakd in weeds and foild to find a road
The choice retirement of the snake and toad   30
Then lost in shallows dimpling restlessly
In fluttering struggles murmuring to be free
Oer gravel stones its depth can scarcly hide
It runs the remnant of its broken tide
Till seemly weary of each choaked controul
It rests collected in some gulled hole
Scoopd by the sudden floods when winters snow
Melts in confusion by a hasty thaw
There bent in hopfull musings on the brink
They watch their floating corks that seldom sink   40
Save when a warey roach or silver bream
Nibbles the worm as passing up the stream
Just urging expectations hopes astray
To view the dodging cork then slink away
Still hopes keep burning with untird delight
Till wobbling curves keep waving like a bite
If but the breezy wind their floats shoud spring
And move the water with a troubling ring
A captive fish still fills the anxious eyes
And willow wicks lie ready for the prize   50
Till evening gales awaken damp and chill

And nip the hopes that morning suns instill
When resting flyes have tired their gauzy wing
Nor longer tempt the watching fish to spring
Who at the worm nor nibbles more repeat
But lunge from night in sheltering flag retreat
Then dissapointed in their days employ
They seek amusement in a feebler joy
Short is the sigh for fancys provd untrue
With humbler hopes still pleasure they pursue   60
Where the rude oak bridge scales the narrow pass
Half hid in rustling reeds and scrambling grass
Or stepping stones stride oer the narrow sloughs
Which maidens daily cross to milk their cows
There they in artless glee for minnows run
And wade and dabble past the setting sun
Chasing the struttle oer the shallow tide
And flat stones turning up were gudgeons hide
Hopes visions with success here runneth high
And on a rush they string the little frye   70
All former hopes their ill success delayd
In this new change they fancy well repayd
And thus they wade and chatter oer their joys
Till night unlookd for young success destroys
Drives home the sons of solitude and streams
And stops uncloyd hopes ever freshning dreams
Who then like school boys that at truant play
In sloomy fear lounge on their homward way
And inly trembling as they gain the town
To meet chastisment from a parents frown   80
Where hazel twigs in readiness prepard
For their long abscence brings a mete reward

Sunday Walks

How fond the rustics ear at leisure dwells
On the soft soundings of his village bells
As on a sunday morning at his ease
He takes his rambles just as fancys please
Down narrow baulks that interscet the fields
Hid in profusions that its produce yields
Long twining peas in faintly misted greens

And wingd leaf multitudes of crowding beans
And flighty oatlands of a lighter hue
And speary barley bowing down with dew   10
And browning wheat ear on its taper stalk
With gentle breezes bending oer the baulk
Greeting the parting hand that brushes near
With patting welcomes of a plentious year
Or narrows lanes were cool and gloomy sweet
Hedges above head in an arbour meet
Meandering down and resting for awhile
Upon a moss clad molhill or a stile
While every scene that on his leisure crowds
Wind waving vallies and light passing clouds   20
In brighter colors seem to meet the eye
Then in the bustle of the days gone bye
A peacful solitude around him creeps
And nature seemly oer its quiet sleeps
No more is heard save sutherings thro the trees
Of brisk wind gushes or a trembling breeze
And song of linnets in the hedgrow thorn
As twittering welcomes to the days return
And hum of bees were labours doomd to stray
In ceasless bustle on his weary way   30
And low of distant cattle here and there
Seeking the stream or dropping down to lare
And bleat of sheep and horses playfull neigh
From rustics whips and plough and waggon free
Biting in carless freedom oer the leas
Or turnd to knap each other at their ease
While neath the bank on which he rests his head
The brook mourns drippling oer its pebbly bed
And wimpers soothingly a calm serene
Oer the lulld comforts of a sunday scene   40
He ponders round and muses with a smile
On thriving produce of his earlier toil
What once was curnels from his hopper sown
Now browning wheat ears and oat bunches grown
And pea pods swelld by blossoms long forsook
And nearly ready for the scythe and hook
He pores wi wonder on the mighty change
Which suns and showers perform and thinks it strange

And tho no philosophic reasoning draws
His musing marvels home to natures cause   50
A simple feeling in him turns his eye
To where the thin clouds smoak along the sky
And there his soul consents the power must reign
Who rules the year and shoots the spindling grain
Lights up the sun and sprinkles rain below
The fount of nature whence all causes flow
Thus much the feelings of his bosom warms
Nor seeks he further then his soul informs
A six days prisoner lifes support to earn
From dusty cobwebs and the murky barn   60
The weary thresher meets the rest thats given
And thankfull sooths him in the boon of heaven
And sabbath walks enjoys along the fields
With loves sweet pledges poddling at his heels
That oft divert him with their childish glee
In fruitless chaces after bird and bee
And eager gathering every flower they pass
Of yellow lambtoe and the totter grass
Oft wimpering round him dissapointments sigh
At sight of blossoms thats in bloom too high   70
And twitching at his sleeve their coaxing powers
To urge his hand to reach the tempting flowers
And as he climbs their eager hopes to crown
On gate or stile to pull the blossoms down
Of pale hedgroseys straggling wild and tall
And scrambling woodbines that outgrows them all
Turns to the days when he himsen woud teaze
His tender father for such toys as these
And smiles with rapture as he plucks the flowers
To meet the feelings of those lovly hours   80
And blesses sundays rest whose peace at will
Retains a portion of those pleasures still
And when the duty of the days expird
And priest and parish offered whats requird
When godly farmer shuts his book again
To talk of profits from advancing grain
Short menory keeping what the parson read
Prayers neath his arm and business in his head
And dread of boys the clerk is left to close

The creaking church door on its weeks repose   90
Then leave me sundays remnant to employ
In seeking sweets of solitary joy
And lessons learning from a simpler tongue
Were nature preaches in a crickets song
Were every tiney thing that lives and creeps
Some feeble language owns its prayer to raise
Were all that lives by noise or silence keeps
An homly sabbath in its makers praise
There free from labour let my musings stray
Were foot paths ramble from the public way   100
In quiet lonliness oer many a scene
This grassy close or Grounds of blossomd bean
Oft winding baulks were groves of willows spread
Their welcome waving shadows over head
And thorns beneath in woodbines often drest
Inviting strongly in their peace to rest
Or wildly left to follow choice at will
Oer many a trackless vale and pathless hill
Or natures wilderness oer heaths of goss
Each foot step sinking anckle deep in moss   110
By pleasing interuptions often tyd
An hedge to clamber or a brook to stryde
Were nought of 'proaching feet or noises rude
Molests the quiet of ones solitude
Save birds song broken by a false alarm
Thro branches fluttering from their fancyd harm
And cows and sheep the startld low and bleat
Disturbd from lare by ones unwelcome feet
The all thats met in sundays slumbering case
That rather adds then checks the power to please   120
And sweet it is to creep ones blinded way
Were woodland boughs shuts out the smiles of day
Were hemmd in glooms that scarce give leave to spy
A passing cloud or patch of purple sky
Tracking half hidden from the world beside
Sweet hermit nature that in woodlands hide
Were namless flowers that never meet the sun
Like bashing modesty the sight to shun
Buds in their snug retreat and bloom and dye
With out one notice of a passing eye   130

There while I drop me in the woody waste
Neath arbours nature fashions to her taste
Entwining oak trees with the ivys gloom
And wood bines propping over boughs to bloom
And scallopt briony mingling round her bowers
Whose fine bright leaves make up the want of flowers
With natures minstrels of the woods let me
Thou lord of sabbaths add a song to thee
A humble offering for the holy day
Which thou most wise and graciously hast given   140
As leisure dropt in labours rugged way
To claim a passport wi the rest to heaven

The Fate of Genius

Far from the life of market towns was seen
The humble hutts and spire of topal green°
Were from the treetops that the hamlet shields
The white spire mounts and over looks the fields
Meeting the distant view of passing eyes
Were gentle memory often points and sighs
For there amidst the ignorance it wears
Wants chilling views and labours ceasless cares
A rustic genius from the darkness sprung
And sought the muses mid his toils and sung   10
And warmd with hopes while nature round him smild
He humd their raptures and his fate beguild
But evil light thro his oblivion gleamd
The world wore smiles his artless hopes esteemd
And warmd with raptures better days to meet
They sought applause and realizd the cheat
Soon envys wasps around his sweets did swarm
And peacfull muses fled the rude alarm
Soon fames vain follys from their ambush rose
Friends while theyre powerless but in public foes   20
This praisd as fine what that as faults accusd
That urgd amendments which the next abusd
Thus mid the wild confusion babel raisd
By one advisd by others scofft and praisd
The damps of dissapointment provd too much

And warm hopes witherd at the chilly touch
Shrinking from life and hopes emblazoned noon
To witness envy had its own too soon
And what remains now linger to be blest
Aside that church were friendship tells the rest   30
Who placd a stone to mark his lowly sleep
That kindred hearts might find the spot to weep
Were the old sexton deaths undaunted slave
Who knew the bard and dug his early grave
To each request enquireys warmth may raise
Oft gives the tale of his unnoticd days
In hopes calm walks ere flattery smild his friend
And black injustice bade their journey end
'I knew him from a child' the clerk woud say
'And often noticd his dislike to play   40
Oft met him then lone left by woods and streams
Muttering about as people do in dreams
And neath lone bushes dropt about the field
Or peacfull hedges that woud shelter yield
With hand beneath his head in silence bent
Oft saw him sit and wonderd what it meant
Nor did his habits alter with his age
Still woods and fields his leisure did engage
Nor friends nor labour woud his thoughts beguile
Still dumb he seemd in company and toil   50
And if ones questions did his dreams supprise
His unconscern oft pausd in wrong replys
We wonderd many times as well we might
And doubted often if his mind was right
Een childern startld from his oddness ran
And shund his wanderings as "the crazy man"
Tho harmless as the things he mixd among
His ways was gentle and unknown to wrong
For ive oft markd his pity passing bye
Disturb the spiders web to save the flye   60
And saw him give to tyrant boys a fee
To buy the captive sparrows liberty
Each sundays leisure brought the woods their guest
And wildest spot which suited him the best
As bushy greens and valleys left untilld
Were weedy brooks went crooking as they willd

Were flags and reeds and sedge disorderd grew
These woud his abscence from his home pursue
And as he rambld in each peacful round
Hed fancy friends in every thing he found   70
Muttering to cattle—aye and even flowers
As one in visions claimd his talk for hours
And hed oft wonder were we nought coud see
On blades of grass and leaves upon the tree
And pointed often in a wild supprise
To trifling hues of gadding butterflys
While if another made new marvels known
That seemd to me far wonderous then his own
Of ghosts hed seen that nightly walks decievd
He heeded not but laughd and disbelievd   80
Nights dismal tongues that hardest hearts affright
And all may hear that travel out at night
Her shadowd howling tenants fierce and grim
Tho trifles struck him—such was nought to him
At length twas known his ways by woods and brooks
Were secret walks for making ryhmes and books
Which strangers bought and with amazment read
And calld him poet when they sought his shed
But men they said like serpents in the grass
That skulk in ways which learning has to pass   90
To slander worth which they woud feign posses
And dissapointment urges to suppress
Snarling at faults too bright for common minds
And hiding beautys wisdom warmly finds
Such marr'd his powers and slanderd in disguise
And tryd to black his merits with their lyes
And tho his friends the cheating fraud descryd
It hurt too earnest to be wipd aside
He dwindld down from too severe a blast
And hopes might wish to live that dyd as fast   100
Still he did live till real life seemd as gone
And his soul lingerd in a shadowd one
And yet he mingld in his favour ways
And bar'd his forhead to the sunny days
Listning the lark on fountains moaning wave
As like a ghost as ever left its grave
And fled the world at last without a sigh

And dyd as gentle as a lamb woud dye
His learned friends said envys aim was blest
That malice killd him—they might know the best   110
Else folks less learnd to different causes led
Who read his books and marveld as they read
Were he so free of ghost and fairey talks
They thought he found them on his lonley walks
And that some secret which he faild to keep
Brought on their anger and his endless sleep
Be as it might his life fell in decay
And that stone tells when it was calld away
Were een the daiseys that around it spread
The gifts of spring to dress his lowly bed   120
Are often stole in garden scenes to grow
As relics of the dust that sleeps below
While the stones verses hid by summers weed
Which strangers eager trample down to read
Are bye the curious often written down
Tho they tell nought of praises or renown
"Here sleeps the hopes of one whose glowing birth
Was found too warm for this unfeeling earth
That frownd and witherd—yet the fruitfull stem
Hides here and buds with others warm as them   130
Waiting that sun that warms their bloom to smile
And welcome heaven as their native soil" '

Winter

From huddling nights embrace how chill
The winters waking days begin
Dull reddening oer the easts blea hill
And creeping sad and shyly in
Now gilds the sun each bare tree top
And pale peeps thro each window light
While from the eaves the 'icles drop
That eke afresh their tails at night

The snows and ryhme lodge every where
Each cot in dazzling white is drest   10
Nor thatch nor witherd weeds appear
Were birds their numbing feet may rest

And every twig thro wood and plain
Were summer hung her greening bough
Wild winters mockerey cloaths again
With hoary shapes and shadows now

The street is throngd with bawling boys
Who pat their reddend fingers warm
And eager after dithering joys
Unheeding brave each pelting storm   20
To roll their jiant forms of snow
Or slide—or seeking rude repast
Hirpling by hedges were the slow
Hangs mellowd by the biting blast

Past noons thawd snow along the street
Stiffend to ice now night has been
Oft baulks the maidens stepping feet
Who falls and blushes to be seen
While amourous feelings inly warms
Some passing clown who turns to steal   30
A glimpse of modestys alarms
Which such like accidents reveal

In winters surley depth how sweet
To meet those comforts we desire
Possesing some snug corner seat
Were blazes nigh the welcome fire
Warming ones toes upon the hearth
And reading poems not too long
While basks the cat in burring mirth
While crickets sing their winter song   40

And winters tiresome hours to cheat
Have means to visit now and then
Were neighbours oer their tankard meet
And there the corner share agen
Each confort suiting best to chuse
To sit and crump warm penny rolls
Or take short snatches oer the news
While warms the nappy on the coals

And when suns creep the warmest height
And north winds wisper nearly still   50
When greening patches meet the sight
On southward slant of bank or hill
And berrys freed from ryhme awhile
Shines red on hedgrow twigs again
One may a midday hour beguile
To walk in shielding wood and plain

To track some woodlands gentle ride
Where hanging branches lend a screen
Or banks slopd down on either side
Were sheltering vallys creep between   60
As down such hollows one proceeds
We instant feel a warmer day
While mong each bank tops rustling weeds
Winds noise their unfelt rage away

Each twig when touchd tho hardly stird
Its white shower litters to the ground
And from the shake of startld bird
The ryhme like powder puthers round
And as one fails those tracks to meet
By shepherds made and foddering boys   70
The snow shrinks from our hastning feet
Harsh crumping with incessant noise

Now view the prospect were we will
On woods above or vales below
Or nigh or distant winter still
Stretches his dazzling scene of snow
The very spire points catch the eye
As changd with winters frowning pride
And were a sunbeam cannot lye
Shine whitend on their northern side   80

The arch of light around us bowd
Stretches for days its cloudless skye
Save freckling shadows of a cloud
That loose to nothing passing bye

Tho clouds oft darken closing day
And round the north disorderd lye
Like rocks with bases torn away
On nothing hung 'tween earth and skye

Nature that pauses nearly dumb
But startles some complaint to make   90
Not like the buried busyed hum
Which banishd summer kept awake—
Were sheep their bleating wants reveal
And hollow noise of bawling cow
That wait the fodderers stinted meal
Is all ones walks can listen now

Save when some clown with beatle breaks
The ponds thick ice for stock to drink
Wild noises round the village wakes
From geese that gabble on the brink   100
Who mope and brood about the snows
When frost their plashy sport destroys
Till such scant chance relief bestows
To urge afresh their squalling joys

Oft oer one flyes the chirping lark
With ryhme hung round his chilly breast
Complaining of some dogs rude bark
That scard him from his chilly rest
And oft from snowbanks ridgy edge
The hare steps hirpling oer the plain   110
Till found a bush or bunch of sedge
Then drops its ears and squats again

And feebly whines the puddocks wail
Slow circling naked woods around
And wild geese ranks that swifter sail
Oft start one with a hoarser sound
While towering at the farthest height
The heron brawls its lonley cry
Who interscepts the dazzld light
And looks a cloud speck in the skye   120

The herdboys drawling noise is oer
And all the scenes his summer saw
His cows now haunt each threshers door
And pick in sullen mood the straw
The ploughmans song is vanishd now
And quawking rooks and chattering pyes
Are silent all—each idle plough
Froze in the snow hid furrow lyes

Made bold by want in many a flock
The ringdoves flye from solitude   130
And mingling share with friendly stock
A portion of their winter food
A meal which providence bestows
Were hardy turnip roots abound
And oft one sees upon the snows
Their little footmarks dinted round

Cold woods the blackbirds gladly shun
Were round their perch the 'icles freeze
And courts less shy the noonday sun
And hops about our garden trees   140
And little birds with hunger tame
To cottage yards undaunted go
Were pity warms some gentle dame
To scatter crumbles round the snow

Yet all save robins will retreat
And shun rude mans forbidding sight
Who seemly welcomes trampling feet
And ruffs its feathers in delight
Brisk hopping from its shielding thorn
As one who woud our steps detain   150
Then droops its wing and sits forlorn
When left to solitude again

In blackening droves the rook and crow
Flap the cold air with heavy wings
To seek what home will not bestow
As soon as morn the summons brings

Full many a weary mile they flye
To try what stranger fields will spare
Till eve returns her freezing sky
Then wearied to their homes repair   160

Tho doled about reservd and shy
As one who hates to please us—still
Beautys will often catch the eye
From snow surrounding wood and hill
Those drops which nights chill finger hings
Froze on the point of every thorn'
Are trifles kin to lovley things
When gilt by slanting beams of morn

And were in midway ripples still
The brook toils on its hasty tides   170
And slides the touch of winter chill
Save on its calmer sleeping sides
There frost his quiet toil resumd
Shoots streaking spars that wildly run
From weed to weed and shine illumnd
Like glittering stars before the sun

Were as one steps its oaken plank
The hollow frozen sounding noise
From flags and sedge beside the bank
The wild ducks brooding peace destroys   180
And snipes with long mishapen bill
Oft startles from intruding fears
Who haunt the brooks in winter chill
And vanish as the spring appears

The ivey greens in brightness now
And round the tree its beauty weaves
With chocolate berrys on its bough
And shoots of paler veined leaves
And beech trees tho their bloom is flown
Still fragments of the autumn wear   190
Muffld in leaves of rustling brown
Coy beautys wildness lingers there

And milking hovels passing bye
In some close nook were shelter dwells
And cows at quiet musing lye
Whose breath steams up in savourey smells
One often meets the healthy lass
As fair and fresh as summer flowers
Which leaves a pleasure as we pass
That gladdens winters lonley hours   200

And when a sudden thaw comes in
And floods like autumn roll and noise
When hills of snow are sunk and gone
Then winter has her added joys
Banks were the north wind never comes
Then greens as with the hopes of spring
And birds fly round their changing homes
Chirping as tho they tryd to sing

Woodpecker too whose glossy wings
Seem leaves upon each witherd oak   210
Were lurd by suns it often clings
And taps for hours its gentle stroak
And ravens croaking on the wing
And crows will clamours dittys raise
All busied with the hopes of spring
When thaws mock winters warmest days

The stock now huddld side to side
From winters nipping rage to brood
Will then disperse and wander wide
Nor wait the fodderers call to food   220
Yon sullen steed that hangs his head
Will prick his ears in pleasure then
And by the pastures promise fed
Will plunge in frolic joys agen

The swain then whistles to his sheep
Nor plods his dog behind his heels
As he was wont from winds to creep
But runs at random oer the fields

Chasing the startld hare by guess
Then stops and barks his master on   230
And in his antic joys excess
Forgets his happy puppy days are gone

Each bank smiles in the sunny hours
As sweet as those the spring provides
Save that they want the daisey flowers
And white lambs basking by their sides
Mays mildness mocks the gladdend sky
And clouds as swiftly clouds pursue
Save that no swallow cares to flye
Nor cuckoo sings the story true   240

Thus some few days may idly dwell
And hold the tempting season still
And tempt the early buds to swell
For lurking winters blast to kill
And many a flower on sunny slopes
That startles up the spring to see
Is doomd to loose their early hopes
And perish in their infancy

And oft one views the hairy leaves
Of woodbines in the shelterd plain   250
Sprouting when winters thaw decieves
To perish when he frowns again
And pity often mourns to meet
A daisey smiling to the sun
Unconsious of the tempting cheat
That fancys gentle spring begun

But short is natures waking hopes
A frowning cloud may cross the skyes
When sun and warmth and all elopes
And shriveld leaf and daisey dyes   260
A cuckoos songs in summer cease
As swallows from the autumn flew
So flyes in mistery winters peace
And storms steal on to frown anew

And give me then as now at eve
The chimney corners idle joys
As days cold scenes my rambles leave
To list the kettles simmering noise
And while the chimney mocks the blast
And windows quake with jarring din   270
Let doors and shutters tightend fast
Keep cold night out and comfort in

Ballad

Where the dark ivy the thorn tree is mounting
Sweet shielding in summer the nest of the dove
There lies the sweet spot by the side of the fountain
Thats dear to all sweetness that dwells upon love
For there setting sunbeams ere evens clouds close em
Once stretchd a long shadow of one I adore
And there I did meet the sweet smiles of a bosom
Of one ever dear tho I meet her no more

And who wi a soul and a share of warm feeling
And who wi a heart that owns love for the fair   10
Can pass by a spot where his first look was stealing
Or first fondness venturd love tales to declare
Ah who can pass by it and notice it never
Can long days forget on first fondness to call
Sure time kindles love to burn brighter then ever
And natures first choice must be dearest of all

I prove it sweet mary I prove it too truly
That fountain once sweetnd wi presence of thee
As oft as I pass it at eve and as duly
As may brings the time round I think upon thee   20
I go and I sit on the soft bed of rushes
As nigh as remembrance the spot can decide
There lonly I wisper in sorrows warm gushes
That bliss when my mary was placd by my side

It grieves me to see the first open may blossom
Mary if still the hours 'membered by thee
Twas just then thou wisht one to place in thy bosom
When scarce a peep showd it self open to me

Each may wi a tear is that flower and I parted
As near that lovd spot it first blooms on the bower   30
'Ive no cause to pluck thee' I sigh broken hearted
'Theres no mary nigh to be pleasd wi the flower'

To the Rural Muse

Simple enchantress, wreathd in summer blooms
Of slender bent stalks topt wi' feathery down
Heaths creeping fetch and glaring yellow brooms
And ash keys wavering on thy rushey crown
Simple enchantress how Ive wooed thy smiles
How often sought thee far from flusht renown
Sought thee unseen where fountain waters fell
Touchd thy wild reed unheard, in weary toils
And tho my heavy hand thy song defiles
Tis hard to leave thee and to bid farwell   10

Simple enchantress ah from all renown
Far far, my soul hath warmd in bliss to see
The varied figures on thy summer gown
That natures fingure works so witchingly
The silken leaf the varied colord flower
Green nestling bower bush and high towering tree
Brooks of the sunny green and shady dell
Ah sweet full many a time they've bin to me
And tho my weak song faulters sung to thee
I cannot wild enchantress bid farwell   20

Still feign to seek thee tho I wind the brook
When morning sunbeams oer the waters glide
And trace thy footsteps in the lonly nook
As evening moists the daisey by thy side
Ah if I wooe thee on thy bed of thyme
If courting thee be deemd ambitions pride
Ah tis so passing sweet wi thee to dwell
If love for thee in clowns be calld a crime
Forgive presumption—O thou queen of ryhme
Ive lovd thee long I cannot bid farwell   30

The Last of March

written at Lolham Brigs°

Though o'er the darksome northern hill
　　Old ambush'd winter frowning flies,
And faintly drifts his threatenings still
　　In snowy sleet and blackening skies;
Yet where the willow leaning lies
　　And shields beneath the budding flower,
Where banks to break the wind arise,
　　Tis sweet to sit and spend an hour.

Though floods of winter bustling fall
　　Adown the arches bleak and blea,　　　　10
Though snow-storms clothe the mossy wall,
　　And hourly whiten oer the lea,
Yet when from clouds the sun is free
　　And warms the learning bird to sing,
'Neath sloping bank and sheltering tree
　　'Tis sweet to watch the creeping spring.

Though still so early, one may spy
　　And track her footsteps every hour;
The daisy with its golden eye,
　　And primrose bursting into flower;　　　20
And snugly where the thorny bower
　　Keeps off the nipping frost and wind,
Excluding all but sun and shower,
　　Their early violets children find.

Here 'neath the shelving bank's retreat
　　The horse-blob swells its golden ball;
Nor fear the Lady-smocks to meet
　　The snows that round their blossoms fall;
Here by the arches' ancient wall
　　The antique Elder buds anew;　　　　　30
Again the bulrush sprouting tall
　　The water wrinkles rippling through.

As Spring's warm herald April comes,
   As Natures sleep is nearly past,
How sweet to hear the wakening hums
   Of aught beside the Winter blast!
Of feather'd minstrels first and last
   The robins song's again begun
And as skies clear when overcast
   Larks rise to hail the peeping sun.   40

The startling pee-wits, as they pass,
   Scream joyous whizzing over head,
Right glad the fields and meadow grass
   Will quickly hide their careless shed:
The rooks where yonder witchens spread
   Quawk clamorous to the spring's approach:
Here silent from its watery bed,
   To hail its coming, leaps the roach.

While stalking oer the fields again
   In stript defiance to the storms,   50
The hardy seedsman spreads the grain,
   And all his hopeful toil performs:
In flocks the timid pigeon swarms
   For scatter'd kernels chance may spare,
And as the plough unbeds the worms
   The crows and magpies gather there.

Yon bullocks low their liberty,
   The young grass cropping to the full;
And colts from straw-yards neighing free
   Spring's opening promise 'joy at will: 60
Along the bank, beside the rill
   The happy lambkins bleat and run,
Then weary, neath a sheltering hill
   Drop basking in the gleaming sun.

At distance from the water's edge,
   An hanging sallows farthest stretch,
The moor hen 'gins her nest of sedge
   Safe from destroying boys to reach.

Fen-sparrows chirp and fly to fetch
    The wither'd reed-down rustling nigh,   70
And by the sunny side the ditch
    Prepare their dwelling warm and dry.

Again a storm encroaches round,
    Thick clouds are darkening deep behind,
And through the arches hoarsely sound
    The risings of the hollow wind:
Springs early hopes seem half resign'd,
    And silent for a while remain,
Till sunbeams broken clouds can find
    And brighten all to life again.   80

Ere yet a hailstone pattering comes,
    Or dimps the pool the rainy squall,
One hears the mighty murmuring hums,
    The Spirit of the tempest call.
Here sheltering 'neath the ancient wall
    I still pursue my musing dreams,
And as the hailstones round me fall
    I mark their bubbles in the streams.

Reflection here is warm'd to sigh,
    Tradition gives these brigs renown,   90
Though heedless Time long pass'd them by
    Nor thought them worthy noting down.
Here in the mouth of every clown
    The 'Roman road' familiar sounds;
All else with everlasting frown
    Oblivions mantling mist surrounds.

These walls the work of Roman hands!
    How may conjecturing Fancy pore,
As lonely here one calmly stands,
    On paths that age has trampled o'er.   100
The builders' names are known no more;
    No spot on earth their memory bears;
And crowds reflecting thus before
    Have since found graves as dark as their's.

The storm has ceas'd,—again the sun
   The ague-shivering season dries;
Short winded March, thou'lt soon be done,
   Thy fainting tempest mildly dies.
Soon April's flowers and dappled skies
   Shall spread a couch for lovely May,   110
Upon whose bosom Nature lies
   And smiles its' joyous Youth away.

Winter

The small wind wispers thro the leafless hedge
Most sharp and chill while the light snowey flakes
Rests on each twig and spike of witherd sedge
Resembling scatterd feathers—vainly breaks
The pale split sunbeam thro the frowning cloud
On winters frowns below—from day to day
Unmelted still he spreads his hoary shroud
In dithering pride on the pale travellers way
Who croodling hastens from the storm behind
Fast gathering deep and black—again to find   10
His cottage fire and corners sheltering bounds
Where haply such uncomfortable days
Makes musical the woodsaps frizzling sounds
And hoarse loud bellows puffing up the blaze

To a Fallen Elm

Old Elm that murmured in our chimney top
The sweetest anthem autumn ever made
And into mellow whispering calms would drop
When showers fell on thy many colored shade
And when dark tempests mimic thunder made
While darkness came as it would strangle light
With the black tempest of a winter night
That rocked thee like a cradle to thy root
How did I love to hear the winds upbraid
Thy strength without while all within was mute   10

It seasoned comfort to our hearts desire
We felt thy kind protection like a friend
And pitched our chairs up closer to the fire
Enjoying comforts that was never penned

Old favourite tree ₋₋oust seen times changes lower
But change till now did never come to thee
For time beheld thee as his sacred dower
And nature claimed thee her domestic tree
Storms came and shook thee with a living power
Yet stedfast to thy home thy roots hath been   20
Summers of thirst parched round thy homely bower
Till earth grew iron—still thy leaves was green
The children sought thee in thy summer shade
And made their play house rings of sticks and stone
The mavis sang and felt himself alone
While in thy leaves his early nest was made
And I did feel his happiness mine own
Nought heeding that our friendship was betrayed

Friend not inanimate—tho stocks and stones
There are and many cloathed in flesh and bones   30
Thou ownd a language by which hearts are stirred
Deeper than by the atribute of words
Thine spoke a feeling known in every tongue
Language of pity and the force of wrong
What cant asumes what hypocrites may dare
Speaks home to truth and shows it what they are

I see a picture that thy fate displays
And learn a lesson from thy destiny
Self interest saw thee stand in freedoms ways
So thy old shadow must a tyrant be   40
Thoust heard the knave abusing those in power
Bawl freedom loud and then oppress the free
Thoust sheltered hypocrites in many a shower
That when in power would never shelter thee
Thoust heard the knave supply his canting powers
With wrongs illusions when he wanted friends
That bawled for shelter when he lived in showers
And when clouds vanished made thy shade amends

With axe at root he felled thee to the ground
And barked of freedom—O I hate that sound   50

It grows the cant terms of enslaving tools
To wrong another by the name of right
It grows a liscence with oer bearing fools
To cheat plain honesty by force of might
Thus came enclosu·e—ruin was her guide
But freedoms clapping hands enjoyed the sight
Tho comforts cottage soon was thrust aside
And workhouse prisons raised upon the scite
Een natures dwelling far away from men
The common heath became the spoilers prey   60
The rabbit had not where to make his den
And labours only cow was drove away
No matter—wrong was right and right was wrong
And freedoms brawl was sanction to the song

Such was thy ruin music making Elm
The rights of freedom was to injure thine
As thou wert served so would they overwhelm
In freedoms name the little that is mine
And these are knaves that brawl for better laws
And cant of tyranny in stronger powers   70
Who glut their vile unsatiated maws
And freedoms birthright from the weak devours

from *The Parish*°

That good old fame the farmers earnd of yore
That made as equals not as slaves the poor
That good old fame did in two sparks expire
A shooting coxcomb and a hunting Squire
And their old mansions that was dignified
With things far better then the pomp of pride
At whose oak table that was plainly spread
Each guest was welcomd and the poor was fed
Were master son and serving man and clown
Without distinction daily sat them down   10

Were the bright rows of pewter by the wall
Se[r]ved all the pomp of kitchen or of hall
These all have vanished like a dream of good
And the slim things that rises were they stood
Are built by those whose clownish taste aspires
To hate their farms and ape the country squires

And weres that lovley maid in days gone bye
The farmers daughter unreserved tho shye
That milked her cows and old songs used to sing
As red and rosey as the lovely spring   20
All these have dwindled to a formal shade
As pale and bed rid as my ladys maid
Who cannot dare to venture in the street
Some times thro cold at other times for heat
And vulgar eyes to shun and vulgar winds
Shrouded in veils green as their window blinds
These taught at school their stations to despise
And view old customs with disdainful eyes
Deem all as rude their kindred did of yore
And scorn to toil or foul their fingers more   30
Prim as the pasteboard figures which they cut
At school and tastful on the chimney put
They sit before their glasses hour by hour
Or paint unnatural daubs of fruit or flowers
Or boasting learning novels beautys quotes
Or aping fashions scream a tune by notes
Een poetry in these high polished days
Is oft profained by their dislike or praise
Theyve read the Speaker till without a look°
Theyll sing whole pages and lay bye the book   40
Then sure their judgment must be good indeed
When ere they chuse to speak of what they read
To simper tastful some devoted line
As somthing bad or somthing very fine
Thus mincing fine airs misconcieved at school
That pride outherods and compleats the fool
Thus housed mid cocks and hens in idle state
Aping at fashions which their betters hate
Affecting high lifes airs to scorn the past
Trying to be somthing makes them nought at last   50

These are the shadows that supply the place
Of farmers daughters of the vanished race
And what are these rude names will do them harm
O rather call them 'Ladys of the Farm'

Miss Peevish Scornful once the Village toast
Deemd fair by some and prettyish by most
Brought up a lady tho her fathers gain
Depended still on cattle and on grain
She followd shifting fashions and aspired
To the high notions baffled pride desired   60
And all the profits pigs and poultry made
Were gave to Miss for dressing and parade
To visit balls and plays fresh hopes to trace
And try her fortune with a simpering face
And now and then in Londons crowds was shown
To know the world and to the world be known
All leisure hours while miss at home sojournd
Past in preparing till new routs returnd
Or tittle tattling oer her shrewd remarks
Of Ladys dresses or attentive sparks   70
How Mr So and so at such a rout
Fixd his eyes on her all the night about
While the good lady seated by his side
Behind her hand her blushes forced to hide
Till consious Miss in pity she woud say
For the poor lady turnd her face away
And young Squire Dandy just returnd from france°
How he first chose her from the rest to dance
And at the play how such a gent resignd
His seat to her and placed himself behind   80
How this squire bowd polite at her approach
And Lords een nodded as she passd their coach
Thus miss in raptures woud such things recall
And Pa and Ma in raptures heard it all
But when an equal woud his praise declare
And told young madam that her face was fair
She might believe the fellows truth the while
And just in sport might condescend to smile
But frownd his further teazing suit to shun
And deemd it rudeness in a farmers son   90

Thus she went on and visited and drest
And deemd things earnest that was spoke in jest
And dreamd at night oer prides uncheckd desires
Of nodding gentlemen and smiling squires
To Gretna green her visions often fled
And rattling coaches lumberd in her head
Till hopes grown weary with too long delay
Caught the green sickness and declined away
And beauty like a garment worse for wear
Fled her pale cheek and left it much too fair   100
Then she gave up sick visits balls and plays
Were whispers turnd to any thing but praise
All were thrown bye like an old fashiond song
Were she had playd show woman much too long
And condecended to be kind and plain
And 'mong her equals hoped to find a swain
Past follys now were hatful to review
And they were hated by her equals too
Notice from equals vain she tryd to court
Or if they noticed twas but just in sport   110
At last grown husband mad away she ran
Not with squire Dandy but the servant man

Young farmer Bigg of this same flimsey class
Wise among fools and with the wise an ass
A farming sprout with more then farmers pride
Struts like the squire and dresses dignified
They call him rich at which his weakness aimd
But others view him as a fool misnamed
Yet dress and tattle ladys hearts can charm
And hes the choice with madams of the farm   120
Now with that lady strutting now with this
Braced up in stays as slim as sickly miss
Shining at christmass rout and vulgar ball
The favourite spark and rival of them all
And oft hell venture to bemean his pride
Tho bribes and mysterys do their best to hide
Teazing weak maidens with his pert deciet
Whose lives are humble but whose looks are sweet
Whose beauty happen[s] to outrival those
With whom the dandy as an equal goes   130

Thus maids are ruind oft and mothers made
As if bewitchd without a fathers aid
Tho nodds and winks and whispers urge a guess
Weakness is bribed and hides its hearts distress
To live dishonourd and to dye unwed
For clowns grow jealous when theyre once misled
Thus pointed fingers brand the passing spark
And whispers often guess his deeds are dark
But friends deny and urge that doubts mislead
And prove the youth above so mean a deed   140
The town agrees and leaves his ways at will
A proud consieted meddling fellow still . . .

Sudden Shower

Black grows the southern clouds betokening rain
And humming hive bees homeward hurry bye
They feel the change—so let us shun the grain
And take the broad road while our feet are dry
Aye there some dropples moistened in my face
And pattered on my hat—tis coming nigh
Lets look about and find a sheltering place
The little things around like you and I
Are hurrying thro the grass to shun the shower
Here stoops an Ash tree—hark the wind gets high   10
But never mind its Ivy for an hour
Rain as it may will keep us dryly here
That little Wren knows well his sheltering bower
Nor leaves his dry house tho we come so near

Home Pictures in May

The sunshine bathes in clouds of many hues
And mornings feet are gemmed with early dews
Warm Daffodils about the garden beds
Peep thro their pale slim leaves their golden heads
Sweet earthly suns of spring—the Gosling broods
In coats of sunny green about the road
Waddle in extacy—and in rich moods
The old hen leads her flickering chicks abroad

Oft scuttling neath her wings to see the kite
Hang waving oer them in the springs blue light   10
The sparrows round their new nests chirp with glee
And sweet the Robin springs young luxury shares
Tuteling its song in feathery Goosberry tree
While watching worms the Gardeners spade unbears

The Wheat Ripening

What time the wheat field tinges rusty brown
And barley bleaches in its mellow grey
Tis sweet some smooth mown baulk to wander down
Or cross the fields on footpaths narrow way
Just in the mealey light of waking day
As glittering dewdrops moist the maidens gown
And sparkling bounces from her nimble feet
Journying to milking from the neighbouring town
Making life bright with song—and it is sweet
To mark the grazing herds and list the clown   10
Urge on his ploughing team with cheering calls
And merry shepherds whistling toils begun
And hoarse tongued bird boy whose unceasing calls
Join the Larks dittys to the rising sun

Careless Rambles

I love to wander at my idle will
In summers luscious prime about the fields
And kneel when thirsty at the little rill
To sip the draught its pebbly bottom yields
And where the maple bush its fountain shields
To lie and rest a swailey hour away
And crop the swelling peascod from the land
Or mid the uplands woodland walks to stray
Where oaks for aye oer their old shadows stand
Neath whose dark foliage with a welcome hand   10
I pluck the luscious strawberry ripe and red
As beautys lips—and in my fancys dreams
As mid the velvet moss I musing tread
Feel life as lovely as her picture seems

To the Rural Muse

Muse of the Fields oft have I said farewell
To thee my boon companion loved so long
And hung thy sweet harp in the bushy dell
For abler hands to wake an abler song
Much did I fear mine homage did thee wrong
Yet loath to leave as oft I turned again
And to its wires mine idle hands would cling
Torturing it into song—it may be vain
Yet still I try ere fancy drops her wing
And hopeless silence comes to numb its every string   10

Muse of the pasture brooks on thy calm sea
Of poesy Ive sailed and tho the will
To speed were greater then my prowess be
Ive ventured with much fear of usage ill
Yet more of joy—tho timid be my skill
As not to dare the depths of mightier streams
Yet rocks abide in shallow ways and I
Have much of fear to mingle with my dreams
Yet lovely Muse I still believe thee bye
And think I see thee smile and so forget I sigh   20

Muse of the cottage hearth oft did I tell
My hopes to thee nor feared to plead in vain
But felt around my heart thy witching spell
That bade me as thy worshiper remain
I did and worship on O once again
Smile on my offerings and so keep them green
Bedeck my fancys like the clouds of even
Mingling all hues which thou from heaven dost glean
To me a portion of thy power be given
If theme so mean as mine may merit aught of heaven   30

For thee in youth I culled the simple flower
That on thy bosom gained a sweeter hue
And took thy hand along lifes sunny hour
Meeting the sweetest joys that ever grew
More friends were needless and my foes were few

Tho freedom then be deemed as rudeness now
And what once won thy praise now meet disdain
Yet the last wreath I braided for thy brow
Thy smiles did so commend it made me vain
To weave another one and hope for praise again   40

With thee the spirit of departed years
Wakes that sweet voice that time hath rendered dumb
And freshens like to spring—loves hopes and fears
That in my bosom found an early home
Wooing the heart to extacys—I come
To thee when sick of care of joys bereft
Seeking the pleasures that are found in bloom
And happy hopes that time hath only left
Around the haunts where thou didst erst sojourn
Then smile sweet cherubim and welcome my return   50

With thee the raptures of lifes early day
Appear and all that pleased me when a boy
Tho pains and cares have torn the best away
And winters crept between us to destroy
Do thou commend the reccompense is joy
The tempest of the heart shall soon be calm
Tho sterner truth against my dreams rebel
Hope feels success and all my spirits warm
To strike with happier mood my simple shell
And seize thy mantles hem O say not fare thee well   60

Still sweet enchantress youths stray feelings move
That from thy presence their existance took
The innocent idolatry and love
Paying thee worship in each secret nook
That fancied friends in tree and flower and brook
Shaped clouds to angels and beheld them smile
And heard commending tongues in every wind
Lifes grosser fancys did these dreams defile
Yet not entirely root them from the mind
I think I hear them still and often look behind   70

Aye I have heard thee in the summer wind
As if commending what I sung to thee
Aye I have seen thee on a cloud reclined
Kindling my fancys into poesy
I saw thee smile and took the praise to me
In beautys past all beauty thou wert drest
I thought the very clouds around thee knelt
I saw the sun to linger in the west
Paying thee worship and as eve did melt
In dews they seemd thy tears for sorrows I had felt   80

Sweeter than flowers on beautys bosom hung
Sweeter than dreams of happiness above
Sweeter than themes by lips of beauty sung
Are the young fancies of a poets love
When round his thoughts thy trancing visions move
In floating melody no notes may sound
The world is all forgot and past his care
While on thine harp thy fingers lightly bound
As winning him its melody to share
And heaven itself with him where is it then but there   90

Een now my heart leaps out from grief and all
The gloom thrown round by cares oershading wing
Een now those sunny visions to recall
Like to a bird I loose dull earth and sing
Lifes tempest swoons to calms on every string
And sweet enchantress if I do but dream
If earthly visions have been only mine
My weakness in thy service wooes esteem
And pleads my truth as almost worthy thine
Surely true worship makes the meanest theme divine   100

And still warm courage calming many a fear
Heartens my hand once more thine harp to try
To join the anthem of the minstrel year
For summers music in thy praise is high
The very winds about thy mantle sigh
Love melodies thy minstrel bards to be
Insects and Birds exerting all their skill
Float in continued song for mastery

While in thy haunts loud leaps the little rill
To kiss thy sweeping dress and how can I be still 110

There still I see thee fold thy mantle grey
To trace the dewy lawn at morn and night
And there I see thee in the sunny day
Withdraw thy veil and shine confest in light
Burning my fancies with a wild delight
To win a portion of the blushing fame
Tho haughty fancies treat thy powers as small
And fashions thy simplicitys disclaim
Should but a corner of thy mantle fall
Oer him who wooes thy love tis reccompense for all 120

Not with the mighty to thy shrine I come
In anxious sighs or self applauding mirth
On mount parnassus as thine heir to roam
I dare not credit that immortal birth
But mingling with the lesser ones on earth
Like as the little lark from off its nest
Beside the mossy hill awakes in glee
To seek thy mornings throne a merry guest
So do I seek thy shrine if that may be
To win by new attempts another smile from thee 130

If without thee neath clouds and storms and winds
Ive roamed the wood and field and meadow lea
And found no flowers but what the vulgar finds
Nor met one breath of living poesy
Among such charms where inspirations be
The fault is mine and I must bear the lot
Of missing praise to merit thy disdain
To feel each idle plea tho urged forgot
I can but sigh—tho foolish to complain
Oer hopes so fair begun to find them end so vain 140

Then will it prove presumption thus to dare
To add fresh failings to each faulty song
Urging thy blessing on an idle prayer
To sanction silly themes it will be wrong
For one so lowly to be heard so long

Yet sweet enchantress yet a little while
Forgo impatience and from frowns refrain
The strong are not debarred thy cheering smile
Why should the weak who need them most complain
Alone in solitude soliciting in vain   150

[*Bloomfield I*]°

Sweet unasuming Minstrel not to thee
The dazzling fashions of the day belong
Natures wild pictures field and cloud and tree
And quiet brooks far distant from the throng
In murmurs tender as the toiling bee
Make the sweet music of thy gentle song
Well—nature owns thee let the crowd pass bye—
The tide of fashion is a stream too strong
For pastoral brooks that gently flow and sing
But nature is their source and earth and sky   10
Their annual offerings to her current bring
Thy injured muse and memory need no sigh
For thine shall murmur on to many a spring
When their proud stream is summer burnt and dry

[*Bloomfield II*]

The shepherd musing oer his summer dreams
The may day wild flowers in the meadow grass
The sunshine sparkling in the valley streams
The singing ploughman and hay making lass
These live the summer of thy rural themes
Thy green memorials these and they surpass
The cobweb praise of fashion—every may
Shall find a native 'Giles' beside his plough
Joining the sky larks song at early day
And summer rustling in the ripened corn   10
Shall meet thy rustic loves as sweet as now
Offering to Marys lips the 'brimming horn'
And seasons round thy humble grave shall be
Fond lingering pilgrims to remember thee

[*Woodland Thoughts*]

How sweet the wood shades the hot summer hours
And stretches oer my head its sheltering green
As I recline mid grass and cooling flowers
And seeded stalks of blossoms that have been
Sure tis a pleasure in such secret nooks
To muse on distant friends in memorys eye
Or glance on passages in favourite books
Whose thoughts like echoes to our own reply
Or shades recall which substance long forsook
From the black nothingness of days gone bye   10
Blessings of infant hope and loves young bliss
Ah thus to think the thoughts of death is sweet
In shaping heaven to a scene like this
With loves and friends and feelings all to meet

Impulses of Spring

Day burnishes the distant hills
    And clouds blush far away
Lifes heart with natures rapture thrills
    To hail this glorious day
The morning falls in dizzy light
    On mountain tops and towers
But speeds with soft and gentle flight
    Among these valley flowers

Theres music in the waking woods
    Theres glory in the air   10
Birds in their merry summer moods
    Now rant and revel there
Joy wakes and wantons all around
    Love laughs in every call
Music in many hearts abound
    And poesy breaths in all

The merry new come Nightingale
  Wooes nights dull hours along
Till daylight at the sound turns pale
  And hastes to share the song   20
A waste of sunny flowers is seen
  And insence fills the air
No sunless place is found too mean
  Springs blushing gems to wear

The horse blob by the water mill
  Blooms in the foaming dam
And pilewort blazes round the hill
  Beside the sleeping lamb
Spring is the happy breathing time
  For young loves stolen joys   30
Spring is the poets luscious prime
  He revels in the noise

Of waking insects humming round
  And birds upon the wing
And all the gushing soul of sound
  That ecchoes of the spring
For in their joys his own are met
  Tho tears stand in his eye
In their gay mirth he half forgets
  He eer knew how to sigh

                                               40

He feeds on springs precarious boon
  A being of her race
Where light and shade and shower and sun
  Are ever changing place
To day he buds and glows to meet
  To morrows coming shower
But crushed by cares intruding feet
  He fades a broken flower

His hopes they change like summer clouds
  And fairey phantasys   50
His pleasures wrapt in gayer shrouds
  Are sorrows in disguise

The sweetest smiles his heart can find
    Posses their tears as well
And highest pleasures leave behind
    Their heart ache and farewell

His are the fading 'joys of grief'
    Care grows his favoured guest
And sorrow gives his heart relief
    Because it knows him best   60
The sweetest flower on pleasures path
    Will bloom on sorrows grave
And earthly love and earthly mirth
    Their share of grief shall have

And poesy owns an haunted mind
    A thirst enduring flame
Burning the soul to leave behind
    The memory of a name
Tho life be deemed as sweetly sold
    For toil so ill repaid   70
The marble epitaph how cold
    Altho with gold inlaid

While the rude clown of thoughtless clay
    In feelings unrefined
Lives out lifes cloudless holiday
    With nothing on his mind
Then sound as ever king hath slept
    On earths green lap he lies
While beautys tear so sweetly wept
    And friendships warmest sighs   80

Are left upon his lowly grave
    And live his only fame
While frowning envy never gave
    One insult to his name
Yet who would from their cares be freed
    For such unconsious bliss
A living blank in life to be
    Pains sympathys to miss

To meet enthusiastic May
        As but dull winters hours   90
And primrose pale and daisey gay
        As white and yellow flowers
And not as friends in our esteem
        To cheer dull lifes sojourn
Let me in its decieving dream
        Much rather feel and mourn

The bliss or grief tho past control
        That in extreems inflame
Blood rushing feelings thro the soul
        Not uttered in a name   100
Where no words live to free the mind
        Of hidden hopes or fears
The only utterance they can find
        Are gushing smiles and tears

Yet woo I not that burning flame
        Enkindling extacy
Blazing in dreams to win a name
        From fames eternity
Fames yearning breath breeds not my sigh
        Nor eats my heart away   110
Burning lifes every channel dry
        To triumph oer decay

Yet with the minstrelsy on earth
        I too would love the lyre
For heaven neer gave the meanest birth
        To quench that holy fire
It owns the muses sweetest smiles
        And scatters life around
Grief sick with hopes heart broken toils
        Glows happy at the sound   120

The lyre is pleasures blest abode
        Around it angels throng
The lyre it is the voice of God
        The prophets spoke in song

And as the sun this day brings forth
  Creations every hour
Cares wreath warms at the muses mirth
  And blushes into flower

The Old Willow

The juicey wheat now spindles into ear
And trailing pea blooms ope their velvet eyes
And weeds and flowers by crowds far off and near
In all their sunny liverys appear
For summers lustre boasts unnumbered dyes
How pleasant neath this willow by the brook
Thats kept its ancient place for many a year
To sit and oer these crowded fields to look
And the soft dropping of the shower to hear
Our selves so sheltered een a pleasant book   10
Might lie uninjured from the fragrant rain
For not a drop gets through the bowering leaves
But dry as housed in my old hut again
I sit and troublous care of half its claim decieves

from *Childhood*

The past it is a magic word
Too beautiful to last
It looks back like a lovely face
Who hath not felt the past
Theres music in its childhood
Thats known in every tongue
Like the music of the wildwood
All chorus to the song

The happy dream the joyous play
The life without a sigh   10
The beauty thoughts can neer pourtray
In those four letters lye
The painters beauty breathing arts
The poets speaking pens
Can neer call back a thousand part
Of what that word contains

And fancy at its sweetest hour
What eer may come to pass
Shall find that magic thrill no more
Time broke it like his glass   20
The sweetest joy the fairest face
The treasures most preferred
Have left the honours of their place
Locked in that silent word

When we look back on what we were
And feel what we are now
A fading leaf is not so drear
Upon a broken bough
A winter seat without a fire
A cold world without friends   30
Doth not such chilly glooms impart
As that one word portends

Like withered wreaths in banquet halls
When all the rout is past
Like sunshine that on ruins fall
Our pleasures are at last
The joy is fled the love is cold
And beautys splendour too
Our first believings all are old
And faith itself untrue . . .   40

Each noise that breathed around us then
Was magic all and song
Where ever pastime found us then
Joy never led us wrong
The wild bee in the blossom hung
The coy birds startled call
To find its home in danger—there
Was music in them all

And oer the first Bumbarrels nest
We wondered at the spell   50
That birds who served no prenticeship
Could build their nests so well

And finding linnets moss was green
And buntings chusing grey
And every buntings nest alike
Our wits was all away

Then blackbirds lining them with grass
And thrushes theirs with dung
So for our lives we could not tell
From whence the wisdom sprung   60
We marvelled much how little birds
Should ever be so wise
And so we guessed some angel came
To teach them from the skys

In winter too we traced the fields
And still felt summer joys
We sought our hips and felt no cold
Cold never came to boys
The sloes appeared as choice as plumbs
When bitten by the frost   70
And crabs grew honey in the mouth
When apple time was past

We rolled in sunshine lumps of snow
And called them mighty men
And tired of pelting Bounaparte
We ran to slide agen
And ponds for glibbest ice we sought
With shouting and delight
And tasks of spelling all were left
To get by heart at night   80

And when it came—and round the fire
We sat—what joy was there
The kitten dancing round the cork
That dangled from a chair
While we our scraps of paper burnt
To watch the flitting sparks
And collect books were often torn
For 'parsons' and for 'clerks'

Nought seemed too hard for us to do
But the sums upon our slates   90
Nought seemed too high for us to win
But the masters chair of state
The 'Town of Troy' we tried and made°
When our sums we could not trye
While we envied een the sparrows wings
From our prison house to flye

When twelve oclock was counted out
The joy and strife began
The shut of books the hearty shout
As out of doors we ran   100
Sunshine and showers who could withstand
Our food and rapture they
We took our dinners in our hands
To loose no time in play

The morn when first we went to school
Who can forget the morn
When the birch whip lay upon the clock
And our horn book it was torn
We tore the little pictures out
Less fond of books then play   110
And only took one letter home
And that the letter 'A'

I love in childhoods little book
To read its lessons thro
And oer each pictured page to look
Because they read so true
And there my heart creates anew
Love for each trifling thing
—Who can disdain the meanest weed
That shows its face at spring   120

The daisey looks up in my face
As long ago it smiled
It knows no change but keeps its place
And takes me for a child

The bunting in the hedgerow thorn
Cries 'pink pink pink' to hear
My footsteps in the early morn
As tho a boy was near

I seek no more the buntings nest
Nor stoop for daisey flowers   130
I grow a stranger to myself
In these delightful hours
Yet when I hear the voice of spring
I can but call to mind
The pleasures which they used to bring
The joys I used to find

The firetail on the orchard wall
Keeps at its startled cry
Of 'tweet tut tut' nor sees the morn
Of boyhoods mischief bye   140
It knows no change of changing time
By sickness never stung
It feeds on hopes eternal prime
Around its brooded young

Ponds where we played at 'Duck and drake'
Where the Ash with ivy grew
Where we robbed the owl of all her eggs
And mocked her as she flew
The broad tree in the spinney hedge
Neath which the gipseys lay   150
Where we our fine oak apples got
On the twenty ninth of may

These all remain as then they were
And are not changed a day
And the ivys crowns as near to green
As mine is to the grey
It shades the pond oerhangs the stile
And the oak is in the glen
But the paths to joy are so worn out
I cant find one agen   160

The merry wind still sings the song
As if no change had been
The birds build nests the summer long
And trees look full as green
As eer they did in childhoods joy
Tho that hath long been bye
When I a happy roving boy
In the fields had used to lye

To tend the restless roving sheep
Or lead the quiet cow   170
Toils that seemed more then slavery then
How more then freedom now
Could we but feel as then we did
When joy too fond to flye
Would flutter round as soon as bid
And drive all troubles bye

But rainbows on an april cloud
And blossoms pluckt in may
And painted eves that summer brings
Fade not so fast away   180
Tho grass is green tho flowers are gay
And every where they be
What are the leaves on branches hung
Unto the withered tree

Lifes happiest gifts and what are they
Pearls by the morning strung
Which ere the noon are swept away
—Short as a cuckoos song
A nightingales the summer is
Can pleasure make us proud   190
To think when swallows flye away
They leave her in her shroud

Youth revels at his rising hour
With more then summer joys
And rapture holds the fairey flower
Which reason soon destroys

O sweet the bliss which fancy feigns
To hide the eyes of truth
And beautious still the charm appears
Of faces loved in youth   200

And spring returns the blooming year
Just as it used to be
And joys in youthful smiles appear
To mock the change in me
Each sight leaves memory ill at ease
And stirs an aching bosom
To think that seasons sweet as these
With me are out of blossom

The finest summer sinks in shade
The sweetest blossom dies   210
And age finds every beauty fade
That youth esteemed a prize
The play breaks up the blossom fades
And childhood dissapears
For higher dooms ambition aims
And care grows into years

But time we often blame him wrong
That rude destroying time
And follow him with sorrows song
When he hath done no crime   220
Our joys in youth are often sold
In follys thoughtless fray
And many feel their hearts grow old
Before their heads are grey

The past there lies in that one word
Joys more then wealth can crown
Now could a million call them back
Tho muses wrote them down
The sweetest joys imagined yet
The beautys that surpast   230
All life or fancy ever met
Are there among the past

Sport in the Meadows

Maytime is in the meadows coming in
And cowslap peeps have gotten eer so big
And water blobs and all their golden kin
Crowd round the shallows by the striding bríg
Daiseys and buttercups and lady smocks
Are all abouten shining here and there
Nodding about their gold and yellow locks
Like morts of folken crowding at a fair
The sheep and cows do flocken for a share
And snatch the blossoms in such eager haste   10
That basket bearing childern running there
Do think within their hearts theyll get them all
And hoot and drive them from their graceless waste
As though there wa'n't a cowslap peep to spare
—For they want some for tea and some for wine
And some to maken up a cucka ball
To throw accross the garlands silken line
That reaches oer the street from wall to wall
—Good gracious me how merrily they fare
One sees a finer cowslap than the rest   20
And off they shout—the foremost bidding fair
To get the prize—and earnest half and jest
The next one pops her down—and from her hand
Her basket falls and out her cowslaps all
Tumble and litter out—the merry band
In laughing friendship round about her fall
To helpen gather up the littered flowers
That she no loss may mourn—and now the wind
In frolic mood among the merry hours
Wakens with sudden start and tosses off   30
Some untied bonnet on its dancing wings
Away they follow with a scream and laugh
(And aye the youngest ever lags behind)
Till on the deep lakes very brink it hings
They shout and catch it and then off they start
The chase for cowslaps merry as before
And each one seems so anxious at the heart
As they would even get them all and more

One climbs a molehill for a bunch of may
One stands on tiptoe for a linnets nest   40
And pricks her hand and throws her flowers away
And runs for plantin leaves to have it drest
So do they run abouten all the day
And teaze the grass hid larks from getting rest
—Scarce give they time in their unruly haste
To tie a shoe string that the grass unties
And thus they run the meadows bloom to waste
Till even comes and dulls their phantasys
When one finds losses out to stifle smiles
Of silken bonnet strings and uthers sigh   50
Oer garments renten clambering over stiles
Yet in the morning fresh afield they hie
Bidding the last days troubles a good bye
When red pied cow again their coming hears
And ere they clap the gate she tosses up
Her head and hastens from the sport she fears
The old yoe calls her lamb nor cares to stoop
To drop a cowslap in their company
Thus merrily the little noisey troop
Along the grass as rude marauders hie   60
For ever noisey and for ever gay
While keeping in the meadows holiday

Wild Bees

These childern of the sun which summer brings
As pastoral minstrels in her merry train
Pipe rustic ballads upon busy wings
And glad the cotters quiet toils again
The white nosed bee that bores its little hole
In mortared walls and pipes its symphonies
And never absent couzin black as coal
That indian-like bepaints its little thighs
With white and red bedight for holiday
Right earlily a morn do pipe and play   10
And with their legs stroke slumber from their eyes
And aye so fond they of their singing seem

That in their holes abed at close of day
They still keep piping in their honey dreams
And larger ones that thrum on ruder pipe
Round the sweet smelling closen and rich woods
Where tawney-white and red flus[h]ed clover buds
Shine bonnily and bean fields blossom ripe
Shed dainty perfumes and give honey food
To these sweet poets of the sunny field   20
Me much delighting as I sawn along
The narrow path that hay laid meadow yields
Catc[h]ing the windings of their wandering song
The black and yellow bumble first on wing
To buzz among the sallows early flowers
Hiding its nest in holes from fickle spring
Who stints his rambles with her frequent showers
And one that may for wiser piper pass
In livery dress half sables and half red
Who laps a moss ball in the meadow grass   30
And hurds her stores when april showers have fled
And russet commoner who knows the face
Of every blossom that the meadow brings
Starting the traveller to a qu[i]cker pace
By threatning round his head in many rings
These sweeten summer in their happy glee
By giving for her honey melodie

Songs Eternity

What is songs eternity
Come and see
Can it noise and bustle be
Come and see
Praises sung or praises said
Can it be
Wait awhile and these are dead
Sigh sigh
Be they high or lowly bred
They die   10

What is songs eternity
Come and see
Melodys of earth and sky
Here they be
Songs once sung to adams ears
Can it be
—Ballads of six thousand years
Thrive thrive
Songs awakened with the spheres
Alive   20

Mighty songs that miss decay
What are they
Crowds and citys pass away
Like a day
Books are writ and books are read
What are they
Years will lay them with the dead
Sigh sigh
Trifles unto nothing wed
They die   30

Dreamers list the honey be[e]
Mark the tree
Where the blue cap tootle tee
Sings a glee
Sung to adam and to eve
Here they be
When floods covered every bough
Noahs ark
Heard that ballad singing now
Hark hark   40

Tootle tootle tootle tee
Can it be
Pride and fame must shadows be
Come and see
Every season own her own
Bird and be[e]

Sing creations music on
Natures glee
Is in every mood and tone
Eternity   50

The eternity of song
Liveth here
Natures universal tongue
Singeth here
Songs Ive heard and felt and seen
Everywhere
Songs like the grass are evergreen
The giver
Said live and be and they have been
For ever   60

Summer Images

Now swathy summer by rude health embrownd
Presedence takes of rosey fingered spring
And laughing joy with wild flowers prankt and crowned
          A wild and giddy thing
With health robust from every care unbound
          Comes on the zephers wing
          And cheers the toiling clown

Happy as holiday enjoying face
Loud tongued and merry as a marriage bell
Thy lightsome step sheds joy in every place   10
          And where the troubled dwell
Thy witching smiles weans them of half their cares
          And from thy sunny spell
          They greet joy unawares

Then with thy sultry locks all loose and rude
And mantle laced with gems of garish light
Come as of wont for I would fain intrude
          And in the worlds despight
Share the rude mirth that thine own heart beguiles
          If haply so I might   20
          Win pleasure from thy smiles

Me not the noise of brawling pleasures cheer
In nightly revels or in city streets
But joys which sooth and not distract mine ear
    That one at leisure meets
In the green woods and meadows summer shorn
    Or fields where bee flye greets
    Ones car with mellow horn

Where green swathed grass hoppers on treble pipe
Singeth and danceth in mad hearted pranks   30
And bees go courting every flower thats ripe
    On baulks and sunny banks
And droning dragon flye on rude bassoon
    Striveth to give god thanks
    In no discordant tune

Where speckled thrush by self delight embued
Singeth unto himself for joys amends
And drinks the honey dew of solitude
    Where happiness attends
With inbred joy untill his heart ocrflows   40
    Of which the worlds rude friends
    Nought heeding nothing knows

Where the gay river laughing as it goes
Plashes with easy wave its flaggy sides
And to the calm of heart in calmness shows
    What pleasure there abides
To trace its sedgy banks from trouble free
    Spots solitude provides
    To muse and happy be

Or ruminating neath some pleasant bush   50
On sweet silk grasses stretch me at mine ease
Where I can pillow on the yielding rush
    And acting as I please
Drop into pleasant dreams or musing lye
    Mark the wind shaken trees
    And cloud betravelled sky

And think me how some barter joy for care
And waste lifes summer health in riot rude
Of nature nor of natures sweets aware
  Where passions vain intrude   60
By calm reflection softened are and still
   And the hearts better mood
   Feels sick of doing ill

Here I can live and at my leisure seek
Joys far from cold restraints—not fearing pride
Free as the winds that breath upon my cheek
  Rude health so long denied
Where poor integrity can sit at ease
   And list self satisfied
   The song of honey bees   70

And green lane traverse heedless where it goes
Naught guessing till some sudden turn espies
Rude battered finger post that stooping shows
  Where the snug mystery lies
And then a mossy spire with ivy crown
   Clears up the short supprise
   And shows the peeping town

And see the wild flowers in their summer morn
Of beauty feeding on joys luscious hours
The gay convolvulus wreathing round the thorn 80
  Agape for honey showers
And slender king cup burnished with the dew
   Of mornings early hours
   Like gold yminted new

And mark by rustic bridge on shallow stream
Cow tending boy to toil unreconsiled
Absorbed as in some vagrant summer dream
  And now in gestures wild
Starts dancing to his shadow on the wall
   Feeling self gratified   90
   Nor fearing human thrall

Then thread the sunny valley laced with streams
Or forrests rude and the oer shadowed brims
Of simple ponds where idle shepherd dreams
　　　And streaks his listless limbs
Or trace hay scented meadow smooth and long
　　　Where joys wild impulse swims
　　　In one continued song

I love at early morn from new mown swath
To see the startled frog his rout pursue　　　100
And mark while leaping oer the dripping path
　　　His bright sides scatter dew
And early Lark that from its bustle flyes—
　　　To hail his mattin new
　　　And watch him to the skyes

And note on hedgerow baulks in moisture sprent
The jetty snail creep from the mossy thorn
In earnest heed and tremolous intent
　　　Frail brother of the morn
That from the tiney bents and misted leaves　　　110
　　　Withdraws his timid horn
　　　And fearful vision weaves

And swallows heed on smoke tanned chimney top
As wont be first unsealing mornings eye
Ere yet the bee hath gleaned one wayward drop
　　　Of honey on his thigh
And see him seek morns airy couch to sing
　　　Untill the golden sky
　　　Besprents his russet wing

And sawning boy by tanning corn espy　　　120
With clapping noise to startle birds away
And hear him bawl to every passer bye
　　　To know the hour of day
And see the uncradled breeze refreshed and strong
　　　With waking blossoms play
　　　And breath eolian song

I love the south west wind or low or loud
And not the less when sudden drops of rain
Moistens my palid cheek from ebon cloud
    Threatning soft showers again   130
That over lands new ploughed and meadow grounds
    Summer[s] sweet breath unchains
    And wakes harmonious sounds

Rich music breaths in summers every sound
And in her harmony of varied greens
Woods meadows hedgrows cornfields all around
    Much beauty intervenes
Filling with harmony the ear and eye
    While oer the mingling scenes
    Far spreads the laughing sky   140

And wind enarmourd Aspin—mark the leaves
Turn up their silver lining to the sun
And list the brustling noise that oft decieves
    And makes the sheep boy run
The sound so mimics fast approaching showers
    He thinks the rain begun
    And hastes to sheltering bowers

And mark the evening curdle dank and grey
Changing her watchet hue for sombre weeds
And moping owls to close the lids of day   150
    On drowsy wing proceeds
While chickering cricket tremolous and long
    Lights farwell inly heeds
    And gives it parting song

While pranking bat its flighty circlet makes
And gloworm burnisheth its lamp anew
Oer meadows dew besprent—and beetle wakes
    Enquiries ever new
Teazing each passing ear with murmurs vain
    As wonting to pursue   160
    His homward path again

And catch the melody of distant bells
That on the wind with pleasing hum rebounds
By fitful starts—then musically swells
    Oer the dim stilly grounds
While on the meadow bridge the pausing boy
    Listens the mellow sounds
    And hums in vacant joy

And now the homebound hedger bundles round
His evening faggot and with every stride   170
His leathern doublet leaves a rushing sound
    Till silly sheep beside
His path start tremolous—and once again
    Look back dissatisfied
    Then scour the dewy plain

And greet the soothing calm that smoothly stills
Oer the hearts every sense its opiate dews
In meek eyed moods and ever balmy trills
    That softens and subdues
With gentle quiets bland and sober train   180
    Which dreamy eve renews
    In many a balmy strain

I love to walk the fields they are to me
A legacy no evil can destroy
They like a spell set every rapture free
    That cheered me when a boy
Play pastime—all times blotting pen conseals
    Come like a new born joy
    To greet me in the fields

For natures objects ever harmonize   190
With emelous taste that vulgar deed anoys
It loves in quiet moods to sympathise
    And meet vibrating joys
Oer natures pleasant things—nor slighting deems
    Pastimes the muse employs
    As vain obtrusive themes

November

Sybil of months and worshiper of winds
I love thee rude and boisterous as thou art
And scraps of joy my wandering ever finds
Mid thy uproarious madness—when the start
Of sudden tempest stirs the forrest leaves
Into hoarse madness till the shower set free
Stills the hugh Wells and ebbs the mighty heaves
That swing the forrest like a troubled sea
I love the wizard noise and rave in turn
Half vacant thoughts and self imagined ryhmes   10
Then hide me from the shower a short sojourn
Neath ivied oak and mutter to the winds
Wishing their melody belonged to me
That I might breath a living song to thee

The Lady Flye

Tennant of leaves and flowers and glossy stalks
The wild profusion that the summer brings
Hiding in crowding beans and benty balks
Where on the knapweed while the cricket sings
I often watch thee prime thy freckled wings
On the smooth stem advancing yet more high
Till with the help the puffing zepher brings
Thoult all uncase thy under wings and flye
In changing scenes more snug and cool to lye
Ah when a cowboy I at ease reclined   10
Upon a thymy hill and thou wert nigh
What fond enquireys filled my curious mind
How have I watched thy pastimes Lady Fly
And thought thee happiest creature of thy kind

Autumn

Autumn comes laden with her ripened load
Of fruitage and so scatters them abroad
That each fern smothered heath and molehill waste
Are black with bramble berrys—where in haste
The chubby urchins from the village hie
To feast them there stained with the purple dye
While painted woods around my rambles be
In draperys worthy of eternity
Yet will the leaves soon patter on the ground
And deaths deaf voice awake at every sound   10
One drops—then others—and the last that fell
Rings for those left behind their passing bell
Thus memory every where her tidings brings
How sad death robs us of lifes dearest things

Nutting

The sun had stooped his westward clouds to win
Like weary traveller seeking for an Inn
When from the hazelly wood we glad descried
The ivied gateway by the pasture side
Long had we sought for nutts amid the shade
Where silence fled the rustle which we made
When torn by briars and brushed by sedges rank
We left the wood and on the velvet bank
Of short sward pasture ground we sat us down
To shell our nutts before we reached the town   10
The near hand stubble field with mellow glower
Showed the dimmed blaze of poppys still in flower
And sweet the mole hills smelt we sat upon
And now the thymes in bloom but where is pleasure gone

The Woodman

Now evening comes and from the new laid hedge
The woodman rustles in his leathern guise
Hiding in dyke ylined with brustling sedge
His bill and mittens from thefts meddling eyes
And in his wallets storing many a pledge
Of flowers and boughs from early sprouting trees
And painted pootys from the ivied hedge
About its mossy roots—his boys to please
Who wait with merry joy his coming home
Anticipating presents such as these   10
Gained far afield where they nor night nor morn
Find no school leisure long enough to go
Where flowers but rarely from their stalks are torn
And birds scarce loose a nest the season through

Hay Making

Tis hay-time and the red complexioned sun
Was scarcely up ere Black birds had begun
Along the meadow hedges here and there
To sing loud songs to the sweet smelling air
Where breath of flowers and grass and breathing cow
Fling oer ones senses streams of fragrance now
While in some pleasant nook the swain and maid
Lean oer their rakes and loiter in the shade
To bend a minute oer the bridge and throw
Crumbs from their pockets to the fish below   10
—Hark at that happy shout—and song between
Tis pleasures birthday in her meadow scene
What joy seems half so rich from rapture won
As the loud laugh of maidens in the sun

The Cottager

True as the church clock hand the hour pursues
He plods about his toils and reads the news
And at the blacksmiths shop his hour will stand
To talk of 'Lunun' as a foreign land
For from his cottage door in peace or strife
He neer went fifty miles in all his life
His knowledge with old notions still combined
Is fifty years behind the march of mind
He views new knowledge with suspicious eyes
And thinks it blasphemy to be so wise   10
Oer steams almighty tales he wondering looks
As witchcraft gleaned from old black letter books
Life gave him comfort but denied him wealth
He toils in quiet and enjoys his health
He smokes a pipe at night and drinks his beer
And runs no scores on tavern screens to clear
He goes to market all the year about
And keeps one hour and never stays it out
Een at St Thomas tide old Rovers bark
Hails Dapples trot an hour before its dark   20
He is a simple worded plain old man
Whose good intents take errors in their plan
Oft sentimental and with saddend vein
He looks on trifles and bemoans their pain
And thinks the angler mad and loudly storms
With emphasis of speech oer murdered worms
And hunters cruel pleading with sad care
Pitys petition for the fox and hare
Yet feels self satisfaction in his woes
For wars crushed myriads of his slaughtered foes   30
He is right scruplous in one pretext
And wholesale errors swallows in the next
He deems it sin to sing yet not to say
A song a mighty difference in his way
And many a moving tale in antique ryhmes
He has for christmass and such merry times
When chevey chase his master piece of song
Is said so earnest none can think it long

Twas the old Vicars way who should be right
For the late Vicar was his hearts delight   40
And while at church he often shakes his head
To think what sermons the old Vicar made
Down right and orthodox that all the land
Who had their ears to [h]ear might understand
But now such mighty learning meets his ears
He thinks it greek or lattin which he hears
Yet church recieves him every sabbath day
And rain or snow he never keeps away
All words of reverence still his heart reveres
Low bows his head when Jesus meets his ears   50
And still he thinks it blasphemy as well
Such names without a capital to spell
In an old corner cupboard by the wall
His books are laid—tho good in number small
His Bible first in place—from worth and age
Whose grandsires name adorns the title page
And blank leaves once now filled with kindred claims
Display a worlds epitome of names
Parents and childern and grandchildern—all
Memorys affections in the list recall   60
And Prayer book next much worn tho strongly bound
Proves him a churchman orthodox and sound
The 'Pilgrims Progress' too and 'Death of Abel'°
Are seldom missing from his sunday table
And prime old Tusser in his homely trim°
The first of Bards in all the world with him
And only poet which his leisure knows
—Verse deals in fancy so he sticks to prose
These are the books he reads and reads again
And weekly hunts the almanacks for rain   70
Here and no further learnings channels ran
Still neighbours prize him as the learned man
His cottage is a humble place of rest
With one spare room to welcome every guest
And that tall poplar pointing to the sky
His own hand planted when an idle boy
It shades his chimney while the singing wind
Hums songs of shelter to his happy mind
Within his cot the 'largest ears of corn'

He ever found his picture frames adorn   80
Brave Granbys Head—De Grasses grand defeat°
He rubs his hands and tells how Rodney beat
And from the rafters upon strings depend
Bean stalks beset with pods from end to end
Whose numbers without counting may be seen
Wrote on the Almanack behind the screen
Around the corner upon worsted strung
Pootys in wreaths above the cupboards hung
Memory at trifling incidents awakes
And there he keeps them for his childerns sakes   90
Who when as boys searched every sedgy lane
Traced every wood and shattered cloaths again
Roaming about on raptures easy wing
To hunt those very Pooty shells in spring
And thus he lives too happy to be poor
While strife neer pauses at so mean a door
Low in the sheltered valley stands his cot
He hears the mountain storm and feels it not
Winter and spring toil ceasing ere tis dark
Rests with the lamb and rises with the lark   100
Content is helpmate to the days employ
And care neer comes to steal a single joy
Time scarcely noticed turns his hair to grey
Yet leaves him happy as a child at play

The Shepherd's Calendar°

JUNE

Now summer is in flower and natures hum
Is never silent round her sultry bloom
Insects as small as dust are never done
Wi' glittering dance and reeling in the sun
And green wood fly and blossom haunting bee
Are never weary of their melody
Round field hedge now flowers in full glory twine
Large bindweed bells wild hop and streakd woodbine
That lift athirst their slender throated flowers
Agape for dew falls and for honey showers   10

These round each bush in sweet disorder run
And spread their wild hues to the sultry sun
Were its silk netting lace on twigs and leaves
The mottld spider at eves leisure weaves
That every morning meet the poets eye
Like faireys dew wet dresses hung to dry
The wheat swells into ear and leaves below
The may month wild flowers and their gaudy show
Bright carlock bluecap and corn poppy red
Which in such clouds of colors wid[e]ly spread   20
That at the sun rise might to fancys eye
Seem to reflect the many colord sky
And leverets seat and lark and partridge nest
It leaves a schoolboys height in snugger rest
And oer the weeders labour overgrows
Who now in merry groups each morning goes
To willow skirted meads wi fork and rake
The scented hay cocks in long rows to make
Were their old visitors in russet brown
The hay time butterflyes dance up and down   30
And gads that teaze like whasps the timid maid
And drive the herdboys cows to pond and shade
Who when his dogs assistance fails to stop
Is forcd his half made oaten pipes to drop
And start and halloo thro the dancing heat
To keep their gadding tumult from the wheat
Who in their rage will dangers overlook
And leap like hunters oer the pasture brook
Brushing thro blossomd beans in maddening haste
And stroying corn they scarce can stop to taste   40
Labour pursues its toil in weary mood
And feign woud rest wi shadows in the wood
The mowing gangs bend oer the beeded grass
Were oft the gipseys hungry journeying ass
Will turn its wishes from the meadow paths
Listning the rustle of the falling swaths
The ploughman sweats along the fallow vales
And down the suncrackt furrow slowly trails
Oft seeking when athirst the brooks supply
Were brushing eager the brinks bushes bye   50
For coolest water he oft brakes the rest

Of ring dove brooding oer its idle nest
And there as loath to leave the swaily place
He'll stand to breath and whipe his burning face
The shepherds idle hours are over now
Nor longer leaves him neath the hedgrow bough
On shadow pillowd banks and lolling stile
Wilds looses now their summer friends awhile
Shrill whistles barking dogs and chiding scold
Drive bleating sheep each morn from fallow fold   60
To wash pits were the willow shadows lean
Dashing them in their fold staind coats to clean
Then turnd on sunning sward to dry agen
They drove them homeward to the clipping pen
In hurdles pent were elm or sycamore
Shut out the sun—or in some threshing floor
There they wi scraps of songs and laugh and [t]ale
Lighten their anual toils while merry ale
Goes round and gladdens old mens hearts to praise
The thread bare customs of old farmers days   70
Who while the shrinking sheep wi trembling fears
Lies neath the snipping of his harmless sheers
Recalls full many a thing by bards unsung
And pride forgot—that reignd when he was young
How the hugh bowl was in the middle set
At breakfast time as clippers yearly met
Filld full of frumity were yearly swum
The streaking sugar and the spotting plumb
Which maids coud never to the table bring
Without one rising from the merry ring   80
To lend a hand who if twas taen amiss
Woud sell his kindness for a stolen kiss
The large stone pitcher in its homly trim
And clouded pint horn wi its copper rim
Oer which rude healths was drank in spirits high
From the best broach the cellar woud supply
While sung the ancient swains in homly ryhmes
Songs that were pictures of the good old times
When leathern bottles held the beer nut brown
That wakd the sun wi songs and sung him down   90
Thus will the old man ancient ways bewail
Till toiling sheers gain ground upon the tale

And brakes it off—when from the timid sheep
The fleece is shorn and wi a fearfull leap
He starts—while wi a pressing hand
His sides are printed by the tarry brand
Shaking his naked skin wi wondering joys
And fresh ones are tugd in by sturdy boys
Who when theyre thrown down neath the sheering swain
Will wipe his brow and start his tale again   100
Tho fashions haughty frown hath thrown aside
Half the old forms simplicity supplyd
Yet their are some prides winter deigns to spare
Left like green ivy when the trees are bare
And now when sheering of the flocks are done
Some ancient customs mixd wi harmless fun
Crowns the swains merry toils—the timid maid
Pleasd to be praisd and yet of praise affraid
Seeks her best flowers not those of woods and fields
But such as every farmers garden yields   110
Fine cabbage roses painted like her face
And shining pansys trimmd in golden lace
And tall tuft larkheels featherd thick wi flowers
And woodbines climbing oer the door in bowers
And London tufts of many a mottld hue
And pale pink pea and monkshood darkly blue
And white and purple jiliflowers that stay
Lingering in blossom summer half away
And single blood walls of a lucious smell
Old fashiond flowers which huswives love so well   120
And columbines stone blue or deep night brown
Their honey-comb-like blossoms hanging down
Each cottage gardens fond adopted child
Tho heaths still claim them were they yet grow wild
Mong their old wild companions summer blooms
Furze brake and mozzling ling and golden broom
Snap dragons gaping like to sleeping clowns
And 'clipping pinks' (which maidens sunday gowns
Full often wear catcht at by tozing chaps)
Pink as the ribbons round their snowy caps   130
'Bess in her bravery' too of glowing dyes
As deep as sunsets crimson pillowd skyes
And marjoram notts sweet briar and ribbon grass

And lavender the choice of every lass
And spr[i]gs of lads love all familiar names
Which every garden thro the village claims
These the maid gathers wi a coy delight
And tyes them up in readiness for night
Giving to every swain tween love and shame
Her 'clipping poseys' as their yearly claim   140
And turning as he claims the custom kiss
Wi stifld smiles half ankering after bliss
She shrinks away and blushing calls it rude
But turns to smile and hopes to be pursued
While one to whom the seeming hint applied
Follows to claim it and is not denyd
No doubt a lover for within his coat
His nosgay owns each flower of better sort
And when the envious mutter oer their beer
And nodd the secret to his neighbor near   150
Raising the laugh to make the mutter known
She blushes silent and will not disown
And ale and songs and healths and merry ways
Keeps up a shadow of old farmers days
But the old beachen bowl that once supplyd
Its feast of frumity is thrown aside
And the old freedom that was living then
When masters made them merry wi their men
Whose coat was like his neighbors russet brown
And whose rude speech was vulgar as his clown   160
Who in the same horn drank the rest among
And joind the chorus while a labourer sung
All this is past—and soon may pass away
The time torn remnant of the holiday
As proud distinction makes a wider space
Between the genteel and the vulgar race
Then must they fade as pride oer custom showers
Its blighting mildew on her feeble flowers

NOVEMBER

The village sleeps in mist from morn till noon
And if the sun wades thro tis wi a face
Beamless and pale and round as if the moon
When done the journey of its nightly race

Had found him sleeping and supplyd his place
For days the shepherds in the fields may be
Nor mark a patch of sky—blindfold they trace
The plains that seem wi out a bush or tree
Wistling aloud by guess to flocks they cannot see

The timid hare seems half its fears to loose   10
Crouching and sleeping neath its grassy lare
And scarcly startles tho the shepherd goes
Close by its home and dogs are barking there
The wild colt only turns around to stare
At passers bye then naps his hide again
And moody crows beside the road forbear
To flye tho pelted by the passing swain
Thus day seems turned to night and trys to wake in vain

The Owlet leaves her hiding place at noon
And flaps her grey wings in the doubting light   20
The hoarse jay screams to see her out so soon
And small birds chirp and startle with affright
Much doth it scare the superstitious wight
Who dreams of sorry luck and sore dismay
While cow boys think the day a dream of night
And oft grow fearful on their lonly way
Who fancy ghosts may wake and leave their graves by day

The cleanly maiden thro the village streets
In pattens clicks down causways never drye
While eves above head drops—were oft she meets   30
The schoolboy leering on wi mischiefs eye
Trying to splash her as he hurrys bye
While swains afield returning to their ploughs
Their passing aid wi gentle speech apply
And much loves rapture thrills when she alows
Their help wi offerd hand to lead her oer the sloughs

The hedger soakd wi the dull weather chops
On at his toils which scarcly keeps him warm
And every stroke he takes large swarms of drops
Patter about him like an april storm   40

The sticking dame wi cloak upon her arm
To guard against a storm walks the wet leas
Of willow groves or hedges round the farm
Picking up aught her splashy wanderings sees
Dead sticks the sudden winds have shook from off the trees

The boy that scareth from the spirey wheat
The mellancholy crow—quakes while he weaves
Beneath the ivey tree a hut and seat
Of rustling flags and sedges tyd in sheaves
Or from nigh stubble shocks a shelter thieves   50
There he doth dithering sit or entertain
His leisure hours down hedges lost to leaves
While spying nests where he spring eggs hath taen
He wishes in his heart twas summer time again

And oft hell clamber up a sweeing tree
To see the scarlet hunter hurry bye
And feign woud in their merry uproar be
But sullen labour hath its tethering tye
Crows swop around and some on bushes nigh
Watch for a chance when ere he turns away   60
To settle down their hunger to supply
From morn to eve his toil demands his stay
Save now and then an hour which leisure steals for play

Gaunt greyhounds now their coursing sports impart
Wi long legs stretchd on tip toe for the chase
And short loose ear and eye upon the start
Swift as the wind their motions they unlace
When bobs the hare up from her hiding place
Who in its furry coat of tallow stain
Squats on the lands or wi a dodging pace   70
Tryes its old coverts of wood grass to gain
And oft by cunning ways makes all their speed in vain

Dull for a time the slumbering weather flings
Its murky prison round then winds wake loud
Wi sudden start the once still forest sings
Winters returning song cloud races cloud

And the orison throws away its shrowd
And sweeps its stretching circle from the eye
Storm upon storm in quick succession crowd
And oer the sameness of the purple skye   80
Heaven paints its wild irregularity

The shepherd oft foretells by simple ways
The weathers change that will ere long prevail
He marks the dull ass that grows wild and brays
And sees the old cows gad adown the vale
A summer race and snuff the coming gale
The old dame sees her cat wi fears alarm
Play hurly burly races wi its tale
And while she stops her wheel her hands to warm
She rubs her shooting corns and prophecys a storm   90

Morts are the signs—the stone hid toad will croak
And gobbling turkey cock wi noises vile
Dropping his snout as flaming as a cloak
Loose as a red rag oer his beak the while
Urging the dame to turn her round and smile
To see his uncooth pride her cloaths attack
Sidling wi wings hung down in vapoury broil
And feathers ruffld up while oer his back
His tail spreads like a fan cross wavd wi bars of black

The hog sturts round the stye and champs the straw   100
And bolts about as if a dog was bye
The steer will cease its gulping cud to chew
And toss his head wi wild and startld eye
At windshook straws—the geese will noise and flye
Like wild ones to the pond—wi matted mane
The cart horse squeals and kicks his partner nigh
While leaning oer his fork the foddering swain
The uproar marks around and dreams of wind and rain

And quick it comes among the forest oaks
Wi sobbing ebbs and uproar gathering high   110
The scard hoarse raven on its cradle croaks
And stock dove flocks in startld terrors flye
While the blue hawk hangs oer them in the skye

The shepherd happy when the day is done
Hastes to his evening fire his cloaths to dry
And forrester crouchd down the storm to shun
Scarce hears amid the strife the poachers muttering gun

The ploughman hears the sudden storm begin
And hies for shelter from his naked toil
Buttoning his doublet closer to his chin   120
He speeds him hasty oer the elting soil
White clouds above him in wild fury boil
And winds drive heavily the beating rain
He turns his back to catch his breath awhile
Then ekes his speed and faces it again
To seek the shepherds hut beside the rushy plain

Oft stripping cottages and barns of thack
Were startld farmer garnerd up his grain
And wheat and bean and oat and barley stack
Leaving them open to the beating rain   130
The husbandman grieves oer his loss in vain
And sparrows mourn their night nests spoild and bare
The thackers they resume their toils again
And stubbornly the tall red ladders bare
While to oerweight the wind they hang old harrows there

Thus wears the month along in checkerd moods
Sunshine and shadow tempest loud and calms
One hour dyes silent oer the sleepy woods
The next wakes loud with unexpected storms
A dreary nakedness the field deforms   140
Yet many rural sounds and rural sights
Live in the village still about the farms
Where toils rude uproar hums from morn till night
Noises in which the ear of industry delights

Hoarse noise of field-free bull that strides ahead
Of the tail switching herd to feed again
The barking mastiff from his kennel bed
Urging his teazing noise at passing swain
The jostling rumble of the starting wain

From the farm yard were freedoms chance to wait   150
The turkey drops his snout and geese in vain
Noise at the signal of the opening gate
Then from the clowns whip flyes and finds the chance
    too late

The pigeon wi its breast of many hues
That spangles to the sun turns round and round
About his timid sidling mate and croos
Upon the cottage ridge were oer their heads
The puddock sails oft swopping oer the pen
Were timid chickens from their parent stray
That skulk and scutter neath her wings agen   160
Nor peeps no more till they have saild away

Such rural sounds the mornings tongue renews
And rural sights swarm on the rustics eye
The billy goat shakes from his beard the dews
And jumps the wall wi country teams to hie
Upon the barn rig at their freedom flye
The spotted guiney fowl—hogs in the stye
Agen the door in rooting whinings stand
The freed colt drops his head and gallops bye
The boy that holds a scuttle in his hand   170
Prefering unto toil the commons rushy land

At length the busy noise of toil is still
And industry awhile her care forgoes
When winter comes in earnest to fulfill
Her yearly task at bleak novembers close
And stops the plough and hides the field in snows
When frost locks up the streams in chill delay
And mellows on the hedge the purple sloes
For little birds—then toil hath time for play
And nought but threshers flails awake the dreary day   180

The Heath

O I love the dear wild and the outstretching heath
With its sweet swelling uplands and downs
When I toil up the path till Im half out of breath
While the oakwood the distance embrowns

With the first hues of spring—and the mossy thorn tree
Shines in its most delicate hue
And the long withered grass reaching up to my knee
Rustles loud as my feet brushes through

Where the furze on the slopes turn from green into gold
With their millions of blossoms—and Ling   10
Blushing red underneath is most sweet to behold
Where the wood lark sits pruning her wing

Such a freshness comes round from the wide spreading air
Such a smell from the blossoms beneath
Such a beautiful somthing refreshes me there
While I ramble about on the heath

The old hills that for a mans lifetime hath stood
Unmolested mid brushes and burrs
The worn ways leading along to the wood
And the rabbit tracks into the furze   20

There nought but a shepherd cries 'whoop' to his sheep
Or a herdsman hails 'hoi' to his cows
And the noise of the waggoner trailing the steep
While crossing the pudges and sloughs

Oft standing to rest them and then with a smack
Of his whip driving onward again
While the wood in an eccho repeateth the crack
And the load of wood creaks on the wain

Though simple to some I delight in the sight
Of such objects that bring unto me   30
A picture of picturesque joy and delight
Where beauty and harmony be

O I love at my heart to be strolling along
Oer the heath a new impulse to find
While I hum to the wind in a ballad or song
Some fancy that starts in the mind

All seem so delightful and bring to the mind
Such quiet and beautiful joys
That the mind when its weary like hermits may find
A retreat from earths follys and noise   40

[*Winter in the Fens*]

So moping flat and low our valleys lie
So dull and muggy is our winter sky
Drizzling from day to day dull threats of rain
And when that falls still threating on again
From one wet week so great an ocean flows
That every village to an island grows
And every road for even weeks to come
Is stopt and none but horsemen go from home
And one wet night leaves travels best in doubt
And horseback travel asks if floods are out   10
Such are the lowland scenes that winter gives
And strangers wonder where our pleasure lives
Yet in a little garden close at home
I watch for spring and there the crocus comes
And in a little close however keen
The winter comes I find a patch of green
And then mayhap a letter from a friend
Just in the bustle of the city penned
And then to show that friendships warmth survives
The winter from the busy town arives   20
A letter spite of flooded roads—with news
—New books old friendships authors and reviews
While the intermediate blanks employ
And though fenced [in] with water meet with joy
Though troubled waters down the meadow roars
And fancy dreads the danger out of doors
When every little window after dark
Lights comfort in like faith in noahs ark

[*The Lament of Swordy Well*]°

Pe[ti]tioners are full of prayers
To fall in pitys way
But if her hand the gift forbears
Theyll sooner swear then pray
They're not the worst to want who lurch
On plenty with complaints
No more then those who go to church
Are eer the better saints

I hold no hat to beg a mite
Nor pick it up when thrown   10
Nor limping leg I hold in sight
But pray to keep my own
Where profit gets his clutches in
Theres little he will leave
Gain stooping for a single pin
Will stick it on his sleeve

For passers bye I never pin
No troubles to my breast
Nor carry round some names
More money from the rest   20
Im swordy well a piece of land
Thats fell upon the town
Who worked me till I couldnt stand
And crush me now Im down

In parish bonds I well may wail
Reduced to every shift
Pity may grieve at troubles tale
But cunning shares the gift
Harvests with plenty on his brow
Leaves losses taunts with me   30
Yet gain comes yearly with the plough
And will not let me be

Alas dependance thou'rt a brute
Want only understands
His feelings wither branch and root
That falls in parish hands
The muck that clouts the ploughmans shoe
The moss that hides the stone
Now Im become the parish due
Is more then I can own   40

Though Im no man yet any wrong
Some sort of right may seek
And I am glad if een a song
Gives me the room to speak
Ive got among such grubbling geer
And such a hungry pack
If I brought harvests twice a year
They'd bring me nothing back

When war their tyrant prices got
I trembled with alarms   50
They fell and saved my little spot
Or towns had turned to farms
Let profit keep an humble place
That gentry may be known
Let pedigrees their honours trace
And toil enjoy its own

The silver springs grown naked dykes
Scarce own a bunch of rushes
When grain got high the tasteless tykes
Grubbed up trees banks and bushes   60
And me they turned me inside out
For sand and grit and stones
And turned my old green hills about
And pickt my very bones

These things that claim my own as theirs
Where born but yesterday
But ere I fell to town affairs
I were as proud as they

I kept my horses cows and sheep
And built the town below   70
Ere they had cat or dog to keep
And then to use me so

Parish allowance gaunt and dread
Had it the earth to keep
Would even pine the bees to dead
To save an extra keep
Prides workhouse is a place that yields
From poverty its gains
And mines a workhouse for the fields
A starving the remains   80

The bees flye round in feeble rings
And find no blossom bye
Then thrum their almost weary wings
Upon the moss and die
Rabbits that find my hills turned oer
Forsake my poor abode
They dread a workhouse like the poor
And nibble on the road

If with a clover bottle now
Spring dares to lift her head   90
The next day brings the hasty plough
And makes me miserys bed
The butterflyes may wir and come
I cannot keep em now
Nor can they bear my parish home
That withers on my brow

No now not een a stone can lie
Im just what eer they like
My hedges like the winter flye
And leave me but the dyke   100
My gates are thrown from off the hooks
The parish thoroughfare
Lord he thats in the parish books
Has little wealth to spare

I couldnt keep a dust of grit
Nor scarce a grain of sand
But bags and carts claimed every bit
And now theyve got the land
I used to bring the summers life
To many a butterflye   110
But in oppressions iron strife
Dead tussocks bow and sigh

Ive scarce a nook to call my own
For things that creep or flye
The beetle hiding neath a stone
Does well to hurry bye
Stock eats my struggles every day
As bare as any road
He's sure to be in somthings way
If eer he stirs abroad   120

I am no man to whine and beg
But fond of freedom still
I hing no lies on pitys peg
To bring a gris to mill
On pitys back I neednt jump
My looks speak loud alone
My only tree they've left a stump
And nought remains my own

My mossy hills gains greedy hand
And more then greedy mind   130
Levels into a russet land
Nor leaves a bent behind
In summers gone I bloomed in pride
Folks came for miles to prize
My flowers that bloomed no where beside
And scarce believed their eyes

Yet worried with a greedy pack
They rend and delve and tear
The very grass from off my back
Ive scarce a rag to wear   140

Gain takes my freedom all away
Since its dull suit I wore
And yet scorn vows I never pay
And hurts me more and more

And should the price of grain get high
Lord help and keep it low
I shant possess a single flye
Or get a weed to grow
I shant possess a yard of ground
To bid a mouse to thrive   150
For gain has put me in a pound
I scarce can keep alive

I own Im poor like many more
But then the poor mun live
And many came for miles before
For what I had to give
But since I fell upon the town
They pass me with a sigh
Ive scarce the room to say sit down
And so they wander bye   160

Though now I seem so full of clack
Yet when yer' riding bye
The very birds upon my back
Are not more fain to flye
I feel so lorn in this disgrace
God send the grain to fall
I am the oldest in the place
And the worst served of all

Lord bless ye I was kind to all
And poverty in me   170
Could always find a humble stall
A rest and lodging free
Poor bodys with an hungry ass
I welcomed many a day
And gave him tether room and grass
And never said him nay

There was a time my bit of ground
Made freemen of the slave
The ass no pindard dare to pound
When I his supper gave   180
The gipseys camp was not affraid
I made his dwelling free
Till vile enclosure came and made
A parish slave of me

The gipseys further on sojourn
No parish bounds they like
No sticks I own and would earth burn
I shouldnt own a dyke
I am no friend to lawless work
Nor would a rebel be   190
And why I call a christian turk
Is they are turks to me

And if I could but find a friend
With no deciet to sham
Who'd send me some few sheep to tend
And leave me as I am
To keep my hills from cart and plough
And strife of mongerel men
And as spring found me find me now
I should look up agen   200

And save his Lordships woods that past
The day of danger dwell
Of all the fields I am the last
That my own face can tell
Yet what with stone pits delving holes
And strife to buy and sell
My name will quickly be the whole
Thats left of swordy well

The Progress of Ryhme

O soul enchanting poesy
Thoust long been all the world with me
When poor thy presence grows my wealth
When sick thy visions gives me health
When sad thy sunny smile is joy
And was from een a tiney boy
When trouble was and toiling care
Seemed almost more then I could bear
While thrashing in the dusty barn
Or squashing in the ditch to earn   10
A pittance that would scarce alow
One joy to smooth my sweating brow
Where drop by drop would chase and fall
—Thy presence triumphed over all
The vulgar they might frown and sneer
Insult was mean   but never near
Twas poesys self that stopt the sigh
And malice met with no reply
So was it in my earlier day
When sheep to corn had strayed away   20
Or horses closen gaps had broke
Ere sunrise peeped or I awoke
My masters frown might force the tear
But poesy came to check and cheer
It glistened in my shamed eye
But ere it fell the swoof was bye
I thought of luck in future days
When even he might find a praise
I looked on poesy like a friend
To cheer me till my life should end   30
Twas like a parents first regard
And love when beautys voice was heard
Twas joy twas hope and may be fear
But still twas rapture every where
My heart were ice unmoved to dwell
Nor care for one I loved so well
Thro rough and smooth thro good and ill
That led me and attends me still

It was an early joy to me
That joy was love and poesy   40
And but for thee my idle lay
Had neer been urged in early day
The harp imagination strung
Had neer been dreamed of—but among
The flowers in summers fields of joy
Id lain an idle rustic boy
No hope to think of fear or care
And even love a stranger there
But poesy that vision flung
Around me as I hummed or sung   50
I glowered on beauty passing bye
Yet hardly turned my sheepish eye
I worshiped yet could hardly dare
To show I knew the goddess there
Lest my presumptious stare should gain
But frowns ill humour or disdain
My first ambition was its praise
My struggles aye in early days
Had I by vulgar boldness torn
That hope when it was newly born   60
By rudeness gibes and vulgar tongue
The curse of the unfeeling throng
Their scorn had frowned upon the lay
And hope and song had passed away
And I with nothing to attone
Had felt myself indeed alone
But promises of days to come
The very fields would seem to hum
Those burning days when I should dare
To sing aloud my worship there   70
When beautys self might turn its eye
Of praise—what could I do but try
Twas winter then—but summer shone
From heaven when I was all alone
And summer came and every weed
Of great or little had its meed
Without its leaves there wa'nt a bower
Nor one poor weed without its flower
Twas love and pleasure all along

I felt that Id a right to song   80
And sung—but in a timid strain
Of fondness for my native plain
For every thing I felt a love
The weeds below the birds above
And weeds that bloomed in summers hours
I thought they should be reckoned flowers
They made a garden free for all
And so I loved them great and small
And sung of some that pleased my eye
Nor could I pass the thistle bye   90
But paused and thought it could not be
A weed in natures poesy
No matter for protecting wall
No matter tho they chance to fall
Where sheep and cows and oxen lie
The kindly shower when theyre a dry
Falls upon them with cheering powers
As when it waters garden flowers
They look up with a blushing eye
Upon a tender watching sky   100
And still enjoy the kindling smile
Of sunshine tho they live with toil
As garden flowers with all their care
For natures love is even there
And so it cheered me while I lay
Among their beautiful array
To think that I in humble dress
Might have a right to happiness
And sing as well as greater men
And then I strung the lyre agen   110
And heartened up oer toil and fear
And lived with rapture every where
Till day shine to my themes did come
Just as a blossom bursts to bloom
And finds its self in thorny ways
So did my musings meet wi praise
And tho no garden care had I
My heart had love for poesy
A simple love a wild esteem
As heart felt as the linnets dream   120

That mutters in its sleep at night
Some notes from extacys delight
Thus did I dream oer joys and lye
Muttering dream songs of poesy
The storm was oer and hue and cry
With her false pictures herded bye
With tales of help where help was not
Of friends who urged to write or blot
Whose taste were such that mine were shame
Had they not helpt it into fame   130
Poh let the idle rumour ill
Their vanity is never still
My harp tho simple was my own
When I was in the fields alone
With none to help and none to hear
To bid me either hope or fear
The bird and bee its chords would sound
The air humed melodys around
I caught with eager ear the strain
And sung the music oer again   140
The Fields and woods are still as mine
Real teachers that are all divine
So if my song be weak or tame
Tis I not they who bear the blame
But hope and cheer thro good and ill
They are my aids to worship still
Still growing on a gentle tide
Nor foes could mar or friends could guide
Like pasture brooks thro sun and shade
Crooked as channels chance hath made   150
It rambled as it loved to stray
And hope and feeling led the way
And birds no matter what the tune
Or croak or tweet—twas natures boon
That brought them joy—and music flung
Its spell oer every mattin sung
And een the sparrows chirp to me
Was song in its felicity
When grief hung oer me like a cloud
Till hope seemed even in her shroud   160
I whispered poesys spells till they

Gleamed round me like a summers day
When tempests oer my labour sung
My soul to its responses rung
And joined the chorus till the storm
Fell all unheeded void of harm
And each old leaning shielding tree
Were princely pallaces to me
Where I would sit me down and chime
My unheard rhapsodies to ryhme   170
All I beheld of grand—with time
Grew up to beautifuls sublime
The arching groves of ancient lime
That into roofs like churches climb
Grain intertwisting into grain
That stops the sun and stops the rain
And spreads a gloom that never smiles
Like ancient halls and minster aisles
While all without a beautious screen
Of summers luscious leaves is seen   180
While heard that everlasting hum
Of bees that haunt them where they bloom
As tho' twas natures very place
Of worship where her mighty race
Of insect life and spirits too
In summer time were wont to go
Both insects and the breath of flowers
To sing their makers mighty powers
Ive thought so as I used to rove
Thro burghley park that darksome grove°   190
Of limes where twilight lingered grey
Like evening in the midst of day
And felt without a single skill
That instinct that would not be still
To think of song sublime beneath
That heaved my bosom like my breath
That burned and chilled and went and came
Without or uttering or name
Untill the vision waked with time
And left me itching after rhyme   200
Where little pictures idly tells
Of natures powers and natures spells

I felt and shunned the idle vein
Laid down the pen and toiled again
But spite of all thro good and ill
It was and is my worship still
No matter how the world approved
Twas nature listened—I that loved
No matter how the lyre was strung
From my own heart the music sprung   210
The cowboy with his oaten straw
Altho he hardly heard or saw
No more of music then he made
Twas sweet—and when I pluckt the blade
Of grass upon the woodland hill
To mock the birds with artless skill
No music in the world beside
Seemed half so sweet—till mine was tried
So my boy worship poesy
Made een the muses pleased with me   220
Untill I even danced for joy
A happy and a lonely boy
Each object to my ear and eye
Made paradise of poesy
I heard the blackbird in the dell
Sing sweet—could I but sing as well
I thought—untill the bird in glee
Seemed pleased and paused to answer me
And nightingales O I have stood
Beside the pingle and the wood   230
And oer the old oak railing hung
To listen every note they sung
And left boys making taws of clay
To muse and listen half the day
The more I listened and the more
Each note seemed sweeter then before
And aye so different was the strain
Shed scarce repeat the note again
—'Chew-chew Chew-chew'—and higher still
'Cheer-cheer Cheer-cheer'—more loud and shrill   240
'Cheer-up Cheer-up cheer-up'—and dropt
Low 'tweet tweet tweet jug jug jug' and stopt
One moment just to drink the sound

Her music made and then a round
Of stranger witching notes was heard
As if it was a stranger bird
'Wew-wew wew-wew chur-chur chur-chur
Woo-it woo-it'—could this be her
'Tee-rew Tee-rew tee-rew tee-rew
Chew-rit chew-rit'—and ever new   250
'Will-will will-will grig-grig grig-grig'
The boy stopt sudden on the brig
To hear the 'tweet tweet tweet' so shill
Then 'jug jug jug'—and all was still
A minute—when a wilder strain
Made boys and woods to pause again
Words were not left to hum the spell
Could they be birds that sung so well
I thought—and may be more then I
That musics self had left the sky   260
To cheer me with its magic strain
And then I hummed the words again
Till fancy pictured standing bye
My hearts companion poesy
No friends had I to guide or aid
The struggles young ambition made
In silent shame the harp was tried
And raptures guess the tune applied
Yet oer the songs my parents sung
My ear in silent musings hung   270
Their kindness wishes did regard
They sung and joy was my reward
All else was but a proud decree
The right of bards and nought to me
A title that I dare not claim
And hid it like a private shame
I whispered aye and felt a fear
To speak aloud tho' none was near
I dreaded laughter more then blame
And dare not sing aloud for shame   280
So all unheeded lone and free
I felt it happiness to be
Unknown obscure and like a tree
In woodland peace and privacy

No not a friend on earth had I
But my own kin and poesy
Nor wealth—and yet I felt indeed
As rich as any body need
To be—for health and hope and joy
Was mine altho a lonely boy   290
And what I felt—as now I sing
Made friends of all and every thing
Save man the vulgar and the low
The polished twas not mine to know
Who paid me in my after days
And gave me even more then praise
Twas then I found that friends indeed
Were needed when Id less to need
—The pea that independant springs
—When in its blossom trails and clings   300
To every help that lingers bye
And I when classed with poesy
Who stood unbrunt the heaviest shower
Felt feeble as that very flower
And helpless all—but beautys smile
Is harvest for the hardest toil
Whose smiles I little thought to win
With ragged coat and downy chin
A clownish silent haynish boy
Who even felt ashamed of joy   310
So dirty ragged and so low
With nought to reccomend or show
That I was worthy een a smile
—Had I but felt amid my toil
That I in days to come should be
A little light in minstrelsy
And in the blush of after days
Win beautys smile and beautys praise
My heart with lonely fancy warm
Had even bursted with the charm   320
And Mary thou whose very name
I loved whose look was even fame
From those delicious eyes of blue
In smiles and rapture ever new
Thy timid step thy fairy form

Thy face with blushes ever warm
When praise my schoolboy heart did move
I saw thy blush and thought it love
And all ambitious thee to please
My heart was ever ill at ease   330
I saw thy beauty grow with days
And tryed song pictures in thy praise
And all of fair or beautiful
Were thine akin—nor could I pull
The blossoms that I thought divine
Lest I should injure aught of thine
So where they grew I let them be
And tho' I dare not look to thee
Of love—to them I talked aloud
And grew ambitious from the crowd   340
With hopes that I should one day be
Beloved Mary een by thee
But I mistook in early day
The world—and so our hopes decay
Yet that same cheer in after toils
Was poesy—and still she smiles

Autumn

Syren of sullen moods and fading hues
Yet haply not incapable of joy
Sweet autumn I thee hail
With welcome all unfeignd
And oft as morning from the lattice peeps
To beckon up the sun I seek with thee
To drink the dewy breath
Of fields left fragrant then

To solitudes where no frequented paths
But what thy own feet makes betray thine home   10
Stealing obtrusive there
To meditate thy end
By overshadowed ponds in woody nooks
With ramping sallows lined and crowding sedge
Who woo the winds to play
And with them dance for joy

And meadow pools torn wide by lawless floods
Where water lilys spread their oily leaves
On which as wont the flye
Oft battens in the sun   20
Where leans the mossy willow half way oer
On which the shepherd crawls astride to throw
His angle clear of weeds
That crowd the waters brim

Or crispy hills and hollows scant of sward
Where step by step the patient lonely boy
Hath cut rude flights of stairs
To climb their steepy sides
Then tracking at their feet grown hoarse with noise
The crawling brook that ekes its weary speed   30
And struggles through the weeds
With faint and sullen brawls

These haunts long favoured and the more as now
With thee thus wandering moralizing on
Stealing glad thoughts from grief
And happy though I sigh
Sweet vision with the wild dishevilled hair
And raiments shadowy of each winds embrace
Fain would I win thine harp
To one accordant theme   40

Now not inaptly craved communing thus
Beneath the curdled arms of this stunt oak
We pillow on the grass
And fondly ruminate
Oer the disordered scenes of woods and fields
Ploughed lands thin travelled with half hungry sheep
Pastures tracked deep with cows
Where small birds seek for seed

Marking the cowboy that so merry trills
His frequent unpremeditated song   50
Wooing the winds to pause
Till echo brawls again

As on with plashy step and clouted shoon
He raves half indolent and self employed
To rob the little birds
Of hips and pendant haws

And sloes dim covered as with dewy veils
And rambling bramble berries pulp and sweet
Arching their prickly trails
Half oer the narrow lane   60
And mark the hedger front with stubborn face
The dank blea wind that whistles thinly bye
His leathern garb thorn proof
And cheek red hot with toil

And oer the pleachy stubbs of mellow brown
The mowers stubbling scythe clog to his foot
The ever eking whisp
With sharp and sudden jerk
Till into formal rows the russet shocks
Crowd the blank lands to thatch time-weathered barns   70
And hovels rude repair
Stript by disturbing winds

While from the rustling scythe the haunted hare
Scampers circuitous with startled ears
Prickt up then squat—as bye
She brushes to the woods
Where seeded grass breast high and undisturbed
Form pleasant clumps through which the sutheing winds
Softens her rigid fears
And lulls to calm repose   80

Wild sorceress me thy restless mood delights
More then the stir of summers crowded scenes
Where jostled in the din
Joy pauled my ear with song
Heart sickening for the silence that is thine
Not broken inharmoniously as now
That lone and vagrant bee
Booms faint with weary chime

And filtering winds thin winnowing through the woods
In tremelous noise that bids at every breath   90
Some sickly cankered leaf
Let go its hold and die
And now the bickering storm with sudden start
In flirting fits of anger carpeth loud
Thee urging to thine end
Sore wept by troubled skys

And yet sublime in grief thy thoughts delight
To show me visions of most gorgeous dies
Haply forgetting now
They but prepare thy shroud   100
Thy pencil dashing its excess of shades
Improvident of waste till every bough
Burns with thy mellow touch
Disorderly divine

Soon must I view thee as a pleasant dream
Droop faintly and so sicken for thine end
As sad the winds sink low
In dirges for their queen
While in the moment of their weary pause
To cheer thy bankrupt pomp the willing lark   110
Starts from his shielding clod
Snatching sweet scraps of song

Thy life is waining now and silence tries
To mourn but meets no sympathy in sounds
As stooping low she bends
Forming with leaves thy grave
To sleep inglorious there mid tangled woods
Till parched lipped summer pines in draught away
Then from thine ivied trance
Awake to glories new   120

The Eternity of Nature

Leaves from eternity are simple things
To the worlds gaze where to a spirit clings
Sublime and lasting—trampled underfoot
The daisey lives and strikes its little root
Into the lap of time—centurys may come
And pass away into the silent tomb
And still the child hid in the womb of time
Shall smile and pluck them when this simple ryhme
Shall be forgotten like a church yard stone
Or lingering lye unnotised and alone   10
When eighteen hundred years our common date
Grows many thousands in their marching state
Aye still the child with pleasure in his eye
Shall cry the daisy a familiar cry
And run to pluck it—in the self same state
As when time found it in his infant date
And like a child himself when all was new
Wonder might smile and make him notice too
—Its little golden bosom frilled with snow
Might win e'en Eve to stoop adown and show   20
Her partner Adam in the silky grass
This little gem that smiled where pleasure was
And loving eve from eden followed ill
And bloomed with sorrow and lives smiling still
As once in eden under heavens breath
So now on blighted earth and on the lap of death
It smiles for ever   Cowslaps golden blooms
That in the closen and the meadow comes
Shall come when kings and empires fade and dye
And in the meadows as times partners lie   30
As fresh two thousand years to come as now
With those five crimson spots upon its brow
And little brooks that hum a simple lay
In green unnoticed spots from praise away
Shall sing—when poets in times darkness hid
Shall lie like memory in a pyramid
Forgetting yet not all forgot though lost
Like a threads end in ravelled windings crost

And the small bumble bee shall hum as long
As nightingales for time protects the song   40
And nature is their soul to whom all clings
Of fair or beautiful in lasting things
The little Robin in the quiet glen
Hidden from fame and all the strife of men
Sings unto time a pastoral and gives
A music that lives on and ever lives
Both spring and autumn years rich bloom and fade
Longer then songs that poets ever made
And think ye these times play things pass p[r]oud skill
Time loves them like a child and ever will   50
And so I worship them in bushy spots
And sing with them when all else notice not
And feel the music of their mirth agree
With that sooth quiet that bestirreth me
And if I touch aright that quiet tone
That soothing truth that shadows forth their own
Then many a year shall grow in after days
And still find hearts to love my quiet lays
Yet cheering mirth with thoughts sung not for fame
But for the joy that with their utterance came   60
That inward breath of rapture urged not loud
—Birds singing lone flye silent past a crowd
So in these pastoral spot[s] which childish time
Makes dear to me I wander out and ryhme
What time the dewy mornings infancy
Hangs on each blade of grass and every tree
And sprents the red thighs of the bumble bee
Who 'gins by times unwearied minstrelsy
Who breakfasts dines and most divinely sups
With every flower save golden buttercups   70
On their proud bosoms he will never go
And passes by with scarcely 'how do ye do'
So in thier showy shining gaudy cells
Maybe the summers honey never dwells
Her ways are mysterys all yet endless youth
Lives in them all unchangeable as truth
With the odd number five strange natures laws
Plays many freaks nor once mistakes the cause
And in the cowslap peeps this very day

Five spots appear which time ne'er wears away   80
Nor once mistakes the counting—look within
Each peep and five nor more nor less is seen
And trailing bindweed with its pinky cup
Five leaves of paler hue goes streaking up
And birds a many keep the rule alive
And lay five eggs nor more nor less then five
And flowers how many own that my[s]tic power
With five leaves ever making up the flower
The five leaved grass mantling its golden cup
Of flowers—five leaves make all for which I stoop   90
And briony in the hedge that now adorns
The tree to which it clings and now the thorns
Grow five star pointed leaves of dingy white
Count which I will all make the number right
And spreading goose grass trailing all abroad
In leaves of silver green about the road
Five leaves make every blossom all along
I stoop for many none are counted wrong
Tis natures wonder and her makers will
Who bade earth be and order owns him still   100
As that superior power who keeps the key
Of wisdom power and might through all eternity

The Mores

Far spread the moorey ground a level scene
Bespread with rush and one eternal green
That never felt the rage of blundering plough
Though centurys wreathed springs blossoms on its brow
Still meeting plains that stretched them far away
In uncheckt shadows of green brown and grey
Unbounded freedom ruled the wandering scene
Nor fence of ownership crept in between
To hide the prospect of the following eye
Its only bondage was the circling sky   10
One mighty flat undwarfed by bush and tree
Spread its faint shadow of immensity
And lost itself which seemed to eke its bounds
In the blue mist the orisons edge surrounds

Now this sweet vision of my boyish hours
Free as spring clouds and wild as summer flowers
Is faded all—a hope that blossomed free
And hath been once no more shall ever be
Inclosure came and trampled on the grave
Of labours rights and left the poor a slave   20
And memorys pride ere want to wealth did bow
Is both the shadow and the substance now
The sheep and cows were free to range as then
Where change might prompt nor felt the bonds of men
Cows went and came with evening morn and night
To the wild pasture as their common right
And sheep unfolded with the rising sun
Heard the swains shout and felt their freedom won
Tracked the red fallow field and heath and plain
Then met the brook and drank and roamed again   30
The brook that dribbled on as clear as glass
Beneath the roots they hid among the grass
While the glad shepherd traced their tracks along
Free as the lark and happy as her song
But now alls fled and flats of many a dye
That seemed to lengthen with the following eye
Moors loosing from the sight far smooth and blea
Where swopt the plover in its pleasure free
Are vanished now with commons wild and gay
As poets visions of lifes early day   40
Mulberry bushes where the boy would run
To fill his hands with fruit are grubbed and done
And hedgrow briars—flower lovers overjoyed
Came and got flower pots—these are all destroyed
And sky bound mores in mangled garbs are left
Like mighty giants of their limbs bereft
Fence now meets fence in owners little bounds
Of field and meadow large as garden grounds
In little parcels little minds to please
With men and flocks imprisoned ill at ease   50
Each little path that led its pleasant way
As sweet as morning leading night astray
Where little flowers bloomed round a varied host
That travel felt delighted to be lost
Nor grudged the steps that he had taen as vain

When right roads traced his journeys end again
Nay on a broken tree hed sit awhile
To see the mores and fields and meadows smile
Sometimes with cowslaps smothered—then all white
With daiseys—then the summers splendid sight   60
Of corn fields crimson oer the 'headach' bloomd
Like splendid armys for the battle plumed
He gazed upon them with wild fancys eye
As fallen landscapes from an evening sky
These paths are stopt—the rude philistines thrall
Is laid upon them and destroyed them all
Each little tyrant with his little sign
Shows where man claims earth glows no more divine
On paths to freedom and to childhood dear
A board sticks up to notice 'no road here'   70
And on the tree with ivy overhung
The hated sign by vulgar taste is hung
As tho the very birds should learn to know
When they go there they must no further go
This with the poor scared freedom bade good bye
And much the[y] feel it in the smothered sigh
And birds and trees and flowers without a name
All sighed when lawless laws enclosure came
And dreams of plunder in such rebel schemes
Have found too truly that they were but dreams   80

Pleasant Places

Old stone pits all with ivy overhung
Rude crooked brooks oer which is idly flung
A rail and plank that bends beneath the tread
Old narrow lanes where trees meet over head
And gaps th[r]ough bramble hedges where we spy
A steeple peeping in the stretching sky
And heaths oer spread with furze blooms sunny shine
Where praise in wonderment exclaims divine
Old ponds dim shado[w]ed with a broken tree
These are the picturesque of taste to me   10

While the wild wind to make compleat the scene
In rich confusion mingles every green
Waving her sketchy pencil in her hand
That tints the moving scene

Shadows of Taste°

Taste with as many hues doth hearts engage
As leaves and flowers do upon natures page
Not mind alone the instinctive mood declares
But birds and flowers and insects are its heirs
Taste is their joyous heritage and they
All choose for joy in a peculiar way
Birds own it in the various spots they chuse
Some live content in low grass gemmed with dews
The yellowhammer like a tasteful guest
Neath picturesque green molehills makes a nest   10
Where oft the shepherd with unlearned ken
Finds strange eggs scribbled as with ink and pen
He looks with wonder on the learned marks
And calls them in his memory writing larks
Birds bolder winged on bushes love to be
While some choose cradles on the highest tree
There rocked by winds they feel no moods of fear
But joy their birthright lives for ever near
And the bold eagle which mans fear enshrouds
Would could he lodge it house upon the clouds   20
While little wrens mistrusting none that come
In each low hovel meet a sheltered home
Flowers in the wisdom of creative choice
Seem blest with feeling and a silent voice
Some on the barren roads delight to bloom
And others haunt the melancholly tomb
Where death the blight of all finds summers hours
Too kind to miss him with her host of flowers
Some flourish in the sun and some the shade
Who almost in his morning smiles would fade   30
These in leaf darkened woods right timid stray
And in its green night smile their lives away

Others in water live and scarcely seem
To peep their little flowers above the stream
While water lilies in their glories come
And spread green isles of beauty round their home
All share the summers glory and its good
And taste of joy in each peculiar mood
Insects of varied taste in rapture share
The heyday luxuries which she comes to heir   40
In wild disorder various routs they run
In water earth still shade and busy sun
And in the crowd of green earths busy claims
They een grow nameless mid their many names
And man that noble insect restless man
Whose thoughts scale heaven in its mighty span
Pours forth his living soul in many a shade
And taste runs riot in her every grade
While the low herd mere savages subdued
With nought of feeling or of taste imbued   50
Pass over sweetest scenes a carless eye
As blank as midnight in its deepest dye
From these and diffcrent far in rich degrees
Minds spring as various as the leaves of trees
To follow taste and all her sweets explore
And Edens make where deserts spread before
In pocsys spells some all their raptures find
And revel in the melodies of mind
There nature oer the soul her beauty flings
In all the sweets and essences of things   60
A face of beauty in a city crowd
Met—passed—and vanished like a summer cloud
In poesys vision more refined and fair
Taste reads oerjoyed and greets her image there
Dashes of sunshine and a page of may
Live there a whole life long one summers day
A blossom in its witchery of bloom
There gathered dwells in beauty and perfume
The singing bird the brook that laughs along
There ceasless sing and never thirsts for song   70
A pleasing image to its page conferred
In living character and breathing word
Becomes a landscape heard and felt and seen

Sunshine and shade one harmonizing green
Where meads and brooks and forrests basking lie
Lasting as truth and the eternal sky
Thus truth to nature as the true sublime
Stands a mount atlas overpeering time

Styles may with fashions vary—tawdry chaste
Have had their votaries which each fancied taste   80
From Donns old homely gold whose broken feet°
Jostles the readers patience from its seat
To Popes smooth ryhmes that regularly play
In musics stated periods all the way
That starts and closes starts again and times
Its tuning gammut true as minster chimes
From these old fashions stranger metres flow
Half prose half verse that stagger as they go
One line starts smooth and then for room perplext
Elbows along and knocks against the next   90
And half its neighbour where a pause marks time
There the clause ends what follows is for ryhme
Yet truth to nature will in all remain
As grass in winter glorifies the plain
And over fashions foils rise proud and high
As lights bright fountain in a cloudy sky

The man of science in discoverys moods
Roams oer the furze clad heath leaf buried woods
And by the simple brook in rapture finds
Treasures that wake the laugh of vulgar hinds   100
Who see no further in his dark employs
Then village childern seeking after toys
Their clownish hearts and ever heedless eyes
Find nought in nature they as wealth can prize
With them self interest and the thoughts of gain
Are natures beautys all beside are vain
But he the man of science and of taste
Sees wealth far richer in the worthless waste
Where bits of lichen and a sprig of moss
Will all the raptures of his mind engross   110
And bright winged insects on the flowers of may
Shine pearls too wealthy to be cast away

His joys run riot mid each juicy blade
Of grass where insects revel in the shade
And minds of different moods will oft condemn
His taste as cruel such the deeds to them
While he unconsious gibbets butterflyes
And strangles beetles all to make us wise
Tastes rainbow visions own unnumbered hues
And every shade its sense of taste pursues   120
The heedless mind may laugh the clown may stare
They own no soul to look for pleasure there
Their grosser feelings in a coarser dress
Mock at the wisdom which they cant possess

Some in recordless rapture love to breath
Natures wild Eden wood and field and heath
In common blades of grass his thoughts will raise
A world of beauty to admire and praise
Untill his heart oerflows with swarms of thought
To that great being who raised life from nought   130
The common weed adds graces to his mind
And gleams in beautys few beside may find
Associations sweet each object breeds
And fine ideas upon fancy feeds
He loves not flowers because they shed perfumes
Or butterflyes alone for painted plumes
Or birds for singing although sweet it be
But he doth love the wild and meadow lea
There hath the flower its dwelling place and there
The butterflye goes dancing through the air   140
He loves each desolate neglected spot
That seems in labours hurry left forgot
The warped and punished trunk of stunted oak
Freed from its bonds but by the thunder stroke
As crampt by straggling ribs of ivy sere
There the glad bird makes home for half the year
But take these several beings from their homes
Each beautious thing a withered thought becomes
Association fades and like a dream
They are but shadows of the things they seem   150
Torn from their homes and happiness they stand
The poor dull captives of a foreign land

Some spruce and delicate ideas feed
With them disorder is an ugly weed
And wood and heath a wilderness of thorns
Which gardeners shears nor fashions nor adorns
No spots give pleasure so forlorn and bare
But gravel walks would work rich wonders there
With such wild natures beautys run to waste
And arts strong impulse mars the truth of taste   160
Such are the various moods that taste displays
Surrounding wisdom in concentring rays
Where threads of light from one bright focus run
As days proud halo circles round the sun

St Martins Eve°

Now that the year grows wearisome with age
And days grow short and nights excessive long
No out door sports the village hinds engage
Still is the meadow romp and harvest song
That wont to echo from each merry throng
At dinner hours beneath hugh spreading tree
Rude winds hath done the landscape mickle wrong
That nature in her mirth did ill foresee
Who clingeth now to hope like shipwrecked folks at sea

The woods are desolate of song—the sky   10
Is all forsaken of its joyous crowd
Martin and swallow there no longer flye
—Hugh seeming rocks and deserts now enshroud
The sky for aye with shadow shaping cloud
None there of all those busy tribes remain
No song is heard save one that wails aloud
From the all lone and melancholly crane
Who like a traveller lost the right road seeks in vain

The childern hastening in from threatening rain
No longer round the fields for wild fruit run   20
But at their homes from morn till night remain
And wish in vain to see the welcome sun

Winters imprisonment is all begun
Yet when the wind grows troubleous and high
Pining for freedom like a love sick nun
Around the gardens little bounds they flye
Beneath the roaring trees fallen apples to espye

But spite of all the melancholly moods
That out of doors poor pleasures heart alarms
Flood bellowing rivers and wind roaring woods   30
The fireside evening owns increasing charms
What with the tale and eldern wine that warms
In purple bubbles by the blazing fire
Of simple cots and rude old fashioned farms
They feel as blest as joys can well desire
And midnight often joins before the guests retire

And such a group on good St Martins eve
Was met together upon pleasure bent
Where tales and fun did cares so well decieve
That the old cottage rung with merriment   40
And even the very rafters groaned and bent
Not so much it would seem from tempests din
That roared without in howling discontent
As from the merry noise and laugh within
That seemed as summers sports had never absent bin

Beside the fire large apples lay to roast
And in a hugh brown pitcher creaming ale
Was warming seasoned with a nutmeg toast
The merry group of gossips to regale
Around her feet the glad cat curled her tail   50
Listening the crickets song with half shut eyes
While in the chimney top loud roared the gale
Its blustering howl of out door symphonies
That round the cottage hearth bade happier moods arise

And circling round the fire the merry folks
Brought up all sports their memory could devise
Playing upon each other merry jokes
And now one shuts his hands and archly cries
Come open wide your mouth and shut your eyes

And see what gifts are sent you—foolish thing   60
He doth as he is bid and quickly rise
The peals of laughter when they up and fling
The ashes in while he goes spitting from the ring

And the old dame tho not in laughing luck
For that same night at one fell sweeping stroke
Mischieving cat that at a mouse had struck
Upon the shelf her best blue china broke
Yet spite of fate so funny was the joke
She laughed untill her very sides did shake
And some so tittled were they could not smoke   70
Laying down their pipes lest they their pipe should break
And laughed and laughed again untill their ribs did ache

Then deftly one with cunning in his eyes
With out stretched hand walks backward in the dark
Encouraged to the feat with proffered prize
If so he right can touch pretended mark
Made on the wall—and happy as a lark
He chuckles oer success by hopes prepared
While one with open mouth like greedy shark
Slives in the place and bites his finger hard   80
He bawls for freedom loud and shames his whole reward

Then came more games of wonderment and fun
Which set poor Hodges wisdom all aghast
Who sought three knives to hide them one by one
While one no conjuror to reveal the past
Blind fold would tell him where he hid the last
Hodge hiding two did for the third enquire
All tittered round and bade him hold it fast
But ah he shook it from his hands in ire
For while he hid the two they warmed it in the fire   90

Then to appease him with his burning hand
They bade him hide himself and they would tell
The very way in which he chose to stand
Hodge thought the matter most impossible
And on his knees behind the mash tub fell

And muttering said 'Ill beat em now or never'
Crying out 'how stand I' just to prove the spell
They answered 'like a fool' and thing so clever
Raised laughter against Hodge more long and loud than ever

Nor can the aged in such boisterous glee   100
Escape the tricks for laugh and jest designed
The old dame takes the bellows on her knee
And puffs in vain to tricks of rougery blind
Nor heeds the urchin who lets out the wind
With crafty finger and with cunning skill
That for her life the cause she cannot find
Untill the group unable to be still
Laughs out and dame though tricked smiles too against
   her will

Yet mid this strife of joy   on corner stool
One sits all silent doomed to worst of fate   110
Who made one slip in love and played the fool
And since condemned to live without a mate
No youth again courts once beguiled kate
Tho hopes of sweet hearts yet perplex her head
And charms to try by gipseys told of late
Beneath her pillow lays an onion red
To dream on this same night with whom she is to wed

And hopes that like to sunshine warming falls
Being all the solace to her withering mind
When they for dancing rise old young and all   120
She in her corner musing sits behind
Her palid cheek upon her hand reclined
Nursing rude melancholly like a child
Who sighs its silence to the sobbing wind
That in the chimney roars with fury wild
While every other heart to joy is reconsiled

One thumps the warming pan with merry glee
That bright as is a mirror decks the cot
Another droning as an humble bee
Plays on the muffled comb till piping hot   130
With over strained exertion—yet the lot

Is such an happy one that still he plays
Fatigue and all its countless ills forgot
All that he wants he wins—for rapture pays
To his unwearied skill right earnest words of praise

Ah happy hearts how happy cant be told
To fancy music in such clamorous noise
Like those converting all they touched to gold
These all they hearken to convert to joys
Thrice happy hearts—old men as wild as boys   140
Feel nought of age creep oer their extacys
—Old women whom no cares of life destroys
Dance with the girls—true did the bard surmise
'Where ignorance is bliss tis folly to be wise'°

When weary of the dance one reads a tale
Tho puzzled oft to spell a lengthy word
Storys though often read yet never stale
But gaining interest every time theyre heard
With morts of wonderment that neer occurred
Yet simple souls their faith it knows no stint   150
Things least to be believed are most preferred
All counterfiets as from truths sacred mint
Are readily believed if once put down in print

Blue beard and all his murders dread parade
Are listened to and mourned for and the tear
Drops from the blue eye of the listening maid
Warm as it fell upon her lovers bier
None in the circle doubt of what they hear
It were a sin to doubt oer tales so true
So say the old whose wisdom all revere   160
And unto whom such reverence may be due
For honest good intents praise that belongs to few

And Tib a Tinkers daughter is the tale
That doth by wonder their rude hearts engage
Oer young and old its witchcraft scenes prevail
In the rude legend of her pilgrimage
How she in servitude did erst engage

To live with an old hag of dreadful fame
Who often fell in freaks of wonderous rage
And played with Tib full many a bitter game   170
Til een the childern round cried out for very shame

They read how once to thrash her into chaff
The fearful witch tied Tibby in a sack
And hied her to the wood to seek a staff
That might be strong enough her bones to whack
But lucky Tib escaped ere she came back
And tied up dog and cat her doom to share
And pots and pans—and loud the howl and crack
That rose when the old witch with inky hair
Began the sack to thrash with no intent to spare   180

And when she found her unrevenged mistake
Her rage more fearful grew but all in vain
For fear no more caused Tibbys heart to ache
She far away from the old hags domain
Ran hartsomely a better place to gain
And here the younkers tongues grew wonder glib
With gladness and the reader stopt again
Declaring all too true to be a fib
And urged full glasses round to drink success to Tib

And when her sorrows and her pilgrimage   190
The plot of most new novels and old tales
Grew to a close her beauty did presage
Luck in the wind—and fortune spread her sails
In favouring bounty to Tibs summer gales
All praised her beauty and the lucky day
At length its rosey smiling face unveils
When Tib of course became a lady gay
And loud the listeners laughed while childern turned to play

Anon the clock counts twelve and mid their joys
The startled blackbird smooths its feathers down   200
That in its cage grew weary of their noise
—The merry maiden and the noisey clown
Prepare for home and down the straggling town

To seek their cottages they tittering go
Heartened with sports and stout ale berry brown
Beside their dames like chanticleer they crow
While every lanthorn flings long gleams along the snow

*To P * * * **

Fair was thy bloom when first I met
Thy summers maiden blossom
And thou art fair and lovely yet
And dearer to my bosom
O thou wast once a wildling flower
All garden flowers excelling
And still I bless the happy hour
That led me to thy dwelling

Though nursed by field and brook and wood
And wild in every feature   10
Spring neer unsealed a fairer bud
Nor formed a blossom sweeter
And of all flowers the spring has met
And it has met with many
Thou art to me the fairest yet
And lovliest of any

Though ripening summers round thee bring
Buds to thy swelling bosom
That wait the cheering smiles of spring
To ripen into blossom   20
These buds shall added blessings be
To make our loves sincerer
For as their flowers resemble thee
Theyll make thy memory dearer

And though thy bloom shall pass away
By winter overtaken
Thoughts of the past will charms display
And many joys awaken
When time shall every sweet remove
And blight thee on my bosom   30
Let beauty fade—to me and love
Thoult neer be out of blossom

Emmonsales Heath°

In thy wild garb of other times
I find thee lingering still
Furze oer each lazy summit climbs
At natures easy will

Grasses that never knew a scythe
Waves all the summer long
And wild weed blossoms waken blythe
That ploughshares never wrong

Stern industry with stubborn toil
And wants unsatisfied   10
Still leaves untouched thy maiden soil
In its unsullied pride

The birds still find their summer shade
To build their nests agen
And the poor hare its rushy glade
To hide from savage men

Nature its family protects
In thy security
And blooms that love what man neglects
Find peaceful homes in thee   20

The wild rose scents thy summer air
And woodbines weave in bowers
To glad the swain sojourning there
And maidens gathering flowers

Creations steps ones wandering meets
Untouched by those of man
Things seem the same in such retreats
As when the world began

Furze ling and brake all mingling free
And grass forever green   30
All seem the same old things to be
As they have ever been

The brook oer such neglected ground
Ones weariness to sooth
Still wildly threads its lawless bounds
And chafes the pebble smooth

Crooked and rude as when at first
Its waters learned to stray
And from their mossy fountain birst
It washed itself a way   40

O who can pass such lovely spots
Without a wish to stray
And leave lifes cares a while forgot
To muse an hour away

Ive often met with places rude
Nor failed their sweet to share
But passed an hour with solitude
And left my blessing there

He that can meet the morning wind
And oer such places roam   50
Nor leave a lingering wish behind
To make their peace his home

His heart is dead to quiet hours
No love his mind employs
Poesy with him neer shares its flowers
Nor solitude its joys

O there are spots amid thy bowers
Which nature loves to find
Where spring drops round her earliest flowers
Uncheckt by winters wind   60

Where cowslips wake the childs supprise
Sweet peeping ere their time
Ere april spreads her dappled skyes
Mid mornings powdered rime

Ive stretched my boyish walks to thee
When maydays paths were dry
When leaves had nearly hid each tree
And grass greened ancle high

And mused the sunny hours away
And thought of little things   70
That childern mutter oer their play
When fancy trys its wings

Joy nursed me in her happy moods
And all lifes little crowd
That haunt the waters fields and woods
Would sing their joys aloud

I thought how kind that mighty power
Must in his splendour be
Who spread around my boyish hour
Such gleams of harmony   80

Who did with joyous rapture fill
The low as well as high
And made the pismires round the hill
Seem full as blest as I

Hopes sun is seen of every eye
The haloo that it gives
In natures wide and common sky
Cheers every thing that lives

The Summer Shower

I love it well oercanopied in leaves
Of crowding woods to spend a quiet hour
And where the woodbine weaves
To list the summer shower

Brought by the south west wind that balm and bland
Breaths luscious coolness loved and felt by all
While on the uplifted hand
The rain drops gently fall

Now quickening on and on the pattering woods
Recieves the coming shower birds trim their wings   10
And in a joyful mood
The little wood chat sings

And blackbird squatting on her mortared nest
Safe hid in ivy and the pathless wood
Pruneth her sooty breast
And warms her downy brood

And little Pettichap like hurrying mouse
Keeps nimbling near my arbour round and round
Aye theres her oven house
Built nearly on the ground   20

Of woodbents withered straws and moss and leaves
And lined with downy feathers saftys joy
Dwells with the home she weaves
Nor fears the pilfering boy

The busy falling rain increases now
And sopping leaves their dripping moisture pour
And from each loaded bough
Fast falls the double shower

Weed climbing hedges banks and meeds unmown
Where rushy fringed brooklet easy curls   30
Look joyous while the rain
Strings their green suit [with] pearls

While from the crouching corn the weeding troop
Run hastily and huddling in a ring
Where the old willows stoop
Their ancient ballads sing

And gabble over wonders ceasless tale
Till from the southwest sky showers thicker come
Humming along the vale
And bids them hasten home   40

With laughing skip they stride the hasty brook
That mutters through the weeds untill it gains
A clear and quiet nook
To greet the dimpling rain

And on they drabble all in mirth not mute
Leaving their footmarks on the elting soil
Where print of sprawling foot
Stirs up a tittering smile

On beautys lips who slipping mid the crowd
Blushes to have her anckle seen so high   50
Yet inly feeleth proud
That none a fault can spy

Yet rudely followed by the meddling clown
Who passes vulgar gibes—the bashful maid
Lets go her folded gown
And pauses half afraid

To climb the stile before him till the dame
To quarrel half provoked assails the knave
And laughs him into shame
And makes him well behave   60

Bird nesting boys ocrtaken in the rain
Beneath the ivied maple bustling run
And wait in anxious pain
Impatient for the sun

And sigh for home yet at the pasture gate
The molehill tossing bull with straining eye
Seemeth their steps to wait
Nor dare they pass him bye

Till wearied out high over hedge they scrawl
To shun the road and through the wet grass roam 70
Till wet and draggled all
They fear to venture home

The plough team wet and dripping plashes home
And on the horse the ploughboy lolls along
Yet from the wet grounds come
The loud and merry song

Now neath the leafy arch of dripping bough
That loaded trees form oer the narrow lane
The horse released from plough
Naps the moist grass again   80

Around their blanket camps the gipseys still
Heedless of showers while black thorns shelter round
Jump oer the pasture hills
In many an idle bound

From dark green clumps among the dripping grain
The lark with sudden impulse starts and sings
And mid the smoking rain
Quivers her russet wings

A joy inspiring calmness all around
Breaths a refreshing sense of strengthening power   90
Like that which toil hath found
In sundays leisure hour

When spirits all relaxed heart sick of toil
Seeks out the pleasant woods and shadowy dells
And where the fountain boils
Lye listening distant bells

Amid the yellow furze the rabbits bed
Labour hath hid his tools and oer the heath
Hies to the milking shed
That stands the oak beneath   100

And there he wiles the pleasant shower away
Filling his mind with store of happy things
Rich crops of corn and hay
And all that plenty brings

The crampt horison now leans on the ground
Quiet and cool and labours hard employ
Ceases while all around
Falls a refreshing joy

Love and Memory

Thou art gone the dark journey
That leaves no returning
Tis fruitless to mourn thee
But who can help mourning
To think of the life
That did laugh on thy brow
In the beautiful past
Left so desolate now

When youth seemed immortal
So sweet did it weave   10
Heavens haloo around thee
Earths hopes to decieve
Thou fairest and dearest
Where many were fair
To my heart thou art nearest
Though this name is but there

The nearer the fountain
More pure the stream flows
And sweeter to fancy
The bud of the rose   20
And now thourt in heaven
More pure is the birth
Of thoughts that wake of thee
Than ought upon earth

As a bud green in spring
As a rose blown in June
Thy beauty looked out
And departed as soon

Heaven saw thee too fair
For earths tennants of clay   30
And ere age did thee wrong
Thou wert summoned away

I know thou art happy
Why in grief need I be
Yet I am and the more so
To feel its for thee
For thy presence possest
As thy abscence destroyed
The most that I loved
And the all I enjoyed   40

So I try to seek pleasure
But vainly I try
Now joys cup is drained
And hopes fountain is dry
I mix with the living
Yet what do I see
Only more cause for sorrow
In loosing of thee

The year has its winter
As well as its May   50
So the sweetest must leave us
And the fairest decay
Suns leave us to night
And their light none may borrow
So joy retreats from us
Overtaken by sorrow

The sun greets the spring
And the blossom the bee
The grass the blea hill
And the leaf the bare tree   60
But suns nor yet seasons
As sweet as they be
Shall ever more greet me
With tidings of thee

The voice of the cuckoo
Is merry at noon
And the song of the nightingale
Gladdens the moon
But the gayest to day
May be saddest to morrow   70
And the loudest in joy
Sink the deepest in sorrow

For the lovely in death
And the fairest must die
Fall once and for ever
Like stars from the sky
So in vain do I mourn thee
I know its in vain
Who would wish thee from joy
To earths troubles again   80

Yet thy love shed upon me
Life more then mine own
And now thou art from me
My being is gone
Words know not my grief
Thus without thee to dwell
Yet in one I felt all
When life bade thee farewell

Insects

Thou tiney loiterer on the barleys beard
And happy unit of a numerous herd
Of playfellows the laughing summer brings
Mocking the sunshine in their glittering wings
How merrily they creep and run and flye
No kin they bear to labours drudgery
Smoothing the velvet of the pale hedge rose
And where they flye for dinner no one knows
The dew drops feed them not—they love the shine
Of noon whose sun may bring them golden wine   10

All day theyre playing in their sunday dress
Till night goes sleep and they can do no less
Then in the heath bells silken hood they flie
And like to princes in their slumber lie
From coming night and dropping dews and all
In silken beds and roomy painted hall
So happily they spend their summer day
Now in the corn fields now the new mown hay
One almost fancys that such happy things
In coloured hoods and richly burnished wings   20
Are fairy folk in splendid masquerade
Disguised through fear of mortal folk affraid
Keeping their merry pranks a mystery still
Lest glaring day should do their secrets ill

Sabbath Bells

Ive often on a sabbath day
Where pastoral quiet dwells
Lay down among the new mown hay
To listen distant bells
That beautifully flung the sound
Upon the quiet wind
While beans in blossom breathed around
A fragrance oer the mind

A fragrance and a joy beside
That never wears away   10
The very air seems deified
Upon a sabbath day
So beautiful the flitting wrack
Slow pausing from the eye
Earths music seemed to call them back
Calm settled in the sky

And I have listened till I felt
A feeling not in words
A love that rudest moods would melt
When those sweet sounds was heard   20

A melancholly joy at rest
A pleasurable pain
A love a rapture of the breast
That nothing will explain

A dream of beauty that displays
Ima[g]inary joys
That all the world in all its ways
Finds not to realize
All idly stretched upon the hay
The wind-flirt fanning bye   30
How soft how sweetly swept away
The music of the sky

The ear it lost and caught the sound
Swelled beautifully on
A fitful melody around
Of sweetness heard and gone
I felt such thoughts I yearned to sing
The humming airs delight
That seemed to move the swallows wing
Into a wilder flight   40

The butterflye in wings of brown
Would find me where I lay
Fluttering and bobbing up and down
And settling on the hay
The waving blossoms seemed to throw
Their fragrance to the sound
While up and down and loud and low
The bells were ringing round

Peggy Band°

O it was a lorn and a dismal night
And the storm beat loud and high
Nor a friendly light to guide me right
Was there shining in the sky
When a lonely hut my wanderings met
Lost in a foreign land
And I found the dearest friend as yet
In my lovely Peggy Band

'O father heres a soldier lad
And weary he seems to be'   10
'Then welcome him in' the old man said—
And she gave her seat to me
The fire she trimmed and my cloaths she dried
With her own sweet lily hand
And oer the soldiers lot she sighed
While I blest my Peggy Band

When I told the tale of my wandering years
And the nights unknown to sleep
She made excuse to hide her tears
And she stole away to weep   20
A pilgrims blessing I seemed to share
As saints of the holy land
And I thought her a guardian angel there
Though he called her his Peggy Band

The night it passed and the hour to part
With the morning winged away
And I felt an anguish at my heart
That vainly bade to stay
I thanked the old man for all he did
And I took his daughters hand   30
But my heart was full and I could not bid
Farewell to my Peggy Band

A blessing on that friendly cot
Where the soldier found repose
And a blessing be her constant lot
Who soothed the strangers woes
I turned a last look on the door
As she held it in her hand
And my heart ached sore as I crossed the moor
To leave my Peggy Band   40

To the weary ways that I have gone
Full many friends befell
And Ive met with maidens many a one
To use the soldier well

But of all the maids I ever met
At home or in foreign land
Ive never seen the equal yet
Of my charming Peggy Band

An Idle Hour

Sauntering at ease I often love to lean
Oer old bridge walls and mark the flood below
Whose ripples through the weeds of oily green
Like happy travellers mutter as they go
And mark the sunshine dancing on the arch
Time keeping to the merry waves beneath
And on the banks see drooping blossoms parch
Thirsting for water in the days hot breath
Right glad of mud drops plashed upon their leaves
By cattle plunging from the steepy brink   10
While water flowers more than their share recieve
And revel to their very cups in drink
Just like the world some strive and fare but ill
While others riot and have plenty still

The Flood

On Lolham Brigs in wild and lonely mood°
Ive seen the winter floods their gambols play
Through each old arch that trembled while I stood
Bent oer its wall to watch the dashing spray
As their old stations would be washed away
Crash came the ice against the jambs and then
A shudder jarred the arches—yet once more
It breasted raving waves and stood agen
To wait the shock as stubborn as before
—While foam brown crested with the russet soil   10
As washed from new ploughed lands—would dart beneath
Then round and round a thousand eddies boil
On tother side—then pause as if for breath
One minute—and ingulphed—like life in death°

Whose wrecky stains dart on the floods away
More swift then shadows in a stormy day
Things trail and turn and steady—all in vain
The engulphing arches shoot them quickly through
The feather dances flutters and again
Darts through the deepest dangers still afloat   20
Seeming as faireys whisked it from the view
And danced it oer the waves as pleasures boat
Light hearted as a merry thought in may—
Trays—uptorn bushes—fence demolished rails
Loaded with weeds in sluggish motions stray
Like water monsters lost each winds and trails
Till near the arches—then as in affright
It plunges—reels—and shudders out of sight

Waves trough—rebound—and fury boil again
Like plunging monsters rising underneath   30
Who at the top curl up a shaggy main
A moment catching at a surer breath
Then plunging headlong down and down—and on
Each following boil the shadow of the last
And other monsters rise when those are gone
Crest their fringed waves—plunge onward and are past
—The chill air comes around me ocean blea
From bank to bank the waterstrife is spread
Strange birds like snow spots oer the huzzing sea
Hang where the wild duck hurried past and fled   40
—On roars the flood—all restless to be free
Like trouble wandering to eternity

Labours Leisure

O for the feelings and the carless health
That found me toiling in the fields—the joy
I felt at eve with not a wish for wealth
When labour done and in the hedge put bye
My delving spade—I homeward used to hie
With thoughts of books I often read by stealth
Beneath the black thorn clumps at dinners hour
It urged my weary feet with eager speed
To hasten home where winter fires did shower

Scant light now felt as beautiful indeed   10
Where bending oer my knees I used to read
With earnest heed all books that had the power
To give me joy in most delicious ways
And rest my spirits after weary days

Mist in the Meadows

The evening oer the meadow seems to stoop
More distant lessens the diminished spire
Mist in the hollows reaks and curdles up
Like fallen clouds that spread—and things retire
Less seen and less—the shepherd passes near
And little distant most grotesquely shades
As walking without legs—lost to his knees
As through the rawky creeping smoke he wades
Now half way up the arches dissappear
And small the bits of sky that glimmer through   10
Then trees loose all but tops—I meet the fields
And now the indistinctness passes bye
The shepherd all his length is seen again
And further on the village meets the eye

Signs of Winter

Tis winter plain the images around
Protentious tell us of the closing year
Short grows the stupid day the moping fowl
Go roost at noon—upon the mossy barn
The thatcher hangs and lays the frequent yaum
Nudged close to stop the rain that drizzling falls
With scarce one interval of sunny sky
For weeks still leeking on that sulky gloom
Muggy and close a doubt twixt night and day
The sparrow rarely chirps the thresher pale   10
Twanks with sharp measured raps the weary frail
Thump after thump right tiresome to the ear
The hedger lonesome brustles at his toil
And shepherds trudge the fields without a song

The cat runs races with her tail—the dog
Leaps oer the orchard hedge and knarls the grass
The swine run round and grunt and play with straw
Snatching out hasty mouthfuls from the stack
Sudden upon the elm tree tops the crow
Uncerimonious visit pays and croaks   20
Then swops away—from mossy barn the owl
Bobs hasty out—wheels round and scared as soon
As hastily retires—the ducks grow wild
And from the muddy pond fly up and wheel
A circle round the village and soon tired
Plunge in the pond again—the maids in haste
Snatch from the orchard hedge the mizled cloaths
And laughing hurry in to keep them dry

Angling

Angling has pleasures that are much enjoyed
By tasteful minds of nature never cloyed
In pleasant solitudes where winding floods
Pass level meadows and oerhanging woods
Verged with tall reeds that rustle in the wind
A soothing music in the anglers mind
And rush right complasant that ever bows
Obesceience to the stream that laughs below
He feels delighted into quiet praise
And sweet the pictures that the mind essays   10
While gentle whispers on the southern wind
Brings health and quiet to the anglers mind
Smooth as the gentle river whirls along
And sweet as memory of some happy song

The morn is still and balmy all that moves
The trees are south gales which the angler loves
That stirs the waveing grass in idle whirls
And flush the cheeks and fan the jetty curls
Of milking maidens at their morns employ
Who sing and wake the dewy fields to joy   20
The sun just rising large and round and dim
Keeps creeping up oer the flat meadows brim

As rising from the ground to run its race
Till up it mounts and shows a ruddy face
Now is the time the angler leaves his dreams
In anxious movements for the silent streams
Frighting the heron from its morning toil
First at the river watching after coil

Now with the rivers brink he winds his way
For a choice place to spend the quiet day   30
Marking its banks how varied things appear
Now cloathed in trees and bushes and now clear
While steep the bank climbs from the waters edge
Then almost choaked with rushes flags and sedge
Then flat and level to the very brink
Tracked deep by cattle running there to drink
At length he finds a spot half shade half sun
That scarcely curves to show the waters run
Still clear and smooth quick he his line unlaps
While fish leap up and loud the water claps   40
Which fills his mind with pleasures of supprise
That in the deep hole some old monster lies

Right cautious now his strongest line to take
Lest some hugh monster should his tackle break
Then half impatient with a cautious throw
He swings his line into the depths below
The water rat hid in the shivering reeds
That feeds upon the slime and water weeds
Nibbling their grassy leaves with crizzling sound
Plunges below and makes his fancys bound   50
With expectations joy—down goes the book
In which glad leisure might for pleasure look
And up he grasps the angle in his hand
In readiness the expected prize to land
While tip toe hope gives expectations dream
Sweet as the sunshine sleeping on the stream

None but true anglers feel that gush of joy
That flushes in the patient minds employ
While expectation upon tip toe sees
The float just wave it cannot be a breeze   60

For not a waver oer the waters pass
Warm with the joyous day and smooth as glass
Now stronger moved it dances round then stops
Then bobs again and in a moment drops
Beneath the water—he with joys elate
Pulls and his rod bends double with the weight
True was his skill in hopes expecting dream
And up he draws a flat and curving bream
That scarcely landed from the tackle drops
And on the bank half thronged in sedges stops   70

Now sport the waterflyes with tiny wings
A dancing crowd imprinting little rings
And the rich lights the suns young splendours throw
Is by the very pebbles caught below
Behind the leaning tree he stoops to lean
And soon the stirring float again is seen
A larger yet from out its ambush shoots
Hid underneath the old trees cranking roots
The float now shakes and quickens his delight
Then bobs a moment and is out of sight   80
Which scarce secured—down goes the cork again
And still a finer pants upon the plain
And bounds and flounces mid the new mown hay
And luck but ceases with the closing day

Winter Fields

O for a pleasant book to cheat the sway
Of winter—where rich mirth with hearty laugh
Listens and rubs his legs on corner seat
For fields are mire and sludge—and badly off
Are those who on their pudgy paths delay
There striding shepherd seeking driest way
Fearing nights wetshod feet and hacking cough
That keeps him waken till the peep of day
Goes shouldering onward and with ready hook
Progs oft to ford the sloughs that nearly meet   10

Accross the lands—croodling and thin to view
His loath dog follows—stops and quakes and looks
For better roads—till whistled to pursue
Then on with frequent jump he hirkles through

Winter Evening

The crib stock fothered—horses suppered up
And cows in sheds all littered down in straw
The threshers gone the owls are left to whoop
The ducks go waddling with distended craw
Through little hole made in the henroost door
And geese with idle gabble never oer
Bate careless hog untill he tumbles down
Insult provoking spite to noise the more
While fowl high perched blink with contemptous frown
On all the noise and bother heard below   10
Over the stable ridge in crowds the crow
With jackdaws intermixed known by their noise
To the warm woods behind the village go
And whistling home for bed go weary boys

Snow Storm

Winter is come in earnest and the snow
In dazzling splendour—crumping underfoot
Spreads a white world all calm and where we go
By hedge or wood trees shine from top to root
In feathered foliage flashing light and shade
Of strangest contrast—fancys pliant eye
Delighted sees a vast romance displayed
And fairy halls descended from the sky
The smallest twig its snowy burthen wears
And woods oer head the dullest eyes engage   10
To shape strange things—where arch and pillar bears
A roof of grains fantastic arched and high
And little shed beside the spinney wears
The grotesque zemblance of an hermitage

On[e] almost sees the hermit from the wood
Come bending with his sticks beneath his arm
And then the smoke curl up its dusky flood
From the white little roof his peace to warm
One shapes his books his quiet and his joys
And in romances world forgetting mood   20
The scene so strange so fancys mind employs
It seems heart aching for his solitude
Domestic spots near home and trod so oft
Seen daily—known for years—by the strange wand
Of winters humour changed—the little croft
Left green at night when morns loth look obtrudes
Trees bushes grass to one wild garb subdued
Are gone and left us in another land

[*Showers*]

The fitful weather changes every hour
And many a footstep hurrys from the shower
The men at plough the shepherd on the lea
Look up and scamper to the nearest tree
The ditcher ere the last showers hardly gone
Runs to the bush and puts his jacket on
And in escaping haste is often seen
To where the ash hangs oer the thistly green
An hollow dotterel wasted to a shell
Large as a little hut and known as well   10
To all the out door tennants in the fields
That from the heaviest tempest shelter yields
Here two or three were met to shun the rain
That slowly cleared and faster fell again

The Meadow Grass

Delicious is a leisure hour
Among the sweet green fields to be
So sweet indeed I have no power
To tell the joys I feel and see

See here the meadows how they lie
So sunny level and so green
The grass is waving mid leg high
A sweeter rest was never seen

I look around and drop me down
And feel delight to be alone   10
Cares hardly dare to show a frown
While mays sweet leisure is my own
Joy half a stranger comes to me
And gives me thoughts to profit bye
I think how happy worlds must be
That dwell above that peaceful sky

That happy sky with here and there
A little cloud that would express
By the slow motions that they wear
They live with peace and quietness   20
I think so as I see them glide
Thoughts earthly tumults cant destroy
So calm so soft so smooth they ride
Im sure their errands must be joy

The sky is all serene and mild
The sun is gleaming far away
So sweet so rich—the very child
Would feel its maker brought the may
For heavens ways are pleasant ways
Of silent quietness and peace   30
And he who musing hither strays
Finds all in such a scene as this

Where no strife comes but in the songs
Of birds half frantic in their glee
Hid from the rude worlds many wrongs
How can they else but happy be
In places where the summer seems
Entirely out of troubles way
Where joy oer out door leisure dreams
As if twas sunday every day   40

For nature here in self delight
Bestows her richest gifts—the green
Luxuriance all around—the light
Seems more then any common scene
And yet appears no looker on
Left to herself and solitude
I seem myself the only one
Intruding on her happy mood

Intruding as of wont to meet
That joyousness she throws around   50
To feel the grass beneath my feet
Heart cheered to hear its brustling sound
Pitpatting at ones legs to feel
Their seeded heads then bounce away
Theres somthing more then joy to steal
A walk oer meadows in the may

A noise now comes on joys repose
That mays right welcome visit brings
Up from the bush the blackbird goes
The fanned leaves dance beneath his wings   60
And up with yet a louder noise
Wood pigeons flusker start—the road way cows
Brouze there and soon the herd boy shows
His head amid the shaking boughs

Theres somthing more to fill the mind
Then words can paint to ears and eyes
A calmness quiet loves to find
In these green summer reveries
A freshness giving youth to age
A health to pain and troubles drear   70
The world has nought but wars to wage
Peace comes and makes her dwelling here

I feel so calm I seem to find
A world I never felt before
A heaven fills my clouded mind
As though it would be dark no more

An endless sunshine glows around
A meadow like a waveless sea
Glows green in many a level ground
A very paradise to me   80

Tis sweeter then the sweetest book
That ever met the poets eye
To read in this delightful nook
The scenes that round about me lie
And yet they are but common things
Green hedges bowering oer the grass
And one old tree that stoops and flings
Its boughs oer water smooth as glass

And on a ledge of gravel crags
Those golden blooms so nobly tower   90
Though but the yellow water flags
They're fine enough for garden flowers
And over head the breadths of sky
Goes spreading gladness everywhere
And oer this meadow grass to lye
It seems to look more happy here

The Pasture

The pewet is come to the green
And swops oer the swain at his plough
Where the greensward in places is seen
Prest down by the lairs of the cow
The mole roots her hillocks anew
For seasons to dress at their wills
In their thyme and their beautiful dew
For the pastures delight is its hills

They invite us when weary to drop
On their cushons awhile and again   10
They invite us when musing to stop
And see how they checker the plain

And the old hills swell out in the sun
So inviting een now—the cow boy
Has his game of peg morris begun
And cuts his rude figures in joy

When I stroll oer the molehilly green
Stepping onward from hillock to hill
I think over pictures Ive seen
And feel them delicously still   20
I think when the glad shepherd lay
On the velvet sward stretched for a bed
On the bosom of sunshiney hay
While an hillock supported his head

I think when in weeding the maid
Made choice of a hill for her seat
When the wind in her curls so delicously played
And her smiles seemed so blushing and sweet
I think of gay groups in the shade
In hay time with noise never still   30
When the green sward their gay cushons made
And their dinner was spread on a hill

I think when in harvest folks lay
Underneath the green shade of a tree
While their childern where busy at play
Running round the hugh trunk in their glee
Joy shouted wherever I went
And een now such a freshness it yields
I could fancy with books and a tent
What delight one could find in the fields   40

BIRD POEMS

To the Snipe°

Lover of swamps
The quagmire overgrown
With hassock tufts of sedge—where fear encamps
Around thy home alone

The trembling grass
Quakes from the human foot
Nor bears the weight of man to let him pass
Where he alone and mute

Sitteth at rest
In safety neath the clump   10
Of hugh flag-forrest that thy haunts invest
Or some old sallow stump

Thriving on seams
That tiney islands swell
Just hilling from the mud and rancid streams
Suiting thy nature well

For here thy bill
Suited by wisdom good
Of rude unseemly length doth delve and drill
The gelid mass for food   20

And here may hap
When summer suns hath drest
The moors rude desolate and spungy lap
May hide thy mystic nest

Mystic indeed
For isles that ocean make
Are scarcely more secure for birds to build
Then this flag-hidden lake

Boys thread the woods
To their remotest shades   30
But in these marshy flats these stagnant floods
Security pervades

From year to year
Places untrodden lye
Where man nor boy nor stock hath ventured near
—Nought gazed on but the sky

And fowl that dread
The very breath of man
Hiding in spots that never knew his tread
A wild and timid clan   40

Wigeon and teal
And wild duck—restless lot
That from mans dreaded sight will ever steal
To the most dreary spot

Here tempests howl
Around each flaggy plot
Where they who dread mans sight the water fowl
Hide and are frighted not

Tis power divine
That heartens them to brave   50
The roughest tempest and at ease recline
On marshes or the wave

Yet instinct knows
Not safetys bounds to shun
The firmer ground where skulking fowler goes
With searching dogs and gun

By tepid springs
Scarcely one stride across
Though brambles from its edge a shelter flings
Thy safety is at loss   60

And never chuse
The little sinky foss
Streaking the moores whence spa-red water spews
From puddles fringed with moss

Free booters there
Intent to kill and slay
Startle with cracking guns the trepid air
And dogs thy haunts betray

From dangers reach
Here thou art safe to roam   70
Far as these washy flag-worn marshes stretch
A still and quiet home

In these thy haunts
Ive gleancd habitual love
From the vague world where pride and folly taunts
I muse and look above

Thy solitudes
The unbounded heaven cstccms
And here my heart warms into higher moods
And dignifying dreams   80

I see the sky
Smile on the meanest spot
Giving to all that creep or walk or flye
A calm and cordial lot

Thine teaches me
Right feelings to employ
That in the dreariest places peace will be
A dweller and a joy

Birds Nests

How fresh the air the birds how busy now
In every walk if I but peep I find
Nests newly made or finished all and lined
With hair and thistle down and in the bough

Of little awthorn huddled up in green
The leaves still thickening as the spring gets age
The Pinks quite round and snug and closely laid
And linnets of materials loose and rough
And still hedge sparrow moping in the shade
Near the hedge bottom weaves of homely stuff   10
Dead grass and mosses green an hermitage
For secresy and shelter rightly made
And beautiful it is to walk beside
The lanes and hedges where their homes abide

Sand Martin

Thou hermit haunter of the lonely glen
And common wild and heath—the desolate face
Of rude waste landscapes far away from men
Where frequent quarrys give thee dwelling place
With strangest taste and labour undeterred
Drilling small holes along the quarrys side
More like the haunts of vermin than a bird
And seldom by the nesting boy descried
Ive seen thee far away from all thy tribe
Flirting about the unfrequented sky   10
And felt a feeling that I cant describe
Of lone seclusion and a hermit joy
To see thee circle round nor go beyond
That lone heath and its melancholly pond

On Seeing Two Swallows Late in October

Lone occupiers of a naked sky
When desolate november hovers nigh
And all your fellow tribes in many crowds
Have left the village with the autumn clouds
Carless of old affections for the scene
That made them happy when the fields were green
And left them undisturbed to build their nests
In each old chimney like to welcome guests

Forsaking all like untamed winds they roam
And make with summers an unsettled home   10
Following her favours to the farthest lands
Oer untraced oceans and untrodden sands
Like happy images they haste away
And leave us lonely till another may

But little lingerers old esteem detains
Ye haply thus to brave the chilly air
When skys grow dull with winters heavy rains
And all the orchard trees are nearly bare
Yet the old chimneys still are peeping there
Above the russet thatch where summers tide   20
Of sunny joys gave you such social fare
As makes you haply wishing to abide
In your old dwellings through the changing year
I wish ye well to find a dwelling here
For in the unsocial weather ye would fling
Gleamings of comfort through the winter wide
Twittering as wont above the old fire side
And cheat the surly winter into spring

The Fern Owls Nest

The weary woodman rocking home beneath
His tightly banded faggot wonders oft
While crossing over the furze crowded heath
To hear the fern owls cry that whews aloft
In circling whirls and often by his head
Wizzes as quick as thought and ill at rest
As through the rustling ling with heavy tread
He goes nor heeds he tramples near its nest
That underneath the furze or squatting thorn
Lies hidden on the ground and teazing round   10
That lonely spot she wakes her jarring noise
To the unheeding waste till mottled morn
Fills the red east with daylights coming sounds
And the heaths echoes mocks the herding boys

The March Nightingale

Now sallow catkins once all downy white
Turn like the sunshine into golden light
The rocking clown leans oer the spinney rail
In admiration at the sunny sight
The while the Blackcap doth his ears assail
With such a rich and such an early song
He stops his own and thinks the nightingale
Hath of her monthly reckoning counted wrong
'Sweet jug jug jug' comes loud upon his ear
Those sounds that unto may by right belong   10
Yet on the awthorn scarce a leaf appears
How can it be—spell struck the wondering boy
Listens again—again the sound he hears
And mocks it in his song for very joy

The Thrushes Nest

Within a thick and spreading awthorn bush
That overhung a molehill large and round
I heard from morn to morn a merry thrush
Sing hymns to sunrise while I drank the sound
With joy and often an intruding guest
I watched her secret toils from day to day
How true she warped the moss to form her nest
And modelled it within with wood and clay
And bye and bye like heath bells gilt with dew
There lay her shining eggs as bright as flowers   10
Ink-spotted over shells of greeny blue
And there I witnessed in the summer hours
A brood of natures minstrels chirp and fly
Glad as the sunshine and the laughing sky

The Wren

Why is the cuckoos melody preferred
And nightingales rich song so fondly praised
In poets ryhmes   Is there no other bird
Of natures minstrelsy that oft hath raised
Ones heart to extacy and mirth as well
I judge not how anothers taste is caught
With mine theres other birds that bear the bell
Whose song hath crowds of happy memories brought
Such the wood Robin singing in the dell
And little Wren that many a time hath sought   10
Shelter from showers in huts where I did dwell
In early spring the tennant of the plain
Tenting my sheep and still they come to tell
The happy stories of the past again

The Happy Bird

The happy white throat on the sweeing bough
Swayed by the impulse of the gadding wind
That ushers in the showers of april—now
Singeth right joyously and now reclined
Croucheth and clingeth to her moving seat
To keep her hold—and till the wind for rest
Pauses—she mutters inward melodys
That seem her hearts rich thinkings to repeat
And when the branch is still—her little breast
Swells out in raptures gushing symphonys   10
And then against her blown wing softly prest
The wind comes playing an enraptured guest
This way and that she swees—till gusts arise
More boisterous in their play—when off she flies

Emmonsails Heath in Winter°

I love to see the old heaths withered brake
Mingle its crimpled leaves with furze and ling
While the old Heron from the lonely lake
Starts slow and flaps his melancholly wing
And oddling crow in idle motions swing
On the half rotten ash trees topmost twig
Beside whose trunk the gipsey makes his bed
Up flies the bouncing wood cock from the brig
Where a black quagmire quakes beneath the tread
The field fare chatters in the whistling thorn   10
And for the awe round fields and closen rove
And coy bumbarrels twenty in a drove
Flit down the hedgerows in the frozen plain
And hang on little twigs and start again

The Firetails Nest

Tweet pipes the robin as the cat creeps bye
Her nestling young that in the elderns lie
And then the bluecap tootles in its glee
Picking the flies from blossomed apple tree
And pink the chaffinch cries its well known strain
Urging its mate to utter pink again
While in a quiet mood hedgsparrows trie
An inward stir of shadowed melody
While on the rotten tree the firetail mourns
As the old hedger to his toil returns   10
And chops the grain to stop the gap close bye
The hole where her blue eggs in safety lie
Of every thing that stirs she dreameth wrong
And pipes her 'tweet tut' fears the whole day long

The Wrynecks Nest

That summer bird its oft repeated note
Chirps from the dotterel ash and in the hole
The green woodpecker made in years remote
It makes its nest—where peeping idlers strole
In anxious plundering moods—and bye and bye
The wrynecks curious eggs as white as snow
While squinting in the hollow tree they spy
The sitting bird looks up with jetty eye
And waves her head in terror too and fro
Speckled and veined in various shades of brown   10
And then a hissing noise assails the clown
And quick with hasty terror in his breast
From the trees knotty trunk he sluthers down
And thinks the strange bird guards a serpents nest

The Nightingales Nest

Up this green woodland ride lets softly rove
And list the nightingale—she dwelleth here
Hush let the wood gate softly clap—for fear
The noise may drive her from her home of love
For here Ive heard her many a merry year
At morn and eve nay all the live long day
As though she lived on song—this very spot
Just where that old mans beard all wildly trails
Rude arbours oer the road and stops the way
And where that child its blue bell flowers hath got   10
Laughing and creeping through the mossy rails
There have I hunted like a very boy
Creeping on hands and knees through matted thorns
To find her nest and see her feed her young
And vainly did I many hours employ
All seemed as hidden as a thought unborn
And where these crimping fern leaves ramp among
The hazels under boughs—Ive nestled down
And watched her while she sung—and her renown

Hath made me marvel that so famed a bird   20
Should have no better dress than russet brown
Her wings would tremble in her extacy
And feathers stand on end as twere with joy
And mouth wide open to release her heart
Of its out sobbing songs—the happiest part
Of summers fame she shared—for so to me
Did happy fancys shapen her employ
But if I touched a bush or scarcely stirred
All in a moment stopt—I watched in vain
The timid bird had left the hazel bush   30
And at a distance hid to sing again
Lost in a wilderness of listening leaves
Rich extacy would pour its luscious strain
Till envy spurred the emulating thrush
To start less wild and scarce inferior songs
For cares with him for half the year remain
To damp the ardour of his speckled breast
While nightingales to summers life belongs
And naked trees and winters nipping wrongs
Are strangers to her music and her rest   40
Her joys are evergreen her world is wide
—Hark there she is as usual lets be hush
For in this black thorn clump if rightly guest
Her curious house is hidden—part aside
These hazle branches in a gentle way
And stoop right cautious neath the rustling boughs
For we will have another search to day
And hunt this fern strown thorn clump round and round
And where this seeded wood grass idly bows
Well wade right through—it is a likely nook   50
In such like spots and often on the ground
Theyll build where rude boys never think to look
Aye as I live her secret nest is here
Upon this white thorn stulp—Ive searched about
For hours in vain—there put that bramble bye
Nay trample on its branshes and get near
How subtle is the bird she started out
And raised a plaintive note of danger nigh
Ere we were past the brambles and now near
Her nest she sudden stops—as choaking fear   60

That might betray her home so even now
Well leave it as we found it—safetys guard
Of pathless solitude shall keep it still
See there shes sitting on the old oak bough
Mute in her fears our presence doth retard
Her joys and doubt turns all her rapture chill
 Sing on sweet bird may no worse hap befall
Thy visions then the fear that now decieves
We will not plunder music of its dower
Nor turn this spot of happiness to thrall   70
For melody seems hid in every flower
That blossoms near thy home—these harebells all
Seems bowing with the beautiful in song
And gaping cuckoo with its spotted leaves
Seems blushing of the singing it has heard
How curious is the nest no other bird
Uses such loose materials or weaves
Their dwellings in such spots dead oaken leaves
Are placed without and velvet moss within
And little scraps of grass—and scant and spare 80
Of what seems scarce materials down and hair
For from mans haunts she seemeth nought to win
Yet nature is the builder and contrives
Homes for her childerns comfort even here
Where solitudes deciples spend their lives
Unseen save when a wanderer passes near
That loves such pleasant places—deep adown
The nest is made an hermits mossy cell
Snug lie her curious eggs in number five
Of deadend green or rather olive brown   90
And the old prickly thorn bush guards them well
And here well leave them still unknown to wrong
As the old woodlands legacy of song

The Sky Lark

 The rolls and harrows lies at rest beside
 The battered road and spreading far and wide
 Above the russet clods the corn is seen
 Sprouting its spirey points of tender green

Where squats the hare to terrors wide awake
Like some brown clod the harrows failed to break
While neath the warm hedge boys stray far from home
To crop the early blossoms as they come
Where buttercups will make them eager run
Opening their golden caskets to the sun   10
To see who shall be first to pluck the prize
And from their hurry up the skylark flies
And oer her half formed nest with happy wings
Winnows the air—till in the clouds she sings
Then hangs a dust spot in the sunny skies
And drops and drops till in her nest she lies
Where boys unheeding past—neer dreaming then
That birds which flew so high—would drop agen
To nests upon the ground where any thing
May come at to destroy had they the wing   20
Like such a bird themselves would be too proud
And build on nothing but a passing cloud
As free from danger as the heavens are free
From pain and toil—there would they build and be
And sail about the world to scenes unheard
Of and unseen—O where they but a bird
So think they while they listen to its song
And smile and fancy and so pass along
While its low nest moist with the dews of morn
Lye safely with the leveret in the corn   30

The Sky Lark Leaving Her Nest

Right happy bird so full of mirth
Mounting and mounting still more high
To meet morns sunshine in the sky
Ere yet it smiles on earth

How often I delight to stand
Listening a minutes length away
Where summer spreads her green array
By wheat or barley land

To see thee with a sudden start
The green and placid herbage leave   10
And in mid air a vision weave
For joys delighted heart

Shedding to heaven a vagrant mirth
When silence husheth other themes
And woods in their dark splendour dreams
Like heaviness on earth

My mind enjoys the happy sight
To watch thee to the clear blue sky
And when I downward turn my eye
Earth glows with lonely light   20

Then nearer comes thy happy sounds
And downward drops thy little wing
And now the valleys hear thee sing
And all the dewy grounds

Gleam into joy now from the eye
Thourt dropping sudden as a stone
And now thourt in the wheat alone
And still the circle of the sky

And abscent like a pleasure gone
Though many come within the way   30
Thy little song to peeping day
Is still remembered on

For who that crosses fields of corn
Where sky larks start to meet the day
But feels more pleasure on his way
Upon a summers morn

Tis one of those heart cheering sights
In green earths rural chronicles
That upon every memory dwells
Among home fed delights   40

The Ravens Nest

Upon the collar of an hugh old oak
Year after year boys mark a curious nest
Of twigs made up a faggot near in size
And boys to reach it try all sorts of schemes
But not a twig to reach with hand or foot
Sprouts from the pillared trunk and as to try
To swarm the massy bulk tis all in vain
They scarce one effort make to hitch them up
But down they sluther soon as ere they try
So long hath been their dwelling there—old men   10
When passing bye will laugh and tell the ways
They had when boys to climb that very tree
And as it so would seem that very nest
That ne'er was missing from that self same spot
A single year in all their memorys
And they will say that the two birds are now
The very birds that owned the dwelling then
Some think it strange yet certaintys at loss
And cannot contradict it so they pass
As old birds living the woods patriarchs   20
Old as the oldest men so famed and known
That even men will thirst into the fame
Of boys at get at schemes that now and then
May captivate a young one from the tree
With iron claums and bands adventuring up
The mealy trunk or else by waggon ropes
Slung over the hugh grains and so drawn up
By those at bottom one assends secure
With foot rope stirruped—still a perrilous way
So perrilous that one and only one   30
In memorys of the oldest man was known
To wear his boldness to intentions end
And reach the ravens nest—and thence acchieved
A theme that wonder treasured for supprise
By every cottage hea[r]th the village through
Nor yet forgot though other darers come
With daring times that scale the steeples top
And tye their kerchiefs to the weather cock

As trophys that the dangerous deed was done
Yet even now in these adventureous days   40
Not one is bold enough to dare the way
Up the old monstrous oak where every spring
Finds the two ancient birds at their old task
Repairing the hugh nest—where still they live
Through changes winds and storms and are secure
And like a landmark in the chronicles
Of village memorys treasured up yet lives
The hugh old oak that wears the ravens nest

The Moorehens Nest

O poesys power thou overpowering sweet
That renders hearts that love thee all unmeet
For this rude world its trouble and its care
Loading the heart with joys it cannot bear
That warms and chills and burns and bursts at last
Oer broken hopes and troubles never past
I pay thee worship at a rustic shrine
And dream oer joys I still imagine mine
I pick up flowers and pebbles and by thee
As gems and jewels they appear to me   10
I pick out pictures round the fields that lie
In my minds heart like things that cannot die
Like picking hopes and making friends with all
Yet glass will often bear a harder fall
As bursting bottles loose the precious wine
Hopes casket breaks and I the gems resign
Pain shadows on till feelings self decays
And all such pleasures leave me is their praise
And thus each fairy vision melts away
Like evening landscapes from the face of day   20
Till hope returns with aprils dewy reign
And then I start and seek for joys again
And pick her fragments up to hurd anew
Like fancy-riches pleasure loves to view
And these associations of the past
Like summer pictures in a winter blast

Renews my heart to feelings as the rain
Falls on the earth and bids it thrive again
Then een the fallow fields appear so fair
The very weeds make sweetest gardens there   30
And summer there puts garments on so gay
I hate the plough that comes to dissaray
Her holiday delights—and labours toil
Seems vulgar curses on the sunny soil
And man the only object that distrains
Earths garden into deserts for his gains
Leave him his schemes of gain—tis wealth to me
Wild heaths to trace—and note their broken tree
Which lightening shivered—and which nature tries
To keep alive for poesy to prize   40
Upon whose mossy roots my leisure sits
To hear the birds pipe oer their amorous fits
Though less beloved for singing then the taste
They have to choose such homes upon the waste
Rich architects—and then the spots to see
How picturesque their dwellings make them be
The wild romances of the poets mind
No sweeter pictures for their tales can find
And so I glad my heart and rove along
Now finding nests—then listening to a song   50
Then drinking fragrance whose perfuming cheats
Tinges lifes sours and bitters into sweets
That heart stirred fragrance when the summers rain
Lays the road dust and sprouts the grass again
Filling the cracks up on the beaten paths
And breathing insence from the mowers swaths
Insence the bards and prophets of old days
Met in the wilderness to glad their praise
And in these summer walks I seem to feel
These bible pictures in their essence steal   60
Around me—and the ancientness of joy
Breath from the woods till pleasures even cloy
Yet holy breathing manna seemly falls
With angel answers if a trouble calls
And then I walk and swing my stick for joy
And catch at little pictures passing bye
A gate whose posts are two old dotterel trees

A close with molehills sprinkled oer its leas
A little footbrig with its crossing rail
A wood gap stopt with ivy wreathing pale   70
A crooked stile each path crossed spinny owns
A brooklet forded by its stepping stones
A wood bank mined with rabbit holes—and then
An old oak leaning oer a badgers den
Whose cave mouth enters neath the twisted charms
Of its old roots and keeps it safe from harms
Pick axes spades and all its strength confounds
When hunted foxes hide from chasing hounds
—Then comes the meadows where I love to see
A flood washed bank support an aged tree   80
Whose roots are bare—yet some with foothold good
Crankle and spread and strike beneath the flood
Yet still it leans as safer hold to win
On tother side and seems as tumbling in
While every summer finds it green and gay
And winter leaves it safe as did the may
Nor does the more hen find its safety vain
For on its roots their last years homes remain
And once again a couple from the brood
Seek their old birth place and in safetys mood   90
Lodge there their flags and lay—though danger comes
It dares and tries and cannot reach their homes
And so they hatch their eggs and sweetly dream
On their shelfed nests that bridge the gulphy stream
And soon the sutty brood from fear elopes
Where bulrush forrests give them sweeter hopes
Their hanging nest that aids their wishes well
Each leaves for water as it leaves the shell
And dive and dare and every gambol trie
Till they themselves to other scenes can fly   100

Sedge Birds Nest

Fixed in a white thorn bush its summer guest
So low een grass oertopt its tallest twig
A sedge bird built its little benty nest
Close by the meadow pool and wooden brig

Where school boys every morn and eve did pass
In robbing birds and cunning deeply skilled
Searching each bush and taller clumps of grass
Where ere was liklihood of bird to build
Yet she did hide her habitation long
And keep her little brood from dangers eye   10
Hidden as secret as a crickets song
Till they well fledged oer widest pools could flye
Proving that providence is often bye
To guard the simplest of her charge from wrong

[*Crows in Spring*]

The crow will tumble up and down
    At the first sight of spring
And in old trees around the town
    Brush winter from its wing

No longer flapping far away
    To naked fen they flye
Chill fare as on a winters day
    But field and valleys nigh

Where swains are stirring out to plough
    And woods are just at hand   10
They seek the uplands sunny brow
    And strut from land to land

And often flap their sooty wings
    And sturt to neighboring tree
And seems to try all ways to sing
    And almost speaks in glee

The ploughman hears and turns his head
    Above to wonder why
And there a new nest nearly made
    Proclaims the winter bye   20

The schoolboy free from winters frown
    That rests on every stile
In wonder sets his basket down
    To start his happy toil

The Robins Nest

Come luscious spring come with thy mossy roots
Thy weed strown banks—young grass—and tender shoots
Of woods new plashed sweet smells of opening blooms
Sweet sunny mornings and right glorious dooms
Of happiness—to seek and harbour in
Far from the ruder worlds inglorious din
Who see no glory but in sordid pelf
And nought of greatness but its little self
Scorning the splendid gift that nature gives
Where natures glory ever breaths and lives   10
Seated in crimping ferns uncurling now
In russet fringes ere in leaves they bow
And moss as green as silk—there let me be
By the grey powdered trunk of old oak tree
Buried in green delights to which the heart
Clings with delight and beats as loath to part
The birds unbid come round about to give
Their music to my pleasures—wild flowers live
About as if for me—they smile and bloom
Like uninvited guests that love to come   20
Their wildwood fragrant offerings all to bring
Paying me kindness like a throned king
Lost in such extacys in this old spot
I feel that rapture which the world hath not
That joy like health that flushes in my face
Amid the brambles of this ancient place
Shut out from all but that superior power
That guards and glads and cheers me every hour
That wraps me like a mantle from the storm
Of care and bids the coldest hope be warm   30
That speaks in spots where all things silent be
In words not heard but felt—each ancient tree
With lickens deckt—times hoary pedigree
Becomes a monitor to teach and bless
And rid me of the evils cares possess
And bid me look above the trivial things
To which prides mercenary spirit clings
The pomps the wealth and artificial toys

That men call wealth beleagued with strife and noise
To seek the silence of their ancient reign   40
And be my self in memory once again
To trace the path of briar entangled holt
Or bushy closen where the wanton colt
Crops the young juicey leaves from off the hedge
In this old wood where birds their passions pledge
And court and build and sing their under song
In joys own cue that to their hearts belong
Having no wish or want unreconsiled
But spell bound to their homes within the wild
Where old neglect lives patron and befriends   50
Their homes with safetys wildness—where nought lends
A hand to injure—root up or disturb
The things of this old place—there is no curb
Of interest industry or slavish gain
To war with nature so the weeds remain
And wear an ancient passion that arrays
Ones feelings with the shadows of old days
The rest of peace the sacredness of mind
In such deep solitudes we seek and find
Where moss grows old and keeps an evergreen   60
And footmarks seem like miracles when seen
So little meddling toil doth trouble here
The very weeds as patriarchs appear
And if a plant ones curious eyes delight
In this old ancient solitude we might
Come ten years hence of trouble dreaming ill
And find them like old tennants peaceful still
Here the wood robin rustling on the leaves
With fluttering step each visitor recieves
Yet from his ancient home he seldom stirs   70
In heart content on these dead teazle burs
He sits and trembles oer his under notes
So rich—joy almost choaks his little throat
With extacy and from his own heart flows
That joy himself and partner only knows
He seems to have small fear but hops and comes
Close to ones feet as if he looked for crumbs
And when the woodman strinkles some around
He leaves the twig and hops upon the ground

And feeds untill his little daintys cloy 80
Then claps his little wings and sings for joy
And when in woodland solitudes I wend
I always hail him as my hermit friend
And naturally enough whenere they come
Before me search my pockets for a crumb
At which he turns his eye and seems to stand
As if expecting somthing from my hand
And thus these feathered heirs of solitude
Remain the tennants of this quiet wood
And live in melody and make their home 90
And never seem to have a wish to roam
Beside this ash stulp where in years gone bye
The thrush had built and taught her young to flye
Where still the nest half filled with leaves remains
With moss still green amid the twisting grains
Here on the ground and sheltered at its foot
The nest is hid close at its mossy root
Composed of moss and grass and lined with hair
And five brun-coloured eggs snug sheltered there
And bye and bye a happy brood will be 100
The tennants of this woodland privacy

The Autumn Robin

Sweet little Bird in russet coat
   The livery of the closing year
I love thy lonely plaintive note
   And tiney whispering song to hear
While on the stile or garden seat
   I sit to watch the falling leaves
Thy songs thy little joys repeat
   My lonliness relieves

And many are the lonely minds
   That hear and welcome thee anew 10
Not taste alone but humble hinds
   Delight to praise and love thee too

The veriest clown beside his cart
   Turns from his song with many a smile
To see thee from the hedgrow start
   And sing upon the stile

The Shepherd on the fallen tree
   Drops down to listen to thy lay
And chides his dog beside his knee
   Who barks and frightens thee away   20
The hedger pauses ere he knocks
   The stake down in the meadow gap
—The Boy who every songster mocks
   Forbears the gate to clap

When in the hedge that hides the post
   Thy ruddy bosom he surveys
Pleased with thy song in pleasure lost
   He pausing mutters scraps of praise
The maiden marks at days decline
   Thee in the yard on broken plough   30
And stops her song to listen thine
   While milking brindled cow

Thy simple faith in mans esteem
   From every heart that favours won
Dangers to thee no dangers seem
   Thou seemest to court them more then shun
The clown in winter takes his gun
   The barn door flocking birds to slay
Yet shouldst thou in the danger run
   He turns the tube away   40

The gipsey boy who seeks in glee
   Blackberrys for a dainty meal
Laughs loud on first beholding thee
   When called so near his presence steal
For sure he thinks thou knew the call
   And tho his hunger ill can spare
The fruit he will not pluck them all
   But leaves some to thy share

Up on the ditchers spade thoult hop
    For grubs and wreathing worms to search   50
Where woodmen in the Forrests chop
    Thoult fearless on their faggots perch
Nay by the gipseys camp I stop
    And mark thee perch a moment there
To prune thy wing awhile then drop
    The littered crumbs to share

Domestic bird thy pleasant face
    Doth well thy common suit commend
To meet thee in a stranger place
    Is meeting with an ancient friend   60
I track the thickets glooms around
    And there as loath to leave agen
Thou comest as if thou knew the sound
    And loved the sight of men

The lonliest wood that man can trace
    To thee a pleasant dwelling gives
In every town and crowded place
    The sweet domestic Robin lives
Go where we will in every spot
    Thy little welcome mates appear   70
And like the daiseys common lot
    Thourt met with every where

The swallow in the chimney tier
    The tittering martin in the eaves
With half of love and half of fear
    Their mortared dwelling shyly weaves
The sparrows in the thatch will shield
    Yet they as well as eer they can
Contrive with doubtful faith to build
    Beyond the reach of man   80

But thourt less timid then the Wren
    Domestic and confiding bird
And spots the nearest haunts of men
    Are oftenest for thy home prefered

In garden walls thoult build so low
  Close where the bunch of fennel stands
That een a child just learned to go
  May reach with tiny hands

Sweet favoured bird thy under notes
  In summers music grows unknown   90
The conscert from a thousand throats
  Leaves thee as if to pipe alone
No listening ear the shepherd lends
  The simple ploughman marks thee not
And then by all thy autumn friends
  Thourt missing and forgot

The far famed nightingale that shares
  Cold public praise from every tongue
The popular voice of music heirs
  And injures much thy under song   100
Yet then my walks thy theme salutes
  And finds their autumn favoured guest
Gay piping on the hazel roots
  Above thy mossy nest

Tis wrong that thou shouldst be despised
  When these gay fickle birds appear
They sing when summer flowers are prized
  Thou at the dull and dying year
Well let the heedless and the gay
  Bepraise the voice of louder lays   110
The joy thou stealst from sorrows day
  Is more to thee then praise

And could my notes steal aught from thine
  My words but immitate thy lay
Time would not then his charge resign
  Nor throw the meanest verse away
But ever at this mellow time
  He should thine Autumn praise prolong
So would they share eternal prime
  With daiseys and thy song   120

The Pettichaps Nest

Well in my many walks I rarely found
A place less likely for a bird to form
Its nest close by the rut gulled waggon road
And on the almost bare foot-trodden ground
With scarce a clump of grass to keep it warm
And not a thistle spreads its spears abroad
Or prickly bush to shield it from harms way
And yet so snugly made that none may spy
It out save accident   and you and I
Had surely passed it in our walk to day   10
Had chance not led us by it—nay e'en now
Had not the old bird heard us trampling bye
And fluttered out—we had not seen it lie
Brown as the road way side—small bits of hay
Pluckt from the old propt-haystacks pleachy brow
And withered leaves make up its outward walls
That from the snub-oak dotterel yearly falls
And in the old hedge bottom rot away
Built like a oven with a little hole
Hard to discover—that snug entrance wins   20
Scarcely admitting e'en two fingers in
And lined with feathers warm as silken stole
And soft as seats of down for painless ease
And full of eggs scarce bigger e'en then peas
Heres one most delicate with spots as small
As dust—and of a faint and pinky red
—We'll let them be and safety guard them well
For fears rude paths around are thickly spread
And they are left to many dangers ways
When green grass hoppers jump might break the shells   30
While lowing oxen pass them morn and night
And restless sheep around them hourly stray
And no grass springs but hungry horses bite
That trample past them twenty times a day
Yet like a miracle in safetys lap
They still abide unhurt and out of sight
—Stop heres the bird that woodman at the gap
Hath frit it from the hedge—tis olive green

Well I declare it is the pettichaps
Not bigger then the wren and seldom seen   40
Ive often found their nests in chances way
When I in pathless woods did idly roam
But never did I dream untill to day
A spot like this would be her chosen home

The Yellowhammers Nest

Just by the wooden brig a bird flew up
Frit by the cowboy as he scrambled down
To reach the misty dewberry—let us stoop
And seek its nest—the brook we need not dread
Tis scarcely deep enough a bee to drown
So it sings harmless oer its pebbly bed
—Aye here it is stuck close beside the bank
Beneath the bunch of grass that spindles rank
Its husk seeds tall and high—tis rudely planned
Of bleached stubbles and the withered fare   10
That last years harvest left upon the land
Lined thinly with the horses sable hair
—Five eggs pen-scribbled over lilac shells
Resembling writing scrawls which fancy reads
As natures poesy and pastoral spells
They are the yellow hammers and she dwells
A poet-like—where brooks and flowery weeds
As sweet as Castaly to fancy seems
And that old molehill like as parnass hill
On which her partner haply sits and dreams   20
Oer all his joy of song—so leave it still
A happy home of sunshine flowers and streams
Yet in the sweetest places cometh ill
A noisome weed that burthens every soil
For snakes are known with chill and deadly coil
To watch such nests and seize the helpless young
And like as though the plague became a guest
Leaving a housless-home a ruined nest
And mournful hath the little warblers sung
When such like woes hath rent its little breast   30

The Yellow Wagtails Nest

Upon an edding in a quiet nook
We double down choice places in a book
And this I noted as a pleasant scene
Hemmed in all round with barleys juicey green
While in its clover grass at holiday
A broken plough as leisures partner lay
A pleasant bench among the grass and flowers
For merry weeders in their dinner hours
From fallow fields released and hot turmoil
It nestled like a thought forgot by toil   10
And seemed so picturesque a place for rest
I een dropt down to be a minutes guest
And as I bent me for a flower to stoop
A little bird cheeped loud and fluttered up
The grasses tottered with their husky seeds
That ramped beside the plough with ranker weeds
I looked—and there a snug nest deep and dry
Of roots and twitches entertained my eye
And six eggs sprinkled ocr with spots of grey
Lay snug as comforts wishes ever lay   20
The yellow wagtail fixed its dwelling there
Sheltered from rainfalls by the shelving share
That leaned above it like a sheltering roof
From rain and wind and tempest comfort proof
Such safety-places little birds will find
Far from the cares and help of human kind
For nature is their kind protector still
To chuse their dwellings farthest off from ill
So thought I— sitting on that broken plough
While evenings sunshine gleamed upon my brow   30
So soft so sweet—and I so happy then
Felt life still eden from the haunts of men
And in the brook-pond waters spread below
Where misty willows wavered too and fro
The setting sun shed such a golden hue
I almost felt the poets fables true
And fashioned in my minds creating eye
Dryads and nymphs like beautys dreams go bye

From the rich arbours of the distant wood
To taste the spring and try its golden flood   40
Thus pleasures to the fancy often shine
Truest when false when fables most divine
And though each sweet consception soon decays
We feel such pleasures after many days

Partridge Coveys

Among the stubbles when the fields grow grey
And mellow harvest gathers to a close
The painful gleaner twenty times a day
Start up the partridge broods that glad repose
Upon the grassy slip or sunny land
Yet ever it would seem in dangers way
Where snufting dogs their rustling haunts betray
And tracking gunners ever seem at hand
Oft frighted up they startle to the shade
Of neighbouring wood and through the yellow leaves   10
Drop wearied where the brakes and ferns hath made
A solitary covert—that decieves
For there the fox prowls its unnoticed round
And danger dares them upon every ground

The Blackcap

Under the twigs the blackcap hangs in vain
With snowwhite patch streaked over either eye
This way and that he turns and peeps again
As wont where silk-cased insects used to lie
But summer leaves are gone the day is bye
For happy holidays and now he fares
But cloudy like the weather yet to view
He flirts a happy wing and inly wears
Content in gleaning what the orchard spares
And like his little couzin capped in blue   10
Domesticates the lonely winter through
In homestead plots and gardens where he wears
Familiar pertness—yet but seldom comes
With the tame robin to the door for crumbs

Hedge Sparrow

The tame hedge sparrow in its russet dress
Is half a robin for its gentle ways
And the bird loving dame can do no less
Then throw it out a crumble on cold days
In early march it into gardens strays
And in the snug clipt box tree green and round
It makes a nest of moss and hair and lays
When een the snow is lurking on the ground
Its eggs in number five of greenish blue
Bright beautiful and glossy shining shells   10
Much like the firetails but of brighter hue
Yet in her garden home much danger dwells
Where skulking cat with mischief in its breast
Catches their young before they leave the nest

The Landrail

How sweet and pleasant grows the way
Through summer time again
While Landrails call from day to day
Amid the grass and grain

We hear it in the weeding time
When knee deep waves the corn
We hear it in the summers prime
Through meadows night and morn

And now I hear it in the grass
That grows as sweet again   10
And let a minutes notice pass
And now tis in the grain

Tis like a fancy every where
A sort of living doubt
We know tis somthing but it neer
Will blab the secret out

If heard in close or meadow plots
It flies if we pursue
But follows if we notice not
The close and meadow through   20

Boys know the note of many a bird
In their birdnesting bounds
But when the landrails noise is heard
They wonder at the sounds

They look in every tuft of grass
Thats in their rambles met
They peep in every bush they pass
And none the wiser get

And still they hear the craiking sound
And still they wonder why   30
It surely cant be under ground
Nor is it in the sky

And yet tis heard in every vale
An undiscovered song
And makes a pleasant wonder tale
For all the summer long

The shepherd whistles through his hands
And starts with many a whoop
His busy dog accross the lands
In hopes to fright it up   40

Tis still a minutes length or more
Till dogs are off and gone
Then sings and louder then before
But keeps the secret on

Yet accident will often meet
The nest within its way
And weeders when they weed the wheat
Discover where they lay

And mowers on the meadow lea
Chance on their noisey guest   50
And wonder what the bird can be
That lays without a nest

In simple holes that birds will rake
When dusting on the ground
They drop their eggs of curious make
Deep blotched and nearly round

A mystery still to men and boys
Who know not where they lay
And guess it but a summer noise
Among the meadow hay   60

The Reed Bird

A little slender bird of reddish brown
With frequent haste pops in and out the reeds
And on the river frequent flutters down
As if for food and so securely feeds
Her little young that in their ambush needs
Her frequent journeys hid in thickest shade
Where danger never finds a path to throw
A fear on comforts nest securely made
In woods of reeds round which the waters flow
Save by a jelted stone that boys will throw   10
Or passing rustle of the fishers boat
It is the reed bird prized for pleasant note
Ah happy songster man can seldom share
A spot as hidden from the haunts of care

The Woodlarks Nest

The woodlark rises from the coppice tree
Time after time untired she upward springs
Silent while up then coming down she sings
A pleasant song of varied melody

Repeated often till some sudden check
The sweet toned impulse of her rapture stops
Then stays her trembling wings and down she drops
Like to a stone amid the crowding kecks
Where underneath some hazels mossy root
Is hid her little low and humble nest   10
Upon the ground larks love such places best
And hers doth well her quiet station suit
As safe as secresy her six eggs lie
Mottled with dusky spots unseen by passers bye

Yet chance will somtimes prove a faithless guest
Leading some wanderer by her hants to roam
And startled by the rustle from her nest
She flutters out and so betrays her home
Yet this is seldom accident can meet
With her weed hidden and surrounded rest   20
Ive often wondered when agen my feet
She fluttered up and fanned the anemonie
That blossomed round in crowds—how birds could be
So wise to find such hidden homes again
And this in sooth oft puzzled me—they go
Far off and then return—but natures plain
She giveth what sufficeth them to know
That they of comfort may their share retain

Field Cricket

Sweet little minstrel of the sunny summer
Housed in the pleasant swells that front the sun
Neighbour to many a happy yearly comer
For joys glad tidings when the winters done
How doth thy music through the silk grass run
That cloaths the pleasant banks with herbage new
A chittering sound of healthy happiness
That bids the passer bye be happy too
Who hearing thee feels full of pleasant moods
Picturing the cheerfulness that summers dress   10

Brings to the eye with all her leaves and grass
In freshness beautified and summers sounds
Brings to the ear in one continued flood
The luxury of joy that knows no bounds

I often pause to seek thee when I pass
Thy cottage in the sweet refreshing hue
Of sunny flowers and rich luxuriant grass
But thou wert ever hidden from the view
Brooding and piping oer thy rural song
In all the happiness of solitude   20
Busy intruders do thy music wrong
And scare thy gladness dumb—where they intrude
Ive seen thy dwelling by the scythe laid bare
And thee in russet garb from bent to bent
Moping without a song in silence there
Till grass should bring anew thy home content
And leave thee to thyself to sing and wear
The summer through without another care

['*And often from the rustling sound*']

And often from the rustling sound
The jay bird calls and starts away
A warning to the birds around
That peeping dangers on the way
The blackbird answers and the rest
Start silent from each mossy nest

A noise in oaks above the head
Keep on throughout the day
Wood peckers nests are neerly made
And natures carpenters are they   10
Through hardest oaks their whimbles go
And thick the sawdust lies below

And oft the squirrels nest is seen
On ashen poles and near the top
And if one shakes the grain
From branch to branch they out and hop
And up the oak trunks mealy white
Theyre in a moment out of sight

[*The Fens*]

Wandering by the rivers edge
I love to rustle through the sedge
And through the woods of reed to tear
Almost as high as bushes are
Yet turning quick with shudder chill
As danger ever does from ill
Fears moment ague quakes the blood
While plop the snake coils in the flood
And hissing with a forked tongue
Across the river winds along   10

In coat of orange green and blue
Now on a willow branch I view
Grey waving to the sunny gleam
King fishers watch the ripple stream
For little fish that nimble bye
And in the gravel shallows lie

Eddies run before the boats
Gurgling where the fisher floats
Who takes advantage of the gale
And hoists his hankerchief for sail   20
On osier twigs that form a mast
And quick his nutshell hurrys past
While idly lies nor wanted more
The sp[i]rit that pushed him on before

There not a hill in all the view
Save that a forked cloud or two
Upon the verge of distance lies
And into mountains cheats the eyes
And as to trees the willows wear
Lopped heads as high as bushes are   30
Some taller things the distance shrouds
That may be trees or stacks or clouds
Or may be nothing still they wear
A zemblance where theres nought to spare

Among the tawny tasseled reed
The ducks and ducklings float and feed
With head oft dabbing in the flood
They fish all day the weedy mud
And tumbler like are bobbing there
Tails topsy turvy in the air   40
Then up and quack and down they go
Heels over head again below
The geese in troops come droving up
Nibble the weeds and take a sup
And closely puzzled to agree
Chatter like gossips over tea
The ganders with their scarlet nose
When strife gets highest interpose
And strecking necks to that and this
With now a mutter now a hiss   50
A nibble at the feathers too
A sort of pray be quiet do
And turning as the matter mends
He stills them into mutual friends
Then in a sort of triumph sings
And throws the water oer his wings
Ah could I see a spinny nigh
A puddock sailing in the sky
Above the oaks with easy sail
On stilly wing and forked tail   60
Or meet a heath of furze in flower
I might enjoy a pleasant hour
Sit down at rest and walk at ease
And find a many things to please
But here my fancys moods admire
The naked levels till they tire
Nor een a molehill cushion meets
To rest on when I want a seat

Here[s] little save the river scene
And grounds of oats in smiling green   70
And crowded growth of wheat and beans
That with the hope of plenty leans
And cheers the farmers gazing brow
Who lives and triumphs in the plough
One sometimes meets a pleasant sward

Of swarthy grass—and quickly marred
The plough soon turns it into brown
And when again one rambles down
The path small hillocks lie
And smoak beneath a burning sky   80
Green paddocks have but little charms
With gain the merchandise of farms
And muse and marvel where we may
Gain mars the landscape every day
The meadow grass turned up and copt
The trees to stumpy dotterels lopt
The hearth with fuel to supply
For rest to smoke and chatter bye
Giving the joy of home delights
The warmest mirth on coldest nights   90
And so for gain that joys repay
Change cheats the landscape every day
No tree no bough about it grows
That from the hatchet can repose
And the orison stooping smiles
Oer treeless fens of many miles
Spring comes and goes and comes again
And all is nakedness and fen

And dunghills hiding snake and toad
Lyes more then half accross the road   100
Where docks and thistles crowd the lane
Cut yearly yet they come again
And those the quaking winter finds
Make dithering whistles on the wind
Picturing to passengers acold
A picture dreary to behold
Where spite of all they eat and kill
A scene that makes the cold achill
Large grounds bethronged with thistles brown
Shivering and swadding up and down   110
Was but a bramble in the place
Twould be a sort of living grace
A shape of shelter in the wind
For stock to chew their cuds behind
But all is level cold and dull
And osier swamps with water full

['*And yonder by the circling stack*']

And yonder by the circling stack
Provoking any eye to smile
A pye perched on the heifers back
Pulls hair to line her nest the while
That winds upon the high oak rocks
The threat of every coming storm
Yet still it stands the rudest shocks
A sweeing cradle snug and warm

['*High overhead that silent throne*']

High overhead that silent throne
Of wild and cloud betravelled sky
That makes ones loneliness more lone
Sends forth a crank and reedy cry
I look the crane is sailing oer
That pathless world without a mate
The heath looked brown and dull before
But now tis more then desolate

[*Autumn Evening*]

I love to hear the evening crows go bye
And see the starnels darken down the sky
The bleaching stack the bustling sparrow leaves
And plops with merry note beneath the eaves
The odd and lated pigeon bounces bye
As if a wary watching hawk was nigh
While far and fearing nothing high and slow
The stranger birds to distant places go
While short of flight the evening robin comes
To watch the maiden sweeping out the crumbs   10
Nor fears the idle shout of passing boy
But pecks about the door and sings for joy
Then in the hovel where the cows are fed
Finds till the morning comes a pleasant bed

[*Birds in Alarm*]

The fire tail tells the boys when nests are nigh
And tweets and flyes from every passer bye
The yellow hammer never makes a noise
But flyes in silence from the noisey boys
The boys will come and take them every day
And still she lays as none were taen away
The nightingale keeps tweeting churring round
But leaves in silence when the nest is found
The pewet hollos chewsit as she flyes
And flops about the shepherd where he lies   10
But when her nest is found she stops her song
And cocks [her] coppled crown and runs along
Wrens cock their tails and chitter loud and play
And robins hollow tut and flye away

['*In the hedge I pass a little nest*']

In the hedge I pass a little nest
Green morning after morning
Where the old ones scared at every guest
Cheeped loud a danger warning
But the young ones cree'd at every tread
Nor knew of danger near
They quivering hold up many a head
At all that passes near

The awbush round their dwelling hings
Which morn with dropples strinkles   10
That wets the old birds eager wings
While the brook at bottom tinkles
A constant guardian running past
Sweet young[ling]s cease your cheeping
For many a clown goes whistling past
When ye're unconscious sleeping

The old ones on a distant bough
With victuals in her bill
Waits back to see me passing now
And tweets in fear of ill   20
But soon as bye she hurrys in
They twitter caw and cree
The laughing brook wont let me win
A peep to reach and see

Right pleasant brook Im glad ye lie
Between them and the road
They're not all friends that wander bye
And faith is ill bestowed
Hid from the world their green retreat
The worlds ways never knew   30
But much I fear they'd quickly meet
Its cares if in its view

I've past the nest so often bye
They seem my neighbours now
And I'd be glad to see 'em flye
And cheep upon the bough
The worlds way is a cheating way
And it would not be long
Before they met a cloudy day
And some to do em wrong   40

Though I have not gone half the ways
That many have to go
Nor met with half the swaily days
That many troubles know
Yet chuse not haunts that many know
Though many much pretend
For ye are sure to find a foe
Where many pass for friends

ANIMAL POEMS

Hares at Play°

The birds are gone to bed the cows are still
And sheep lie panting on each old mole hill
And underneath the willows grey-green bough
Like toil a resting—lies the fallow plough
The timid hares throw daylights fears away
On the lanes road to dust and dance and play
Then dabble in the grain by nought deterred
To lick the dewfall from the barleys beard
Then out they sturt again and round the hill
Like happy thoughts—dance—squat—and loiter still   10
Till milking maidens in the early morn
Gingle their yokes and sturt them in the corn
Through well known beaten paths each nimbling hare
Sturts quick as fear—and seeks its hidden lair

[*The Marten*]

The martin cat long shaged of courage good
Of weazle shape a dweller in the wood
With badger hair long shagged and darting eyes
And lower then the common cat in size
Small head and running on the stoop
Snuffing the ground and hind parts shouldered up
He keeps one track and hides in lonely shade
Where print of human foot is scarcely made
Save when the woods are cut the beaten track
The woodman[s] dog will snuff cock tailed and black   10
Red legged and spotted over either eye
Snuffs barks and scrats the tree and passes bye
The great brown horned owl looks down below
And sees the shaggy martin come and go

The martin hurrys through the woodland gaps
And poachers shoot and make his skin for caps
When any woodman come and pass the place
He looks at dogs and scarcely mends his pace
And gipseys often and birdnesting boys
Look in the hole and hear a hissing noise   20
They climb the tree such noise they never heard
And think the great owl is a foreign bird
When the grey owl her young ones cloathed in down
Seizes the boldest boy and drives him down
They try agen and pelt to start the fray
The grey owl comes and drives them all away
And leaves the martin twisting round his den
Left free from boys and dogs and noise and men

[*The Fox*]

The shepherd on his journey heard when nigh
His dog among the bushes barking high
The ploughman ran and gave a hearty shout
He found a weary fox and beat him out
The ploughman laughed and would have ploughed him in
But the old shepherd took him for the skin
He lay upon the furrow stretched and dead
The old dog lay and licked the wounds that bled
The ploughman beat him till his ribs would crack
And then the shepherd slung him at his back   10
And when he rested to his dogs supprise
The old fox started from his dead disguise
And while the dog lay panting in the sedge
He up and snapt and bolted through the hedge

He scampered [to] the bushes far away
The shepherd call[ed] the ploughman [to] the fray
The ploughman wished he had a gun to shoot
The old dog barked and followed the pursuit
The shepherd threw his hook and tottered past
The ploughman ran but none could go so fast   20
The woodman threw his faggot from the way
And ceased to chop and wondered at the fray

But when he saw the dog and heard the cry
He threw his hatchet but the fox was bye
The shepherd broke his hook and lost the skin
He found a badger hole and bolted in
They tryed to dig but safe from dangers way
He lived to chase the hounds another day

[*The Badger*]

The badger grunting on his woodland track
With shaggy hide and sharp nose scrowed with black
Roots in the bushes and the woods and makes
A great hugh burrow in the ferns and brakes
With nose on ground he runs a awkard pace
And anything will beat him in the race
The shepherds dog will run him to his den
Followed and hooted by the dogs and men
The woodman when the hunting comes about
Go round at night to stop the foxes out   10
And hurrying through the bushes ferns and brakes
Nor sees the many hol[e]s the badger makes
And often through the bushes to the chin
Breaks the old holes and tumbles headlong in

When midnight comes a host of dogs and men
Go out and track the badger to his den
And put a sack within the hole and lye
Till the old grunting badger passes bye
He comes and hears they let the strongest loose
The old fox hears the noise and drops the goose   20
The poacher shoots and hurrys from the cry
And the old hare half wounded buzzes bye
They get a forked stick to bear him down
And clapt the dogs and bore him to the town
And bait him all the day with many dogs
And laugh and shout and fright the scampering hogs
He runs along and bites at all he meets
They shout and hollo down the noisey streets

He turns about to face the loud uproar
And drives the rebels to their very doors   30
The frequent stone is hurled where ere they go
When badgers fight and every ones a foe
The dogs are clapt and urged to join the fray
The badger turns and drives them all away
Though scar[c]ely half as big dimute and small
He fights with dogs for hours and beats them all
The heavy mastiff savage in the fray
Lies down and licks his feet and turns away
The bull dog knows his match and waxes cold
The badger grins and never leaves his hold   40
He drive[s] the crowd and follows at their heels
And bites them through the drunkard swears and reels

The frighted women takes the boys away
The blackguard laughs and hurrys on the fray
He trys to reach the woods a awkard race
But sticks and cudgels quickly stop the chace
He turns agen and drives the noisey crowd
And beats the many dogs in noises loud
He drives away and beats them every one
And then they loose them all and set them on   50
He falls as dead and kicked by boys and men
Then starts and grins and drives the crowd agen
Till kicked and torn and beaten out he lies
And leaves his hold and cackles groans and dies

Some keep a baited badger tame as hog
And tame him till he follows like the dog
They urge him on like dogs and show fair play
He beats and scarcely wounded goes away
Lapt up as if asleep he scorns to fly
And siezes any dog that ventures nigh   60
Clapt like a dog he never bites the men
But worrys dogs and hurrys to his den
They let him out and turn a barrow down
And there he fights the pack of all the town
He licks the patting hand and trys to play
And never trys to bite or run away
And runs away from noise in hollow tree[s]
Burnt by the boys to get a swarm of bees

[*The Hedgehog*]

The hedgehog hides beneath the rotten hedge
And makes a great round nest of grass and sedge
Or in a bush or in a hollow tree
And many often stoops and say they see
Him roll and fill his prickles full of crab[s]
And creep away and where the magpie dabs
His wing at muddy dyke in aged root
He makes a nest and fills it full of fruit
On the hedge bottom hunts for crabs and sloes
And whistles like a cricket as he goes   10
It rolls up like a ball a shapeless hog
When gipseys hunt it with their noisey dogs
Ive seen it in their camps they call it sweet
Though black and bitter and unsavoury meat

But they who hunt the fields for rotten meat
And wash in muddy dyke and call it sweet
And eat what dogs refuse where ere they dwell
Care little either for the taste or smell
They say they milk the cows and when they lye
Nibble their fleshy teats and make them dry   20
But they whove seen the small head like a hog
Rolled up to meet the savage of a dog
With mouth scarce big enough to hold a straw
Will neer believe what no one ever saw
But still they hunt the hedges all about
And shepherd dogs are trained to hunt them out
They hurl with savage force the stick and stone
And no one cares and still the strife goes on

[*The Vixen*]

Among the taller wood with ivy hung
The old fox plays and dances round her young
She snuffs and barks if any passes bye
And swings her tail and turns prepared to flye

The horseman hurrys bye she bolts to see
And turns agen from danger never free
If any stands she runs among the poles
And barks and snaps and drives them in the holes
The shepherd sees them and the boy goes bye
And gets a stick and progs the hole to try   10
They get all still and lie in safty sure
And out again when safety is secure
And start and snap at blackbirds bouncing bye
To fight and catch the great white butterflye

POEMS OF THE NORTHBOROUGH
PERIOD
1832–1837

The Flitting°

Ive left my own old home of homes
Green fields and every pleasant place
The summer like a stranger comes
I pause and hardly know her face
I miss the hazels happy green
The blue bells quiet hanging blooms
Where envys sneer was never seen
Where staring malice never comes

I miss the heath its yellow furze
Molehills and rabbit tracks that lead   10
Through beesom ling and teazel burrs
That spread a wilderness indeed
The woodland oaks and all below
That their white powdered branches shield
The mossy pads—the very crow
Croaked music in my native fields

I sit me in my corner chair
That seems to feel itself from home
I hear bird music here and there
From awthorn hedge and orchard come   20
I hear but all is strange and new
—I sat on my old bench in June
The sailing puddocks shrill 'peelew'
Oer royce wood seemed a sweeter tune°

I walk adown the narrow lane
The nightingale is singing now
But like to me she seems at loss
For royce wood and its shielding bough

I lean upon the window sill
The trees and summer happy seem   30
Green sunny green they shine—but still
My heart goes far away to dream

Of happiness and thoughts arise
With home bred pictures many a onc
Green lancs that shut out burning skies
And old crooked stiles to rest upon
Above them hangs the maple tree
Below grass swells a velvet hill
And little footpads sweet to see
Goes seeking sweeter places still   40

With bye and bye a brook to cross
Oer which a little arch is thrown
No brook is here I feel the loss
From home and friends and all alone
—The stone pit with its shelvey sides
Seemed hanging rocks in my esteem
I miss the prospect far and wide
From Langley bush and so I seem°

Alone and in a stranger scene
Far far from spots my hcart esteems   50
The closen with their ancient green
Heath woods and pastures sunny streams
The hawthorns here were hung with may
But still they seem in deader green
The sun e'en seems to loose its way
Nor knows thc quarter it is in

I dwell on trifles like a child
I feel as ill becomes a man
And still my thoughts like weedlings wild
Grow up to blossom where they can   60
They turn to places known so long
And feel that joy was dwelling there
So homebred pleasure fills the song
That has no present joys to heir

I read in books for happiness
But books mistake the way to joy
They change as well give age the glass
To hunt its visage when a boy
For books they follow fashions new
And throw all old esteems away   70
In crowded streets flowers never grew
But many there hath died away

Some sing the pomps of chivalry
As legends of the ancient time
Where gold and pearls and my[s]tery
Are shadows painted for sublime
But passions of sublimity
Belong to plain and simpler things
And David underneath a tree
Sought when a shepherd Salems springs   80

Where moss did unto cushions spring
Forming a seat of velvet hue
A small unnoticed trifling thing
To all but heavens daily dew
And Davids crown hath passed away
Yet poesy breaths his shepherd-skill
His palace lost—and to this day
The little moss is blooming still

Strange scenes mere shadows are to me
Vague unpersonifying things   90
I love with my old hants to be
By quiet woods and gravel springs
Where little pebbles wear as smooth
As hermits beads by gentle floods
Whose noises doth my spirits sooth
And warms them into singing moods

Here every tree is strange to me
All foreign things where ere I go
Theres none where boyhood made a swee
Or clambered up to rob a crow   100

No hollow tree or woodland bower
Well known when joy was beating high
Where beauty ran to shun a shower
And love took pains to keep her dry

And laid the shoaf upon the ground
To keep her from the dripping grass
And ran for stowks and set them round
Till scarse a drop of rain could pass
Through—where the maidens they reclined
And sung sweet ballads now forgot   110
Which brought sweet memorys to the mind
But here a memory knows them not

There have I sat by many a tree
And leaned oer many a rural stile
And conned my thoughts as joys to me
Nought heeding who might frown or smile
Twas natures beautys that inspired
My heart with rapture not its own
And shes a fame that never tires
How could I feel myself alone   120

No—pasture molehills used to lie
And talk to me of sunny days
And then the glad sheep listing bye
And still in ruminating praise
Of summer and the pleasant place
And every weed and blossom too
Was looking upward in my face
With friendships welcome 'how do ye do'

All tennants of an ancient place
And heirs of noble heritage   130
Coeval they with adams race
And blest with more substantial age
For when the world first saw the sun
These little flowers beheld him too
And when his love for earth begun
They were the first his smiles to woo

These little lambtoe bunches springs
In red tinged and begolden dye
For ever and like china kings
They come but never seem to die   140
These may-blooms with its little threads
Still comes upon the thorny bowers
And ne'er forgets those pinky heads
Like fairy pins amid the flowers

And still they bloom as in the day
They first crow[n]ed wilderness and rock
When abel haply crowned with may
The firstlings of his little flock
And Eve might from the matted thorn
To deck her lone and lovely brow   150
Reach that same rose that heedless scorn
Misnames as the dog rosey now

Give me no high flown fangled things
No haughty pomp in marching chime
Where muses play on golden strings
And splendour passes for sublime
Where citys stretch as far as fame
And fancys straining eye can go
And piled untill the sky for shame
Is stooping far away below   160

I love the verse that mild and bland
Breaths of green fields and open sky
I love the muse that in her hand
Bears wreaths of native poesy
Who walks nor skips the pasture brook
In scorn—but by the drinking horse
Leans oer its little brig to look
How far the sallows lean accross

And feels a rapture in her breast
Upon their root-fringed grains to mark   170
A hermit morehens sedgy nest
Just like a naiads summer bark

She counts the eggs she cannot reach
Admires the spot and loves it well
And yearns so natures lessons teach
Amid such neighbourhoods to dwell

I love the muse who sits her down
Upon the molehills little lap
Who feels no fear to stain her gown
And pauses by the hedgerow gap   180
Not with that affectation praise
Of song to sing and never see
A field flower grow in all her days
Or e'en a forests aged tree

E'en here my simple feelings nurse
A love for every simple weed
And e'en this little shepherds purse
Grieves me to cut it up—Indeed
I feel at times a love and joy
For every weed and every thing   190
A feeling kindred from a boy
A feeling brought with every spring

And why—this 'shepherds purse' that grows
In this strange spot in days gone bye
Grew in the little garden rows
Of that old hut now left—and I
Feel what I never felt before
This weed an ancient neighbour here
And though I own the spot no more
Its every trifle makes it dear   200

The ivy at the parlour end
The woodbine at the garden gate
Are all and each affections friend
That renders parting desolate
But times will change and friends must part
And nature still can make amends
Their memory lingers round the heart
Like life whose essence is its friends

Time looks on pomp with careless moods
Or killing apathys disdain   210
—So where old marble citys stood
Poor persecuted weeds remain
She feels a love for little things
That very few can feel beside
And still the grass eternal springs
Where castles stood and grandeur died

Decay A Ballad

O poesy is on the waine
For fancys visions all unfitting
I hardly know her face again
Nature herself seems on the flitting
The fields grow old and common things
The grass the sky the winds a blowing
And spots where still a beauty clings
Are sighing 'going all a going'
O poesy is on the wain
I hardly know her face again   10

The bank with brambles over spread
And little molehills round about it
Was more to me then laurel shades
With paths and gravel finely clouted
And streaking here and streaking there
Thro[u]gh shaven grass and many a border
With rutty lanes had no compare
And heaths were in a richer order
But poesy is in its wane
I hardly know her face again   20

I sat with love by pasture stream
Aye beautys self was sitting bye
Till fields did more then edens seem
Nor could I tell the reason why

I often drank when not a dry
To pledge her health in draught divine
Smiles made it nectar from the sky
Love turned een water into wine
O poesy is on its wane
Nor love nor joy is mine again   30

The sun those mornings used to find
When clouds were other country mountains
And heaven looked upon the mind
With groves and rocks and mottled fountains
These heavens are gone—the mountains grey
Turned mist—the sun a homless ranger
Pursues a naked weary way
Unnoticed like a very stranger
O poesy is on its wain
I cannot find her face again   40

Loves sun went down without a frown
For very joy it used to grieve us
I often think that west is gone
Ah cruel time to undecieve us
The stream it is a naked stream
Where we on sundays used to ramble
The sky hangs oer a broken dream
The brambles nothing but a bramble
O poesy is on its wane
I cannot find her hants again   50

Mere withered stalks and fading trees
And pastures spread with hills and rushes
Are all my fading vision sees
Gone gone is raptures flooding gushes
When mushrooms they were fairy bowers
Their marble pillars overswelling
And danger paused to pluck the flowers
That in their swarthy rings were dwelling
But poesys spells are on the wane
Nor joy nor fear is mine again   60

Aye poesy hath passed away
And fancys visions undecieve us
The night hath taen the place of day
And why should passing shadows grieve us
I thought the flowers upon the hills
Were flowers from Adams open gardens
And I have had my summer thrills
And I have had my hearts rewardings
So poesy is on its wane
I hardly know her face again   70

And friendship it hath burned away
Just like a very ember cooling
A make believe on april day
That sent the simple heart a fooling
Mere jesting in an earnest way
Decieving on and still decieving
And hope is but a fancy play
And joy the art of true believing
For poesy is on the wane
O could I feel her faith again   80

Remembrances°

Summer pleasures they are gone like to visions every one
And the cloudy days of autumn and of winter cometh on
I tried to call them back but unbidden they are gone
Far away from heart and eye and for ever far away
Dear heart and can it be that such raptures meet decay
I thought them all eternal when by Langley bush I lay°
I thought them joys eternal when I used to shout and play
On its bank at 'clink and bandy' 'chock' and 'taw' and ducking
     stone
Where silence sitteth now on the wild heath as her own
Like a ruin of the past all alone   10

When I used to lie and sing by old eastwells boiling spring°
When I used to tie the willow boughs together for a 'swing'

And fish with crooked pins and thread and never catch a thing
With heart just like a feather—now as heavy as a stone
When beneath old lea close oak I the bottom branches broke°
To make our harvest cart like so many working folk
And then to cut a straw at the brook to have a soak
O I never dreamed of parting or that trouble had a sting
Or that pleasures like a flock of birds would ever take to
    wing
Leaving nothing but a little naked spring   20

When jumping time away on old cross berry way°
And eating awes like sugar plumbs ere they had lost the may
And skipping like a leveret before the peep of day
On the rolly polly up and downs of pleasant swordy well°
When in round oaks narrow lane as the south got black again°
We sought the hollow ash that was shelter from the rain
With our pockets full of peas we had stolen from the grain
How delicious was the dinner time on such a showry day
O words are poor receipts for what time hath stole away
The ancient pulpit trees and the play   30

When for school oer 'little field' with its brook and wooden
    brig
Where I swaggered like a man though I was not half so big
While I held my little plough though twas but a willow twig
And drove my team along made of nothing but a name
'Gee hep' and 'hoit' and 'woi'—O I never call to mind
These pleasant names of places but I leave a sigh behind
While I see the little mouldywharps hang sweeing to the wind
On the only aged willow that in all the field remains
And nature hides her face where theyre sweeing in their chains
And in a silent murmuring complains   40

Here was commons for their hills where they seek for freedom
    still
Though every commons gone and though traps are set to kill
The little homeless miners—O it turns my bosom chill
When I think of old 'sneap green' puddocks nook and hilly
    snow°

Where bramble bushes grew and the daisy gemmed in dew
And the hills of silken grass like to cushions to the view
Where we threw the pissmire crumbs when we'd nothing else
    to do
All leveled like a desert by the never weary plough
All vanished like the sun where that cloud is passing now
All settled here for ever on its brow   50

O I never thought that joys would run away from boys
Or that boys would change their minds and forsake such summer
    joys
But alack I never dreamed that the world had other toys
To petrify first feelings like the fable into stone
Till I found the pleasure past and a winter come at last
Then the fields were sudden bare and the sky got overcast
And boyhoods pleasing haunts like a blossom in the blast
Was shrivelled to a withered weed and trampled down and
    done
Till vanished was the morning spring and set that summer
    sun
And winter fought her battle strife and won   60

By Langley bush I roam but the bush hath left its hill
On cowper green I stray tis a desert strange and chill°
And spreading lea close oak ere decay had penned its will
To the axe of the spoiler and self interest fell a prey
And cross berry way and old round oaks narrow lane
With its hollow trees like pulpits I shall never see again
Inclosure like a Buonaparte let not a thing remain
It levelled every bush and tree and levelled every hill
And hung the moles for traitors—though the brook is running
    still
It runs a naked brook cold and chill   70

O had I known as then joy had left the paths of men
I had watched her night and day besure and never slept agen
And when she turned to go O I'd caught her mantle then
And wooed her like a lover by my lonely side to stay
Aye knelt and worshiped on as love in beautys bower
And clung upon her smiles as a bee upon a flower
And gave her heart my poesys all cropt in a sunny hour

As keepsakes and pledges all to never fade away
But love never heeded to treasure up the may
So it went the common road with decay 80

['*Ive ran the furlongs to thy door*']

Ive ran the furlongs to thy door
And thought the way as miles
With doubts that I should see thee not
And scarcely staid for stiles
Lest thou should think me past the time
And change thy mind to go
Some other where to pass the time
The quickest speed was slow

But when thy cottage came in sight
And showed thee at the gate 10
The very scene was one delight
And though we parted late
Joy scarcely seemed a minute long
When hours their flight had taen
And parting welcomed from thy tongue
Be sure and come again

For thou wert young and beautiful
A flower but seldom found
That many hands were fain to pull
Who wouldnt care to wound 20
But there was no delight to meet
Where crowds and folly be
The fields found thee companion sweet
And kept loves heart for me

To follys ear twas little known
A secret in a crowd
And only in the fields alone
I spoke thy name aloud

And if to cheer my walk along
A pleasant book was mine   30
Then beautys name in every song
Seemed nobodys but thine

Far far from all the world I found
Thy pleasant home and thee
Heaths woods a stretc[h]ing circle round
Hid thee from all but me
And o so green those ways when I
On sundays used to seek
Thy company they gave me joy
That cheered me all the week   40

And when we parted with the pledge
Right quickly to return
How lone the wind sighed through the hedge
Birds singing seemed to mourn
My old home was a stranger place
It told the story plain
My home was in thy happy face
That saw me soon again

['*The hoar frost lodges on every tree*']

The hoar frost lodges on every tree
On the round hay stack and the rushy lea
And the boy ere he fothers behind the stack stands
A stamping his feet and a knocking his hands
The shepherd goes tucking his hook in his arm
And makes the dog bark up the sheep to the farm
The ploughman though noisey goes silently now
And rubs off the ryhme with his arm from the plough
Kop kop to his horses he sings and no more
For winter grins keenly and singing is oer   10
Save just now and then in the midst of the day
When hoar feathered frost is all melted away
Then larks from the thurrows takes sunshine for spring
And mounts oer his head just a minute to sing
And cleaning his plough at the end of the land
He'll hum lovely Jessey and sweet Peggy Band°

[*The Mouse's Nest*]

I found a ball of grass among the hay
And proged it as I passed and went away
And when I looked I fancied somthing stirred
And turned agen and hoped to catch the bird
When out an old mouse bolted in the wheat
With all her young ones hanging at her teats
She looked so odd and so grotesque to me
I ran and wondered what the thing could be
And pushed the knapweed bunches where I stood
When the mouse hurried from the crawling brood   10
The young ones squeaked and when I went away
She found her nest again among the hay
The water oer the pebbles scarce could run
And broad old cesspools glittered in the sun

[*Sheep in Winter*]

The sheep get up and make their many tracks
And bear a load of snow upon their backs
And gnaw the frozen turnip to the ground
With sharp quick bite and then go noising round
The boy that pecks the turnips all the day
And knocks his hands to keep the cold away
And laps his legs in straw to keep them warm
And hides behind the hedges from the storm
The sheep as tame as dogs go where he goes
And try to shake their fleeces from the snows   10
Then leave their frozen meal and wander round
The stubble stack that stands beside the ground
And lye all night and face the drizzling storm
And shun the hovel where they might be warm

['*The seeding done the fields are still at morn*']

The seeding done the fields are still at morn
The old roll lies till over grown with corn

And serves the weeders for a dinner seat
The thistle runs and grows above the wheat
The plough lies in the dyke behind the hedge
And harrows stand till overgrown with sedge
The lither ploughman has more work to do
And hodge has fifty calls and cannot go
So there they lye at rest from every call
Till turnip seeding comes and needs them all   10
The maiden with the shepherd stays to play
Then starts and goes accross the nearest way
The hare bolts out and nearly whipes her gown
And the dogs runs and nearly frights her down
The partridge dusting in the milking shed
Starts up and almost settles on her head

[*Wild Bees' Nest*]

The mower tramples on the wild bees nest
And hears the busy noise and stops the rest
Who carless proggle out the mossy ball
And gather up the honey comb and all
The boy that seeks dewberrys from the sedge
And lays the poison berrys on the hedge
Will often find them in the meadow hay
And take his bough and drive the bees away
But when the maiden goes to turn the hay
She whips her apron up and runs away   10
The schoolboy eats the honey comb and all
And often knocks his hat agen the wall
And progs a stick in every hole he sees
To steal the honey bag of black nosed bees

[*Storm in the Fens*]

The f[l]aggy forrest beat the billows breast
And roared and frit the wild duck from her nest
Who hurried up from gunners and from harm
And sought the skys and went above the storm

The boat lay splashing where the waters play
And lay like safety in a dangerous way
The fisher wet and drownded to the skin
Tied up his net and boat and hurried in
To his low hut that stood beside the flood
And lit a fire of flags for want of wood   10
The billows rolled and rolled in frothy spray
And bigger followed as they lashed away
The fisher started as the storm went oer
And thought a stranger knocked agen the door

And looked about and started none to find
The open door brought nothing but the wind
The heron only started from the mud
And stretched his lazy wings accross the flood
The wild duck hurried oer the crane went bye
And flopped about and scarcely cared to flye   20
His careless boat the lonely tempest braves
And lashes in a wilderness of waves
The tempest could not loose her when he tried
And squabd about and lashed agen the side
He tied her to the tree agen the door
And made her safer till the storm was oer
Then made a bigger fire from danger free
And read a book of songs about the sea

[*The Fen*]

The dreary fen a waste of water goes
With nothing to be seen but royston crows
The traveller journeying on the road for hours
Sees nothing but the dyke and water flowers
The lonely lodges scattered miles away
Lock up from fear and robbers all the day
The merry maiden that no place dislikes
Runs out and fills her kettle from the dykes
She hurrys wildly from the face of men
And knows no company but cocks and hens   10

Here highland maidens see in sundays hour
The glorious sight of sinkfoin grounds in flower
And meets the savoury smells that wake the morn
The woodbine hedges and the poppied corn

[*Autumn Morning*]

The mist lies on the weeds but clears away
And half the fields lie open to the day
The ditcher hollos out and cleans his spade
To see the dogs go where his dinners laid
They snuff about and stare and hurry bye
The silly sheep that need not start and flye
The[y] snuff the morning gale and hurry on
And only follow where the game is gone
And bite the weeds in wantoness and play
And leap along the stubbles all the day   10
Then sit on end with pointed foot and eye
The partridge brood that round the bushes lye
And soon the shooters thunder loudly calls
And half the covey in the stubble falls

[*November*]

The shepherds almost wonder where they dwell
And the old dog for his night journey stares
The path leads somewhere but they cannot tell
And neighbour meets with neighbour unawares
The maiden passes close beside her cow
And wonders on and think[s] her far away
The ploughman goes unseen behind his plough
And seems to loose his horses half the day
The lazy mist creeps on in journey slow
The maidens shout and wonder where they go   10
So dull and dark are the november days
The lazy mist high up the evening curled
And now the morn quite hides in smokey haze
The place we occupy seems all the world

[*Autumn Birds*]

The wild duck startles like a sudden thought
And heron slow as if it might be caught
The flopping crows on weary wing go bye
And grey beard jackdaws noising as they flye
The crowds of starnels wiz and hurry bye
And darken like a cloud the evening sky
The larks like thunder rise and suthy round
Then drop and nestle in the stubble ground
The wild swan hurrys high and noises loud
With white necks peering to the evening cloud   10
The weary rooks to distant woods are gone
With length of tail the magpie winnows on
To neighbouring tree and leaves the distant crow
While small birds nestle in the hedge below

[*Farmer's Boy*]

He waits all day beside his little flock
And asks the passing stranger whats o clock
But those who often pass his daily task
Look at their watch and tell before he asks
He mutters storys to himself and lies
Where the thick hedge the warmest house supplys
And when he hears the hunters far and wide
He climbs the highest tree to see them ride
He climbs till all the fields are blea and bare
And makes the old crows nest an easy chair   10
And soon his sheep are got in other grounds
He hastens down and fears his master come
And stops the gap and keeps them all in bounds
And tents them closely till its time for home

['*With hook tucked neath his arm that now and then*']

With hook tucked neath his arm that now and then
He throweth out to leap oer dyke or stile
He soodling totters down the lonely glen
And talks with all he meets in idle toil

His dogs long shaggy coat all claged with dirt
That rattles as he goes keeps in his pace
Nor ever plays in idle sport
He never follows in a foolish race
But smells the leverets seat and passes on
And often lies upon an easy place   10
And easy finds his master when hes gone
Who stands and finds a tale for every one
Leans oer his hook awhile then shools along
And never sings but always hums a song

[*The Squirrel's Nest*]

One day when all the woods where bare and blea
I wandered out to take a pleasant walk
And saw a strange formed nest on stoven tree
Where startled piegon buzzed from bouncing hawk
I wondered strangley what the nest could be
And thought besure it was some foreign bird
So up I scrambled in the highest glee
And my heart jumpt at every thing that stirred
Twas oval shaped strange wonder filled my breast
I hoped to catch the old one on the nest   10
When somthing bolted out I turned to see
And a brown squirrel puttered up the tree
Twas lined with moss and leaves compact and strong
I sluthered down and wondering went along

[*Quail's Nest*]

I wandered out one rainy day
And heard a bird with merry joys
Cry wet my foot for half the way
I stood and wondered at the noise

When from my foot a bird did flee
The rain flew bouncing from her breast
I wondered what the bird could be
And almost trampled on her nest

The nest was full of eggs and round
I met a shepherd in the vales   10
And stood to tell him what I found
He knew and said it was a quails

For he himself the nest had found
Among the wheat and on the green
When going on his daily round
With eggs as many as fifteen

Among the stranger birds they feed
Their summer flight is short and slow
Theres very few know where they breed
And scarcely any where they go   20

[*Morris Dancers*]

Deckt out in ribbons gay and papers cut
Fine as a maidens fancy off they strut
And act the morris dance from door to door
Their highest gains a penny nothing more
The childern leave their toys to see them play
And laughing maidens lay their work away
The stolen apple in her apron lies
To give her lover in his gay disguise
Een the old woman leaves her knitting off
And lays the bellows in her lap to laugh   10
Upon the floor the stool made waggons lie
And playing scholars lay the lesson bye
The cat and dog in wonder run away
And hide beneath the table from the fray

[*'A hugh old tree all wasted to a shell'*]

A hugh old tree all wasted to a shell
Stood in the pleasant fields where I did dwell
As shelter for the shepherd from the shower
Who made his fire and wasted many an hour

The cowboys house to live in lonely ease
Who hurried there to eat his stolen peas
And bird boy often hid him there to play
Bawling aloud to shoo the crows away
Then made a fire the blustry cold to shun
And watched his roasted crabs till day was done   10
And all the roosting crows had flocked away
To teaze his idle toil another day
The gipsey stole his stubble shock and there
In the old shelter found a pleasant lare
A shelter from the storm and from the wind
Leaving the fragments of their stay behind
Black coats and rags to mark their wayward tracks
That would no longer hang upon their backs

[*Stone Pit*]

The passing traveller with wonder sees
A deep and ancient stone pit full of trees
So deep and very deep the place has been
The church might stand within and not be seen
The passing stranger oft with wonder stops
And thinks he een could walk upon their tops
And often stoops to see the busy crow
And stands above and sees the eggs below
And while the wild horse gives his head a toss
The squirrel dances up and runs accross   10
The boy that stands and kills the black nosed bee
Dares down as soon as magpies nests are found
And wonders when he climbs the highest tree
To find it reaches scarce above the ground

[*Wild Duck's Nest*]

As boys where playing in their schools dislike
And floating paper boats along the dyke
They laid their baskets down a nest to see
And found a small hole in a hollow tree

When one looked in and wonder filled his breast
And halloed out a wild duck on her nest
They doubted and the boldest went before
And the duck bolted when they waded oer
And suthied up and flew against the wind
And left the boys and wondering thoughts behind   10
The eggs lay hid in down and lightly prest
They counted more then thirty in the nest
They filled their hats with eggs and waded oer
And left the nest as quiet as before

['*The schoolboys in the morning soon as drest*']

The schoolboys in the morning soon as drest
Went round the fields to play and look for nests
They found a crows but dare not climb so high
And looked for nests when any bird was nigh
At length they got agen a bush to play
And found a pinks nest round and mossed with grey
And lined about with feathers and with hair
They tryed to climb but brambles said forbear
One found a stone and stronger then the rest
And took another up to reach the nest   10
Heres eggs they hollowed with a hearty shout
Small round and blotched they reached and tore them out
The old birds sat and hollowed pink pink pink
And cattle hurried to the pond to drink

[*The Green Woodpecker's Nest*]

The green woodpecker flying up and down
With wings of mellow green and speckled crown
She bores a hole in trees with crawking noise
And pelted down and often catched by boys
She makes a lither nest of grass and whool
Men fright her oft that go the sticks to pull
Ive up and clumb the trees with hook and pole
And stood on rotten grains to reach the hole

And as I trembled upon fear and doubt
I found the eggs and scarce could get them out   10
I put them in my hat a tattered crown
And scarcely without breaking brought them down
The eggs are small for such a bird they lay
Five eggs and like the sparrows spotted grey

[*Woodpecker's Nest*]

There is a small woodpecker red and grey
That hides in woods and forrests far away
They run like creepers up and down the tree
And few can find them when they stand to see
They seldom fly away but run and climb
A man may stand and look for twenty time
And seldom see them once for half a day
Ive stood nor seen them till they flew away
Ive swarmed the grain and clumb with hook and pole
But scarce could get three fingers in the hole   10
They build on grains scarse thicker then ones legs
Ive found the nests but never got the eggs
But boys who wish to see what eggs they lay
Will climb the tree and saw the grain away

[*The Puddock's Nest*]

The sailing puddock sweeps about for prey
And keeps above the woods from day to day
They make a nest so large in woods remote
Would fill a womans apron with the sprotes
And schoolboys daring doing tasks the best
Will often climb and stand upon the nest
They find a hugh old tree and free from snaggs
And make a flat nest lined with wool and rags
And almost big enough to make a bed
And lay three eggs and spotted oer with red   10
The schoolboy often hears the old ones cry°
And climbs the tree and gets them ere they fly
And takes them home and often cuts their wing
And ties them in the garden with a string

[*The Groundlark*]

Close where the milking maidens pass
In roots and twitches drest
Within a little bunch of grass
A groundlark made her nest
The maiden touched her with her gown
And often frit her out
And looked and set her buckets down
But never found it out
The eggs where large and spotted round
And dark as is the fallow ground   10
The schoolboy kicked the grass in play
But danger never guest
And when they came to mow the hay
They found an empty nest

[*Turkeys*]

The turkeys wade the close to catch the bees
In the old border full of maple trees
And often lay away and breed and come
And bring a brood of chelping chickens home
The turkey gobbles loud and drops his rag
And struts and sprunts his tail and drags
His wing on ground and makes a huzzing noise
Nauntles at passer bye and drives the boys
And bounces up and flyes at passer bye
The old dogs snaps and grins nor ventures nigh   10
He gobbles loud and drives the boys from play
They throw their sticks and kick away
And turn agen the stone comes huzzing bye
He drops his quiet tail and forced to flye

Draws up his scarlet snout and cools to grey
And drops his gobble noise and sneaks away
He drives the noisey ducks as soon as loose
And fights with awkard haste the hissing goose

And tramples round and fairly beats him down
And quarrels with the maidens sunday gown   20
He often gives the cock and hens the chase
And drives the stranger till he leaves the place
And runs and gobbles up and when he beats
They all come up and follow the retreat
And when a beggar comes he nauntling steals
And gobbles loud and pecks the strangers heels
He fights the dunghill cock that quarrels hard
And hobbles round the master of the yard

The idle turkey gobbling half the day
Goes hobbling through the grass and lays away   30
Five and red spotted eggs where many pass
But none ere thinks of turkeys in the grass
The old dogs sees her on and goes away
The old dame calls and wonders where they lay
Among the old and thickest grass they lie
The fox unnotices and passes bye
The blackbird breeds above a cunning guest
And hides the shells cause none should find the nest
The old crow crawks around them every day
And trys to steal the turkeys eggs away   40
The magpie cackles round for any prey
And finds the wounded snake and goes away

[Rook's Nest]

The rooks begin to build and pleasant looks
The homestead elms now almost black with rooks
The birds at first for mastership will try
They fight for sticks and squabble as they flye
And if a stranger comes they soon invade
And pull his nest in pieces soon as made
The carrion crow and hawk dare never come
They dare to fight like armys round their home
The boughs will hardly bear their noisey guests
And storms will come and over turn the nests   10

They build above the reach of clauming clowns
They climb and fast but cunning cuts them down
Others with reaching poles the nest destroys
While off and up they flye with deafening noise

['*The old pond full of flags and fenced around*']

The old pond full of flags and fenced around
With trees and bushes trailing to the ground
The water weeds are all around the brink
And one clear place where cattle go to drink
From year to year the schoolboy thither steals
And muddys round the place to catch the eels
The cowboy often hiding from the flies
Lies there and plaits the rushcap as he lies
The hissing owl sits moping all the day
And hears his song and never flies away   10
The pinks nest hangs upon the branch so thin
The young ones caw and seem as tumbling in
While round them thrums the purple dragon flye
And great white butter flye goes dancing bye

[*Dyke Side*]

The frog croaks loud and maidens dare not pass
But fears the noisome toad and shuns the grass
And on the sunny banks they fear to go
Where hissing snakes run to the floods below
The nuthatch noises loud in wood and wild
Like women turning skreekers to a child
The schoolboy hears and brushes through the trees
And runs about till drabbled to the knees
The old hawk winnows round the old crows nest
The schoolboy hears and wonder fills his breast   10
He throws his basket down to climb the tree
And wonders what the red blotched eggs can be
The green woodpecker bounces from the view
And hollow as they buzz along kew kew

[*The Partridge*]

One day accross the fields I chancd to pass
When chickens chelped and skuttled in the grass
And as I looked about to find the seat
A wounded partridge dropped agen my feet
She fluttered round and calling as she lay
The chickens chelpd and fluttered all away
I stooped to pick her up when up she drew
Her wounded wing and cackled as she flew
I wondered much to hear the chickens lye
As still as nothing till I wandered bye   10
And soon she came agen with much ado
And swept the grass and called them as she flew
But still they kept their seat and left no trace
And old cows snorted when they passed the place

[*The Crane's Nest*]

The passer bye oft stops his horse to look
To see strange birds sit building like the rook
And every stranger ere he passes bye
Will stop and hollow shoo to see them flye
They swee about the trees a flopping herd
He goes and thinks them some outlandish bird
They bring their sticks nor fear the noisey clown
And load the trees till nearly broken down
They little think the crane will leave the floods
And make their nests like crows among the woods   10
They lay their sticks so thick each awkard guest
That boys might stand and walk from nest to nest
Their eggs are long and green and spotted brown
And winds will come and often throw them down

[*The Nuthatch*]

In summer showers a skreeking noise is heard
Deep in the woods of some uncommon bird

It makes a loud and long and loud continued noise
And often stops the speed of men and boys
They think somebody mocks and goes along
And never thinks the nuthatch makes the song
Who always comes along the summer guest
The birdnest hunters never found the nest
The schoolboy hears the noise from day to day
And stoops among the thorns to find a way   10
And starts the jay bird from the bushes green
He looks and sees a nest he's never seen
And takes the spotted eggs with many joys
And thinks he found the bird that made the noise

[*The Partridge's Nest*]

The partridge makes no nest but on the ground
Lays many eggs and I have often found
Sixteen or eighteen in a beaten seat
When tracing oer the fields or weeding wheat
They lay in furrows or an old land rig
Brown as the pheasants only not so big
Theyre often found by pasture boys at play
And by the weeders often taen away
The boys will often throw the eggs abroad
And stay and play at blind eggs on the road   10
They lay in any hole without a nest
And oft a horses footing pleases best
And there they safely lie till weeders come
When boys half fill their hats and take them home

POEMS WRITTEN IN EPPING FOREST
AND NORTHAMPTON ASYLUM
1837–1864

The Water Lilies°

The Water Lilies, white and yellow flowers,
  How beautiful they are upon the lake!
I've stood and looked upon the place for hours,
  And thought how fine a garden they would make.
The pleasant leaves upon the water float;
  The dragon-fly would come and stay for hours,
And when the water pushed the pleasure boat,
  Would find a safer place among the flowers:
They lay like Pleasure in a quiet place,
  Close where the moor-hen loved her nest to make,—   10
They lay like beauty with a smiling face,
  And I have called them 'Ladies of the Lake!'
I've brought the longest pole and stood for hours,
And tried for years, before I got those flowers!

The Gipsy Camp°

The snow falls deep; the Forest lies alone:
The boy goes hasty for his load of brakes,
Then thinks upon the fire and hurries back;
The Gipsy knocks his hands and tucks them up,
And seeks his squalid camp, half hid in snow,
Beneath the oak, which breaks away the wind,
And bushes close, with snow like hovel warm:
There stinking mutton roasts upon the coals,
And the half-roasted dog squats close and rubs,
Then feels the heat too strong and goes aloof;   10
He watches well, but none a bit can spare,
And vainly waits the morsel thrown away:
'Tis thus they live—a picture to the place;
A quiet, pilfering, unprotected race.

Child Harold°

Many are poets—though they use no pen
To show their labours to the shuffling age
Real poets must be truly honest men
Tied to no mongrel laws on flatterys page
No zeal have they for wrong or party rage
—The life of labour is a rural song
That hurts no cause—nor warfare tries to wage
Toil like the brook in music wears along—
Great little minds claim right to act the wrong

BALLAD

Summer morning is risen   10
And to even it wends
And still Im in prison
Without any friends

I had joys assurance
Though in bondage I lie
—I am still left in durance
Unwilling to sigh

Still the forest is round me
Where the trees bloom in green
As if chains ne'er had bound me   20
Or cares had ne'er been

Nature's love is eternal
In forest and plain
Her course is diurnal
To blossom again

For home and friends vanished
I have kindness not wrath
For in days care has banished
My heart possessed both

My hopes are all hopeless   30
My skys have no sun
Winter fell in youths mayday
And still freezes on

But Love like the seed is
In the heart of a flower
It will blossom with truth
In a prosperous hour

True love is eternal
For God is the giver
And love like the soul will   40
Endure—and forever

And he who studies natures volume through
And reads it with a pure unselfish mind
Will find Gods power all round in every view
As one bright vision of the almighty mind
His eyes are open though the world is blind
No ill from him creations works deform
The high and lofty one is great and kind
Evil may cause the blight and crushing storm
His is the sunny glory and the calm   50

SONG

The sun has gone down with a veil on his brow
While I in the forest sit museing alone
The maiden has been oer the hills for her cow
While my hearts affections are freezing to stone
Sweet Mary I wish that the day was my own
To live in a cottage with beauty and thee
The past I will not as a mourner bemoan
For abscence leaves Mary still dearer to me

How sweet are the glooms of the midsummer even
Dark night in the bushes seems going to rest   60
And the bosom of Mary with fancys is heaving
Where my sorrows and feelings for seasons were blest

Nor will I repine though in love we're divided
She in the Lowlands and I in the glen
Of these forest beeches—by nature we're guided
And I shall find rest on her bosom agen

How soft the dew falls on the leaves of the beeches
How fresh the wild flower seems to slumber below
How sweet are the lessons that nature still teaches
For truth is her tidings wherever I go   70
From school days of boyhood her image was cherished
In manhood sweet Mary was fairer then flowers
Nor yet has her name or her memory perished
Though abscence like winter oer happiness lowers

Though cares still will gather like clouds in my sky
Though hopes may grow hopeless and fetters recoil
While the sun of existance sheds light in my eye
I'll be free in a prison and cling to the soil
I'll cling to the spot where my first love was cherished
Where my heart nay my soul unto Mary I gave   80
And when my last hope and existance is perished
Her memory will shine like a sun on my grave

Mary thou ace of hearts thou muse of song
The pole star of my being and decay
Earths coward foes my shattered bark may wrong
Still thourt the sunrise of my natal day
Born to misfortunes—where no sheltering bay
Keeps off the tempest—wrecked where'er I flee
I struggle with my fate—in trouble strong—
Mary thy name loved long still keeps me free   90
Till my lost life becomes a part of thee

SONG *a*

I've wandered many a weary mile
Love in my heart was burning
To seek a home in Mary[s] smile
But cold is loves returning

The cold ground was a feather bed
Truth never acts contrary
I had no home above my head
My home was love and Mary

I had no home in early youth   100
When my first love was thwarted
But if her heart still beats with truth
We'll never more be parted
And changing as her love may be
My own shall never vary
Nor night nor day I'm never free
But sigh for abscent Mary

Nor night nor day nor sun nor shade
Week month nor rolling year
Repairs the breach wronged love hath made   110
There madness—misery here
Lifes lease was lengthened by her smiles
—Are truth and love contrary
No ray of hope my life beguiles
I've lost love home and Mary

Love is the main spring of existance—It
Becomes a soul wherebye I live to love
On all I see that dearest name is writ
Falsehood is here—but truth has life above
Where every star that shines exists in love   120
Skys vary in their clouds—the seasons vary
From heat to cold—change cannot constant prove
The south is bright—but smiles can act contrary
My guide star gilds the north—and shines with Mary

SONG *b*

Heres where Mary loved to be
And here are flowers she planted
Here are books she loved to see
And here the kiss she granted

Here on the wall with smileing brow
Her picture used to cheer me   130
Both walls and rooms are naked now
No Marys nigh to hear me

The church spire still attracts my eye
And leaves me broken hearted
Though grief hath worn their channels dry
I sigh o'er days departed

The churchyard where she used to play
My feet could wander hourly
My school walks there was every day
Where she made winter flowery   140

But where is angel Mary now
Loves secrets none disclose 'em
Her rosey cheeks and broken vow
Live in my aching bosom

My life hath been one love—no blot it out
My life hath been one chain of contradictions
Madhouses Prisons wh–re shops—never doubt
But that my life hath had some strong convictions
That such was wrong—religion makes restrictions
I would have followed—but life turned a bubble   150
And clumb the jiant stile of maledictions
They took me from my wife and to save trouble
I wed again and made the error double

Yet abscence claims them both and keeps them too
And locks me in a shop in spite of law
Among a low lived set and dirty crew
Here let the Muse oblivions curtain draw
And let man think—for God hath often saw
Things here too dirty for the light of day
For in a madhouse there exists no law—   160
Now stagnant grows my too refined clay
I envy birds their wings to flye away

How servile is the task to please alone
Though beauty woo and love inspire the song
Mere painted beauty with her heart of stone
Thinks the world worships while she flaunts along
The flower of sunshine butterflye of song
Give me the truth of heart in womans life
The love to cherish one—and do no wrong
To none—O peace of every care and strife   170
Is true love in an estimable wife

How beautifull this hill of fern swells on
So beautifull the chappel peeps between
The hornbeams—with its simple bell—alone
I wander here hid in a palace green
Mary is abscent—but the forest queen
Nature is with me—morning noon and gloaming
I write my poems in these paths unseen
And when among these brakes and beeches roaming
I sigh for truth and home and love and woman   180

I sigh for one and two—and still I sigh
For many are the whispers I have heard
From beautys lips—loves soul in many an eye
Hath pierced my heart with such intense regard
I Looked for joy and pain was the reward
I think of them I love each girl and boy
Babes of two mothers—on this velvet sward
And nature thinks—in her so sweet employ
While dews fall on each blossom weeping joy

Here is the chappel yard enclosed with pales   190
And oak trees nearly top its little bell
Here is the little bridge with guiding rail
That leads me on to many a pleasant dell
The fernowl chitters like a startled knell
To nature—yet tis sweet at evening still—
A pleasant road curves round the gentle swell
Where nature seems to have her own sweet will
Planting her beech and thorn about the sweet fern hill

I have had many loves—and seek no more—
These solitudes my last delights shall be   200
The leaf hid forest—and the lonely shore
Seem to my mind like beings that are free
Yet would I had some eye to smile on me
Some heart where I could make a happy home in
Sweet Susan that was wont my love to be
And Bessey of the glen—for I've been roaming
With both at morn and noon and dusky gloaming

Cares gather round I snap their chains in two
And smile in agony and laugh in tears
Like playing with a deadly serpent—who   210
Stings to the death—there is no room for fears
Where death would bring me happiness—his sheers
Kills cares that hiss to poison many a vein
The thought to be extinct my fate endears
Pale death the grand phis[i]cian cures all pain
The dead rest well—who lived for joys in vain

Written in a Thunder storm July 15th 1841

The heavens are wrath—the thunders rattling peal
Rolls like a vast volcano in the sky
Yet nothing starts the apathy I feel
Nor chills with fear eternal destiny   220

My soul is apathy—a ruin vast
Time cannot clear the ruined mass away
My life is hell—the hopeless die is cast
And manhoods prime is premature decay

Roll on ye wrath of thunders—peal on peal
Till worlds are ruins and myself alone
Melt heart and soul cased in obdurate steel
Till I can feel that nature is my throne

I live in love sun of undying light
And fathom my own heart for ways of good   230
In its pure atmosphere day without night
Smiles on the plains the forest and the flood

Smile on ye elements of earth and sky
Or frown in thunders as ye frown on me
Bid earth and its delusions pass away
But leave the mind as its creator free

This twilight seems a veil of gause and mist
Trees seem dark hills between the earth and sky
Winds sob awake and then a gusty hist
Fanns through the wheat like serpents gliding bye   240
I love to stretch my length 'tween earth and sky
And see the inky foliage oer me wave
Though shades are still my prison where I lie
Long use grows nature which I easy brave
And think how sweet cares rest within the grave

Remind me not of other years or tell
My broken hopes of joys they are to meet
While thy own falshood rings the loudest knell
To one fond heart that aches too cold to beat
Mary how oft with fondness I repeat   250
That name alone to give my troubles rest
The very sound though bitter seemeth sweet—
In my loves home and thy own faithless breast
Truths bonds are broke and every nerve distrest

Life is to me a dream that never wakes
Night finds me on this lengthening road alone
Love is to me a thought that ever aches
A frost bound thought that freezes life to stone
Mary in truth and nature still my own
That warms the winter of my aching breast   260
Thy name is joy nor will I life bemoan—
Midnight when sleep takes charge of natures rest
Finds me awake and friendless—not distrest

Tie all my cares up in thy arms O sleep
And give my weary spirits peace and rest
I'm not an outlaw in this midnight deep
If prayers are offered from sweet womans breast
One and one only made my being blest

And fancy shapes her form in every dell
On that sweet bosom I've had hours of rest   270
Though now through years of abscence doomed to dwell
Day seems my night and night seems blackest hell

England my country though my setting sun
Sinks in the ocean gloom and dregs of life
My muse can sing my Marys heart was won
And joy was heaven when I called her wife
The only harbour in my days of strife
Was Mary when the sea roiled mountains high
When joy was lost and every sorrow rife
To her sweet bosom I was wont to flye   280
To undecieve by truth lifes treacherous agony

Friend of the friendless from a host of snares
From lying varlets and from friendly foes
I sought thy quiet truth to ease my cares
And on the blight of reason found repose
But when the strife of nature ceased her throes
And other hearts would beat for my return
I trusted fate to ease my world of woes
Seeking loves harbour—where I now sojourn
—But hell is heaven could I cease to mourn   290

For her for one whose very name is yet
My hell or heaven—and will ever be
Falsehood is doubt—but I can ne'er forget
Oaths virtuous falsehood volunteered to me
To make my soul new bonds which God made free
Gods gift is love and do I wrong the giver
To place affections wrong from Gods decree
—No when farewell upon my lips did quiver
And all seemed lost—I loved her more then ever

I loved her in all climes beneath the sun   300
Her name was like a jewel in my heart
Twas heavens own choice—and so Gods will be done
Love ties that keep unbroken cannot part
Nor can cold abscence sever or desert

That simple beauty blessed with matchless charms
Oceans have rolled between us—not to part
E'en Icelands snows true loves delirium warms
For there Ive dreamed—and Mary filled my arms

SONG

O Mary sing thy songs to me
Of love and beautys melody   310
My sorrows sink beneath distress
My deepest griefs are sorrowless
So used to glooms and cares am I
My tearless troubles seem as joy
O Mary sing thy songs to me
Of love and beautys melody

'To be beloved is all I need
And them I love are loved indeed'°
The soul of woman is my shrine
And Mary made my songs divine   320
O for that time that happy time
To hear thy sweet Piana's chime
In music so divine and clear
That woke my soul in heaven to hear

But heaven itself without thy face
To me would be no resting place
And though the world was one delight
No joy would live but in thy sight
The soul of woman is my shrine
Then Mary make those songs divine   330
For music love and melody
Breath all of thee and only thee

SONG

Lovely Mary when we parted
I ne'er felt so lonely hearted
As I do now in field and glen
When hope says 'we shall meet agen'

And by yon spire that points to heaven
Where my earliest vows was given
By each meadow field and fen
I'll love thee till we meet agen   340

True as the needle to the pole
My life I love thee heart and soul
Wa'n't thy love in my heart enrolled
Though love was fire 't'would soon be cold
By thy eyes of heavens own blue
My heart for thine was ever true
By sun and moon by sea and shore
My life I love thee more and more

And by that hope that lingers last
For heaven when lifes hell is past   350
By time the present—past and gone
I've loved thee—and I love thee on
Thy beauty made youths life divine
Till my soul grew a part of thine
Mary I mourn no pleasures gone—
The past hath made us both as one

Now melancholly autumn comes anew
With showery clouds and fields of wheat tanned brown
Along the meadow banks I peace pursue
And see the wild flowers gleaming up and down   360
Like sun and light—the ragworts golden crown
Mirrors like sunshine when sunbeams retire
And silver yarrow—there's the little town
And oer the meadows gleams that slender spire
Reminding me of one—and waking fond desire

I love thee nature in my inmost heart
Go where I will thy truth seems from above
Go where I will thy landscape forms a part
Of heaven—e'en these fens where wood nor grove
Are seen—their very nakedness I love   370
For one dwells nigh that secret hopes prefer
Above the race of women—like the dove
I mourn her abscence—fate that would deter
My hate for all things—strengthens love for her

Thus saith the great and high and lofty one
Whose name is holy—home eternity
In the high and holy place I dwell alone
And with them also that I wish to see
Of contrite humble spirits—from sin free
Who trembles at my word—and good recieve   380
—Thou high and lofty one—O give to me
Truths low estate and I will glad believe
If such I am not—such I'm feign to live

That form from boyhood loved and still loved on
That voice—that look—that face of one delight
Loves register for years, months, weeks—time past and gone
Her looks was ne'er forgot or out of sight
—Mary the muse of every song I write
Thy cherished memory never leaves my own
Though cares chill winter doth my manhood blight   390
And freeze like Niobe my thoughts to stone—
Our lives are two—our end and aim is one

BALLAD

Sweet days while God your blessings send
I call your joys my own
—And if I have an only friend
I am not left alone

She sees the fields the trees the spires
Which I can daily see
And if true love her heart inspires
Life still has joys for me   400

She sees the wild flower in the dells
That in my rambles shine
The sky that oer her homstead dwells
Looks sunny over mine

The cloud that passes where she dwells
In less then half an hour
Darkens around these orchard dells
Or melts a sudden shower

The wind that leaves the sunny south
And fans the orchard tree   410
Might steal the kisses from her mouth
And waft her voice to me

O when will autumn bring the news
Now harvest browns the fen
That Mary as my vagrant muse
And I shall meet again

Tis pleasant now days hours begin to pass
To dewy Eve—To walk down narrow close
And feel ones feet among refreshing grass
And hear the insects in their homes discourse   420
And startled blackbird flye from covert close
Of white thorn hedge with wild fears fluttering wings
And see the spire and hear the clock toll hoarse
And whisper names—and think oer many things
That love hurds up in truths imaginings

Fame blazed upon me like a comets glare
Fame waned and left me like a fallen star
Because I told the evil what they are
And truth and falshood never wished to mar
My Life hath been a wreck—and I've gone far   430
For peace and truth—and hope—for home and rest
—Like Edens gates—fate throws a constant bar—
Thoughts may o'ertake the sunset in the west
—Man meets no home within a womans breast

Though they are blazoned in the poets song
As all the comforts which our lifes contain
I read and sought such joys my whole life long
And found the best of poets sung in vain
But still I read and sighed and sued again
And lost no purpose where I had the will   440
I almost worshiped when my toils grew vain
Finding no antidote my pains to kill
I sigh a poet and a lover still

SONG

Dying gales of sweet even
How can you sigh so
Though the sweet day is leaving
And the sun sinketh low
How can you sigh so
For the wild flower is gay
And her dew gems all glow   450
For the abscence of day

Dying gales of sweet even
Breath music from toil
Dusky eve is loves heaven
And meets beautys smile
Love leans on the stile
Where the rustic brooks flow
Dying gales all the while
How can you sigh so

Dying gales round a prison   460
To fancy may sigh
But day here hath risen
Over prospects of joy
Here Mary would toy
When the sun it got low
Even gales whisper joy
And never sigh so

Labour lets man his brother
Retire to his nest
The babe meets its mother   470
And sleeps on her breast—
The sun in the west
Has gone down in the ocean
Dying gales gently sweep
O'er the hearts ruffled motion
And sing it to sleep

SONG

The spring may forget that he reigns in the sky
And winter again hide her flowers in the snow
The summer may thirst when her fountains are dry
But I'll think of Mary wherever I go   480
The bird may forget that her nest is begun
When the snow settles white on the new budding tree
And nature in tempests forget the bright sun
But I'll ne'er forget her—that was plighted to me

How could I—how should I—that loved her so early
Forget—when I've sung of her beauty in song
How could I forget—what I've worshiped so dearly
From boyhood to manhood—and all my life long—
As leaves to the branches in summer comes duly
And blossoms will bloom on the stalk and the tree   490
To her beauty I'll cling—and I'll love her as truly
And think of sweet Mary wherever I be

SONG

No single hour can stand for nought
No moment hand can move
But calenders a aching thought
Of my first lonely love

Where silence doth the loudest call
My secrets to betray
As moonlight holds the night in thrall
As suns reveal the day   500

I hide it in the silent shades
Till silence finds a tongue
I make its grave where time invades
Till time becomes a song

I bid my foolish heart be still
But hopes will not be chid
My heart will beat—and burn—and chill
First love will not be hid

When summer ceases to be green
And winter bare and blea—   510
Death may forget what I have been
But I must cease to be

When words refuse before the crowd
My Marys name to give
The muse in silence sings aloud
And there my love will live

Now harvest smiles embrowning all the plain
The sun of heaven oer its ripeness shines
'Peace-plenty' has been sung nor sung in vain
As all bring forth the makers grand designs   520
—Like gold that brightens in some hidden mines
His nature is the wealth that brings increase
To all the world—his sun forever shines
—He hides his face and troubles they increase
He smiles—the sun looks out in wealth and peace

This life is made of lying and grimace
This world is filled with whoring and decieving
Hypocrisy ne'er masks an honest face
Story's are told—but seeing his believing
And I've seen much from which there's no retrieving   530
I've seen deception take the place of truth
I've seen knaves flourish—and the country grieving
Lies was the current gospel in my youth
And now a man—I'm farther off from truth

SONG

They near read the heart
Who would read it in mine
That love can desert
The first truth on his shrine
Though in Lethe I steep it
And sorrows prefer   540
In my hearts core I keep it
And keep it for her

For her and her only
Through months and through years
I've wandered thus lonely
In sorrow and fears
My sorrows I smother
Though troubles anoy
In this world and no other
I cannot meet joy   550

No peace nor yet pleasure
Without her will stay
Life looses its treasure
When Mary's away
Though the nightingale often
In sorrow may sing
—Can the blast of the winter
Meet blooms of the spring

Thou first best and dearest
Though dwelling apart   560
To my heart still the nearest
Forever thou art
And thou wilt be the dearest
Though our joys may be o'er
And to me thou art nearest
Though I meet thee no more

SONG

Did I know where to meet thee
Thou dearest in life
How soon would I greet thee
My true love and wife   570
How soon would I meet thee
At close of the day
Though cares would still cheat me
If Mary would meet me
I'd kiss her sweet beauty and love them away

And when evening discovers
The sun in the west
I long like true lovers
To lean on thy breast
To meet thee my dearest   580
—Thy eyes beaming blue
Abscent pains the severest
Feel Mary's the dearest
And if Mary's abscent—how can I be true

How dull the glooms cover
This meadow and fen
Where I as a lover
Seek Mary agen
But silence is teazing
Wherever I stray   590
There's nothing seems pleasing
Or aching thoughts easing
Though Mary live's near me—she seems far away

O would these gales murmur
My love in her ear
Or a birds note inform her
While I linger here
But nature contrary
Turns night into day
No bird—gale—or fairy   600
Can whisper to Mary
To tell her who seeks her—while Mary's away

Dull must that being live who sees unmoved
The scenes and objects that his childhood knew
The school yard and the maid he early loved
The sunny wall where long the old Elms grew
The grass that e'en till noon retains the dew
Beneath the wallnut shade I see them still
Though not such fancys do I now pursue
Yet still the picture turns my bosom chill   610
And leaves a void—nor love nor hope may fill

After long abscence how the mind recalls
Pleasing associations of the past
Haunts of his youth—thorn hedges and old walls
And hollow trees that sheltered from the blast
And all that map of boyhood overcast
With glooms and wrongs and sorrows not his own
That oer his brow like the scathed lightening past
That turned his spring to winter and alone
Wrecked name and fame and all—to solitude unknown   620

So on he lives in glooms and living death
A shade like night forgetting and forgot
Insects that kindle in the springs young breath
Take hold of life and share a brighter lot
Then he the tennant of the hall and Cot
The princely palace too hath been his home
And Gipseys camp when friends would know him not
In midst of wealth a beggar still to roam
Parted from one whose heart was once his home

And yet not parted—still loves hope illumes   630
And like the rainbow brightest in the storm
It looks for joy beyond the wreck of tombs
And in lifes winter keeps loves embers warm
The oceans roughest tempest meets a calm
Cares thickest cloud shall break in sunny joy
O'er the parched waste showers yet shall fall like balm
And she the soul of life for whom I sigh
Like flowers shall cheer me when the storm is bye

SONG

O Mary dear three springs have been
Three summers too have blossomed here   640
Three blasting winters crept between
Though abscence is the most severe
Another summer blooms in green
But Mary never once was seen

I've sought her in the fields and flowers
I've sought her in the forest groves
In avanues and shaded bowers
And every scene that Mary loves
E'en round her home I seek her here
But Marys abscent every where   650

Tis autumn and the rustling corn
Goes loaded on the creaking wain
I seek her in the early morn
But cannot meet her face again
Sweet Mary she is abscent still
And much I fear she ever will

The autumn morn looks mellow as the fruit
And ripe as harvest—every field and farm
Is full of health and toil—yet never mute
With rustic mirth and peace the day is warm   660
The village maid with gleans upon her arm
Brown as the hazel nut from field to field
Goes cheerily—the valleys native charm—
I seek for charms that autumn best can yield
In mellowing wood and time ybleaching field

SONG

Tis autumn now and natures scenes
The pleachy fields and yellowing trees
Looses their blooming hues and greens
But nature finds no change in me
The fading woods the russet grange   670
The hues of nature may desert
But nought in me shall find a change
To wrong the angel of my heart
For Mary is my angel still
Through every month and every ill

The leaves they loosen from the branch
And fall upon the gusty wind
But my hearts silent love is staunch
And nought can tear her from my mind

The flowers are gone from dell and bower   680
Though crowds from summers lap was given
But love is an eternal flower
Like purple amaranths in heaven
To Mary first my heart did bow
And if she's true she keeps it now

Just as the summer keeps the flower
Which spring conscealed in hoods of gold
Or unripe harvest met the shower
And made earths blessings manifold
Just so my Mary lives for me   690
A silent thought for months and years
The world may live in revellry
Her name my lonely quiet cheers
And cheer it will what e'er may be
While Mary lives to think of me

Sweet comes the misty mornings in september
Among the dewy paths how sweet to stray
Greensward or stubbles as I well remember
I once have done—the mist curls thick and grey
As cottage smoke—like net work on the sprey   700
Or seeded grass the cobweb draperies run
Beaded with pearls of dew at early day
And oer the pleachy stubbles peeps the sun
The lamp of day when that of night is done

What mellowness these harvest days unfold
In the strong glances of the midday sun
The homesteads very grass seems changed to gold
The light in golden shadows seems to run
And tinges every spray it rests upon
With that rich harvest hue of sunny joy   710
Nature lifes sweet companion cheers alone—
The hare starts up before the shepherd boy
And partridge coveys wir on russet wings of joy

The meadow flags now rustle bleached and dank
And misted oer with down as fine as dew
The sloe and dewberry shine along the bank
Where weeds in blooms luxuriance lately grew
Red rose the sun and up the morehen flew
From bank to bank the meadow arches stride
Where foamy floods in winter tumbles through   720
And spread a restless ocean foaming wide
Where now the cowboys sleep nor fear the coming tide

About the medows now I love to sit
On banks bridge walls and rails as when a boy
To see old trees bend oer the flaggy pit
With hugh roots bare that time does not destroy
Where sits the angler at his days employ
And there Ivy leaves the bank to climb
The tree—and now how sweet to weary joy
—Aye nothing seems so happy and sublime   730
As sabbath bells and their delightfull chime

Sweet solitude thou partner of my life
Thou balm of hope and every pressing care
Thou soothing silence oer the noise of strife
These meadow flats and trees—the Autumn air
Mellows my heart to harmony—I bear
Lifes burthen happily—these fenny dells
Seem Eden in this sabbath rest from care
My heart with loves first early memory swells
To hear the music of those village bells   740

For in that hamlet lives my rising sun
Whose beams hath cheered me all my lorn life long
My heart to nature there was early won
For she was natures self—and still my song
Is her through sun and shade through right and wrong
On her my memory forever dwells
The flower of Eden—evergreen of song
Truth in my heart the same love story tells
—I love the music of those village bells

SONG

Heres a health unto thee bonny lassie O   750
Leave the thorns o' care wi' me
And whatever I may be
Here's happiness to thee
Bonny lassie O

Here's joy unto thee bonny lassie O
Though we never meet again
I well can bear the pain
If happiness is thine
Bonny lassie O

Here is true love unto thee bonny lassie O   760
Though abscence cold is ours
The spring will come wi' flowers
And love will wait for thee
Bonny lassie O

So heres love unto thee bonny lassie O
Aye wherever I may be
Here's a double health to thee
Till life shall cease to love
Bonny lassie O

The blackbird startles from the homestead hedge   770
Raindrops and leaves fall yellow as he springs
Such images are natures sweetest pledge
To me there's music in his rustling wings
'Prink prink' he cries and loud the robin sings
The small hawk like a shot drops from the sky
Close to my feet for mice and creeping things
Then swift as thought again he suthers bye
And hides among the clouds from the pursueing eye

SONG

Her cheeks are like roses
Her eyes they are blue   780
And her beauty is mine
If her heart it is true

Her cheeks are like roses—
And though she's away
I shall see her sweet beauty
On some other day

Ere the flowers of the spring
Deck the meadow and plain
If theres truth in her bosom
I shall see her again   790

I will love her as long
As the brooks they shall flow
For Mary is mine and
Whereso ever I go

Honesty and good intentions are
So mowed and hampered in with evil lies
She hath not room to stir a single foot
Or even strength to break a spiders web
—So lies keep climbing round loves sacred stem
Blighting fair truth whose leaf is evergreen   800
Whose roots are the hearts fibres and whose sun
The soul that cheers and smiles it into bloom
Till heaven proclaims that truth can never die

The lightenings vivid flashes—rend the cloud
That rides like castled crags along the sky
And splinters them to fragments—while aloud
The thunders heavens artillery vollies bye
Trees crash, earth trembles—beast prepare to flye
Almighty what a crash—yet man is free
And walks unhurt while danger seems so nigh—   810
Heavens archway now the rainbow seems to be
That spans the eternal round of earth and sky and sea

A shock, a moment, in the wrath of God
Is long as hell's eternity to all
His thunderbolts leave life but as the clod
Cold & inna[ni]mate—their temples fall
Beneath his frown to ashes—the eternal pall
Of wrath sleeps oer the ruins where they fell
And nought of memory may their creeds recall
The sin of Sodom was a moments yell   820
Fires death bed theirs their first grave the last hell

The towering willow with its pliant boughs
Sweeps its grey foliage to the autumn wind
The level grounds where oft a group of cows
Huddled together close—or propped behind
An hedge or hovel ruminate and find
The peace—as walks and health and I pursue
For natures every place is still resigned
To happiness   new life's in every view
And here I comfort seek and early joys renew   830

The lake that held a mirror to the sun
Now curves with wrinkles in the stillest place
The autumn wind sounds hollow as a gun
And water stands in every swampy place
Yet in these fens peace harmony and grace
The attributes of nature are alied
The barge with naked mast in sheltered place
Beside the brig close to the bank is tied
While small waves plashes by its bulky side

SONG

The floods come oer the meadow leas   840
The dykes are full and brimming
Field furrows reach the horses knees
Where wild ducks oft are swimming
The skyes are black the fields are bare
The trees their coats are loosing
The leaves are dancing in the air
The sun its warmth refusing

Brown are the flags and fadeing sedge
And tanned the meadow plains
Bright yellow is the osier hedge   850
Beside the brimming drains
The crows sit on the willow tree
The lake is full below
But still the dullest thing I see
Is self that wanders slow

The dullest scenes are not so dull
As thoughts I cannot tell
The brimming dykes are not so full
As my hearts silent swell
I leave my troubles to the winds   860
With none to share a part
The only joy my feeling finds
Hides in an aching heart

Abscence in love is worse then any fate
Summer is winters desert and the spring
Is like a ruined city desolate
Joy dies and hope retires on feeble wing
Nature sinks heedless—birds unheeded sing
Tis solitude in citys—crowds all move
Like living death—though all to life still cling—   870
The strongest bitterest thing that life can prove
Is womans undisguise of hate and love

SONG

I think of thee at early day
And wonder where my love can be
And when the evening shadows grey
O how I think of thee

Along the meadow banks I rove
And down the flaggy fen
And hope my first and early love
To meet thee once agen   880

I think of thee at dewy morn
And at the sunny noon
And walks with thee—now left forlorn
Beneath the silent moon

I think of thee I think of all
How blest we both have been—
The sun looks pale upon the wall
And autumn shuts the scene

I can't expect to meet thee now
The winter floods begin   890
The wind sighs through the naked bough
Sad as my heart within

I think of thee the seasons through
In spring when flowers I see
In winters lorn and naked view
I think of only thee

While life breaths on this earthly ball
What e'er my lot may be
Wether in freedom or in thrall
Mary I think of thee   900

Tis winter and the fields are bare and waste
The air one mass of 'vapour clouds and storms'
The suns broad beams are buried and oercast
And chilly glooms the midday light deforms
Yet comfort now the social bosom warms
Friendship of nature which I hourly prove
Even in this winter scene of frost and storms
Bare fields the frozen lake and leafless grove
Are natures grand religion and true love   /

SONG

Thourt dearest to my bosom   910
As thou wilt ever be
While the meadows wear a blossom
Or a leaf is on the tree

I can forget thee never—
While the meadow grass is green
While the flood rolls down the river
Thou art still my bonny queen

While the winter swells the fountain
While the spring awakes the bee
While the chamois loves the mountain   920
Thou'lt be ever dear to me
Dear as summer to the sun
As spring is to the bee
Thy love was soon as won
And so twill ever be

Thou'rt loves eternal summer
The dearest maid I prove
With bosom white as ivory
And warm as virgin love
No falsehood gets between us   930
Theres nought the tie can sever
As cupid dwells with venus
Thou'rt my own love forever

SONG

In this cold world without a home
Disconsolate I go
The summer looks as cold to me
As winters frost and snow
Though winters scenes are dull and drear
A colder lot I prove
No home had I through all the year   940
But Marys honest love

But Love inconstant as the wind
Soon shifts another way
No other home my heart can find
Life wasting day by day
I sigh and sit and sit and sigh
For better days to come
For Mary was my hope and joy
Her truth and heart my home

Her truth and heart was once my home   950
And May was all the year
But now through seasons as I roam
Tis winter everywhere
Hopeless I go through care and toil
No friend I e'er possest
To reccompence for Marys smile
And the love within her breast

My love was ne'er so blest as when
It mingled with her own
Told often to be told agen   960
And every feeling known
But now loves hopes are all bereft
A lonely man I roam
And abscent Mary long hath left
My heart without a home

27

The Paigles Bloom In Shower's In Grassy Close
How Sweet To Be Among Their Blossoms Led
And Hear Sweet Nature To Herself Discourse
While Pale The Moon Is Bering Over Head
And Hear The Grazeing Cattle Softly Tread   970
Cropping The Hedgerows Newly Leafing Thorn
Sounds Soft As Visions Murmured Oer In Bed
At Dusky Eve Or Sober Silent Morn
For Such Delights Twere Happy Man Was Born

3

Green bushes and green trees where fancy feeds
On the retireing solitudes of May
Where the sweet foliage like a volume reads
And weeds are gifts too choice to throw away
How sweet the evening now succeeds the day
The velvet hillock forms a happy seat   980
The white thorn bushes bend with snowey may
Dwarf furze in golden blooms and violets sweet
Make this wild scene a pleasure grounds retreat

18

Where are my 'friends' and childern where are they
The childern of two mothers born in joy
One roof has held them—'all' have been at play
Beneath the pleasures of a mothers eye
—And are my late hope's blighted—need I sigh
Hath care commenced his long perpetual reign
The spring and summer hath with me gone bye   990
Hope views the bud a flower and not in vain
Long is the night that brings no morn again

4

Now Come The Balm And Breezes Of The Spring
Not With The Pleasure's Of My Early Day's
When Nature Seemed One Endless Song To Sing
A Joyous Melody And Happy Praise
Ah Would They Come Agen—But Life Betrays
Quicksands And Gulphs And Storms That Howl And Sting
All Quiet Into Madness And Delays
Care Hides The Sunshine With Its Raven Wing   1000
And Hell Glooms Sadness Oer The Songs Of Spring

5

Like Satans Warcry First In Paradise
When Love Lay Sleeping On The Flowery Slope
Like Virtue Wakeing In The Arms Of Vice
Or Deaths Sea Bursting In The Midst Of Hope
Sorrows Will Stay—And Pleasures Will Elope
In The Uncertain Cartnty Of Care
Joys Bounds Are Narrow But A Wider Scope
Is Left For Trouble Which Our Life Must Bear
Of Which All Human Life Is More Or Less The Heir   1010

6

My Mind Is Dark And Fathomless And Wears
The Hues Of Hopeless Agony And Hell
No Plummet Ever Sounds The Souls Affairs
There Death Eternal Never Sounds The Knell
There Love Imprisoned Sighs The Long Farewell
And Still May Sigh In Thoughts No Heart Hath Penned
Alone In Loneliness Where Sorrows Dwell
And Hopeless Hope Hopes On And Meets No End
Wastes Without Springs And Homes Without A Friend

SONG

Say What Is Love—To Live In Vain   1020
To Live And Die And Live Again

Say What Is Love—Is It To Be
In Prison Still And Still Be Free

Or Seem As Free—Alone And Prove
The Hopeless Hopes of Real Love

Doe's Real Love On Earth Exist
Tis Like A Sun beam On The Mist

That Fades And No Where Will Remain
And Nowhere Is Oertook Again

Say What Is Love—A Blooming Name   1030
A Rose Leaf On The Page Of Fame

That Blooms Then Fades—To Cheat No More
And Is What Nothing Was Before

Say What Is Love—What E'er It be
It Center's Mary Still With Thee

7

What Is The Orphan Child without A Friend
That Knows No Fathers Care Or Mothers Love
No Leading Hand His Infant Steps Defend
And None To Notice But His God Above

No Joy's Are Seen His Little Heart To Move   1040
Care Turns All Joys to Dross And Nought To Gold
And Smiles In Fancys Time May Still Disprove
Growing To Cares And Sorrow's Menifold
Bird Of The Waste A Lamb Without A Fold

8

No Mothers Love or Fathers Care Have They
Left To The Storms Of Fate Like Creatures Wild
They Live Like Blossoms In The Winters Day
E'en Nature Frowns Upon The Orphan Child
On Whose Young Face A Mother Never Smiled
Foolhardy Care Increasing With His Years   1050
From Friends And Joys Of Every Kind Exiled
Even Old In Care The Infant Babe Appears
And Many A Mother Meets Its Face in Tears

9

The Dog Can Find A Friend And Seeks His Side
The Ass Can Know Its Owner And Is Fed
But None Are Known To Be The Orphans Guide
Toil Breaks His Sleep And Sorrow Makes His Bed
No Mothers Hand Holds Out The Sugared Bread
To Fill His Little Hand—He Hears No Song
To Please His Pouting Humours—Love Is Dead   1060
With Him And Will Be All His Whole Life Long
Lone Child Of Sorrow And Perpetual Wrong

10

But Providence That Grand Eternal Calm
Is With Him Like The Sunshine In The Sky
Nature Our Kindest Mother Void of Harm
Watches The Orphan's Lonely Infancy
Strengthening The Man When Childhoods Cares Are Bye
She Nurses Still Young Unreproached Distress
And Hears The Lonely Infants Every Sigh
Who Finds At Length To Make Its Sorrows Less   1070
Mid Earths Cold Curses There Is One To Bless

11

Sweet Rural Maids Made Beautifull By Health
Brought Up Where Natures Calm Encircles All
Where Simple Love Remains As Sterling Wealth
Where Simple Habits Early Joys Recall
Of Youthfull Feelings Which No Wiles Enthrall
The Happy Milk Maid In Her Mean Array
Fresh As The New Blown Rose Outblooms Them All
E'en Queens Might Sigh To Be As Blest As They
While Milkmaids Laugh And Sing Their Cares Away   1080

12

How Doth Those Scenes Which Rural Mirth Endears
Revise Old Feelings That My Youth Hath Known
And Paint The Faded Bloom Of Earlier Years
And Soften Feelings Petrefied To Stone
Joy Fled And Care Proclaimed Itself My Own
Farewells I Took Of Joys In Earliest Years
And Found The Greatest Bliss To Be Alone
My Manhood Was Eclipsed But Not In Fears
—Hell Came In Curses And She Laughd At Tears

13

But Memory Left Sweet Traces Of Her Smiles   1090
Which I Remember Still And Still Endure
The Shadows Of First Loves My Heart Beguiles
Time Brought Both Pain And Pleasure But No Cure
Sweet Bessey Maid Of Health And Fancys Pure
How Did I Woo Thee Once—Still Unforgot
But Promises In Love Are Never Sure
And Where We Met How Dear Is Every Spot
And Though We Parted Still I Murmur Not

14

For Loves However Dear Must Meet With Clouds
And Ties Made Tight Get Loose And May Be Parted   1100
Springs First Young Flowers The Winter Often Shrouds
And Loves First Hopes Are Very Often Thwarted

E'en Mine Beat High And Then Fell Broken Hearted
And Sorrow Mourned In Verse To Reconscile
My Feelings To My Fate Though Lone And Parted
Loves Enemies Are Like The Scorpion Vile
That Oer Its Ruined Hopes Will Hiss And Smile

BALLAD

The Blackbird Has Built In The Pasture Agen
And The Thorn Oer The Pond Shows A Delicate Green
Where I Strolled With Patty Adown In The Glen   1110
And Spent Summer Evenings And Sundays Unseen
How Sweet The Hill Brow
And The Low Of The Cow
And The Sunshine That Gilded The Bushes So Green
When Evening Brought Dews Natures Thirst To Allay
And Clouds Seemed To Nestle Round Hamlets And Farms
While In The Green Bushes We Spent The Sweet Day
And Patty Sweet Patty Was Still In My Arms

The Love Bloom That Redded Upon Her Sweet Lips
The Love Light That Glistened Within Her Sweet Eye   1120
The Singing Bees There That The Wild Honey Sips
From Wild Blossoms Seemed Not So Happy As I
How Sweet Her Smile Seemed
While The Summer Sun Gleamed
And The Laugh Of The Spring Shadowed Joys From On
    High
While The Birds Sung About Us And Cattle Grazed Round
And Beauty Was Blooming On Hamlets And Farms
How Sweet Steamed The Inscence Of Dew From The
    Ground
While Patty Sweet Patty Sat Locked In My Arms

15

Yet Love Lives On In Every Kind of Weather   1130
In Heat And Cold In Sunshine And In Gloom
Winter May Blight And Stormy Clouds May Gather
Nature Invigorates And Love Will Bloom

It Fears No Sorrow In A Life To Come
But Lives Within Itself From Year To Year
As Doth The Wild Flower In Its Own Perfume
As In The Lapland Snows Springs Blooms Appear
So True Love Blooms And Blossoms Every Where

BALLAD

The Rose Of The World Was Dear Mary To Me
In The Days Of My Boyhood And Youth   1140
I Told Her In Songs Where My Heart Wished To Be
And My Songs Where The Language of Truth

I Told Her In Looks When I Gazed In Her Eyes
That Mary Was Dearest To Me
I Told Her In Words And The Language Of Sighs
Where My Whole Hearts Affections Would Be

I Told her in love that all nature was true
I convinced her that nature was kind
But love in his trials had labour to do
[   ] Mary would be in the mind   1150

Mary met me in spring where the speedwell knots grew
And the king cups were shining like flame
I chose her all colours red yellow and blue
But my love was one hue and the same

Spring summer and winter and all the year through
In the sunshine the shower and the blast
I told the same tale and she knows it all true
And Mary's my blossom at last

16

Love is of heaven still the first akin
Twas born In paradise and left its home   1160
For desert lands stray hearts to nurse and win
Though pains like plagues pursue them where they roam

Its joys are ever green and blooms at home
The sailors rocking on the giddy mast
The soldier when the cannons cease to boom
And every heart its doubts or dangers past
Beats on its way for love and home at last

17

Nature thou truth of heaven if heaven be true
Falsehood may tell her ever changeing lie
But natures truth looks green in every view   1170
And love in every Landscape glads the eye
How beautifull these slopeing thickets lie
Woods on the hills and plains all smooth and even
Through which we see the ribboned evening skie
Though Winter here in floods and snows was driven
Spring came like God and turned it all to heaven

18

There Is A Tale For Every Day To Hear
For Every Heart To Feel And Tongue To Tell
The Daughters Anzious Dread The Lovers Fear
Pains That In Cots And Palaces May Dwell   1180
Not Short And Passing Like The Friends Farewell
Where Tears May Fall And Leave A Smile Beneath
Eternal Grief Rings In The Passing Bell
Tis Not The Sobs Of Momentary Breath
Ties Part Forever In The Tale Of Death

19

The Dew falls on the weed and on the flower
The rose and thistle bathe their heads in dew
The lowliest heart may have its prospering hour
The sadest bosom meet its wishes true
E'en I may joy love happiness renew   1190
Though not the sweets of my first early days
When one sweet face was all the loves I knew
And my soul trembled on her eyes to gaze
Whose very censure seemed intended praise

20

A soul within the heart that loves the more
Giving to pains and fears eternal life
Burning the flesh till it consumes the core
So Love is still the eternal calm of strife
Thou soul within a soul thou life of life
Thou Essence of my hopes and fears and joys   1200
M—y my dear first love and early wife
And still the flower my inmost soul enjoys
Thy love's the bloom no canker worm destroys

21

Flow on my verse though barren thou mayest be
Of thought—Yet sing and let thy fancys roll
In Early days thou sweept a mighty sea
All calm in troublous deeps and spurned controul
Thou fire and iceberg to an aching soul
And still an angel in my gloomy way
Far better opiate then the draining bowl   1210
Still sing my muse to drive cares fiends away
Nor heed what loitering listener hears the lay

22

My themes be artless cots and happy plains
Though far from man my wayward fancies flee
Of fields and woods rehearse in willing strains
And I mayhap may feed on joys with thee
These cowslip fields this sward my pillow be
So I may sleep the sun into the west
My cot this awthorn hedge this spreading tree
—Mary and Martha once my daily guests   1220
And still as mine both wedded loved and blest

23

I rest my wearied life in these sweet fields
Reflecting every smile in natures face
And much of joy this grass—These hedges yields
Not found in citys where crowds daily trace

Heart pleasures there hath no abideing place
The star gemmed early morn the silent even
Hath pleasures that our broken hopes deface
To love too well leaves nought to be forgiven
The Gates of Eden is the bounds of heaven   1230

24

The apathy that fickle love wears through
The doubts and certaintys are still akin
Its every joy has sorrow in the view
Its holy truth like Eve's beguileing sin
Seems to be losses even while we win
Tormenting joys and cheating into wrong
And still we love—and fall into the Gin
My sun of love was short—and clouded long
And now its shadow fills a feeble song

SONG

I saw her in my springs young choice   1240
Ere loves hopes looked upon the crowd
Ere loves first secrets found a voice
Or dared to speak the name aloud

I saw her in my boyish hours
A Girl as fair as heaven above
When all the world seemed strewn with flowers
And every pulse and look was love

I saw her when her heart was young
I saw her when my heart was true
When truth was all the themes I sung   1250
And Love the only muse I knew

Ere infancy had left her brow
I seemed to love her from her birth
And thought her then as I do now
The dearest angel upon earth

25

O she was more then fair—divinely fair
Can language paint the soul in those blue eyes
Can fancy read the feelings painted there
—Those hills of snow that on her bosom lies
Or beauty speak for all those sweet replies   1260
That through loves visions like the sun is breaking
Wakeing new hopes and fears and stifled sighs
From first love's dreame's my love is scarcely waking
The wounds might heal but still the heart is aching

26

Her looks was like the spring her very voice
Was springs own music more then song to me
Choice of my boyhood nay my souls first choice
From her sweet thralldom I am never free
Yet here my prison is a spring to me
Past memories bloom like flowers where e'er I rove   1270
My very bondage though in snares—is free
I love to stretch me in this shadey Grove
And muse upon the memories of love

Hail Solitude still Peace and Lonely good
Thou spirit of all joys to be alone
My best of friends these glades and this green wood
Where nature is herself and loves her own
The hearts hid anguish here I make it known
And tell my troubles to the gentle wind
Friends cold neglects have froze my heart to stone   1280
And wrecked the voyage of a quiet mind
With wives and friends and every hope disjoined

Wrecked of all hopes save one to be alone
Where Solitude becomes my wedded mate
Sweet Forest with rich beauties overgrown
Where solitude is queen and riegns in state
Hid in green trees I hear the clapping gate
And voices calling to the rambling cows
I Laugh at Love and all its idle fate
The present hour is all my lot alows   1290
An age of sorrow springs from lovers vows

Sweet is the song of Birds for that restores
The soul to harmony the mind to love
Tis natures song of freedom out of doors
Forests beneath free winds and clouds above
The Thrush and Nightingale and timid dove
Breathe music round me where the gipseys dwell—
Pierced hearts left burning in the doubts of love
Are desolate where crowds and citys dwell—
The splendid palace seems the gates of hell   1300

Don Juan A Poem°

'Poets are born'—and so are whores—the trade is
Grown universal—in these canting days
Women of fashion must of course be ladies
And whoreing is the business—that still pays
Playhouses Ball rooms—there the masquerade is
—To do what was of old—and now adays
Their maids—nay wives so innocent and blooming
Cuckold their spouses to seem honest women

Milton sung Eden and the fall of man
Not woman for the name implies a wh—e   10
And they would make a ruin of his plan
Falling so often they can fall no lower
Tell me a worse delusion if you can
For innoscence—and I will sing no more
Wherever mischief is tis womans brewing
Created from manself—to be mans ruin

The flower in bud hides from the fading sun
And keeps the hue of beauty on its cheek
But when full blown they into riot run
The hue turns pale and lost each ruddy streak   20
So 't'is with woman who pretends to shun
Immodest actions which they inly seek
Night hides the wh—e—cupboards tart and pasty
Flora was p–x–d—and womans quite as nasty

Marriage is nothing but a driveling hoax
To please old codgers when they're turned of forty
I wed and left my wife like other folks
But not untill I found her false and faulty
O woman fair—the man must pay thy jokes
Such makes a husband very often naughty   30
Who falls in love will seek his own undoing
The road to marriage is—'the road to ruin'°

Love worse then debt or drink or any fate
It is the damnest smart of matrimony
A hell incarnate is a woman-mate
The knot is tied—and then we loose the honey
A wife is just the protetype to hate
Commons for stock and warrens for the coney
Are not more tresspassed over in rights plan
Then this incumberance on the rights of man   40

There's much said about love and more of women
I wish they were as modest as they seem
Some borrow husbands till their cheeks are blooming
Not like the red rose blush—but yellow cream
Lord what a while those good days are in coming—
Routs Masques and Balls—I wish they were a dream
—I wish for poor men luck—an honest praxis
Cheap food and cloathing—no corn laws or taxes

I wish—but there is little got bye wishing
I wish that bread and great coats ne'er had risen   50
I wish that there was some such word as 'pishun'
For ryhme sake for my verses must be dizen
With dresses fine—as hooks with baits for fishing
I wish all honest men were out of prison
I wish M.P's. would spin less yarn—nor doubt
But burn false bills and cross bad taxes out

I wish young married dames were not so frisky
Nor hide the ring to make believe they're single
I wish small beer was half as good as whiskey
And married dames with buggers would not mingle   60

There's some too cunning far and some too frisky
And here I want a ryhme—so write down 'jingle'
And there's such putting in—in whores crim con
Some mouths would eat forever and eat on

Childern are fond of sucking sugar candy
And maids of sausages—larger the better
Shopmen are fond of good sigars and brandy
And I of blunt—and if you change the letter
To C or K it would be quite as handy
And throw the next away—but I'm your debtor   70
For modesty—yet wishing nought between us
I'd hawl close to a she as vulcan did to venus

I really cant tell what this poem will be
About—nor yet what trade I am to follow
I thought to buy old wigs—but that will kill me
With cold starvation—as they're beaten hollow°
Long speeches in a famine will not fill me
And madhouse traps still take me by the collar
So old wig bargains now must be forgotten
That oil that dressed them fine has made them rotten°   80

I wish old wigs were done with ere they're mouldy
I wish—but heres the papers large and lusty
With speeches that full fifty times they've told ye
—Noble Lord John to sweet Miss Fanny Fusty°
Is wed—a lie good reader I ne'er sold ye
—Prince Albert goes to Germany and must he°
Leave the queens snuff box where all fools are strumming
From addled eggs no chickens can be coming

Whigs strum state fiddle strings untill they snap
With cuckoo cuckold cuckoo year by year   90
The razor plays it on the barbers strap
—The sissars grinder thinks it rather quere
That labour wont afford him 'one wee drap'
Of ale or gin or half and half or beer
—I wish prince Albert and the noble dastards
Who wed the wives—would get the noble bastards

I wish prince Albert on his german journey
I wish the Whigs were out of office and
Pickled in law books of some good atorney
For ways and speeches few can understand   100
They'll bless ye when in power—in prison scorn ye
And make a man rent his own house and land—
I wish prince Alberts queen was undefiled
—And every man could get his *wife* with child

I wish the devil luck with all my heart
As I would any other honest body
His bad name passes bye me like a f—t
Stinking of brimstone—then like whisky toddy
We swallow sin which seems to warm the heart
—There's no imputing any sin to God—he   110
Fills hell with work—and is'n't it a hard case
To leave old whigs and give to hell the carcass

Me b—ne may throw his wig to little Vicky°
And so resign his humbug and his power
And she with the young princess mount the dickey°
On ass milk diet for her german tour°
Asses like ministers are rather tricky
I and the country proves it every hour
W–ll—gt–n and M–lb—n in their station
Coblers to queens—are phisic to the nation   120

These batch of toadstools on this rotten tree
Shall be the cabinet of any queen
Though not such coblers as her servants be
They're of Gods making—that is plainly seen
Nor red nor green nor orange—they are free
To thrive and flourish as the Whigs have been
But come tomorrow—like the Whigs forgotten
You'll find them withered stinking dead and rotten

Death is an awfull thing it is by God
I've said so often and I think so now   130
Tis rather droll to see an old wig nod
Then doze and die the devil don't know how

Odd things are wearisome and this is odd—
Tis better work then kicking up a row
I'm weary of old Whigs and old whigs heirs
And long been sick of teazing God with prayers

I've never seen the cow turn to a bull
I've never seen the horse become an ass
I've never seen an old brawn cloathed in whool—
But I have seen full many a bonny lass   140
And wish I had one now beneath the cool
Of these high elms—Muse tell me where I was
O—talk of turning I've seen Whig and Tory
Turn imps of hell—and all for Englands glory

I love good fellowship and wit and punning
I love 'true love' and God my taste defend
I hate most damnably all sorts of cunning—
I love the Moor and Marsh and Ponders end—°
I do not like the song of 'cease your funning'
I love a modest wife and trusty friend   150
—Bricklayers want lime as I want ryhme for fillups
—So here's a health to sweet Eliza Phillips°

SONG

Eliza now the summer tells
Of spots where love and beauty dwells
Come and spend a day with me
Underneath the forest tree
Where the restless water flushes
Over mosses mounds and rushes
And where love and freedom dwells
With orchis flowers and fox glove bells   160
Come dear Eliza set me free
And oer the forest roam with me

Here I see the morning sun
Among the beachtree's shadows run
That into gold the short sward turns
Where each bright yellow blossom burns

With hues that would his beams out shine
Yet nought can match those smiles of thine
I try to find them all the day
But none are nigh when thou'rt away   170
Though flowers bloom now on every hill
Eliza is the fairest still

The sun wakes up the pleasant morn
And finds me lonely and forlorn
Then wears away to sunny noon
The flowers in bloom the birds in tune
While dull and dowie all the year
No smiles to see no voice to hear
I in this forest prison lie
With none to heed my silent sigh   180
And underneath this beachen tree
With none to sigh for Love but thee

Now this new poem is entirely new
As wedding gowns or money from the mint
For all I know it is entirely true
For I would scorn to put a lie in print
—I scorn to lie for princes—so would you
And ere I shoot I try my pistol flint
—The cattle salesman—knows the way in trying
And feels his bullocks ere he thinks of buying   190

Lord bless me now the day is in the gloaming
And every evil thought is out of sight
How I should like to purchase some sweet woman
Or else creep in with my two wives to night—
Surely that wedding day is on the comeing
Abscence like phisic poisons all delight—
Mary and Martha both an evil omen
Though both my own—they still belong to no man

But to our text again—and pray where is it
Begin as parsons do at the beginning   200
Take the first line friend and you cannot miss it
'Poets are born' and so are whores for sinning

—Here's the court circular—o Lord is this it
Court cards like lists of—not the naked meaning
Here's Albert going to germany they tell us
And the young queen down in the dumps and jealous

Now you have seen a tramper on race courses
Seeking an honest penny as his trade is
Crying a list of all the running horses
And showing handbills of the sporting ladies   210
—In bills of fare you'll find a many courses
Yet all are innoscent as any maid is
Put these two dishes into one and dress it
And if there is a meaning—you may guess it

Don Juan was Ambassador from russia
But had no hand in any sort of tax
His orders hung like blossoms of the fushia
And made the ladies hearts to melt like wax
He knew Napoleon and the king of prusia
And blowed a cloud oer spirits wine or max   220
But all his profits turned out losses rather
To save one orphan which he forced to father

Theres Docter Bottle imp who deals in urine
A keeper of state prisons for the queen
As great a man as is the Doge of Turin
And save in London is but seldom seen
Yclep'd old A–ll–n—mad brained ladies curing
Some p–x–d like Flora and but seldom clean
The new road oer the forest is the right one
To see red hell and further on the white one   230

Earth hells or b–gg–r sh–ps or what you please
Where men close prisoners are and women ravished
I've often seen such dirty sights as these
I've often seen good money spent and lavished
To keep bad houses up for docters fees
And I have known a b–gg–rs tally travers'd
Till all his good intents began to falter
—When death brought in his bill and left the halter

O glorious constitution what a picking
Ye've had from your tax harvest and your tythe   240
Old hens which cluck about that fair young chicken
—Cocks without spurs that yet can crow so blythe
Truth is shut up in prison while ye're licking
The gold from off the gingerbread—be lythe
In winding that patched broken old state clock up
Playhouses open—but mad houses lock up

Give toil more pay where rank starvation lurches
And pay your debts and put your books to rights
Leave whores and playhouses and fill your churches
Old clovenfoot your dirty victory fights   250
Like theft he still on natures manor poaches
And holds his feasting on anothers rights
To show plain truth you act in bawdy farces
Men show their tools—and maids expose their arses

Now this day is the eleventh of July°
And being sunday I will seek no flaw
In man or woman—but prepare to die
In two days more I may that ticket draw
And so may thousands more as well as I
To day is here—the next who ever saw   260
And In a madhouse I can find no mirth pay
—Next tuesday used to be Lord Byrons birthday°

Lord Byron poh—the man wot rites the werses
And is just what he is and nothing more
Who with his pen lies like the mist disperses
And makes all nothing as it was before
Who wed two wives and oft the truth rehearses
And might have had some twenty thousand more
Who has been dead so fools their lies are giving
And still in Allens madhouse caged and living   270

If I do wickedness to day being sunday
Can I by hearing prayers or singing psalms
Clear off all debts twixt god and man on monday
And lie like an old hull that dotage calms

And is there such a word as Abergundy
I've read that poem called the 'Isle of Palms'°
—But singing sense pray tell me if I can
Live an old rogue and die an honest man

I wish I had a quire of foolscap paper
Hot pressed—and crowpens—how I could endite   280
A silver candlestick and green wax taper
Lord bless me what fine poems I would write
The very tailors they would read and caper
And mantua makers would be all delight
Though laurel wreaths my brows did ne'er environ
I think myself as great a bard as Byron

I have two wives and I should like to see them
Both by my side before another hour
If both are honest I should like to be them
For both are fair and bonny as a flower   290
And one o Lord—now do bring in the tea mem
Were bards pens steamers each of ten horse power
I could not bring her beautys fair to weather
So I've towed both in harbour blest together

Now i'n't this canto worth a single pound
From anybodys pocket who will buy
As thieves are worth a halter I'll be bound
Now honest reader take the book and try
And if as I have said it is not found
I'll write a better canto bye and bye   300
So reader now the money till unlock it
And buy the book and help to fill my pocket

[*'Tis martinmass from rig to rig'*]°

Tis martinmass from rig to rig
Ploughed fields and meadow lands are blea
In hedge and field each restless twig
Is dancing on the naked tree

Flags in the dykes are bleached and brown
Docks by its sides are dry and dead
All but the ivy bows are brown
Upon each leaning dotterels head

Crimsoned with awes the awthorns bend
Oer meadow dykes and rising floods   10
The wild geese seek the reedy fen
And dark the storm comes oer the woods
The crowds of lapwings load the air
With buzes of a thousand wings
There flocks of starnels too repair
When morning oer the valley springs

['*Lord hear my prayer when trouble glooms*']°

Lord hear my prayer when trouble glooms
Let sorrow find a way
And when the day of trouble comes
Turn not thy face away
My bones like hearth stones burn away
My life like vapoury smoke decays

My heart is smitten like the grass
That withered lies and dead
And I so lost to what I was
Forget to eat my bread   10
My voice is groaning all the day
My bones prick through this skin of clay

The wildernesses pelican
The deserts lonely owl
I am their like a desert man
In ways as lone and foul
As sparrows on the cottage top
I wait till I with faintness drop

I bear my enemies reproach
All silently I mourn   20
They on my private peace encroach
Against me they are sworn
Ashes as bread my trouble shares
And mix my food with weeping cares

Yet not for them is sorrows toil
I fear no mortals frown
But thou hast held me up awhile
And thou hast cast me down
My days like shadows waste from view
I mourn like withered grass in dew   30

But thou Lord shalt endure forever
All generations through
Thou shalt to Zion be the giver
Of joy and mercey too
Her very stones are in their trust
Thy servants reverence her dust

Heathens shall hear and fear thy name
All kings of earth thy glory know
When thou shalt build up Zions fame   40
And live in glory there below
He'll not despise their prayers though mute
But still regard the destitute

Spring°

The sweet spring now is come'ng
In beautifull sunshine
Thorns bud and wild flowers blooming
Daisey and Celadine
Somthing so sweet there is about the spring
Silence is music ere the birds will sing

And theres the hedgerow pootys
Blackbirds from mossy cells
Pick them where the last year's shoot is
Hedge bottoms and wood dells   10
Stript, spotted, yellow, red, to spring so true
For which the schoolboy looks with pleasures new

On gates the yellow hammer
As bright as Celadine
Sits—green linnets learn to stammer
And Robins sing divine
On brown land furrows stalks the crow
And magpies on the moor below

In small hedged closes lambkins stand
Its cud the heifer chews   20
Like snow clumps upon fallow land
They shine among the Ewes
Or sheets of water by moonlight
The Lambkins shine so very white

The lane the narrow lane
With daisy beds beneath
You scarce can see the light again
Untill you reach the heath
Thorn hedges grow and meet above
For half a mile a green alcove   30

The netles by garden walls°
Stand angrily and dun
Summer on them like poison falls
And all their blossoms shun
The abby's haunted heaps of stone
Is by their treachery overgrown

Theres verdure in the stony street
Decieving earnest eyes
The bare rock has its blossom's sweet
The micriscope espies   40
Flowers leaves and foliage every where
That cloaths the animated year

Fields meadows woods and pastures
Theres spring in every place
From winters wild disasters
All wear her happy face
Beast on their feet and birds upon the wing
The very clouds upon the sky look spring

Sunshine presses by the hedge
And there's the pileworts sure to come   50
The primrose by the rustling sedge
And largest cowslips first in bloom
All show that spring is every where
The flowery herald of the year

Song Last Day

There is a day a dreadfull day
Still following the past
When sun and moon are past away
And mingle with the blast
There is a vision in my eye
A vacuum oer my mind
Sometimes as on the sea I lye
Mid roaring waves and wind

When valleys rise to mountain waves
And mountains sink to seas   10
When towns and cities temples graves
All vanish like a breeze
The skyes that was are past and oer
That almanack of days
Year chronicles are kept no more
Oblivions ruin pays

Pays in destruction shades and hell
Sin goes in darkness down
And therein sulphurs shadows dwell
Worth wins and wears the crown   20

The very shore if shore I see
All shrivelled to a scroll
The Heaven's rend away from me
And thunders sulphurs roll

Black as the deadly thunder cloud
The stars shall turn to dun
And heaven by that darkness bowed
Shall make days light be done
When stars and skys shall all decay
And earth no more shall be   30
When heaven itself shall pass away
Then thou'lt remember me

['*The red bagged bee on never weary wing*']

The red bagged bee on never weary wing
Pipe's his small trumpet round the early flowers
And the white nettles by the hedge in spring
Hears his low music all the sunny hours
Till clouds come on and leaves the falling showers
Herald of spring and music of wild blooms
It seems the minstrel of springs early flowers
On banks where the red nettle flowers it comes
And there all the long sunny morning hums

['*Summer is on the earth and in the sky*']

Summer is on the earth and in the sky
The days all sunny and the fields all green
The woods spread oer her hills a canophy
Of beautys harmony in every scene
Like to a map the fields and valleys lie
Winds dash in wildest motions the woods green
And every wave of leaves and every billow
Lies in the sun like Beauty on a pillow

There is a freshness in the leafy sprays
That dashes oer the forest from the wind   10
The wild sublimity of windy days
Like the rich thinkings of a master mind
Or dashes on the canvass none can find
In works inferior—when the woods all blaze
With a wild sunset and the winds unbind
Their foliage to the heavens wild amaze
Field meadow wood rolling oer stormy days

The roaring of the woods is like a sea
All thunder and comotion to the shore
The old oaks toss their branches to be free   20
And urge the fury of the storm the more
Louder then thunder is the sobbing roar
Of leafy billows to their shore the sky
Round which the bloodshot clouds like fields of gore
In angry silence did at anchor lie
As if the battles roar was not yet bye

Anon the wind has ceased the woods are still
The winds are sobbed to sleep and all is rest
The clouds like solid rocks too jagged for hills
Lie quietly ashore upon the west   30
The cottage ceases rocking—each tired guest
Sleeps sounder for the heavy storm's uproar
—How calm the sunset blazes in the west
As if the waking storm would burst no more
And this still even seems more calmer than before

Song

The bird cherrys white in the dews o' the morning
The wildings are blushing along the hedgeside
The gold blossomed furze the wild heaths are adorning
And the brook in the hollow runs light by my side
But where is the charmer the voice of the maiden
Whose presence once charmed me the whole summers day
The bushes wi' gold and wi' silver oerlaiden
Looks cold i' the morning when Phebe's away

The sun rises bright oer the oaks in the spinney
Bringing gold unto gold on the winbushes there   10
Blossoming bright as a new minted guinea
And moist wi' the mist of the morns dewy air
The flower is bowed down and I let the tired Bee be
All wet wi' night dew and unable to flye
Such a kindness in me would be pleasure to Phebe
A poor trampled Insect would cause her to sigh

The white thorn is coming wi' bunches of blossoms
The broad sheets of daiseys spread out on the lea
The bunches of cowslips spread out their gold bosoms
While the oak balls appear on the old spinney tree   20
Come forward my Phebe wi' dews of the morning
By the old crooked brook let thy early walk be
Where the brambles arched stalks—glossy leaves are adorning
And bits o' woo' hang on the bark o' the tree

Come forward my Phebe by times in the morning
Come forward my Phebe in blebs o' the dew
They bead the young cowslip like pearls i' the dawning
And we'll mark the young shower where the green linnet flew
I'll court thee and woo thee from morning to e'ening
Where the primrose looks bright in the ivy's dark green   30
And the oak oer the brook in its white bark is leaning
There let me and Phebe wi' morning be seen

['*The thunder mutters louder and more loud*']

The thunder mutters louder and more loud
With quicker motion hay folks ply the rake
Ready to burst slow sails the pitch black cloud
And all the gang a bigger haycock make
To sit beneath—the woodland winds awake
The drops so large wet all thro' in an hour
A tiney flood runs down the leaning rake
In the sweet hay yet dry the hay folks cower
And some beneath the waggon shun the shower

[*'Look through the naked bramble and black thorn'*]

Look through the naked bramble and black thorn
And see the arum show its vivid green
Glossy and rich and some ink spotted like the morn
Ing sky with clouds—in sweetest neuks Ive been°
And seen the arum sprout its happy green
Full of spring visions and green thoughts o' may
Dead leaves a' litter where its leaves are seen
Broader and brighter green from day to day
Beneath the hedges in their leafless spray

[*'I love the little pond to mark at spring'*]

I love the little pond to mark at spring
When frogs and toads are croaking round its brink
When blackbirds yellow bills gin first to sing
And green woodpecker rotten trees to clink
I love to see the cattle muse and drink
And water crinkle to the rude march wind
While two ash dotterels flourish on its brink
Bearing key bunches children run to find
And water buttercups they're forced to leave behind

Spring

Pale sun beams gleam
That nurtur a few flowers
Pile wort and daisey and a sprig o' green
On white thorn bushes
In the leaf strewn hedge

These harbingers
Tell spring is coming fast
And these the schoolboy marks
And wastes an hour from school
Agen the old pasture hedge

10

Cropping the daisey
And the pile wort flowers
Pleased with the Spring and all he looks upon
He opes his spelling book
And hides her blossoms there

Shadows fall dark
Like black in the pale Sun
And lye the bleak day long
Like black stock under hedges
And bare wind rocked trees   20

Tis chill but pleasant
In the hedge bottom lined
With brown seer leaves the last
Year littered there and left
Mopes the hedge Sparrow

With trembling wings and cheeps
Its welcome to pale sunbeams
Creeping through and further on
Made of green moss
The nest and green blue eggs are seen   30

All token spring and every day
Green and more green hedges and close
And every where appears
Still tis but March
But still that March is Spring

[*The wind blows happily on every thing*]

The wind blows happily on every thing
The very weeds that shake beside the fold
Bowing they dance—do any thing but sing
And all the scene is lovely to behold
Blue mists of morning evenings of gold
How beautifull the wind will play with spring
Flowers beam with every colour light beholds
Showers oer the Landscape flye on wet pearl wings
And winds stir up unnumbered pleasant things

I love the luscious green before the bloom   10
The leaves and grass and even beds of moss
When leaves gin bud and spring prepares to come
The Ivys evergreen the brown green gorse
Plots of green weeds that barest roads engross
In fact I love the youth of each green thing
The grass the trees the bushes and the moss
That pleases little birds and makes them sing
I love the green before the blooms of spring

[*'God looks on nature with a glorious eye'*]

God looks on nature with a glorious eye
And blesses all creation with the sun
Its drapery of green and brown earth ocean lie
In morning as Creation just begun
That safforn east fortells the riseing sun
And who can look upon that majesty
Of light brightness and splendour nor feel won
With love of him whose bright all seeing eye
Feeds the days light with Immortallity

[*'I'll come to thee at even tide'*]°

I'll come to thee at even tide
When the west is streaked wi grey
I'll wish the night thy charms to hide
And daylight all away
I'll come to thee at set o' sun
Where white thorns i' the May
I'll come to thee when work is done
And love thee till the day

When Daisey stars are all turned green
And all is meadow grass   10
I'll wander down the bank at e'en
And court the bonny Lass

The green banks and the rustleing sedge
I'll wander down at e'en
All slopeing to the waters edge
And in the water green

And theres the luscious meadow sweet
Beside the meadow drain
My lassie there I once did meet
Who I wish to meet again   20
The water lilies where in flower
The yellow and the white
I met her there at even's hour
And stood for half the night

We stood and loved in that green place
When sundays sun got low
Its beams reflected in her face
The fairest thing below
My sweet Ann Foot my bonny Ann°
The Meadow banks are green   30
Meet me at even when you can
Be mine as you have been

['Spring comes and it is may—white as are sheets']

Spring comes and it is may—white as are sheets
Each orchard shines besides its little town
Childern at every bush a poesy meets
Bluebells and primroses—wandering up and down
To hunt birds nests and flowers and a stones throw from town
And hear the blackbird in the coppice sing
Green spots appear like doubling a book down
To find the place agen and strange birds sing
We have [no] name for in the burst of Spring

The Sparrow comes and chelps about the Slates   10
And pops in to her hole beneath the Eaves
While the cock piegon amourously awaits
The Hen on barn ridge cooing and then leaves

With crop all ruffles—where the sower heaves
The hopper at his side his beans to sow
There he with timid coveys harmless thieves
And whirls around the teams and then drops low—
While plops the sudden Gun and great the overthrow

Song

O Love is so decieving
Like bee's it wears a sting
I thought it true believing
But its no such a thing
They smile but to decieve you
They kiss and then they leave you
Speak truth they wont believe you
Their honey wears a Sting

What's the use o' pretty faces
Ruby Lips and cheeks so red   10
Flowers grows in pleasant places
So does a maidenhead
The fairest wont believe you
The foulest all decieve you
The many laugh and grieve you
Untill your coffin dead

Love's Pains°

1

This love, I canna' bear it,
It cheats me night and day;
This love, I canna' wear it,
It takes my peace away.

2

This love, wa' once a flower;
But now it is a thorn,—
The joy o' evening hour,
Turn'd to a pain e're morn.

3

This love, it wa' a bud,
And a secret known to me;   10
Like a flower within a wood;
Like a nest within a tree.

4

This love, wrong understood,
Oft' turned my joy to pain;
I tried to throw away the bud,
But the blossom would remain.

July 13th 1844

Haymaking

1

Among the meadow hay cocks
    'Tis beautiful to lie
When pleasantly the day looks
    And gold like is the sky

2

How lovely looks the hay-swarth
    When turning to the sun
How richly looks the dark path
    When the rickings all are done

3

There's nothing looks more lovely
    As a meadow field in cock   10
There's nothing sounds more sweetly
    As the evenings six o'clock

4

There's nothing sounds so welcome
    As their singing at their toil
Sweet maidens with tan'd faces
    And bosoms fit to broil

5

And its beautiful to look on
  How the hay-cleared meadow lies
How the sun pours down his welcome heat
  Like gold from yonder skies   20

6

There's a calm upon the level
  When the sun is getting low
Smooth as a lawn is the green level
  Save where swarths their pointings shew

7

There the mother makes a journey
  With a babbie at her breast
While the sun is fit to burn ye
  On the sabath day at rest

8

There's nothing like such beauty
  With a woman ere compares   30
Unless the love within her arms
  The infant which she heirs.

Song°

O WERT THOU IN THE STORM

1

O wert thou in the storm,
  How I would shield thee:
To keep thee dry and warm,
  A camp I would build thee.

2

Though the clouds pour'd again,
  Not a drop should harm thee;
The music of wind, and rain,
  Rather should charm thee.

3

O wert thou in the storm,
  A shed I would build thee;   10
To keep thee dry and warm,—
  How I would shield thee.—

4

The rain should not wet thee,
  Nor thunder clap harm thee.
By thy side I would sit me,—
  To comfort, and warm thee.

5

I would sit by thy side love,
  While the dread storm was over;—
And the wings of an angel,
  My charmer would cover.   20

July 25th 1844

Mary

1

It is the evening hour,
  How silent all doth lie,
The horned moon she shews her face,
  In the river, with the sky;
Just by the path on which we pass,
The flaggy lake, lies still, as glass.

2

Spirit of her I love,
  Wispering to me:
Stories of sweet visions, as I rove:
  Here stop and crop with me,   10
Sweet flowers, that in the still hour grew,
We'll take them home, nor shake off the bright dew.

3

Mary, or sweet spirit of thee,
  As the bright sun shines tomorrow;
Thy dark eyes these flowers shall see,
  Gathered by me in sorrow,
In the still hour, when my mind was free,
To walk alone—yet wish I walk'd with thee.

To Mary

1

I sleep with thee, and wake with thee,
And yet thou art not there:—
I fill my arms, with thoughts of thee,
And press the common air.—
Thy eyes are gazing upon mine,
When thou art out of sight;
My lips are always touching thine,
At morning, noon, and night.

2

I think, and speak of other things,
To keep my mind at rest: 10
But still to thee, my memory clings,
Like love in womans breast;—
I hide it from the worlds-wide eye;
And think, and speak contrary;
But soft, the wind comes from the sky,
And wispers tales of Mary.—

3

The night wind wispers in my ear,
The moon shines in my face;
A burden still of chilling fear,
I find in every place.—   20
The breeze is wispering in the bush;
And the dew-fall from the tree,
All; sighing on, and will not hush,
Some pleasant tales of thee.—

A Vision

1

I lost the love, of heaven above;
I spurn'd the lust, of earth below;
I felt the sweets of fancied love,—
And hell itself my only foe.

2

I lost earths joys, but felt the glow,
Of heaven's flame abound in me:
'Till loveliness, and I did grow,
The bard of immortality.

3

I loved, but woman fell away;
I hid me, from her faded fame: 10
I snatch'd the sun's eternal ray,—
And wrote 'till earth was but a name.

4

In every language upon earth,
On every shore, o'er every sea;
I gave my name immortal birth,
And kep't my spirit with the free.

Augst 2nd 1844

The Droneing Bee

1

The droneing bee has wakened up,
And humming round the buttercup:
And round the bright star daisy hums;—
O'er every blade of grass he passes—
The dew-drop shines like looking glasses;
In every drop a bright sun comes:—
'Tis march, and spring, bright days we see,—
Round every blossom hums the bee.

2

As soon as daylight in the morning,
The crimson curtains of the dawning,—   10
We hear, and see, the humming bee,—
Searching for hedge row violets,
Happy with the food he gets:—
Swimming o'er brook, and meadow lea;—
Then sits on maple stools at rest,
On the green mosses velvet breast.

3

About the molehill, round, and round,
The wild bee hums with honied sound,—
Singing a song, of spring, and flowers,—
To school-boys heard in sunny hours.   20
When all the waters seem a blaze,
Of fire, and sunshine in such days;
When bee's buzz on with coal black eye;
Joined by the yellow butterfly.

4

And when it comes, a summer shower;
It still will go from flower, to flower;
Then underneath the rushes,—
It sees the silver daisy flower,
And there it spends a little hour
Then hides among the bushes   30
But whence they come from, where they go
None but the wiser schoolboy's know.

To the Lark

Bird of the morn
When roseate clouds begin
To shew the opening dawn
Thy singing does begin
And oer the sweet green fields and happy vales
Thy pleasant song is heard mixed with the morning gales

Bird of the morn
What time the ruddy sun
Smiles on the pleasant corn
Thy singing is begun   10
Heartfelt and cheering over labours toil
Who chop in coppice wild and delve the russet soil

Bird of the sun
How beautifull art thou
When morning has begun
To gild the mountains brow
How beautifull it is to see thee soar so blest
Winnowing thy russet wings above thy twitchy nest

Bird of the summers day
How oft I stand to hear   20
Thee sing thy airy way
With music wild and clear
Till thou becomes a speck upon the sky
Small as those clods that crumble where I lye

Thou bird of happiest song
The spring and summer too
Is thine the months along
The woods and vales to view
If climes were ever green thy song would be
The sunny music of eternal glee   30

Sonnet

Enough of misery keeps my heart alive
To make it feel more mental agony
Till even life itself becomes all pain
And bondage more than hell to keep alive
And still I live, nor murmer nor complain
Save that the bonds which hold me may make free
My lonely solitude, and give me rest
When every foe hath ceased to trouble me
On the soft throbbings of a womans breast

Where love and truth and feeling live confest 10
The little cottage with those bonds of joy
My family—lifes blood within my breast
Is not more dear—than is each girl and boy
Which times matures and nothing can destroy.

A Lament

1

The sun looks from a cloudy sky,
    On yellow bleaching reeds.—
The river streams run muddy by,
    Among the flags and reeds.
And nature seems so lost and coy,
    All silent and alone;
Left here without a single joy,
    Or love to call my own.

2

How mournful now the river seems,
    Adown the vale to run; 10
That ran so sweet in my young dreams,
    And glittered in the sun.
Now cold and dead, the meadow lies,
    And muddy runs the stream:
The lark on drooping pinion flies,—
    And spoiled is pleasures dream.

3

The wind comes moaning through the trees,—
    No maiden passes by.
And all the summer melodies,—
    Are uttered in a sigh. 20
On many a knoll I set me down,
    Beneath a silent sky,
And of the past all seem to frown,
    And pass in sorrow by.

Song°

A seaboy on the giddy mast
Sees nought but ocean waves
And hears the wild inconstant blast
Where loud the tempest raves

My life is like the ocean wave
And like the inconstant sea
In every hope appears a grave
And leaves no hope for me

My life is like the oceans lot
Bright gleams the morning gave   10
But storms oerwhelmed the sunny spot
Deep in the ocean wave

My life hath been the ocean storm
A black and troubled sea
When shall I find my life a calm
A port and harbour free

Song

The daiseys golden eye
On the fallow land doth lie
Though the spring is just begun
Pewets watch it all the day
And the sky larks nest of hay
Leans agen its group of leaves in the sun

Theres the pilewort all in gold
Neath that ridge of finest mould
Blooms to cheer the ploughmans eye
There the mouse his hole hath made   10
And beneath its golden shade
Hides secure when the hawk is prowling bye

Heres the speedwells sapphire blue
Was there anything more true
To the vernal season still
Here it decks the bank alone
Where the milkmaid throws a stone
At morn to cross the flooded rill

Here the cowslap chill with cold
On the rushy bed behold   20
Looking for [the] spring all day
Where the heavy bee will come
And find no sweets at home
Then quakes his weary wings and flyes away

And here are nameless flowers
Culled from cold and rawky hours
For Marys happy home
They grew in murky blea
Rush fields and naked lea
But suns will shine and pleasing spring will come   30

Autumn

I

The autumn day it fades away,
The fields are wet and dreary;
The rude storm takes the flowers of may,
And nature seemeth weary.
The partridge coveys shunning fate,
Hide in the bleaching stubble;
And many a bird without its mate,
Mourns o'er its lonely trouble.

2

On awthorns shine the crimson awe,
Where spring brought may-day blossoms;   10
Decay is natures cheerless law,
Life's winter in our bosoms.

The fields are brown and naked all,
But hedges still are green:
But storms shall come at autumns fall,
And not a leaf be seen!

3

Yet happy love that warms the heart,
Through darkest storms severe;
Keeps many a tender flower to start,—
When spring shall reappear,   20
Affections hope shall roseys meet;
Like those of summer bloom:—
And joys, and flowers, smell as sweet,
In seasons yet to come.

Sonnet

The flag top quivers in the breeze,
That sighs among the willow trees:
In gentle waves the river heaves,
That sways like boats the lily leaves:
The bent grass trembles, as with cold;
And crow flowers nod their cups of gold,
Till every dew-drop in them found,
Is gently shook upon the ground.
Each wild weed, by the river side,
In different motions dignified,   10
Bows to the wind, quakes to the breeze,
And charms sweet summers harmonies.
The very nettle quakes away,
To glad the summers happy day.

Out of Door Pleasures

The day is all round me the woods and the fields
And sweet is the singing their birds music yields
The waterfall music, there's none such at home
It spreads like a sheet, and then falls into foam

The meadows are mown, what a beautiful hue
There is in green closes as I wander through
A green of all colors, yellow, brown and dark grey
While the footpaths all darkly goes winding away
Creeping on to a foot-brig that crosses a brook
Or a gate, or a stile, and how rustic they look   10
Some leaning so much that the maidens will go
Lower down with their buckets, and try to creep through
There is nothing more sweet in the fields and the sun
Than those dear little footpaths that o'er the fields run
They lead us by maidens all making of hay
While we seem to steal kisses as we bid them good day
They lead us to springs with a stone by the brink
All ready to kneel on, to stoop down and drink
They lead us by bushes, all bowering and sweet
Where the wild thyme has cushioned mole-hills for a seat   20
And the wild thyme smells sweet, as we sit by the stile
And the green-linnet keeps on her nest all the while
The road smokes with dust as the oxen and sheep
Go mile after mile 'till they scarcely can creep
A hugh cloud of dust all the coaches conceals
They are hid in the smoak that flies up from the wheels
The dust like a cloud whirleth up all the day
As coaches and coaches keep flying away
Here nothing in nature displeases the eye
Out of doors there's the fields and the beautiful sky   30
There's the weeds by the hedge and the flowers in the grass
And everything pleases, wherever we pass
This grove of tall elms with their dark sombre green
How sweet their old shadows beneath them are seen
In the heat of the day how delicious to pass
As cool as an ice house, or the dews on the grass
Where every where else, it is scorching, and sear
But here it is pleasant throughout the whole year
The closes are mown, and the haytime is done
And the stacks stand about bleaching brown in the sun   40
The naked shorn sheep, and the sleek looking cows
Are turned in the eddish in quiet to browse
Out of doors we see nothing but pleasure and good
'Tis the greenness of childhood in valley and wood
Good health out of doors is all that we see

Where nature and quiet are happy and free
Oh! there's nought so delightful as the woods and the fields
And the out-of-doors pleasures their sweet music yields.
O powers of mans destiny give me but these
With my wife and my children at evening to please.   50

An Invite to Eternity

1

Wilt thou go with me sweet maid
Say maiden wilt thou go with me
Through the valley depths of shade
Of night and dark obscurity
Where the path hath lost its way
Where the sun forgets the day
Where there's nor life nor light to see
Sweet maiden wilt thou go with me

2

Where stones will turn to flooding streams
Where plains will rise like ocean waves   10
Where life will fade like visioned dreams
And mountains darken into caves
Say maiden wilt thou go with me
Through this sad non-identity
Where parents live and are forgot
And sisters live and know us not

3

Say maiden wilt thou go with me
In this strange death of life to be
To live in death and be the same
Without this life, or home, or name   20
At once to be, and not to be
That was, and is not—yet to see
Things pass like shadows—and the sky
Above, below, around us lie

4

The land of shadows wilt thou trace
And look—nor know each others face
The present mixed with reasons gone
And past, and present all as one
Say maiden can thy life be led
To join the living with the dead   30
Then trace thy footsteps on with me
We're wed to one eternity

Sonnet

The silver mist more lowly swims
And each green bosomed valley dims
And o'er the neighbouring meadow lies
Like half seen visions by dim eyes
Green trees look grey, bright waters black
The lated crow has lost her track
And flies by guess her journey home

She flops along and cannot see
Her peaceful nest on odlin tree
The lark drops down and cannot meet   10
The taller black grown clumps of wheat
The mists that rise from heat of day
Fades field and meadow all away

Morning

The morning comes—the drops of dew
Hang on the grass and bushes too
The sheep more eager bite the grass
Whose moisture gleams like drops of glass
The hiefer licks in grass and dew
That makes her drink and fodder too
The little bird his morn song gives
His breast wet with the dripping leaves

Then stops abruptly just to fly
And catch the wakened butterfly   10
That goes to sleep behind the flowers
Or backs of leaves from dews and showers
The yellowhammer haply blest
Sits by the dyke upon her nest
The long grass hides her from the day
The water keeps the boys away
The morning sun is round and red
As crimson curtains round a bed
The dew drops hang on barley horns
As beads the necklace thread adorns   20
The dew drops hang wheat ears upon
Like golden drops against the sun
Hedge-sparrows in the bush cry 'tweet'
O'er nests larks winnow in the wheat
'Till the sun turns gold and gets more high
And paths are clean, and grass gets dry
And longest shadows pass away
And brightness is the blaze of day.

Wild Flowers

1

Beautiful mortals of the glowing earth
And children of the season crowd together
In showers and sunny weather
Ye beautiful spring hours
Sunshine and all together
  I love wild flowers

2

The rain drops lodge on the swallows wing
Then fall on the meadow flowers
Cowslips and enemonies all come with spring
Beaded with first showers   10
The skylarks in the cowslips sing
  I love wild flowers

3

Blue-bells and cuckoo's in the wood
And pasture cuckoo's too
Red yellow white and blue
Growing where herd cows meet the showers
And lick the morning dew
　　I love wild flowers

4

The lakes and rivers—summer hours
All have their bloom as well　　　　　　　　　　20
But few of these are childrens flowers
They grow where dangers dwell
In sun and shade and showers
　　I love wild flowers

5

They are such lovely things
And make the very seasons where they come
The nightingale is smothered where she sings
Above their scented bloom
O what delight the cuckoo music brings
　　I love wild flowers　　　　　　　　　　　30

The Invitation

1

Let us go in the fields love and see the green tree
Let's go in the meadows and hear the wild bee
There's plenty of pleasure for you love and me
　　In the mirth and the music of nature
We can stand in the path love and hear the birds sing
And see the woodpigeon snap loud on the wing
While you stand beside me a beautiful thing
　　Health and beauty in every feature.

2

We can stand by the brig-foot and see the bright things
On the sun shining water, that merrily springs   10
Like sparkles of fire in their mazes and rings
    While the insects are glancing and twitters
You see naught in shape but hear a deep song
That lasts through the sunshine the whole summer long
That pierces the ear as the heat gathers strong
    And the lake like a burning fire glitters.

3

We can stand in the field love and gaze o'er the corn
See the lark from her wing shake the dews of the morn
Through the dew beaded woodbine the gale is just born
    And there we can wander my dearie   20
We can walk by the wood where the rabbits pop in
Where the bushes are few, and the hedge gapped and thin
There's a wild-rosy bower and a place to rest in
    So we can walk in and rest when we're weary.

4

The skylark my love from the barley is singing
The hare from her seat of wet clover is springing
The crow to its nest on the tall elm swinging
    Bears a mouthful of worms for its young
We'll down the green meadow, and up the lone glen
And down the woodside far away from all men   30
And there we'll talk over our love tales again
    Where last year the nightingale sung.

Sonnet

THE NIGHTINGALE

This is the month, the Nightingale, clod-brown,
    Is heard among the woodland shady boughs;
This is the time when, in the vale, grass-grown
    The maiden hears at eve, her lovers vows.
    What time the blue mist, round her patient cows,

Dim rises from the grass, and half conceals
   Their dappled hides,—I hear the Nightingale,
That from the little blackthorn spinny steals,
   To the old hazel hedge that skirts the vale,
And still unseen, sings sweet:—the ploughman feels   10
   The thrilling music, as he goes along,
And imitates and listens,—while the fields
   Lose all their paths in dusk, to lead him wrong
Still sings the Nightingale her sweet melodious song.

June 12./44.

Spring

1

How beautiful is Spring! the sun gleams gold,
   Reflecting like a mirror, burnished ever;
The skylark from the eddings near the fold,
   Mounts up and sings!—bright gleams the flowing river
Full to the brim!—Winter is gone! and never
   Attempts his scattered force to bring
Against such burnished scenes;—the true believer
   Sees flowers in bloom and hears the woodlands ring,
   With joys awake:—how beautiful is Spring!—

2

Poesy of seasons! scripture of the year!   10
   Whose buds put forth in promise to the sun,
And at their resurrection shall appear
   Hued in all colours, as from rainbows won,—
Gold, blue, green, red, and white! the meadows run,
A garden world of bloom, and richly fling
   Incense to every wind, and shower, and sun;
Music unceasing, woods and valleys bring
From birds about their nests! how beautiful is Spring!

3

The daisy's golden eye and silver rim
  Crow every pasture like a fall of snow   20
And pilewort, where earth's diadems grow dim,
    Stud emerald grass with gold where'er they grow
    Spring flowers flood earth in showers to overflow;—
Meadow and close and pingle, where suns cling,
    And shine on earliest flowers,—there they shew
Their rainbow maps of loveliness; and bring
Their painted crowds,—so beautiful is Spring!

4

Anemonies and lilies of the valley
  Cover whole acres of the forest glade;
And blue-bells, that in woods and spinneys dally,   30
    Beneath the oak tree and the hazel's shade.
    The bushiest place is like a carpet made;
No copse so thick, but there their blooms they bring,
    No spot so cold but meets their purple shade;
In every place where feathered warblers sing,
Wild flowers in armies come!—so beautiful is Spring.

5

The garish Summer comes with many tribes
  Of gay and gaudy flowers, in bright array;
But the hot sun the cloudy morning bribes,
    And dries all moisture with his scorching ray;—   40
    Corn-poppies oft a scarlet host display,—
The oak woods green, like rocky masses hing
    On wooded hills,—the willows waving grey,
Hang mournful in the stream;—birds cease to sing:—
The sweetest poesy of the year is Spring!—

Ballad

1

We'll walk among the tedded hay,
  That smel[l]s as sweet as flowers;
While the meadow water winds its way
  Beneath the hawthorn bowers.

2

And when the bright green haycocks throw
  Their shadows from the sun,
When thou art weary there we'll go,
  And rest, the heat to shun.

3

We'll to the hawthorn shades retire,
  Where blooms the wild dog rose;   10
And smell the sweetly scented briar,
  Where the shining river flows.

4

We'll talk o'er joys we once could prove,
  And blithely spend the day,
For those pleasant dreams of early youth
  Can never pass away.

                  June 18/44.

Evening

1

It is the silent hour when they who roam,
  Seek shelter, on the earth, or ocean's breast;
It is the hour when travel finds a home,
  On deserts, or within the cot to rest.
  It is the hour when joy and grief are blest,
And Nature finds repose where'er she roves;
  It is the hour that lovers like the best,
When in the twilight shades, or darker groves,
The maiden wanders with the swain she loves.

2

The balmy hour when fond hearts fondly meet;   10
  The hour when dew like welcome rest descends
On wild-flowers, shedding forth their odours sweet;
  The hour when sleep lays foes as quiet friends;—

The hour when labour's toilworn journey ends,
And seeks the cot for sweet repose till morn;—
    The hour when prayer from all to God ascends;—
At twilight's hour love's softest sighs are born,
When lovers linger neath the flowering thorn.

3

Oh! at this hour I love to be abroad,
    Gazing upon the moonlit scene around   20
'Looking through Nature up to Nature's God'°
    Regarding all with reverence profound!
The wild flowers studding every inch of ground,
And trees, with dews bespangled, looking bright
    As burnished silver;—while the entrancing sound
Of melody, from the sweet bird of night,
Fills my whole soul with rapture and delight.

Stanzas

1

The spring is come forth, but no spring is for me,
Like the spring of my boyhood, on woodland and lea,
When flowers brought me heaven, and knew me again
In the joy of their blooming o'er mountain and plain
My thoughts are confined, and imprisoned—O when
Will freedom find me my own vallies again?

2

The wind breath[e]s so sweet, and the day is so calm;
In the woods and the thicket the flowers look so warm,
And the grass is so green, so delicious and sweet,
O when shall my manhood my youth's vallies meet,   10
The scenes where my children are laughing at Play,
The scenes where my memory is fading away.

3

The primrose looks happy in every field
In strange woods the violets their odours will yield

And flowers in the sunshine all brightly arrayed,
Will bloom just as fresh and as sweet in the shade:
But the wild flowers that bring me most joy and content
Are the blossoms that blow where my childhood was spent.

4

Then I played like a flower in the shade and the sun
And slept as in Eden when daylight was done   20
There I lived with my parents, and felt my heart free,
And love—that was yet joy or sorrow to be,
Joy and sorrow it has been, like sunshine and showers
And their sun is still bright o'er my happiest hours.

5

The trees they are naked, the bushes are bare
And the fields they are brown, as if winter lay there;
But the violets are there by the dykes and the dell,
Where I played 'hen and chickens'—and heard the church bell
Which called me to prayer-book and sermons in vain
O when shall I see my own vallies again?—   30

6

The churches look bright as sun at noon day,
There meadows look green e're the winter's away,
There the pooty still lies for the school boy to find
And a thought often brings these sweet places to mind
Where the trees waved like thunder no music so well
Then nought sounded harsh but the school-calling bell.

7

There are spots where I played, there are spots where I loved,
There are scenes where the tales of my choice were approved
As green as at first—and their memory will be
The dearest of lifes recollections to me!—   40
The objects seen there in the care of my heart
Are as fair as at first—and will never depart.

8

Though no names are mentioned to sanction my themes
Their heart's beat with mine and make real my dreams:

Their memories with mine their diurnal course run,
True as night to the stars, and as day to the sun.
And as they are now so their memories will be
'Long as sense, truth, and reason, remaineth with me.

'I Am'

1

I am—yet what I am, none cares or knows;
  My friends forsake me like a memory lost:—
I am the self consumer of my woes;—
  They rise and vanish in oblivion's host,
Like shadows in love's frenzied stifled throes:—
And yet I am, and live—like vapours tost

2

Into the nothingness of scorn and noise,—
  Into the living sea of waking dreams,
Where there is neither sense of life or joys,
  But the vast shipwreck of my lifes esteems;   10
Even the dearest, that I love the best
Are strange—nay, rather stranger than the rest.

3

I long for scenes, where man hath never trod
  A place where woman never smiled or wept
There to abide with my Creator, God;
  And sleep as I in childhood, sweetly slept,
Untroubling, and untroubled where I lie,
The grass below—above the vaulted sky.

Sonnet

'I AM'

I feel I am;—I only know I am,
And plod upon the earth, as dull and void:
Earth's prison chilled my body with its dram
Of dullness, and my soaring thoughts destroyed,

I fled to solitudes from passions dream,
But strife persued—I only know, I am,
I was a being created in the race
Of men disdaining bounds of place and time:—
A spirit that could travel o'er the space
Of earth and heaven,—like a thought sublime,   10
Tracing creation, like my maker, free,—
A soul unshackled—like eternity,
Spurning earth's vain and soul debasing thrall
But now I only know I am,—that's all.

Sleep of Spring

O for that sweet untroubled rest
That Poets oft have sung
The babe upon its Mothers breast
The bird upon its young
The heart asleep without a pain
When shall I know that sleep again

When shall I be as I have been
Upon my Mothers breast
Sweet nature's garb of verdant green
To woo my former rest   10
Lone in the meadow field and plain
And in my native wilds again

The sheep within the fallow field
The bird upon the green
The Larks that in the thistle's shield
And pipe from morn to e'en
O for the pasture fields and fen
When shall I see such rest agen

I love the weeds along the fen
More sweet then garden flowers   20
Freedom haunts the humble glen
That blest my happiest hours
Here prisons injure health and me
I love sweet freedom and the free

The crows upon the swelling hills
The cows upon the lea
Sheep feeding by the pasture rills
Are ever dear to me
Because sweet freedom is their mate
While I am lone and desolate   30

I loved the winds when I was young
When life was dear to me
I loved the song which nature sung
Endearing Liberty
I loved the wood the dale the stream
For then my boyhood used to dream

Then toil itself was even play
'Twas pleasure e'en to weep
Twas joy to think of dreams by day
The beautifull of sleep   40
When shall I see the wood and plain
And dream those happy dreams again

Song

Love lives beyond
The tomb—the earth—which fades like dew
I love the fond
The faithfull and the true

Love lives in sleep
The happiness of healthy dreams
Eve's dews may weep
But love delightfull seems

Tis seen in flowers
And in the evens pearly dew   10
On earths green hours
And in the heavens eternal blue

Tis heard in spring
When light and sunbeams warm and kind
On angels wing
Bring love and music to the mind

And where is voice
So young and beautifully sweet
As natures choice
When spring and lovers meet   20

Love lives beyond
The tomb the earth the flowers and dew
I love the fond
The faithfull young and true

Some Days Before the Spring

1

There's a gladness of heart in the first days of Spring
There's a pleasure in memory to hear the birds sing
The Pink or Hedgesparrow will sing at day break
Though a leaf on the hedges is hardly awake
As for flowers on the grass there's not one to be seen
And the grass in the fields scarce enough to be green
The ruts full of water all muddy and thick
Which the boy tries to stop with a bit of a stick

2

The bits of brown haystacks all cut to the core
In the grassy close corners show winter is o'er   10
With the oaks frowning o'er them all mossy and grey
They will stand in the shelter 'till they cut the new hay
The field-fare is there a seeking hedge fruits
And the crow on the grass, is boreing for roots
With the jackdaw that nauntles among the molehills
In their grey powdered wigs, and bright yellow bills

3

The stones in the brooks, are all covered with green
All trailing and spreading as mosses are seen
In the woods at the spring and the close of the year
When violets and primroses like sisters appear   20
How level the meadow, how saffron the sun
How fine is the web that the spider has spun
Round the twigs of the hedge and the bents of the vales
In the soft mornings sunshine and sweet evening gales

4

Then come let us walk and enjoy the brisk air
And fancy the change when sweet spring it is there
Wild flowers in the grass, and nests in the tree
A hedge for the bird and a flower for the bee
So away let us walk while the sun's in the sky
And the paths o'er the greensward and rushes are dry   30
And Mary will see what there is to be seen
The hedges swelled buds, and the meadows more green

The Blackbird

1

The blackbird is a bonny bird
   That singeth in the wood
His song is in the evening heard
   When the red cow chews her cud
His song is heard in morning loud
   Upon the bright white thorn
While the blythe milkmaid sings as proud
   And holds the world in scorn

2

O bonny is the blackbird still
   On top of yon fir tree   10
On which he wipes his golden bill
   And blithely whistles he

He sings upon the sapling oak
 In notes all rich and mellow
Oft' have I quit towns noise, and folk
 In springs sweet summers weather

3

The blackbird is a bonny bird
 I love his mourning suit
And song in the spring mornings heard
 As mellow as the flute   20
How sweet his song in April showers
 Pipes from his golden bill
As yellow as the kingcup flowers
 The sweetest ditty still

My Early Home was This

1

Here sparrows built upon the trees
 And stock-doves hide their nest
The leaves where winnowed by the breeze
 Into a calmer rest
The black-caps song was very sweet
 That used the rose to kiss
It made the paradise complete
 My early home was this

2

The red breast from the sweet briar bush
 Drop't down to pick the worm   10
On the horse chesnut sang the thrush
 O'er the home where I was born
The dew morn like a shower of pearls
 Fell o'er this 'bower of bliss'°
And on the bench sat boys and girls
 —My early home was this

3

The old house stooped just like a cave
 Thatched o'er with mosses green

Winter around the walls would rave
    But all was calm within   20
The trees they were as green agen
    Where bees the flowers would kiss
But flowers and trees seemed sweeter then
    —My early home was this—

Hesperus

Hesperus the day is gone
Soft falls the silent dew
A tear is now on many a flower
And heaven lives in you

Hesperus the evening mild
Falls round us soft and sweet
'Tis like the breathings of a child
When day and evening meet

Hesperus the closing flower
Sleeps on the dewy ground   10
While dews fall in a silent shower
And heaven breathes around

Hesperus thy twinkling ray
Beams in the blue of heaven
And tells the traveller on his way
That earth shall be forgiven

The Round Oak°

I

The Apple top't oak in the old narrow lane
And the hedge row of bramble and thorn
Will ne'er throw their green on my visions again
As they did on that sweet dewy morn
When I went for spring pooteys and birds nests to look
Down the border of bushes ayont the fair spring
I gathered the palm grass close to the brook
And heard the sweet birds in thorn bushes sing

2

I gathered flat gravel stones up in the shallows
To make ducks and drakes when I got to a pond   10
The reed sparrows nest it was close to the sallows
And the wrens in a thorn bush a little beyond
And there did the stickleback shoot through the pebbles
As the bow shoots the arrow quick darting unseen
Till it came to the shallows where the water scarce drebbles
Then back dart again to the spring head of green

3

The nest of the magpie in the low bush of white thorn
And the carrion crows nest on the tree o'er the spring
I saw it in march on many a cold morn
When the arum it bloomed like a beautiful thing   20
And the apple top't oak aye as round as a table
That grew just above on the bank by the spring
Where every saturday noon I was able
To spend half a day and hear the birds sing

4

But now there's no holidays left to my choice
That can bring time to sit in thy pleasures again
Thy limpid brook flows and thy waters rejoice
And I long for that tree—but my wishes are vain
All that's left to me now I find in my dreams
For fate in my fortune's left nothing the same   30
Sweet Apple top't oak that grew by the stream
I loved thy shade once—now I love but thy name

June 19/46

Twilight

1

Sweet twilight, nurse of dews
And mother of sweet hours
With thee a walk I choose
Among the hawthorn bowers
That overhang the molehil greenly gray
Made as it were to intercept the way

2

Beetles are thy trumpeters
And to thy silence play
Where the soft still rustle stirs
O'er dead winds of the day   10
Mid marshy sedge dull aspens and pasture rushes
O'er green corn fields and hedge row bushes

3

Thy hours have one light place
Streaky and dunly grey
As if the night was giving place
And bringing back the day
The sun seems coming so the eye beleives
But darkness deepens round and undeceives

4

O'er brooks the weeping ash
Hangs cool and grimly dark   20
I hear the water splash
And then half fearing mark
In ivy'd ash a robber near the stream
'Till from a nearer view I find it but a dream

5

Sweet twilight nurse of night
Thy path the milk maid treads
With nimble step so light
Scarce bends the cowslips heads
But hastening on ere by thy light forsook
She leaves her cows all resting by the brook   30

6

Sweet twilight thy cool dews
Are beautifully spread
Where the nightingale its song renews
Close by the old cow shed
In that low hazel oft' I've heard her sing
While sombre evening came on downy wing

7

The playful rabit too
Its white scut glancing
Amid the silver dew
I've seen them oft advancing   40
In troops from spiney's where they love to dwell
Dancing on molehills in the open dell

8

Spring leaves seem old in green
And the dull thorn is lost in the[e]—
Dun twilight—but the hazel still is seen
In sleeping beauty by the old oak tree
Giving the woods a beauty and a power
While earth seems Eden in such an hour

9

Sweet twilight in thy dews
And silence I rejoice
Thy odd stars bid me muse   50
And give to silence voice
Now twilight ceases on the verge of even'
And darkness like a pawl spreads over heaven

Song

I

I fly from all I prize the most
I shun what I loved best to see
My joy seems gone—my peace seems lost
And all I loved is hate to me
I shun green fields and hate the light
The glorious sun the peaceful moon
More welcome is the darkest night
Then glaring daylight comes to[o] soon

2

'Tis not the kiss that pouts to leave
The lips of woman that we love   10
'Tis not the world—that will deceive
Or any doubt of that above
'Tis something that my heart hath been
'Tis something that my heart approvd
'Tis something that my eyes have seen
And felt they loved—

3

I grieve not those I loved are gone
That happy years have pass'd away
That time to day keeps stealing on
To that ye call eternity   20
I grieve not that the seasons fade
That winter chills the summer dew
While mortal things are heavenly made
And all now doubt will soon be true

4

To thee my love, and only thee
The spring and summer seemeth true
Thy looks are like the flowers I see
Thy eyes like air-bells filled with dew
Thy look is that of happiest love
And playful as the summer sea   30
Thy health is from the skies above
And heaven itself is full of thee—

Larks and Spring

The sunny end of March is nigh
And not a cloud is in the sky
Along the footpath o'er the farm
The school-boy basket on his arm
Seeks the birds nest therein to look
He takes a stone to cross the brook

Made wider by the rainy night
And hums the music of delight
To see the rabits seek their burrow
Or ground lark from the fallow'd furrow   10
Start up and shiver while he sings
Then drop as though he'd lost his wings
As stunt and heavy as a stone
In the brown furrow still and lone
And still I love the ground-larks flight
Starting up the ploughmans height
And more and more unseal his eye
When rose leaves pave the eastern sky
To see the skylark as he springs
Shake mornings moisture from his wings   20
And rise and sing in music proud
Small as a bee beneath a cloud
'Till mixing with the vapours dun
He's lost in valleys of the sun
And singing on in springs delight
Some moments e're he comes in sight
It drops, and drops from breezy morn
To seek its mate amid the corn
A happy song the skylark brings
And spring's in every note he sings   30
With coppled crown, and speckled breast
The pilewort blooms above his nest
In rain it seeks the sheltering furrow
But sings when sunshine comes tomorrow
In every field they mount and sing
The song of Nature and of Spring.

The Autumn Wind

I

The Autumn wind on suthering wings
    Plays round the oak-tree strong
And through the hawthorn hedges sings
    The years departing song

There's every leaf upon the whirl
Ten thousand times an hour
The grassy meadows crisp and curl
With here and there a flower
There's nothing in the world I find
That pleases like the Autumn wind 10

2

The chaffinch flies from out the bushes
The bluecap 'tee hees' on the tree
The wind sues on in merry gushes
His murmuring autumns minstrelsy
The robin sings his autumn song
Upon the crabtree overhead
The clouds like smoak slow sail along
Leaves rustle like the human tread
There's nothing suits my musing mind
So pleasant as the Autumn wind 20

3

How many miles it suthers on
And stays to dally with the leaves
And when the first broad blast is gone
A stronger gust the foliage heaves
The poplar tree it turns to gray
As leaves lift up their underside
The birch it dances all the day
To rippling billows petrified
There's nothing calms the quiet mind
So welcome as the Autumn wind 30

4

Sweet twittering o'er the meadow grass
Soft sueing o'er the fallow ground
The lark starts up as on they pass
With many a gush and moaning sound
It fans the feathers of the bird
And ruffs the robins ruddy breast
As round the hovel end it whirled
Then sobs and gallops o'er the west
In solitude the musing mind
Must ever love the Autumn wind 40

Oct 15th/45

Song

1

I would not be a wither'd leaf
Twirled in an autumn sky
Mine should not be a life so brief
To fade and fall and die

2

Nor would I be a wither'd flower
Whose stalk was broke before
The bud showed bloom in springs young hour
Heart sicken'd at the core

3

But I would be a happy thought
With thy sweet sleep to lie   10
To live unknown, unseen, unsought
And keep my lonely joy

4

Yes I would be a ray of light
In the apple of thy eye
And watch o'er thee the live long night
In beauty, and in joy

                                    March 3rd/47

The Winters Spring

1

The winter comes I walk alone
I want no birds to sing
To those who keep their hearts their own
The winter is the Spring
No flowers to please—no bees to hum
The coming Springs already come

2

I never want the christmas rose
To come before its time
The seasons each as God bestows
Are simple and sublime   10
I love to see the snow storm hing
'Tis but the winter garb of Spring

3

I never want the grass to bloom
The snow-storm's best in white
I love to see the tempest come
And love its piercing light
The dazzled eyes that love to cling
O'er snow white meadows sees the Spring

4

I love the snow the crimpling snow
That hangs on every thing   20
It covers every thing below
Like white doves brooding wing
A landscape to the aching sight
A vast expance of dazzling light

5

It is the foliage of the woods
That winter's bring—The dress
White easter of the year in bud
That makes the winter Spring
The frost and snow his poseys bring
Natures white spirits of the Spring   30

Feby 23rd/47

Sonnet

WOOD ANEMONIE

The wood anemonie through dead oak leaves
And in the thickest woods now blooms anew
And where the green briar, and the bramble weaves
Thick clumps o' green, anemonies thicker grew

And weeping flowers, in thousands pearled in dew
People the woods and brakes, hid hollows there
White, yellow and purple hued the wide wood through
What pretty, drooping weeping flowers they are
The clipt' frilled leaves the slender stalk they bear
On which the drooping flower hangs weeping dew   10
How beautiful through april time and may
The woods look, filled with wild anemonie
And every little spinney now looks gay
With flowers mid brush wood and the hugh oak tree.

Sonnet

THE CROW

How peaceable it seems for lonely men
To see a crow fly in the thin blue sky
Over the woods and fealds, o'er level fen
It speaks of villages, or cottage nigh
Behind the neighbouring woods—when march winds high
Tear off the branches of the hugh old oak
I love to see these chimney sweeps sail by
And hear them o'er the knarled forest croak
Then sosh askew from the hid woodmans stroke
That in the woods their daily labours ply   10
I love the sooty crow nor would provoke
Its march day exercises of croaking joy
I love to see it sailing to and fro
While fealds, and woods and waters spread below

Silent Love

I

The dew it trembles on the thorn
Then vanishes so love is born
Young love that speaks in silent thought
'Till scorned, then withers and is nought

2

The pleasure of a single hour
The blooming of a single flower
The glitter of the morning dew
Such is young love when it is new

3

The twitter of the wild birds wing
The murmur of the bees   10
Lays of hay crickets when they sing
Or other things more frail than these

4

Such is young love when silence speaks
Till weary with the joy it secks
Then fancy shapes sup[p]lies
'Till sick of its own heart it dies

5

The dew drop falls at mornings hour
When none are standing by
And noiseless fades the broken flower
So lovers in their silence die   20

Loves Story

I do not love thee
So I'll not deceive thee
I do not love thee
Yet I'm lothe to leave thee

I do not love thee
Yet joys very essence
Comes with thy footstep
Is complete in thy presence

I do not love thee
Yet when gone I sigh   10
And think about thee
'Till the stars all die

I do not love thee
Yet thy black bright eyes
Bring to my hearts soul
Heaven and paradise

I do not love thee
Yet thy handsome ways
Bring me in absence
Almost hopeless days   20

I cannot hate thee
Yet my love seems debtor
To love thee more
So hating, love thee better

[‘*I love thee nature with a boundless love*’]

1

I love thee nature with a boundless love
The calm of earth, the storms of roaring woods
The winds breathe happiness where e’er I rove
Theres lifes own music in the swelling floods
My harp is in the thunder melting clouds
The snow capt mountain, and the rolling sea
And hear ye not the voice where darkness shrouds
The heavens,—there lives happiness for me

2

Death breathes its pleasures when it speaks of him
My pulse beats calmer while its lightnings play   10
My eye with earths delusions waxing dim
Clears with the brightness of eternal day
The elements crash round me—it is he
And do I hear his voice and never start
From Eve’s posterity I stand quite free
Nor feel her curses rankle round my heart

3

Love is not here—hope is—and in his voice
The rolling thunder and the roaring sea
My pulse they leap and with the hills rejoice
Then strife and turmoil is a peace to me   20
No matter where lifes ocean leads me on
For nature is my mother and I rest
When tempests trouble and the sun is gone
Like to a weary child upon her breast—

['*How hot the sun rushes*']

1

How hot the sun rushes
Like fire in the bushes
The wild flowers look sick at the foot of the tree
Birds nest are left lonely
The pewit sings only
And all seems disheartened, and lonely like me

2

Baked earth and burnt furrows
Where the rabbit he burrows
And yet it looks pleasant beneath the green tree
The crows nest look darkly   10
O'er fallows dried starkly
And the sheep all look restless as nature and me

3

Yet I love a meadow dwelling
Where nature is telling
A tale to the clear stream—its dearest to me
To sit in green shadows
While the herd turns to gadders
And runs from the hums of the fly and the bee

4

This spot is the fairest
The sweetest and rarest   20
This sweet sombre shade of the bright green tree
Where the morehens flag-nest
On the waters calm breast
Lies near to this sweet spot thats been mother to me

Song

I

Tis evening the sky is one broad dim of gray
The hedges look dull as if mourning in green
The wind winnows chill now the sun is away
Yet still there is comfort while viewing the scene
The grass troubles by as if hushing to sleep
And something seems chearing where ever I roam
For here in the core of my heart I can keep
The smileing endearments that blest me at home

2

But love shall be nameless and I will be free
To think of those joys when I wander alone   10
While the beetle booms by in his night reverie
And the lady bird climbs the tall grass as her own
Sweet dwelling without either neighbour or guest
I envy her ginnet I envy her home
Compared with my home oh how happy her rest
Whilst troubles pursue me where ever I roam

3

No comfort for me lived in palace or hall
But the cottage that stood in a garden of flowers
Where the vine and the woodbine climb'd up by the wall
Twas there that I lived in my happiest hours   20
Tis there I shall live when the strife is gone by
For the sun that shines there shines on vally and plain
Where green fields and bushes will gladden my eye
And make me contented and happy again

Song

1

The rain is come in misty showers
The landscape lies in shrouds
Patches of sunshine like to flowers
Fall down between the clouds
And gild the earth else where so cold
With shreds like flowers of purest gold

2

And now it sweeps along the hills
Just like a falling cloud
The cornfields into silence stills
Where musty moisture shrouds   10
And now a darker cloud sweeps o'er
The rain drops faster than before

3

The cattle graze along the ground
The lark she wets her wings
And chatters as she whirls around
Then to the wet corn sings
And hides upon her twitchey nest
Refreshed with wet and speckled breast

4

And I the calm delight embrace
To walk along the fields   20
And feel the rain drops in my face
That sweetest pleasure yeilds
They come from heaven and there the free
Sends down his blessings upon me

5

I love to walk in summer showers
When the rain falls gently down
I love to walk a lecture hours
A distance from the Town
To see the drops on bushes hing
And Blackbirds prune a dabbled wing   30

Sonnet

How beautiful the white thorn shews its leaves
The first in springs beginnings march or close
Of April and how very green it weaves
The branches in the underwood they burst
More green than grass the common eye receives
Pleasures o'er green white thorn clumps in the wood
So beautifully green it seems at first
It does the eye that gazes on it good
The green enthusaism of young spring
The Blackbird chooses it from all the wood   10
With moss to build his early nest and sing
Among the leaves the young are snugly nurst
Mornings young dew wets each pinfeathered wing
Before a bunch of May was from its white knobs burst.

Autumn

1

I love the fitfull gusts that shakes
    The casement all the day
And from the mossy elm tree takes
    The faded leaf away
Twirling it by the window pane
With thousand others down the lane

2

I love to see the shaking twig
    Dance till the shut of eve
The sparrow on the cottage rig
    Whose chirp would make believe   10
That spring was just now flirting by
In summers lap with flowers to lie

3

I love to see the cottage smoke
Curl upwards through the naked trees
The pigeons nestled round the coat
On dull november days like these
The cock upon the dunghill crowing
The mill sails on the heath agoing

4

The feather from the ravens breast
   Falls on the stubble lea   20
The acorns near the old crows nest
   Fall pattering down the tree
The grunting pigs that wait for all
Scramble and hurry where they fall

Evening

How beautiful the eve comes in
The grazing kine the village din
Of happy children, cocks and hens
And chickens cheeping in their pens
And hogs that grunt the roots to eat
And dogs asleep on their fore-feet
And sparrows on the mossy thatch
Waiting whatever they may catch
Beneath the oak the old cart shed
There the capon goes to bed   10
On the old crippled waggon-see
Propped up with an axle-tree
By the wall on broken rail
Tweets red breasted firetail
And their neighbours pied flycatch
Build cobweb nest in the old thatch
Where beesom weed—that high wind leaves
Blossoms and blooms above the eaves
The old cow-crib is mossed and green
As if it just had painted been   20

The ramping kecks in orchard gaps
Shake like green neighbours in white caps
On which the snail will climb and dwell
For three weeks in its painted shell
There the white nosed 'clock a clay'
Red and black spot[t]ed sits all day
Round which the white nosed bee will hum
To which the black nosed bee will come
More than a hundred times a day
Till evening shadows cool in grey   30
Wormwood, burdock—the cart conceals
Rotting and wanting both the wheels
The battered waggon wanting three
Stands prop't with broken axle-tree
A hen pen with two slats away
And hen and chickens gone astray
A barrow left without a wheel
Since spring, which nettles now conceal
From free stones getting on the moor
The creeping donkeys pass the door   40
The geese on dunghills clean their quills
And squabble o'er the dainty pills
Thrown out by the huswifes cares
Who supper for her man prepares
Labour returning from its toils
Ditcher that the earth besoils
Hedgers from the wattled thorn
Scaring birdboy with his horn
Who blows it to the wandering moon
And thinks the village knows the tune   50
The shepherd in the nearly dark
Followed by his dogs gruff bark
The milkmaid tripping through the dew
Singing all the evening through
The owlet through the barn hole peeps
And all the village hides and sleeps.

Song

The autumns come again
And the clouds descend in rain
And the leaves they are falling from the wood
The summer's voice is still
Save the clacking of the mill
And the lowly muttered thunder of the flood

There's nothing in the mead
But the rivers muddy speed
And the willow leaves all littered by its side
Sweet voices all are still   10
In the vale and on the hill
And the summer's blooms are withered in their pride

Fled is the cuckoo's note
To countries far remote
And the nightingale is vanished from the wood
If you search the Lordship round
There is not a blossom found
And where the haycock scented is the flood

My true loves fled away
Since we walked in cocks of hay   20
On the sabbath in the summer of the year
And she's nowhere to be seen
On the meadow or the green
But she's coming when the happy spring is near

When the birds begin to sing
And the flowers begin to spring
And the cowslips in the meadows reappear
When the woodland oaks are seen
In their monarchy of green
Then Mary and loves pleasure will be here   30

Recolections of Home

1

When we stray far away from the old pleasant village
We love it the fonder the further away
The sweet pleasant songs of ploughmen oer their tillage
Are more pleasant sounds than the strange calls to day
That sweet little homestead with pollard ash and pond
Leads back a hundred miles wherever I may roam
A dove cotes wooden home where the pigeons coo so fond
Soon brings to my eye my own at the old house at home

2

The very layer of crab that's wattled in the hedge
The old post in its red paint crushed with waggons rushing
    through   10
The teazles prickly burrs or the little hubs of sedge
Will bring me to the old place where I lived a moon ago
But the flowers here they tell me in their brown, red, white and
    blue
That their sisters are now in the fields around my house at home
Though the sun here shines as bright, and as christal be the dew
They are not so sweet as those flowers that in our meadows grew

3

A mossy plank across the flood though weedy be the dyke
Here fifty miles away and I cross another stream
It brings me to my own fields the brigs so very like
So here I only wander in the middle of a dream   20
At home I did right cozie and lived as I would choose
And saw nothing but my sweet fields day after day
'Till I was forced to flee my corner and the muse
As the linnet from its nest by the awk is drove away

4

I always see a bit of home in every likely thing
A white-thorn hedge, or bramble bush or pollard willow tree
Brings me my own snug homestead, and the budding of the
    spring

[*The rest of the stanza is missing, though a space is left for it in the transcript*]

Boys and Spring

1

To see the Arum early shoot
Its cone curled leaves of green
About the white green mossy root
Where violet buds are seen

2

The little round hole in the roots
Looks battered hard and round
The mice come out to chimble fruits
And take hips under ground

3

The husks of hips and awes lie round
All chimbled seed and skin   10
There noses now peep from the ground
And there the tails bob in

4

The nettles yellow roots are bare
Where sun shine looks about
Where thin and pricked the hedges are
The leaves are sprouting out

5

The violets blossom where they dwell
The childrens fingers smart
They kiss the place to make it well
And all is joy of heart   20

6

There's something yet in childhoods ways
On which I love to dwell
And oft I hunt in springs first days
The painted pooty shell

7

Children e're they go to school
Hunt hedges and thorn roots
They're badgers by the sedgy pool
And b[u]y the [painted poots]

8

And then they crush them nib to nib
Agen the meadow brig   30
And don't their little tongues run glib
At running such a rig

9

They call them cocks and so they fight
A little 'cocking day'
The hardest breaks the whole outright
As heroe of the day

The Bean Field

A Bean field full in blossom smells as sweet
As Araby or Groves of orange flowers
Black eyed and white and feathered to ones feet
How sweet they smell in mornings dewy hours
When seething night is left upon the flowers
And when morns bright sun shines oer the field
The pea bloom glitters in the gems o' showers
And sweet the fragrance which the union yields
To battered footpaths crossing o'er the fields.

Spring Wind

I

The wind blows the trees about
In the green field
The wind blows the bees about
Which bushes shield

'Tis the green wind of May time
That suddenly wakes
That starts in the day time
When every thing shakes
The trees and the bushes, the grasses and grain
Like the waves of the ocean roll over the plain   10

2

The wind what can beat it
So frolic and playful
The beast cannot eat it
Though it fills all the day full
'Tis the grass in the meadow
All tossing in billows
The wheat where streams glidder
Waving under the willows
Now the trees in the hedges are heaving like hair
And bushes are shaking like living things there   20

3

The water all curdles
Like wrinkles in ice
Like ribbed floating hurdles
That look rather nice
It swabbs the bullrushes
The flags it swirls through
By the ozier bed pushes
Where the white lilies grew
Whose broad leaves are wet with the plash o' the wave
Where the froth binds the bullrush like snow on the grave   30

4

It blows in my face now
Though I do'nt see it pass
It breathes on the flowers now
Now billows the grass
It sweeps the grey willows
Like the roof of a house
Swirls the sedges i' billows
O'er the nest o' the mouse
Flys Bees and crickets are singing all day
And winds mooving every green thing in its way   40

['*There is a charm in Solitude that cheers*']

There is a charm in Solitude that cheers
A feeling that the world knows nothing of
A green delight the wounded mind endears
After the hustling world is broken off
Whose whole delight was crime at good to scoff
Green solitude his prison pleasure yields
The bitch fox heeds him not—birds seem to laugh
He lives the Crusoe of his lonely fields
Which dark green oaks his noontide leisure shields

The Shepherd Boy

1

The fly or beetle on their track
Are things that know no sin
And when they whemble on their back
What terror they seem in
The shepherd boy wi' bits o' bents
Will turn them up again
And start them where they nimbly went
Along the grassy plain
And such the shepherd boy is found
While lying on the sun crackt ground   10

2

The lady-bird that seldom stops
From climbing all the day
Climbs up the rushes tassle tops
Spreads wings and flies away
He sees them—lying on the grass
Musing the whole day long
And clears the way to let them pass
And sings a nameless song
He watches pismires on the hill
Always busy never still   20

3

He sees the traveller beetle run
Where thick the grass wood weaves
To hide the black-snail from the sun
He props up plantain leaves
The lady-cows have got a house
Within the cowslip pip
The spider weaving for his spouse
On threads will often slip
So looks and lyes the shepherd boy
The summer long his whole employ—   30

['*Swift goes the sooty swallow o'er the heath*']

Swift goes the sooty swallow o'er the heath°
Swifter then skims the cloud rack of the skies
As swiftly flies its shadow underneath
And on his wing the twittering sunbeam lies
As bright as water glitters in the eyes
Of those it passes—'tis a pretty thing
The ornament of meadows—and clear skies
With dingy breast and narrow pointed wing
Its daily twittering is a song to spring.

Clock a Clay

I

In the cowslips peeps I lye
Hidden from the buzzing fly
While green grass beneath me lies
Pearled wi' dew like fishes eyes
Here I lye a Clock a clay
Waiting for the time o' day

2

While grassy forests quake surprise
And the wild wind sobs and sighs
My gold home rocks as like to fall
On its pillars green and tall   10
When the pattering rain drives bye
Clock a Clay keeps warm and dry

3

Day by day and night by night
All the week I hide from sight
In the cowslips peeps I lye
In rain and dew still warm and dry
Day and night and night and day
Red black spotted clock a clay

4

My home it shakes in wind and showers
Pale green pillar top't wi' flowers   20
Bending at the wild winds breath
Till I touch the grass beneath
Here still I live lone clock a clay
Watching for the time of day

The Wind

1

The frolicksome wind through the trees and the bushes
Keeps sueing and sobbing and waiving all day
Frighting magpies from trees and from white thorns the thrushes
And waveing the river in wrinkles and spray
The unresting wind is a frolicksome thing
O'er hedges in floods and green fields of the spring

2

It plays in the smoke of the chimney at morn
Curling this way and that i' the morns dewy light
It curls from the twitch heap among the green corn
Like the smoke from the cannon i' th' midst of a fight   10
But report there is none to create any alarm
From the smoke an old ground full hiding meadow and farm°

3

How sweet curls the smoke oer the green o' the field
How majestic it rolls o'er the face o' the grass
And from the low cottage the elm timbers shield
In the calm o' the evening how sweet the curls pass
I' the sunset how sweet to behold the cot smoke
From the low red brick chimney beneath the dark oak

4

How sweet the wind wispers o' midsummers eves
And fans the winged elder leaves o'er the old pales   20
While the cottage smoke o'er them a bright pillar leaves
Rising up and turns clouds by the strength of the gales
O' sweet is the cot neath its colums of smoke
While dewy eve brings home the labouring folk

Song

1

I went my Sunday mornings rounds
  One pleasant summer day
And stood i' the green meadow grounds
  'Mong cocks and swaths o' hay
Up the green rush the Lady bird
  Clomb to its very tops
And there the crickets songs were heard
  Like organs without stops

2

The sun was climbing up the sky
  A looking glass of gold   10
It melts and quivers on the eye
  And blinds us to behold
Melting and shining to its height
  It shines from pole to pole
And sliddering down at dewy night
  Goes out a dying coal

3

I stood among the swathes and cocks
  How sweet the light did seem
When a sweet lass with inky locks
  Came tripping by the stream   20
Sweet one I said I do prefer
  To ask you why you walk
'Tis merely for my pleasure sir
  As you stand there to talk

4

The wind came from the southern sky
  And tokened flying showers
The busy bee and butterfly
  Her ribbons took for flowers
The wasp it buzzed about her mouth
  Her lips seemed cherries red   30
The wind shook from the balmy south
  The curls about her head

5

Young man she said you'l marry me
  And waited for reply
Why yes my dear but do'nt you see
  Love is the stronger tie
And then I kissed her lips and cheeks
  And made her merry hearted
I wed the maid in just three weeks
  From the first day we parted   40

Childhood

I

O dear to us ever the scenes of our childhood
The green spots we played in the school where we met
The heavy old desk where we thought of the wild-wood
Where we pored o'er the sums which the master had set
I loved the old church-school, both inside and outside
I loved the dear Ash trees and sycamore too
The graves where the Buttercups burning gold outvied
And the spire where pelitory dangled and grew

2

The bees i' the wall that were flying about
The thistles the henbane and mallows all day   10
And crept in their holes when the sun had gone out
And the butterfly ceased on the blossoms to play
O dear is the round stone upon the green hill
The pinfold hoof printed with oxen—and bare
The old princess-feather tree growing there still
And the swallows and martins wheeling round in the air

3

Where the chaff whipping outward lodges round the barn door
And the dunghill cock struts with his hens in the rear
And sings 'Cockadoodle' full twenty times oer
And then claps his wings as he'd fly in the air   20
And there's the old cross with its round about steps
And the weathercock creaking quite round in the wind
And theres the old hedge with its glossy red heps
Where the green-linnets nest I have hurried to find—

4

—To be in time for the school or before the bell rung.
There's the odd martins nest o'er the shoemakers door
On the shoemakers chimney the Old swallows sung
That had built and sung there in the season before
Then we went to seek pooty's among the old furze
On the heaths, in the meadows beside the deep lake   30
And return'd with torn cloathes all covered wi' burrs
And oh what a row my fond mother would make

5

Then to play boiling kettles just by the yard door
Seeking out for short sticks and a bundle of straw
Bits of pots stand for teacups after sweeping the floor
And the children are placed under school-mistress's awe
There's one set for pussy another for doll
And for butter and bread they'll each nibble an awe
And on a great stone as a table they loll
The finest small teaparty ever you saw   40

6

The stiles we rode upon 'all a cock-horse'
The mile a minute swee
On creaking gates—the stools o' moss
What happy seats had we
There's nought can compare to the days of our childhood
The mole-hills like sheep in a pen
Where the clodhopper sings like the bird in the wild wood
All forget us before we are men

Oct. 15th/48

['*O could I be as I have been*']

1

O could I be as I have been
　And ne'er can be no more
A harmless thing in meadows green
　Or on the wild sea shore

2

O could I be what once I was
　In heaths and valleys green
A dweller in the summer grass
　Green fields and places green

3

A tennant of the happy fields
　By grounds of wheat and beans　　　　　10
By gipsey's camps and milking bield
　Where lussious woodbine leans

4

To sit on the deserted plough
　Left when the corn was sown
In corn and wild weeds buried now
　In quiet peace unknown

5

The harrows resting by the hedge
  The roll within the Dyke
Hid in the Ariff and the sedge
  Are things I used to like   20

6

I used to tread through fallow lands
  And wade through paths of grain
When wheat ears pattered on the hands
  And head-aches left a stain

7

I wish I was what I have been
  And what I was could be
As when I roved in shadows green
  And loved my willow tree

8

To gaze upon the starry sky
  And higher fancies build   30
And make in solitary joy
  Loves temple in the field

Clifford Hill°

I

The river rambles like a snake
  Along the meadow green
And loud the noise the mill wheels make
  I' summer time at e'en
And there as swift the waters pass
  So runs the life of man
I sit me down upon the grass
  These beauties for to scan

2

Tis summers day and dewy eve
  And sweet the sun sinks low   10
I smile, and yet my heart will greive
  To see the waters flow
To see the flags that look so green
  The sun gilt waves so bright
I wander here this lovely e'en
  In wonder and delight

3

The firs look dark on Clifford hill
  The river bright below
All foamed beneath the water mill
  While beautious flowers do blow   20
'Tis here I'd wander morn and night
  With fondly gazing eye
To see the sunny golden light
  Go down in yonder sky—

4

Yes dearly do these scenes I love
  And dear that fir clad hill
There all secure does build the dove
  While click-clack goes the mill
And now in natures sweet repose
  I leave this spot awile   30
The bee is buried in the rose
  A man gone from his toil

First Love

I ne'er was struck before that hour
  With love so sudden and so sweet
Her face it bloomed like a sweet flower
  And stole my heart away complete
My face turned pale a deadly pale
  My legs refused to walk away
And when she looked what could I ail
My life and all seemed turned to clay

And then my blood rushed to my face
    And took my eyesight quite away   10
The trees and bushes round the place
    Seemed midnight at noon day
I could not see a single thing
    Words from my eyes did start
They spoke as chords do from the string
    And blood burnt round my heart

Are flowers the winters choice
    Is love's bed always snow
She seemed to hear my silent voice
    Not loves appeals to know   20
I never saw so sweet a face
    As that I stood before
My heart has left its dwelling place
    And can return no more—

The Humble Bee

1

When lifes tempests blow high
In seclusion I tread
Where the primroses lie
And the green mosses spread
Where the bottle tit hangs
At the end of a twig
Where the humble bee bangs
That is almost as big

2

Where I feel my heart lonely
I am solitudes own   10
Talking to myself only
And walking woods lone
In the wood briars and brambles
Hazel stools and oak trees
I enjoy such wood rambles
And hear the wood bees

3

That sing their wood journey
And stop at wood blooms
Where the primroses burn ye
And the violet perfumes   20
There to myself talking
I rub through the bushes
And the boughs where I'm walking
Like a sudden wind rushes

4

The wood gate keeps creaking
Opened ever so slow
And from boughs bent to breaking
Often starts the odd crow
Right down the green riding
Gladly winds the wild bee   30
Then through the wood side in
He sucks flowers in glee

5

He flies through the stovens
Brown hazel and grey
Through fern leaves like ovens
Still singing his way
He rests on a moss bed
And perks up his heels
And strokes o'er his small head
Then hies to the fields   40

6

I enjoy these wood rambles
And the juicey wheat fields
Where the wood rose—and brambles
A showers covert yields
I love the wood journey
Where the violets melt blue
And primroses burn ye
With flames the day through

Little Trotty Wagtail°

1

Little trotty wagtail he went in the rain
And tittering tottering sideways he near got straight again
He stooped to get a worm and look'd up to catch a fly
And then he flew away e're his feathers they were dry

2

Little trotty wagtail he waddled in the mud
And left his little foot marks trample where he would
He waddled in the water pudge and waggle went his tail
And chirrupt up his wings to dry upon the garden rail

3

Little trotty wagtail you nimble all about
And in the dimpling water pudge you waddle in and out 10
Your home is nigh at hand and in the warm pigsty
So little Master Wagtail I'll bid you a 'Good bye'

Augst 9th/49

The Swallow

1

Pretty Swallow once again
Come and pass me i' the rain
Pretty swallow why so shy
Pass again my window by

2

The horse pond where he dips his wings
The wet day prints it full o' rings
The rain drops on his [airy] track
Lodge like pearls upon his back

3

Then agen he dips his wing
In the wrinkles of the spring   10
Then o'er the rushes flies again
And pearls roll off his back like rain

4

Pretty little swallows fly
Village doors and windows by
Whisking o'er the garden pales
Where the blackbird finds the snails

5

Whewing by the ladslove tree
For something only seen by thee
Pearls that on the red rose hings
Falls off shaken by thy wings   20

6

On yon low that[c]hed cottage stop
In the sooty chimney pop
Where thy wife and family
Every evening wait for thee—

The Gardeners Bonny Daughter

The chaffinch in the hedge row sings In the brown naked thorn
And by its tail the titmouse hings Searching the buds at morn
And I'll wish dirty roads away And meadows flooded water
And court before I end the day The gardeners bonny daughter

She's sweeter than the first o' spring More fair than Christmas
  roses
When robins by the hovel sing Sweet smiles the maid discloses
Her hair so brown her eye so bright As clear as the spring water
I'll go and have a word tonight With the gardeners bonny
  daughter

Her cheeks are like the coloured rose A kiss would surely burn ye
Her lips are gems more red than those For love I'll go the
    journey   10
And when the white thorn comes in leaf And the chaffinch lays
    her lauter
I walk where singing birds are brief Wi' the gardeners bonny
    daughter

I passed the gardeners house one night My heart burnt to a
    cynder
When I saw her face and eyes so bright A looking through the
    window
And when I'd passed the house agen I'd been pounded in a
    mortar
But she looked and smiled upon me then So I love the gardeners
    bonny daughter

The Red Robin

Cock Robin he got a neat tippet at spring
And he sat in a shed and heard other birds sing
And he whistled a ballad as loud as he could
And built him a nest of oak leaves by the wood

And furnished it just as the ccladine pressed
Like a bright burning blaze by the edge o' its nest
All glittering with sunshine and beautiful rays
Like high polished brass or the fire in a blaze

Then sung a new song on the bend o' the brere
And so it kept singing the whole of the year   10
Till cowslips and wild roses blossomed and died
The red Robin sung by the old spring side

The Ladybird

Ladybird ladybird where art thou gone E're the daisy was open
    or the rose it was spread
On the cabbage flower early thy scarlet wings shone I saw thee
    creep off to the tulip bed
Ladybird ladybird where art thou flown
Thou wert here in the morning before the sun shone

Just now up the bowl o' the damson tree You passed the gold
    lichen and got to the grey
Ladybird ladybird where can you be You climb up the tulips
    and then fly away
You crept up the flowers while I plucked them just now
    And crept to the top and then flew from the flowers
    O sleep not so high as the damson tree bough
    But come from the dew i' the eldern tree bowers   10

    Here's lavender trees that would hide a lone mouse
    And lavender cotton wi' buttons o' gold
    And bushes o' lads love as dry as a house
    Here's red pinks and daisies so sweet to behold
    Ladybird ladybird come to thy nest
    Thy gold beds i' the rose o the sweet brier tree
    Wi rose coloured curtains to pleasure thee best
    Come Ladybird back to thy Garden and Me

The Corn Craiks Rispy Song

The corncraik rispt her summer call Just as the sun went down
Copper red a burning ball In woods behind the town
I wandered forth a maid to meet So bonny and so fair
No other flower was half so sweet And cole black was her hair

Upon the grasses stood the dew Bead drop O' clearest pearl
Her hair was black her eyes were blue O what a lovely Girl
Her neck was like the lilly white Her breast was like the swan
She was in heart and loves delight A worship for a Man

The corncraiks rispy song was oer The sun had left the light
    [alone]
I love dusk kisses on the Moor To lewder life unknown   10
Hid in the bosom of a flower Its lifetime there to dwell
Eternity would seem an hour And I'd be resting well

Autumn

The thistle down's flying Though the winds are all still
On the green grass now lying Now mounting the hill
The spring from the fountain Now boils like a pot
Through stones past the counting It bubbles red hot

The ground parched and cracked is Like over baked bread
The greensward all wrecked is Bents dried up and dead
The fallow fields glitter Like water indeed
And gossamers twitter Flung from weed unto weed

Hill tops like hot iron Glitter hot i' the sun
And the Rivers we're eyeing Burn to gold as they run   10
Burning hot is the ground Liquid gold is the air
Who ever looks round Sees Eternity there

The Peartree Lane°

There's places in our village streets
Where I dearly loved to be
The round cross full o' stoney seats
At the Stable and the tree
The brown bleached Oaks they sit upon
Where the old Roll still remain
And still I love to walk alone
Down the Peartree Lane

The Elm trees o'er our Garden wall
How beautiful they grew   10
Where ring Doves from their nest would call
And the vein leaved Ivy grew

At the old house end while one hugh Elm
That turned a whole days rain
Storm roared as 'twould the town o'erwhelm
Twas shelter down the lane

The blacksmiths shed the Coblers shop
Chock holes and marble rings
By the Cross steps the spinning top
Are memorable things   20
The schoolboys love at morn and eve'
When spring comes in again
But nought can beat the primrose leaves
Down Peartrees dirty lane

There the Bumbarrel build[s] her nest
On early green white thorn
The Chaffinch shews her ruddy breast
O'er her Lichen nest at morn
The Mavis there at Christmas time
Begins his early strain   30
And dead Oak leaves though glazed i' rime
Look dear in Peartree Lane

The woodland stile the broken gap
And day lights peeping moon
Where red cloaked goody fills her lap
To boil the kettle soon
Anemonies peep through the hedge
Hedgesparrows find a strain
Theres nothing i' the world I pledge
Like dear old Peartree Lane   40

The Crow Sat on the Willow

The crow sat on the willow tree
A lifting up his wings
And glossy was his coat to see
And loud the ploughman sings

I love my love because I know
The milkmaid she loves me
And hoarsely croaked the glossy crow
Upon the willow Tree
I love my love the ploughman sung
And all the field wi' music rung   10

I love my love a bonny lass
She keeps her pails so bright
And blythe she t[r]ips the dewy grass
At morning and at night
A cotton drab her morning gown
Her face was rosey health
She traced the pastures up and down
And nature was her wealth
He sung and turned each furrow down
His sweethearts love in cotton gown   20

My love is young and handsome
As any in the Town
She's worth a ploughmans ransom
In the drab cotton gown
He sung and turned his furrows o'er
And urged his Team along
While on the willow as before
The old crow croaked his song
The ploughman sung his rustic Lay
And sung of Phebe all the day   30

The crow was in love no doubt
And wi a many things
The ploughman finished many a bout
And lustily he sings
My love she is a milking maid
Wi' red and rosey cheek
O' cotton drab her gown was made
I loved her many a week
His milking maid the ploughman sung
Till all the fields around him rung   40

In Green Grassy Places

In the white thorn hedges the blackbird sings
Where the hedgesparrow flutters his dirty brown wings
And the skylark he trembles above the green wheat
While the thrush in the spinny is singing so sweet
So come lovely Susan we'll walk i' the fields
And meet all the pleasures the lovely spring yields
For of all the gay lasses sweet Susan I see
There's none that I fancy my sweetheart but thee

So come my dear Susan and where the thrush sings
The primrose and violets the earliest springs   10
The Chaffinch is building his nest on the brere
And the bottle tit hangs up his pudding bag near
I' the ribs o the hedge the hedgesparrow builds
And the brown o' his feathers the morning sun gilds
I long my dear Susan to walk out wi thee
In green grassy places thy sweetheart to be

We'll walk where the barley is hiding the clod
We'll walk where the daisy blooms stars on the sod
Where the Herrinshaw builds in the flags by the streams°
There Susan we'll loiter in green summer dreams   20
By the side o' the river running like glass
We'll seek early cowslips that quake i' the grass
And there bonny Susan I'll love you so true
And kiss you and court you and ne'er bid adieu

The Peasant Poet

He loved the brook's soft sound
The swallow swimming by
He loved the daisy covered ground
The cloud bedappled sky
To him the dismal storm appeared
The very voice of God
And where the Evening rock was reared
Stood Moses with his rod

And every thing his eyes surveyed
The insects I' the brake   10
Where Creatures God almighty made
He loved them for his sake
A silent man in lifes affairs
A thinker from a Boy
A Peasant in his daily cares—
The Poet in his joy

Lines on 'Cowper'

Cowper the Poet of the field
   Who found the muse on common ground
The homesteads that each Cottage shields
   He loved and made them Classic ground

The lonely house the rural walk
   He sang so musically true
E'en now they share the peoples talk
   Who love the poet Cowper too

Who has not read the 'Winter storm'°
   And does not feel the fallen snow   10
And Woodmen keeping noses warm
   With pipes where ever Forests grow

In France in Germany and Spain
   The same delightful pictures show
The Cowpers 'Woodmens' seen again
   And Lurchers tracking thro the snow

The 'Winters walk' and 'Summers Noon'
   We meet together by the fire
And think the 'walks' are o'er too soon
   When books are read and we retire   20

Who travels o'er those sweet fields now
   And brings not Cowper to his mind
Birds sing his name on every bough
   Nature repeats it in the wind

And every place the Poet trod
And every place the Poet sung
Are like the holy land of God
In every Mouth on every tongue

['*The Even comes and the Crow flies low*']

The Even comes and the Crow flies low
And the swallow he dips at the spring
The Leveret starts in the corn from the crow
And frights up the Lark to take wing
The Shrew Mice and Crickets they sing
I' the rushes and grass on the baulk
The swallows have gone from the spring
And the Shepherds have gone from their talk
While lovers only take their Evening walk

['*Know God is every where*']

Know God is every where
Not to one narrow, partial, spot confined
No not to chosen Israel
He extends through all the vast infinitude
    of space At his command the furious
    Tempests rise, the blasting of the
breath of his displeasure.

He tells the world of waters when to war
And at his bidding winds and seas are calm
    In him not in an arm of flesh I trust
    In him whose promise never yet
    has failed I place my confidence

10

Song

I hid my love when young while I
Coud'nt bear the buzzing of a flye
I hid my love to my despite
Till I could not bear to look at light
I dare not gaze upon her face
But left her memory in each place
Where ere I saw a wild flower lye
I kissed and bade my love good bye

I met her in the greenest dells
Where dew drops pearl the wood blue bells　　10
The lost breeze kissed her bright blue eye
The Bee kissed and went singing bye
A sun beam found a passage there
A gold chain round her neck so fair
As secret as the wild bees song
She lay there all the summer long

I hid my love in field and town
Till e'en the breeze would knock me down
The Bees seemed singing ballads oe'r
The flyes buzz turned a Lions roar　　20
And even silence found a tongue
To haunt me all the summer long
The Riddle nature could not prove
Was nothing else but secret love

Song

I wish I was where I would be
With love alone to dwell
Was I but her or she but me
Then love would all be well
I wish to send my thoughts to her
As quick as thoughts can fly
But as the winds the waters stir
The mirrors change and flye

Song

She tied up her few things
And laced up her shoe strings
And put on her bonnet worn through at the crown
Her apron tied tighter
Than snow her caps whiter
She lapt up her earnings and left our old town

The Dog barked again
All the length o' his chain
And licked her hand kindly and huffed her good bye
Old hens prated loudly   10
The Cock strutted proudly
And the horse at the gate turned to let her go bye

The Thrasher man stopping
The old barn floor wopping
Wished oer the door cloth her luck and no harm
Bees hummed round the thistle
While the red Robins whistle
And she just one look on the old mossy farm

Twas Michaelmas season
They'd got corn and pears in   20
And all the Fields cleared save some ru[c]kings and tythes
Cote piegon flocks muster
Round beans shelling cluster
And done are the whettings o reap hooks and scythes

Next years flowers a springing
Will miss Jinneys singing
She opened her Bible and turned a leaf down
In her bosoms forewarnings
She lapt up her earnings
And ere the suns set 'll be in her own town   30

Song

I peeled bits o straws and I got switches too
From the grey peeling Willow as Idlers do
And I switched at the flyes as I sat all alone
Till my flesh blood and marrow wasted to dry bone
My illness was love though I knew not the smart
But the beauty o love was the blood o my heart

Crowded places I shunned them as noises to[o] rude
And flew to the silence of sweet solitude
Where the flower in green darkness, buds, blossoms and fades
Unseen of a shepherds and flower loving maids   10
The hermit bees find them but once and away
There I'll burry alive and in silence decay

I looked on the eyes o' fair woman too long
Till silence and shame stole the use o' my tongue
When I tried to speak to her I'd nothing to say
So I turned myself round and she wandered away
When she got too far off—why I'd something to tell
So I sent sighs behind her and talked to my sell

Willow switches I broke, and I peeled bits o straws
Ever lonely in crowds in natures own laws   20
My ball room the pasture my music the Bees
My drink was the fountain my church the tall trees
Whoever would love or be tied to a wife
When it makes a man mad a' the days o' his life

['*The dew drops on every blade of grass*']

The dew drops on every blade of grass are so much like silver
drops that I am obliged to stoop down as I walk to see if they are
pearls, and those sprinkled on the Ivy woven beds of Primroses
underneath the hazels, white thorns and Maples are so like gold beads
that I stooped down to feel if they were hard but they melted from my
finger—And where the dew lies on the Primroses the violets and white

thorn leaves they are emerald and berryl yet nothing more than the
dews of the morning on the budding leaves nay the road grasses are
cover'd with gold and silver beads and the further we go the brighter
they seem to shine like solid gold and silver—It is nothing more than
the suns light and shade upon them in the dewy morning—every
thorn point and every bramble spear has its trembling ornament till
the wind gets a little brisker and then all is shaken off and all the
shining jewelry passes away into a common spring morning full of
budding leaves Primroses Violets Vernal Speedwell Blue Bell and
Orchis—and common place objects—

The Winters Come

1

Sweet chesnuts brown, like soleing leather turn,
The larch trees, like the colour of the sun,
That paled sky in the Autumn seem'd to burn.
What a strange scene before us now does run,
Red, brown, and yellow, russet black, and dun,
White thorn, wild cherry, and the poplar bare,
The sycamore all withered in the sun,
No leaves are now upon the birch tree there,
All now is stript to the cold wintry air.

2

See! not one tree but what has lost its leaves,   10
And yet, the landscape wears a pleasing hue,
The winter chill on his cold bed receives,
Foliage which once hung oer the waters blue,
Naked, and bare, the leafless trees repose,
Blue headed titmouse now seeks maggots rare,
Sluggish, and dull, the leaf strewn river flows,
That is not green, which was so through the year,
Dark chill November draweth to a close.

3

'Tis winter! and I love to read in-doors,
When the moon hangs her crescent upon high: 20
While on the window shutters the wind roars,
And storms like furies pass remorseless by,

How pleasant on a feather bed to lie,
Or sitting by the fire, in fancy soar,
With Milton, or with Dante to regions high,
Or read fresh volumes we've not seen before,
Or o'er old Bartons 'melancholy' pore.°

Birds: Why are ye Silent?

1

Why are ye silent
Birds where do ye fly
    Winters not violent
Wi such a spring sky
The wheatlands are green snow and frost is away
Birds why are ye silent on such a sweet day

2

By the slated pigstye
The red breast whispers
    Where brown leave's lye
The hedge sparrow lispers   10
But why is the chaffinch and bullfinch so still
While the sulphur primroses bedeck the wood hill

3

The bright yellowhammers
Are strutting about
    All still and none stammers
A single note out
From the hedge starts the Blackbird at brookside to drink
I thought he'd have whistled but he only said prink

4

The tree creeper hustles
Up firs rusty bark   20
    All silent he bustles
We needn't say hark
There's no song in the forest in field or in wood
Though the sun gilds the grass as tho' come in for good

5

February the tenth and
Even sparrows scarce chirp
The lark in the bents ran
And dodging round whirp
All silent they winnow o'er grass i the glen
Then drop like a stone i' the stibbles agen   30

6

How bright the odd daisies
Peep under the stubbs
How bright pilewort blazes
Where riddled sheep rubs
The old willow trunk by the side o' the brook
Where soon for Blue Violets the children will look

7

By the cot green and mossy
Feed sparrows and hens
On the ridge brown and glossy
They chirp now and then   40
The wren cocks his tail oer his back by the sty
Where his green bottle nest will be made by and by

8

Here's bunches o chickweed
Wi' small starry flow'rs
Where Red caps oft pick seed
From weeds in Spring hours
And Blue Cap and Black Cap in glossy spring coat
A peeping in buds wi' out singing a note

9

Why silent? should birds be
And sunshine so warm   50
Larks hide where the herds be
By cottage and farm
If wild flowers were blooming and fully set in the Spring
Maybe all the Birdies would cheerfully sing—

The Yellowhammer

When shall I see the white thorn leaves agen
And Yellowhammers gath'ring the dry bents
By the Dyke side on stilly moor or fen
Feathered wi love and natures good intents
Rude is the nest this Architect invents
Rural the place wi cart ruts by dyke side
Dead grass, horse hair and downy headed bents
Tied to dead thistles she doth well provide
Close to a hill o' ants where cowslips bloom
And shed o'er meadows far their sweet perfume   10
In early Spring when winds blow chilly cold
The yellow hammer trailing grass will come
To fix a place and choose an early home
With yellow breast and head of solid gold

Primroses

1

I love the rath primroses pale brimstone primroses
  That bloom in the thick wood and i' the green closes
I love the primroses whenever they come
  Where the blue fly sits pensive and humble bees hum
The pale brimstone primroses come at the spring
  Swept over and fann'd by the wild thrushes wing
Bow'd down to the leaf cover'd ground by the bees
  Who sing their spring ballads thro bushes and trees

2

Like patches o' flame i' the Ivy so green
  And dark green oak leaves where the Autumn has been   10
Put on thy straw hat love and russet stuff gown
  And see the pale primroses grow up and down
The pale brimstone primroses wild wood primroses
  Which maids i' the dark woods make into posies
Put on thy stuff gown love and off let us be
  To seek brimstone primroses neath the Oak tree

3

Spring time is come love primroses bloom fair
  The sun o' the morning shines in thy bright hair
The ancient wood shadows are bonny dark green
  That throw out like giants the stovens between   20
While brimstone primroses like patches o' flame
  Blaze through the dead leaves making Ivy look tame
I love the rath primrose in hedgerows and closes
  Together lets wander to gather primroses—

Meet Me in the Green Glen

Love meet me in the green glen
  Beside the tall Elm tree
Where the Sweet briar smells so sweet agen
  There come wi me
      Meet me in the green glen

Meet me at the sunset
  Down in the green glen
Where we've often met
  By hawthorn tree and foxes den
      Meet me in the green glen   10

Meet me by the sheep pen
  Where briers smell at een
Meet me i the green glen
  Where white thorn shades are green
      Meet me in the green glen

Meet me in the green glen
  By sweet briar bushes there
Meet me by your own sen
  Where the wild thyme blossoms fair
      Meet me in the green glen   20

Meet me by the sweet briar
  By the mole hill swelling there
When the west glows like a fire
  Gods crimson bed is there
      Meet me in the green glen

Perplexities

1

I talk to the birds as they sing i' the morn
The larks and the Sparrow's that spring from the corn
The Chaffinch and Linnet that sings in the bush
Till the zephyr like breezes all bid me to hush
Then silent I go and in fancy I steal
A kiss from the lips of a name I conceal
But should I meet her I've cherish'd for years
I pass by in silence in fondness and fears

2

Yes I pass her in silence and say not a word
And the noise o' my footsteps may scarcely be heard 10
I scarcely presume to cast on her my eye
And then for a week I do nothing but sigh
If I look on a wild flower I see her face there
There it is in its beauty all radient and fair
And should she pass by I've nothing to say
We are both of us silent and have our own way

3

I talk to the birds the wind and the rain
My love to my dear one I never explain
I talk to the flower's which are growing all wild
As if one was herself and the other her child 20
I utter sweet words in my fanciful way
But if *she* come's by I've nothing to say
To look for a kiss I would if I dare
But I feel myself lost when near to my fair—

Spring

1

In every step we tread appears fresh spring
   Hedge weeds all juicy run up tall and flowers
Birds near their nests in early morning sing
   By yonder Chaffinch there the Leveret cowers

Unseen and nestles through the days warm hours
  Then plays at eve tide in the grass and dew
The old field barn is based with wild spring flowers
  The old cart wheel agen the hovel threw
Leans neath the thatch where last year robins flew

2

The summers messenger the sooty swallow   10
  O'er level meadows like a shadow swims
Then darts with nimbler speed oer the brown fallow
  On o'er the farm within a minute skims
His flight to mark the keenest vision dims
  Now o'er the green wheat field it playful springs
Then oer the meadow field its flight begins
  There drops and drinks and twitters round and sings
The happiest welcomer of early spring

3

The children shout to see a swallow fly
  When they come first where the bow'd cowslips bloom   20
Down valleys where lone lodge and hamlets lie
  They eager bawl and halloo 'Here they come'
'And there they go' as thoughts do to their home
  They hasten quickly to warm chimney pots
Day after day the children watch them come
  The sight of swallow[s] their flower gathring stops
Skiming the valley, brooks, through woods he pops

4

Above the Quick set blooms 'Jack by the hedge'
  His white flowers shine all down the narrow lane
In April sunshine still a welcome pledge   30
  To show warm weather brings wild flowers again
Primrose to woods and cowslips to the plain
  The Arum red or white their flower shows
The grass gets darker with the sun and rain
  The yellow rocket by the dyke side grows
And every wild weed in perfection glows—

The Rawk o' the Autumn

The rawk o' the Autumn hangs over the woodlands
Like smoke from a City dismember'd and pale
The sun without beams burns dim o'er the floodlands
Where white Cawdymaws slow swiver and sail
The flood froths away like a fathomless ocean
The wind winnows chill like a breeze from the sea
And thoughts of my Susan give the heart an emotion
To think does she e'er waste a thought upon me

Full oft I think so on the banks of the meadows
While the pale Cawdymawdy flies swooping all day   10
I think of our true love where grass and flowers hid us
As by the dyke side o' the meadows we lay
The seasons have chang'd since I sat wi my true love
Now the flood roars and raves o'er the bed where we lay
There the bees kiss'd the flowers—Has she got a new love
I feel like a wreck of the flood cast away

The rawk of the Autumn hangs over the woodland
Like smoke from a City sulphurously grey
The Heronshaw lonely hangs over the floodland
And cranks its lone story throughout the dull day   20
There's no green on the hedges no leaves on the darkwood
No cows on the pasture or sheep on the lea
The Linnets cheep still and how happy the lark would
Sing songs to sweet Susan to remind her of me

Woman had we Never Met

Woman had we never met
I nor thou had felt regret
Never had a cause to sigh
Never had a wish to die
     To part and cease to love thee

Had I shared the smallest part
Of friendship from a womans heart
Never had I felt the pains
Of these ever galling chains
      Or ever ceased to love thee   10

And never on my burning brow
Felt the cain curses I do now
That withers up the anxious brain
Blighting what never blooms again
      When woman ceased to love me

The Spring may come the sun may shine
The earth may send forth sweets divine
What pain I've felt have still to know
There's nought in Nature e'er to show
      Since woman ceased to love me   20

Woman had we never met
Love had witnessed no regret
Never left us cause to sigh
Or me a vainer wish to die
      To part and cease to love thee

Written in Prison

I envy e'en the fly its gleams of joy
In the green woods from being but a boy
Among the vulgar and the lowly bred
I envied e'en the hare her grassy bed
Innured to strife and hardship from a child
I traced with lonely step the desert wild
Sigh'd o'er bird pleasures but no nest destroyed
With pleasure felt the singing they enjoyed
Saw nature smile on all and shed no tears
A slave through ages though a child in years   10
The mockery and scorn of those more old
An Esop in the worlds extended fold
The fly I envy settling in the sun
On the green leaf and wish my goal was won

The Maple Tree

The Maple with its tassell flowers of green
That turns to red a stag horn shaped seed
Just spreading out its scallopped leaves is seen
Of yellowish hue yet beautifully green
Bark ribb'd like corderoy in seamy screed
That farther up the stem is smoother seen
Where the white hemlock with white umbel flowers
Up each spread stoven to the branches towers
And mossy round the stoven spread dark green
And blotched leaved orchis and the blue bell flowers   10
Thickly they grow and neath the leaves are seen
I love to see them gemm'd with morning hours
I love the lone green places where they be
And the sweet clothing of the Maple tree

The Chiming Bells

How peaceful sound the chiming bells
From yonder lonely tower
That o'er the cornfield valley swells
And beanfields all in flower
Calmly they reach the shepherds ear
As he oer upland climbs
No day to him is half so dear
As sunday with its chimes

The beanfields make the air so sweet
In pink and purple plea   10
How beautiful the lake we meet
And the willow weeping tree
Decayed by time a very shell
And bent as tumbling in
The pit so deep we cannot tell
Much deeper than the chin

How beautiful the sunday looks
To any other day
How green the fields how clear the brooks
Beneath the white thorn may   20
How beautiful from yon old tower
The chimes their story tells
Theres little in the summer hour
So sweet as chiming bells—

Come dear Amanda walk with me
Let us enjoy the prime
Of field and meadow scenery
And hear the sabbath chime
We'll walk beneath the willow row
Where screaming plover dwells   30
And with the winding river go
And hear the Sabbath bells

Mary Helen from the Hill

The flaggy wheat is in the ear
At the low end of the town
And the barley horns begin to spear
Frae the spindle through the crown
The black snail he has crept abroad
In dangers ways to run
And midges oer the road
Are dancing in the sun
Where firdales darkest shadows leave
Sweet Mary Hellen walks at eve   10

In the deep dyke grows the reed
The bullrush wabbles deeper still
And oval leaves of water weed
The dangerous deeper places fill
The river winds and feels no ill
How lovely sinks the setting sun
The fish leaps up with trembling trill

Grasshoppers chirrup on the reed
The mead so green the air so still
Evening assembles sweet indeed   20
With Mary Hellen from the Hill
Who wanders by that rivers brim
In dewy flowers and shadows dim

Right merrily the midges dance
Above the river stream
Their wings like silver atoms glance
In evenings golden beam
The boat track by the rivers side
Where Mary Hellen roves
The cloud sky where the river wide   30
The banks of willow groves
And Mary Hellen in young pride
Rambling by the river side—

Born upon an Angels Breast

I' crime and enmity they lie
Who sin and tell us love can die
Who say to us in slanders breath
That love belongs to sin and death
From Heaven it came on Angels wing
To bloom on earth eternal spring
In falsehoods enmity they lie
Who sin and tell us love can die

Twas born upon an angels breast
The softest dreams the sweetest rest   10
The brightest sun the bluest sky
Are loves own home and canopy
The thought that cheers this heart of mine
Is that of Love—Love so divine
They sin who say in slanders breath
That love belongs to Sin and death

The sweetest voice that lips contain
The sweetest thought that leaves the brain
The sweetest feelings of the heart
Theres pleasure even in its smart   20
The scent of Rose and Cinnamon
Is hot like Love remem[b]ered on
In falsehoods enmity they lie
Who sin and tell us love can die

Flow on Winding River

Flow on winding river in silence for ever
The sedge and flags rustle about in a bustle
You are dear to my fancy thou smooth flowing river
The bullrush bows calm and theres peace in the hustle
      As the boat gently glides
      Oer thy soft flowing tides
As the young maidens sail on a sweet summer day

The wavelets in ridges by osiers through bridges
Neath the grey willows shade and the nestling reeds made
Were dear to my fancy as onward they sail   10
The osiers they dip in the rings lilys made
      And the maiden look'd red
      As the corn poppy bed
Or dog rose that blushed in the shade

The day was delightful where but gadflies where spiteful
The hum of the Bee carolled merrily there
The Butterflies danced round the wild flowers delightful
And the old willows toss'd their grey locks in the air
      The boat softly rippled
      Suspended oars drippled   20
While the maidens were lovely and beauteously fair

The boat gently pushes aside the bullrushes
All gilt by the water and summer sunbeams
How soft the oar dashes the stream as it splashes
By the side of the boat wi its burden o dreams
      The rushing of waters
      The songs o' earths daughters
How sweetly they sound in the plash of the streams

Fragment

The Elm tree's heavy foliage meets the eye
Propt in dark masses on the evening sky
The lighter ash but half obstructs the view
Leaving grey openings where the light looks through

To John Clare°

Well honest John how fare you now at home
The spring is come and birds are building nests
The old cock robin to the stye is come
With olive feathers and its ruddy breast
And the old cock with wattles and red comb
Struts with the hens and seems to like some best
Then crows and looks about for little crumbs
Swept out bye little folks an hour ago
The pigs sleep in the sty the bookman comes
The little boys lets home close nesting go   10
And pockets tops and tawes where daiseys bloom
To look at the new number just laid down°
With lots of pictures and good stories too
And Jack the jiant killers high renown

Birds Nests°

Tis Spring warm glows the South
Chaffinchs carry the moss in his mouth
To the filbert hedges all day long
And charms the poet with his beautifull song
The wind blows blea oer the sedgey fen
But warm the sunshines by the little wood
Where the old Cow at her leisure chews her cud

[*Autobiographical Passages*]

[I]

. . . the continued sameness of a garden cloyed me and I resumed
my old employments with pleasure were I coud look on the wild
heath, the wide spreading variety of cultured and fallow fields, green
meadows, and crooking brooks, and the dark woods waving to the
murmering winds   these were my delights and here I coud mutter
to myself as usual unheard and unnoticd by the sneering clown and
conscieted coxcomb, and here my old habits and feelings returnd with
redoubled ardour for they left me while I was a gardiner   I now
venturd to commit my musings readily to paper but with all secresy
possible, hiding them when written in an old unused cubbard in the
chamber which when taken for other purposes drove me to the
nessesity of seeking another safety in a hole under it in the wall   here
my mother when clearing the chamber found me out and secretly took
my papers for her own use as occassion calld for them and as I had
no other desire in me but to keep them from being read when laid in
this fancied safe repository that desire seemd compleated and I rarely
turnd to a reperusal of them   consequently my stolen fugitives went
a long time ere they was miss'd   my mother thought they was
nothing more then Copies as attempts at improving my self in
writing   she knew nothing of poetry, at least little dreamed her
son was employd in that business . . .

[II]°

About now all my stock of learning was gleancd from the Sixpenny
Romances of 'Cinderella', 'Little Red Riding Hood', 'Jack and the
bean Stalk', 'Zig Zag', 'Prince Cherry', etc., and great was the
pleasure, pain or surprise increased by allowing them authenticity for
I firmly believed every page I read and considerd I possesd in these
the chief learning and literature of the country   But as it is common
in villages to pass judgment on a lover of books as a sure indication
of laziness I was drove to the narrow nessesity of stinted oppertunitys to hide in woods and dingles of thorns in the fields on
Sundays to read these things which every sixpence, thro the indefati-
gible savings of a penny and halfpenny, when collected was willingly
thrown away for them as oppertunity offered when hawkers offerd
them for sale at the door . . .

[III]

... as to my schooling, I think never a year passd me till I was 11
or 12 but 3 months or more at the worst of times was luckily spared
for my improvment, first with an old woman in the village and latterly
with a master at a distance from it.   here soon as I began to learn
to write the readiness of the Boys always practising urgd and
prompted my ambition to make the best use of my abscence from
school, as well as at it, and my master was always supprisd to find
me improved every fresh visit instead of having lost what I had
learned before, for which to my benefit he never faild to give me
tokens of encouragment   never a leisure hour passd me, without
making use of it   every winter night our once unletterd hut was
wonderfully changd in its appearence to a school room   the old table,
which, old as it was, doubtless never was honourd with higher employment all its days then the convenience of bearing at meal times
the luxury of a barley loaf or dish of potatoes, was now coverd with
the rude begg[in]ings of scientifical requ[i]sitions, pens, ink and paper
one hour, jobbling the pen at sheep hooks and tarbottles, and another
trying on a slate a knotty question in Numeration or Pounds Shillings
and Pence, at which times my parents triumphant anxiety was
pleasingly experiencd for my mother woud often stop her wheel or
look off from her work to urge with a smile of the warmest rapture
in my fathers face her prophesy of my success, saying 'shed be bound
I shoud one day be able to reward them with my pen for the trouble
they had taken in giveing me schooling.'   and I have to return hearty
thanks to a kind providence in bringing her prophesy to pass . . .

. . . I at length got an higher notion of learning by going to school and
every leisure minute was employ'd in drawing squares and triangles
upon the dusty walls of the barn   this was also my practice in learning to write   I also devourd for these purposes every morsel of
brown or blue paper (it matterd not which) that my mother had her
tea and sugar lapt in from the shop but this was in cases of poverty
when I coud not muster three farthings for a sheet of writing
paper   the saying of 'a little learning is a dangerous thing'° is not
far from fact   after I left school for good, (nearly as wise as I went
save reading and writing), I felt an itching after every thing   I now
began to provide my self with books of many puzzling systems
Bonnycastles Mensuration, Fennings Arithmetic and Algebra° was
now my constant teachers and as I read the rules of each Problem

with great care I preseverd so far as to solve many of the questions
in those books   my pride fancyd it self climbing the ladder of learning very rapidly on the top of which harvests of unbounded wonders
was concieved to be bursting upon me and was sufficient fire to promt
my ambition . . .

[IV]

. . . the Romance of 'Robinson Crusoe' was the first book of any
merit I got hold of after I coud read   twas in the winter and I
borrowd it of a boy at s[c]hool who said it was his uncles and seemed
very loath to lend it me, but pressing him with anxious persuasions
and asuring him of its saftey while in my hands he lent it me that
day to be returnd in the morning when I came to school, but in the
night a great snow fell which made it impossible to keep my promise
as I coud not get, Glinton being 2 miles from our village were I
went to school so I had the pleasure of this delightful companion for a
week   new ideas from the perusal of this book was now up in arms,
new Crusoes and new Islands of Solitude was continually mutterd
over in my journeys to and from school . . .

[*Journey out of Essex*]°

July 18—1841—Sunday—Felt very melancholly—went a walk on the forest in the afternoon—fell in with some gipseys one of whom offered to assist in my escape from the mad house by hideing me in his camp to which I almost agreed but told him I had no money to start with but if he would do so I would promise him fifty pounds and he agreed to do so before saturday   on friday I went again but he did not seem so willing so I said little about it—On sunday I went and they were all gone—an old wide awake hat and an old straw bonnet of the plumb pudding sort was left behind— and I put the hat in my pocket thinking it might be usefull for another oppertunity—as good luck would have it, it turned out to be so

July 19—Monday—Did nothing

July 20—Reconnitered the rout the Gipsey pointed out and found it a legible one to make a movement and having only honest courage and myself in my army I Led the way and my troops soon followed but being careless in mapping down the rout as the Gipsey told me I missed the lane to Enfield town and was going down Enfield highway till I passed 'The Labour in vain' Public house where A person I knew comeing out of the door told me the way°

I walked down the lane gently and was soon in Enfield Town and bye and bye on the great York Road where it was all plain sailing and steering ahead meeting no enemy and fearing none I reached Stevenage where being Night I got over a gate crossed over the corner of a green paddock where seeing a pond or hollow in the corner I forced to stay off a respectable distance to keep from falling into it for my legs were nearly knocked up and began to stagger   I scaled some old rotten paleings into the yard and then had higher pailings to clamber over to get into the shed or hovel which I did with difficulty being rather weak and to my good luck I found some trusses of clover piled up about 6 or more feet square which I gladly mounted and slept on   there was some trays in the hovel on which I could have reposed had I not found a better bed   I slept soundly but had a very uneasy dream   I thought my first wife lay on my left arm and somebody took her away from my side which made me wake up rather unhappy   I thought as I awoke somebody said

'Mary' but nobody was near—I lay down with my head towards the north to show myself the steering point in the morning

July 21—[when I awoke] Daylight was looking in on every side and fearing my garrison might be taken by storm and myself be made prisoner I left my lodging by the way I got in and thanked God for his kindness in procureing it (for any thing in a famine is better then nothing and any place that giveth the weary rest is a blessing)   I gained the north road again and steered due north—on the left hand side the road under the bank like a cave I saw a Man and boy coiled up asleep which I hailed and they woke up to tell me the name of the next village°

Some where on the London side the 'Plough' Public house° a Man passed me on horseback in a Slop frock and said 'here's another of the broken down haymakers' and threw me a penny to get a half pint of beer which I picked up and thanked him for and when I got to the plough I called for a half pint and drank it and got a rest and escaped a very heavy shower in the bargain by having a shelter till it was over—afterwards I would have begged a penny of two drovers who were very saucey so I begged no more of any body meet who I would

—I passed 3 or 4 good built houses on a hill and a public house on the road side in the hollow below them   I seemed to pass the Milestones very quick in the morning but towards night they seemed to be stretched further asunder   I got to a village further on and forgot the name   the road on the left hand was quite over shaded by some trees and quite dry so I sat down half an hour and made a good many wishes for breakfast but wishes was no hearty meal so I got up as hungry as I sat down—I forget here the names of the villages I passed through but reccolect at late evening going through Potton in Bedfordshire where I called in a house to light my pipe in which was a civil old woman and a young country wench makeing lace on a cushion as round as a globe and a young fellow all civil people—I asked them a few questions as to the way and where the clergyman and overseer lived but they scarcely heard me or gave me no answer°

I then went through Potton and happened with a kind talking country man who told me the Parson lived a good way from where I was or overseer I do'n't know which so I went on hopping with a crippled foot for the gravel had got into my old shoes one of which I had now nearly lost the sole   Had I found the overseers house at hand or the Parsons I should have gave my name and begged for

a shilling to carry me home but I was forced to brush on pennyless
and be thankfull I had a leg to move on—I then asked him wether he
could tell me of a farm yard any where on the road where I could
find a shed and some dry straw and he said yes and if you will go
with me I will show you the place—its a public house on the left
hand side the road at the sign of the 'Ram'° but seeing a stone or
flint heap I longed to rest as one of my feet was very painfull so I
thanked him for his kindness and bid him go on—but the good
natured fellow lingered awhile as if wishing to conduct me and then
suddenly reccolecting that he had a hamper on his shoulder and a lock
up bag in his hand cram full to meet the coach which he feared
missing—he started hastily and was soon out of sight—I followed
looking in vain for the country mans straw bed—and not being able
to meet it I lay down by a shed side under some Elm trees
between the wall and the trees being a thick row planted some 5 or
6 feet from the buildings   I lay there and tried to sleep but the
wind came in between them so cold that I lay till I quaked like the
ague and quitted the lodging for a better at the Ram which I could
hardly hope to find—It now began to grow dark apace and the odd
houses on the road began to light up and show the inside tennants
lots very comfortable and my outside lot very uncomfortable and
wretched—still I hobbled forward as well as I could and at last came
to the Ram   the shutters were not closed and the lighted window
looked very cheering but I had no money and did not like to go
in   there was a sort of shed or gighouse at the end but I did not like
to lie there as the people were up—so I still travelled on   the road
was very lonely and dark in places being overshaded with trees   at
length I came to a place where the road branched off into two turn-
pikes one to the right about and the other straight forward and on
going bye my eye glanced on a mile stone standing under the hedge
so I heedlessly turned back to read it to see where the other road led
too and on doing so I found it led to London   I then suddenly
forgot which was North or South and though I narrowly examined
both ways I could see no tree or bush or stone heap that I could
reccolect I had passed so I went on mile after mile almost convinced
I was going the same way I came and these thoug[h]ts were so strong
upon me that doubt and hopelessness made me turn so feeble that
I was scarcely able to walk yet I could not sit down or give up but
shuffled along till I saw a lamp shining as bright as the moon which
on nearing I found was suspended over a Tollgate°   before I got
through the man came out with a candle and eyed me narrowly but

having no fear I stopt to ask him wether I was going northward and he said when you get through the gate you are; so I thanked him kindly and went through on the other side and gathered my old strength   as my doubts vanished I soon cheered up and hummed the air of highland Mary as I went on°   I at length fell in with an odd house all alone near a wood but I could not see what the sign was though the sign seemed to stand oddly enough in a sort of trough or spout   there was a large porch over the door and being weary I crept in and glad enough I was to find I could lye with my legs straight   the inmates were all gone to roost for I could hear them turn over in bed as I lay at full length on the stones in the poach—I slept here till daylight and felt very much refreshed as I got up—I blest my two wives and both their familys when I lay down and when I got up and when I thought of some former difficultys on a like occasion I could not help blessing the Queen   Having passed a Lodge on the left hand within a mile and half or less of a town I think it might be St Ives but I forget the name° I sat down to rest on a flint heap° where I might rest half an hour or more and while sitting here I saw a tall Gipsey come out of the Lodge gate and make down the road towards where I was sitting   when she got up to me on seeing she was a young woman with an honest looking countenance rather handsome I spoke to her and asked her a few questions which she answered readily and with evident good humour so I got up and went on to the next town with her—she cautioned me on the way to put somthing in my hat to keep the crown up and said in a lower tone 'you'll be noticed' but not knowing what she hinted—I took no notice and made no reply   at length she pointed to a small tower church which she called Shefford Church and advised me to go on a footway which would take me direct to it and I should shorten my journey fifteen miles by doing so°   I would gladly have taken the young womans advice feeling that it was honest and a nigh guess towards the truth but fearing I might loose my way and not be able to find the north road again I thanked her and told her I should keep to the road when she bade me 'good day' and went into a house or shop on the left hand side the road   I have but a slight reccolection of my journey between here and Stilton for I was knocked up and noticed little or nothing—one night I lay in a dyke bottom from the wind and went sleep half an hour when I suddenly awoke and found one side wet through from the sock in the dyke bottom so I got out and went on—I remember going down a very dark road hung over with trees on both sides very thick which seemed to extend

a mile or two   I then entered a town and some of the chamber
windows had candle lights shineing in them—I felt so weak here that
I forced to sit down on the ground to rest myself and while I sat here
a Coach that seemed to be heavy laden came rattling up and stopt
in the hollow below me and I cannot reccolect its ever passing by
me°   I then got up and pushed onward seeing little to notice for
the road very often looked as stupid as myself and I was very often
half asleep as I went   on the third day I satisfied my hunger by
eating the grass by the road side which seemed to taste something
like bread   I was hungry and eat heartily till I was satisfied and in
fact the meal seemed to do me good   the next and last day I
reccollected that I had some tobacco and my box of lucifers being
exausted I could not light my pipe so I took to chewing Tobacco all
day and eat the quids when I had done and I was never hungry
afterwards—I remember passing through Buckden and going a length
of road afterwards but I dont reccolect the name of any place untill
I came to stilton where I was compleatly foot foundered and broken
down   when I had got about half through the town a gravel
causeway invited me to rest myself so I lay down and nearly went
sleep   a young woman (so I guessed by the voice) came out of a
house and said 'poor creature' and another more elderly said 'O he
shams' but when I got up the latter said 'o no he don't' as I
hobbled along very lame   I heard the voices but never looked back
to see where they came from—when I got near the Inn at the end
of the gravel walk I met two young women and I asked one of them
wether the road branching to the right° bye the end of the Inn did
not lead to Peterborough and she said 'Yes' it did so as soon as ever
I was on it I felt myself in homes way and went on rather more
cheerfull though I forced to rest oftener then usual   before I got
to Peterborough a man and woman passed me in a cart and on hailing
me as they passed I found they were neighbours from Helpstone
where I used to live—I told them I was knocked up which they
could easily see and that I had neither eat or drank any thing since
I left Essex   when I told my story they clubbed together and threw
me fivepence out of the cart   I picked it up and called at a small
public house near the bridge were I had two half pints of ale and
twopenn'oth of bread and cheese   when I had done I started quite
refreshed only my feet was more crippled then ever and I could
scarcely make a walk of it over the stones and being half ashamed
to sit down in the street I forced to keep on the move and got through
Peterborough better then I expected   when I got on the high road

I rested on the stone heaps as I passed till I was able to go on afresh and bye and bye I passed Walton and soon reached Werrington and was making for the Beehive° as fast as I could when a cart met me with a man and woman and a boy in it when nearing me the woman jumped out and caught fast hold of my hands and wished me to get into the cart but I refused and thought her either drunk or mad but when I was told it was my second wife Patty I got in and was soon at Northborough   but Mary was not there neither could I get any information about her further then the old story of her being dead six years ago which might be taken from a bran new old Newspaper printed a dozen years ago but I took no notice of the blarney having seen her myself about a twelvemonth ago alive and well and as young as ever—so here I am homeless at home and half gratified to feel that I can be happy any where

> 'May none those marks of my sad fate efface
> 'For they appeal from tyranny to God'
>
> Byron°

July 24th 1841 Returned home out of Essex and found no Mary— her and her family are as nothing to me now though she herself was once the dearest of all—and how can I forget

[*The Farmer and the Vicar*]

Just as pride and fashion was creeping out of the citys like a plague to infest the Village Ralph Wormstall° one of the last of the oppulent Farmers of the old school flourished in his popularity whose fame for fat oxen and old Ale got wind even beyond the out skirts of the county   he was a very rich plain and superstitious man whose enemys called him 'horse shoe Ralph' from a failing he had in believing in witches and a practice which he indulged in of nailing old horse shoes about the thresholds of his house and stables to prevail as a spell against their nightly depredations as he firmly believed that they rode his sheep trays and cow cribs about the yard on Winter nights and terrified himself and his horses till he tryed the above to prevent them which has branded the old farmer for ever with the name of 'Horse shoe Ralph' and he was a plain rich old farmer and a good fellow in spite of his nick name and it was once whispered about the village that he got the Vicar to conjure some evil spirits in his cellar in a barrel of Ale which he fancied haunted his stock when his sheep dyed of the rot one wet season and his swine of the murrain in acorn time°   his enemys vouched it for truth and his friends did not contradict it but smiled when they heard it and calld it an 'innoscent weakness'   be as it woud the Vicar was as superstitious as himself and always quoted the witch of Endor° as a knockdown to unbelievers in witchcraft for he swallowed every story with the most credulous faith and because a farmer once doubted his authority of the 'Witch of Endor' as a proof of their existance he instantly set him down as an Atheist and declared that he shoud not be buried in the churchyard if he could help it—the Old farmer was very rich but he never purchased a hunting horse and made it his boast among Sportsmen of confessing that he never followed a Fox in his life except to drive him from the henroost and seldom got astride of a saddle save when he gave old Dobbin a holiday from the Plough to carry his Dame to the Fair° to sell her Stilton cheese and while the young coxcomb was praising himself as a 'good shot' he woud confess it as a boast of being no Sportsman and considered it as a mark of his wisdom for such ignorance   when they talked of their certificates to kill game he would cock his pipe higher and dryly observe that his Lordships Gamekeeper always sent a Hare at Christmass to his old tennants and he shoud be a fool to buy a certificate to shoot one—one Hare a year satisfied his wants and he

fancied one liscence enabled them to shoot no more   he was famous
in Obstinacys and as famous for keeping them   he kept an old Gun
for no other purpose as it woud seem then to hang among the fire
Irons above the kitchen chimney but he found it useful to shoot
sparrows in harvest and fright the Fox from the hen roost in Winter—
he always made it a rule to go to Market a foot and sold his Eggs
and Butter himself as he thought it a better scheme then trusting to
servants and he even took a pride to crack of his Orchard in good
fruit years and sold both the Apples and Pears as he considered it a
shame to devour any thing in his own house that might be done
without and that woud turn into money—he always sat at the
same table at Harvest suppers with his men—and woud never suffer
the Oven stone to be opend till the Vicar made his appearance When
they shook hands drank a horn together as a pledge of thanks for a
good harvest and then the supper was instantly on the table—he
always made it a rule to sing all the songs he knew on that night
which were not many and 'When this Old Hat was new' 'Toby
Fillpot' and 'Speed the Plough'° were always sung at a heat in quick
succession for he never waited to be asked to sing or stopt to let any
one else till he was done   and he prided himself in knowing 3 such
good Songs for he coud not aspire to much praise in singing them
as he had but a bad voice and readily acknowledgd that his old
friend the Vicar had a better who was fond of a Song tho he always
excused himself in a mixed company and the old Farmer woud get
him off by saying that he did it for the sake of his 'cloth' tho at the
same time he woud urge him to say 'Chevey Chase' instead of singing
it as there coud be no harm in [that which he] always readily agreed
to   and he woud listen to any Song except the Vicar of Bray when
he woud instantly get up though his pipe was just lighted and make
excuse to leave the room which never happened at the old Farmers
house where none offered to offend him for the old farmer woud not
laugh at the Vicars expence tho he was fond of jokes and had two
or three 'old Joe Millars' which served for all seasons at which none
laughd so heartily as himself   he always had his brown earthern
pitcher of his old ale over a pipe after dinner and he never emptied
it without drinking 'Long life to the King' tho 'peace and plenty' was
his favourite toast in company and he felt it nessesary to appologize
for its frequent use at his sunday dinner partys (for he never invited
friends at another time except the vicar as he had no time to attend
to them) by saying 'heres my old health gentlemen "Peace and
Plenty" for want of a better' tho he thought at the same time that a

better never existed and Vicar woud often confess so when he said
it needed no appology   he was a great stickler for 'good old ways'
as he called them and woud not suffer any of his family to reach a
glass from the cupboard to drink out of when there was no company
and the old Vicar always joined him in believing that the clear horn
with its silver rim was far better then glasses   and he seldom was in a
passion with the wenches unless they wanted to follow the fashions
and never thought his old dame a fool but once when she joind her
daughters in thinking that a 'beautiful set of blue China' woud be a
better ornament to the cupboard then the old Delf Teapot and white
cups and saucers when he declared that they shoud all go without
tea the instant they bought them   whenever genteel company made
glasses a nessesary appendage to the dinner table he appologized
for the use of the old horn to himself by saying it was a gift of his
mothers and he coud not discard it—but his wife woud often let out
his secret pregudice to glasses by laughing and saying that he never
made it a rule to drink healths out of glasses and the old man woud
laugh likewise as it gave him an oppertunity of begining up a long
praise of his young days when horns and brown earthern ware pitchers
were in fashion and if he was a little warm with liquor he woud lay
down his pipe without bidding and sing his old favourite 'When this
old hat was new' and the Daughters were often terribly anoyed with
his meddlings in their dresses and his staunch canvasings for the old
fashion of stays and stumachers and hair hanging down the back
instead of being stuck up in combs but the Vicar sided for the girles
dresses and thought it 'better for them to dress like other people
then to go otherways' and the old dame woud finish the Vicars story
not giving time to say further—'and to be every bodys laughing
stock'°—so they wearied his objections and he suffered them at last
to go without stays and dress up their hair as they pleased tho he
never woud agree to their following the 'Hoggs fashion' as he called it
to wear ear rings so they were always obliged to wear caps in his
presence to hide them   when they talked of new fashions he woud
instantly tell the history of his sunday suit which was a grey
colored coat with hugh buttons and a waistcoat of the same color with
large pockets and flaps that hung over his hips big enough for a
modern squires shooting jacket   it was his 'wedding suit' and he
seldom had it on without mentioning the surcumstance and his wife
often declared to her guests tho her husband had been married 40
years that his sunday suit were as clean and as good as when they
were first put on for the wedding   this always made the old man

smile and at the same time reach his hand to the shelf for the
cloathsbrush to give it a stroke down   his first wish had been to
learn them all to be good Dairey wives by sending them to milk and
do the kitchen work and make the cheese and butter themselves but
his wife told the Vicar it was nothing but a mizardly turn to save the
wages of servants and ruin his daughters by making them fit for
nothing but servants them selves   the old Vicar woud laugh and say
that her 'spark of pride' might be right enough for what he knew—
and she over ruled her husband against sending them to school by
reminding him that Moll Huggings° won a nobleman by the
accomplishments she learned there—so he let them go with the hopes
of making them ladys—he was very cautious in remembering old
customs and considerd the forgetting one an ill omen   he was
always punctual in having the old bowl of frumitory at sheep shearing
ready in time for the shepherds suppers and never let the old year
go out without warming the old can of ale for the ringers well
pepperd with ginger and he woud always have his Yule cake cut at
Twelfth night for the Morris dancers to taste of with their beer let
the old dame mutter as she might   he always got the fattest goose
for christmass and a couple of the best ducks in the yard for lammass
tide and he kept almost every Saint day in the almanack with an
additional pitcher after dinner and another pipe at night with the
Vicar which he called 'a honoring the day' and often remarked as they
were all of the same 'cloth' with his good old neighbour (meaning
the Vicar for he thought all the saints had been Vicars) they were
worth remembering   and as the good old Vicar liked to wet his pipe
in a moderate way he never once contradicted the custom or objected
to catholics—tho King Charles the Martyr and a few others by way of
distinction were honoured with a prayer 'for the occasion' and a
'proper lesson' in the Bible read aloud to the family by the Vicar
whom the old farmer always complimented as being the best reader
in England   tho he did not pretend to much learning himself yet
he fancied he coud read a chapter in the Bible with any man except
the Vicar and he always made a point of reading one every sunday
night aloud to his family and it was generaly from 'Proverbs' for he
considered them as the finest parts of Scripture as he said a man coud
not be made too wise for the world and the Vicar often tryed in vain
to convince him that they aluded to spiritual conserns for he never
coud be beat out of his own way—as he said nothing had two
meanings in his mind—so it was no use talking   he professed a little
knowledge of books tho his whole acquai[n]tance took up no more

then a spare corner on the mantlepiece were the Bible and Mores
Almanack° stood together which he considered two of the best books
that were ever printed   there was the 'Whole duty of man'° too
which he prized as being a heir long to the family and had belonged
to his grandfather but he had never read it and Elliots Husbandry°
he had but he woud not confess that it was of any use to him and
only kept as a family legacy for he used to say that farmers had
done going school now adays and coud farm without Books at least
ought to do   with these lay a heap of pamphlets among which was
the 'History of Jane Shore' 'The King and the Cobler' 'Johnney
Armstrong' and a fragment of an old book on Cookery with 'Hamlet
a tradegy by Will Shakspear Esqr' but these belongd to the Wife and
the last to his daughters who woud often attempt to read passages of
Shakspear on a winters evening to him a taste which they had brought
from school—but they coud not beat him out of his old favourite
opinion that 'George Barnwell'° which his mother took him to see
acted when a boy was a better play then 'Shakspear' for he always
confounded the name with the subject and thought that Shakspear
was the title of a Play the same as 'George Barnwell'   and trying
to correct his errors was of no use for he always stuck to his first
opinions of things wether right or wrong   he prided himself in such
obst[i]nacys by calling those turncoats that were willing to be
corrected out of their old opinions for so he called his errors—they
woud often try to get the Vicar on their side but he only confessed a
dislike for Plays and stopt there—tho the old farmer had no
knowledge of Poetry—'His music long had been the plough'°—yet
like tha true Critic he was ever ready with his opinion in every thing
and argued with the Vicars Latin as stoutly as if he had been
at colledge half his life   he was acqua[i]nted with Old Tussers
Husbandry° and set him down as the greatest poet on Earth and the
Vicar shook his head in vain quoting scraps from Horace to prove
him before Tusser tho nobody understood a word of the latin but
himself and the old farmer always fancied that if a man coud read
english they coud read any thing if it was readable   therefor he
always called Horace a fool and his latin nonsense because he coud
not read it—his Book of old Tusser had been 'time out of mind' in
his family and the favourite passages of his father were doubld down
still as he left them at the 'lessons on Thrift' for his father had
often called him 'the greatest poet that ever lived' and he deemed
the book of sufficient importance to insert in his 'Will' as a family
legacy which he 'desired might never go out of the family' nor was it

placed on the corner shelf with the rest but carefully kept in his coffer with a piece of green bays stretched round the covers to preserve them°—the Vicar like his old neeghbour was not much given to books   he neither read much or pretended to it by talking about it   his chief discourse was like the old farmers about markets and the weather   and tho religion seldom shared their conversation—the old farmer and his family were regular churchgoers

'True to the Church no sunday shower
'Kept him at home in that important hour'°

and he somtimes remarked to the Vicar over their pipes of his never missing going to church of a Sunday but once in twenty years and that was when he got his hay out of that meadow before the 'great July flood'° came down for it was a memorable day with him and he often wondered why Moor did not put it among the remarkable things in his Almanack as well as the 'hot Wednesday'°   and tho those who lost their hay blamed him for breaking the sabbath the Old Vicar excused it and said he was right and preached a sermon on the right of using urgent nessesitys—the Vicar always stiled his neeghbour a rare churchman and wished the rest of his flock had attended as regular and heeded as well to his counsels tho the old Farmer thought it no sin to talk about taxes in the porch or set the Clerk to give notice of to the congregation of new rates under the pulpit as soon as the Sermon was ended and this the Vicar agreed to as right likewise and he was beloved in the Parish by most as he always prayed for fair or wet weather as the farmer required

The Vicar was a great favourite with the family and especially with Mrs Thrifty as he had won her favour by two or three little kindnesses he had paid her one of which was his taking the pains to search the 'Parish Register' to supply the loss of the geneology of her family which one of her childern when young tore out of the bible being all written down on a blank leaf and he not only supplied the defficiency but added several names of kin to the family list which the neglect of different chroniclers had ommitted to put down and another was his chusing a fine name for her eldest son being the heir and over ruling the objections of her husband knowing it was taken from scripture— he was more over a good judge of the weather and reckoned very usefull in hay time and harvest for his opinion as he once prophecied a wet harvest upon its happening to fall a shower on St Swithens day which happened exactly as he had said and they believed him ever after while the old farmer always prefered his opinion to the weather glass—he was a regular Visitor and made it a rule as he woud say when he enterd wether he was welcome or not of paying two visits in a year without the ceremony of asking   one was to talk about tythes at lamas and the other a few days before christmass when the dame broached her elder berry wine of whose merit he was reckoned an excellent judge—for the Vicar was one that woud not seem ignorant of any thing   tho he woud not contradict any one he woud not suffer to be contradicted himself that is he woud take no heed of a contrary opinion no more then if he never heard it—and he woud believe every extravagant story that did not attempt to overthrow his own notions— if any one told any News to him before dinner he woud tell it over again to them afterward as his own News and expected them to listen as attentivly as if they had never known it—he was not fond of long graces at dinner always reckoning that it did little else then cool it as long speeches made the heart weary of listning and made a prayer only uttered by the lips an abomination—he was like the old farmer in good health and troubled with nothing but a sharp stomach—he was very zealous about religion over his sermon but it seldom seemed to trouble him else were except when he went round the village to caution the boys against playing marbles on sundays and the servants to keep out of the Publice in church time and tho they often broke his good counsils they contrived to keep out of his sight which was as well as keeping them as he did not dwell upon trifles   he was somtimes disposed to be merry and woud ramp with the servant wenches in hay time about the Cocks and rarely missed kissing them beneath the missletoe at christmass which he considered as a nessesary preface to good luck thro the year for like his old neeghbour he was a stickler for old customs—and it was whispered about the Village in his young days that he was fond of women but when ever it was hinted to the farmers wife she woud fall in a passion and declare that he was as honest a man as her husband°

[*Apology for the Poor*]°

Mr Editor

In this suprising stir of patrioutism and wonderful change in the
ways and opinions of men when your paper is weekly loaded with the
free speech[e]s of county meetings can you find room for mine—or
will you hear the voice of a poor man—I only wish to ask you a few
plain questions

Amidst all this stir about taxation and tythes and agricultural
distress—are the poor to recieve corresponding benefits   they have
been told so I know but it is not the first time they have heard that and
been dissapointed—when the tax was taken from leather they was told
they should have shoes almost for nothing and they heard the
parliment speeches of patriots as the forthcoming prophecys of a
political millineum but their hopes were soon frost bitten—for the tax
has long vanished and the price of shoes remains just were it did nay I
believe they are a trifle dearer then they was then—thats the only
difference   then there was a hue and cry about taking off the duty on
Sp[i]ritous liquors and the best Gin was to be little more in price then
small beer—the poor man shook his head over such speeches and
looking at his shoes had no faith to believe any more of these cheap
wonders so he was not dissapointed in finding gin as dear as ever—for
which he had little to regret for he prefered good ale to any spirits and
now the Malt and beer tax is in full cry what is the poor man to
expect—it may benefit the farmers a little and the common brewers a
good deal and there no doubt the matter will end   the poor man will
not find the refuse of any more use to him then a dry bone to a hungry
dog—excuse the simile reader for the poor have been likened unto
dogs before now

And many other of these time serving hue and cries might be
noticed in which the poor man was promised as much benefit as
the stork was in the fable for pulling out the bone from the Wolfs
throat and who got just as much at last as the stork did for his
pains

Some of the patriots of these meetings seem to consider the corn
law as a bone sticking in the throat of the countrys distresses but I
am sure that the poor man will be no better off in such a matter—he
will only be 'burning his fingers' and not filling his belly by har-
bouring any notions of benefit from that quarter for he is so many

degrees lower in the Thremometer [of] distress that such benefits to others will not reach him and tho the Farmers should again be in their summer splendour of 'high prices' and 'better markets' as they phrase it the poor man would still be found very little above freezing point—at least I very much fear so for I speak from experience and not from hearsay and hopes as some do—some years back when grain sold at 5 and 6 guineas a quarter I can point out a many villages where the Farmers under a combination for each others inter[e]sts would give no more in winter then 10 Shillings per Week—I will not say that all did so for in a many places and at that very time Farmers whose good intentions was 'to live and let live' gave from 12 to 15 shillings per week and these men would again do the same thing but they could not compel others and there it is were the poor man looses the benefit that ought to fall to him from the farmers 'better markets' and 'high prices' for corn—I hope Mr Editor that I do not offend by my plain speaking for I wish only to be satisfied about these few particulars—and I am so little of a politician that I would rather keep out of the crowd then that my hobnails should trample on the gouty toes of any one tho I cannot help thinking when I read your paper that there is a vast number of taxable advocates wearing barrack shoes or they would certainly not leave the advocates for reform to acchieve their triumphs without a struggle—I wish the good of the people may be found at the end and that in the general triumph the poor man may not be forgotten for the poor have many oppressors and no voice to be heard above them—he is a dumb burthen in the scorn of the worlds prosperity yet in its adversity they are found ever ready to aid and assist and tho that be but as the widows mite yet his honest feelings in the cause are as worthy as the orators proudest orations   Being a poor man myself I am naturally wishing to see some one become the advocate and Champion for the poor not in his speeches but his actions for speeches are now adays nothing but words and sound Politicians are known to be exceedingly wise as far as regards themselves and we have heard of one who tho his whole thoughts seemd constantly professing the good of his country yet he was cunning enough to keep one thought to himself in the hour of danger when he luckily hit upon the thought of standing on his hat to keep himself from catching cold and to die for the good of their country as some others did and to be alive as he is at this moment   now if the poor mans chance at these meetings is any thing better then being a sort of foot cushion for the benefit of others I shall be exceedingly

happy to hear but as it is I much fear it as the poor mans lot seems
to have been so long remembered as to be entirely forgotten

I am sir your humble S[ervan]t

A Poor Man

['*If the nessesitys of the poor*']

If the nessesitys of the poor are always to be left to the mercey of
anothers prosperity—their oppressions in a general way will always
be permanant and their benefits ever precarious   thousands of poor
will be left as destitute of comfort under the high prices of the Farmers
interests as thousands of the poor are now—I wish to see some one
become the champion of the poor so far in disinterested honesty as
to forget his own interests and partial[i]tys of bettering himself and
his class by attempting some simple plan for bettering the community
at large for any thing universally attempted for the benefit of all will
benefit the poor man   partial blessings to those above him will be
no use to him—the manna must be scattered in the wilderness for the
poor to claim as a right and not left in the power of anothers
charity for them to solicit as a blessing for then thousands will be
sent empty away

As to taking off the malt tax that will benefit the poor next to
nothing for if he could have malt at even the price that corn makes
now the poor man who has a family could not get it and if the Malt and
beer tax are all taken off together the poor mans general good will be a
minus in the matter tho to be sure a pint of beer will be cheaper and
tho he can purchase that when he cannot get a bushel of malt to brew
good ale yet he must give so much interest out of his money to the
publican and brewer and what he buys as cheap ale is nothing better
then slow poison or at best small beer under a new name—for let
times be as they will common brewers and pot house retailers will
have their profits or they will not sell

A general reduction of taxes in general and a total abolishment of
such that press so hard on the nessesitys of life and like pharoahs lean
kine swallow up the fatness of the earth making a famine where we
might enjoy plenty—I repeat the abolition of these taxes that would
confer benefit to all would in the end benefit the poor—like a sun
burst from a cloud it would smile upon them in time for I dare say
they would be the last that struggled out of the shadow of poverty

[*'Every farmer is growing into an orator'*]°

Every farmer is growing into an orator and every village into a Forum of speech making and political squabbles—the general good is the universal out cry of these speakers and peti[ti]oners but self interest is the undoubted spirit that puts all in motion—the poor cottager and the little freeholder is called upon to back their intentions that good may come—and yet I am as full of doubt respecting the good of the poor man by this bustle and bother of helping him as I was when he sank alone in his poverty and not a hand was raised to help him or a voice was heard in his favour—there was a time when the prosperity of other[s] was universaly popular yet at that very time the poor man was as an alien in a strange land—he was not suffered even to open his mouth about his distresses for if he had he would have been instantly thrust into jail as a raiser of mobs and seditions   and who were the lords and tyrants of every village that treated the rights of the poor with such contempt as not even to let the murmurs of sorrow to go unpunished—why these very farmers who are now raising up mobs themselves—they were metamorphosed into special constables and paraded the dirty streets with shouldered muskets in all the swaggering awkwardness of the raw lobsters that now infest the metropolis—and if a poor man only smiled upon the ridiculous groups of armed animals when it was almost impossible to resist laughter he was instantly seized and guarded to prison by these files of reduculous assumptions these treasons upon honour and libels on courage who would have retreated from the bray of a jackass as the cannon of the enemy and turned their backs on a scare crow if it had been invested with a red jacket as from a file of soldiers . . .

[*'I never meddle with politics'*]

I never meddle with politics in fact you would laugh at my idea of that branch of art for I consider it nothing more or less then a game at hide and seek for self interest and the terms wig and tory are nothing more in my mind then the left and right hand of that monster the only difference being that the latter lyes nearer the windfalls of wills for self interest then the other—that there are some and many who have the good of the people at heart is not to be doubted but with the others who have only the good of themselves in view when balloted I fear that they will always be as the few

['*I say what good has been yet done*']

I say what good has been yet done by the partial reduction of particular taxes   why as yet nothing but a cheese paring of comfort for the poor and that was the removal of the tax on salt   and the Malt and beer duty will I fear be nothing but another morsel for a camelion and the worst is the poor cannot feed on air—the common brewer and the pot house retailers so long as their respective monopolies are sanctioned and reserved in so long will they recieve every benefit from the deducting of those taxes and the trifleing refuse that falls to the poor will be as much benefit to them as throwing dishwas[h]ings to a hungry dog—to benefit the poor would be to take off the tax on beer and the power from the brewing magistrates disolving the spell of the liscensing system altogether and leaving every body to sell ale as chose to do so and then the poor would be benefited and not till then

['*long speeches*']

long speeches are quite in unison with theory but very unwieldy and cumbersome for the every day business of practical ages . . .—when a mans house is on fire there should be no ceremony insisted on in putting it out—the schoolmaster who insisted on the maxim that a boy ought to think thrice before he spoke once had the inconvenience of his theory illustrated on himself in a very convincing manner—The boy one day seeing an urgent occasion to speak put the masters theory to practice by remarking that he had thought once—the master applauded him for his adherence to good counsel—I have thought twice said the boy   now speak said the master very deliberately— your coat is on fire said the boy—and thus the master notoriously sacraficed a coat to his principles but had nearly fell a martyr to them by the loss of his life—having thereby a convincing proof that however excellent a quallity caution may be to come to right conclusions or prevent wrong theories Dispatch was the only expedient to put in practice in urgent nesses[i]tys . . .

['*These out of place patriots*']

These out of place patriots have grown into as fierce a perception of the countrys wrongs and grievances as the boy in the Tales of the fa[i]ries had of the secrets of nature who could hear the flowers grow and see the wind—yet a twelvemonth is scarcely past since these perceptible nervous ambitionists in the countrys welfare where as silent and as ignorant of all but their own interests as a deaf man is of the distinction between noise and silence and a blind man of that of light and darkness . . .

['. . . *I fear these tory radicals*']

. . . I fear these tory radicals these out of place patriots (or parrots) who are so loud in their insults against the present ministry only want to make paddles of the people to sail into their harbours of old sinecures and then to be again themselves they will be as silent of suffering people and all such alusions—as an old maid of her age or an old borough monger of common honesty

[*The Poor Man* Versus *the Rich Man*]

A poor man is insulted by every prosperity—his struggles to better himself meet with rebukes where if he recieved kindness it would have been the only profit he had met with—his plain honesty is inspected and his every good intention is met by careless inattentions and disregard—to sum up the matter he is looked upon as a being despised for his poverty—and no feeling but that of profitable speculations can bring him into notice with the world—therefore the advice of Solomon is just 'My son it is better to die then to be poor'°

If he be a jiant seven foot high he may arrive at the honour of being exibited in a cage as a jiant if he be well proportioned he may become a soldier and strut in plumes—if he be strong he may win independancy by the sweat of his brow—but he should keep the 'Life of the race horse'° in his memory and lay bye for age   if he should reach writing and reading as it were by a accident he may by accident become an author but it must not be forgotten that the writer is a poor man or the matter looses all its attraction—merit is nothing with the poor man—untill time forces the conviction of his merit into the face of his readers and then his struggles his rebuffs and his poverty is forgotten and he is written down Esqr. with the rest of the million—such is a poor man—who is a combatant with difficulty and a steeple climber all his life—while wealth meets the world as smooth as a bowling green and as easy as a velvet cushion—the world is nigh bursting for oppertunitys to applaud—if they copy a sentiment from the ancients—the world sings the beauty and the wit and wisdom upon them as their own—if they become authors they are Bacons and Miltons and Shakspears and Newtons, in a twinkling— nay a greater then these   tho he only copy that which has been ten thousand times repeated from them no matter he is rich and a greater then Newton is there—such is the magic of wealth—and yet reader fill not thy head with the vanitys of wealth—let facts be thy illustrations of value—look at the riches of Shakspear and see if money ever made one—no not a shadow that was even worthy to unloose the latchets of his shoes—flattery wrote such praises but time whiped them away like a picture of eternity drawn in crayons

Men make a boast of pedigree—as well might the descendants of Richard Turpin boast of their's for both honours spring from robbery and spoliation—what was William the Conquerer but a robber by wholesale and what were his followers but highway men by his authority recieving titles by their expertness at plunder for which Turpin (a more noble plunderer if absence from fear or dareing achievements make one) recieved a halter because he dared to rob and could show only his courage for the liscence—the ancestors of Newton have something to boast of—but pedigree belongs to a race horse and confers nothing to the mind or the man

[*Nature Notes*]

Winter Primroses—I have gathered a handful of primrose[s] in hilly wood° on christmass day in the midst of a severe frost not only once but many years

Wild ducks always rise against the wind that is to face it   they never rise with it to have it behind them

Magpies have always two openings into their nest one to enter into it and one to escape from it—I have often got my hand into the nest before the old one has left it when she has sat hard on her eggs and she always escaped at another hole

Magpies always line their nests with twitch and dried roots—Crows use twitch roots old rags and wool—but the magpie never uses wool or any thing but roots and twitch

Jaybirds use dead roots and twitch like the magpie but they are generally of finer texture

Those little beetles called yules that eat holes in beans and other grain—as soon as touched drop down and lie as if dead

Spiders will coil up their legs and lie still and the hogbeetle will roll itself into a round ball and scarcely open if laid by a fire

The long legged Shepherd will emit a drop of water if imprisoned in the hand and a flat beetle of a dull purple brown will emit a red sort of fluid if stopt in its journeys by the childern in harvest who provoke it on purpose to make do so

The blue Crow builds on thorn bushes in the fens—seldom venturing on trees   its eggs are similar to common Crows but of a paler colour and slenderer in shape

The Heronshaws build in the fir trees on the Island pond in Milton gardens°   they make their nests in clusters and associate like the rook but their nests are of a more clumbsy and heavy appearance and yet are perched on the tops of the trees and grains in such places that appear incapable of bearing such a load of rough thorny sticks as their nest[s] appear below   Their eggs are long and very slender at the small end of a greenish white colour spotted with brown and faintly streakd with a paler colour—they never meddle with the fish in the pond but go a great distance for their food

The Fern Owl or Goat sucker or Night jar or night hawk while several more or's might be added no doubt to fresh names is a curious bird   they are found about us in summer on a wild heath calld Emmingsales° and I believe that is the only spot which they visit   they make an odd noise in the evening begin[n]ing at dew fall and continuing it at intervals all night   it is a beautifull object in Poetic Nature—(nay all nature is poetic) from that peculiarity alone   one cannot pass over a wild heath in a summer evening without being stopt to listen and admire its novel and pleasing noise   it is a trembling sort of crooing sound which may be nearly imitated by making a crooing noise and at the same time patting the finger before the mouth to break the sound like stopping a hole in the German flute to quaver a double sound on one note   this noise is generally made as it descends from a bush or tree for its prey   It is said to feed on insects that breed on the fox fern whense its name   it is a beautiful mottld bird variously shadowd with the colors of black and brown   it appears of the hawk tribe   its eye is keen its bill hookshapd and its mouth very wide with long bristle like hairs growing at each corner   my friend Artis° has one in his collection of specimens and knows a great deal more about its habits then I do   there was a nest of one of these birds found on Emmingsales last year by the Cowkeepers with 3 eggs in it   wether the whole number I cannot say   they was describd to me as short and smallish eggs blotchd with umber colord spots   I believe the nest was found among the brakes   it was sent to Dʳ Skrimshire of Peterbro° who is a curious man and collects the eggs of English birds   I never found a nest of these birds in my life so I cannot say were they build but the next time I visit Artis or Henderson° I will enquire and send you further particulars   as beautiful an object as this bird must have been in the summer dew-fall rambles of Poets I have never read one that mentions it except Mʳˢ Smith in her Sonnets° which I had the pleasure to meet with last summer in a friends book case   her poems may be only pretty but I felt much pleasd with them because she wrote more from what she had seen of nature then from what she had read of it   there fore those that read her poems find new images which they have not read of before tho they have often felt them and from those assosiatons poetry derives the power of pleasing in the happiest manner   When

I workd at Casterton I met with another nocturnal bird called a 'night hawk' I say another because I am certain it was not the Fern owl it was larger I have started it in the night from among the short stumpy bushes on the cow pasture often but coud not distinguish the color or make of the bird all I coud tell of it was that it seemd very swift on the wing and from that I imagind it of the hawk kind—My Love rambles then made me acquainted with many of the privacys of night which she seemd wishing to keep as secrets I was then the companion of the Evening and very often the morning Star Pattys Lodge° stood in a lone spot and the very path seemd to loose itself in the solitudes and was glad to take the direction of rabbit tracks ere it coud lead one to the door nature revelld in security this bird was one of her curositys it very often startld me with its odd noise which was a dead thin whistling sort of sound which I fancied was the whistle call of robbers for it was much like the sound of a man whistling in fear of being heard by any but his companions tho it was continued much longer then a man coud hold his breath it had no trembling in it like a game keeps dog-whistle but was of one thin continued sound I was supprisd when I mentiond it to them to find it was the noise of a bird and of one very common about there it was not only heard in sumer but at all seasons of the year they knew no other name for it then that of the Night hawk and they supposd it preyd on the young rabbits by night and made their burrows its hiding place by day as it was never seen after the mornings twilight began it made no noise when it was startld up in my hearing so I supposd from that it was mostly sitting when it made its fear creeping and danger haunting cry—Querie—May it not be very natural to suppose that the frequent whistles which people have heard while crossing wild heaths under the horrible apprehe[n]sions of being pursued by robbers came from this bird—I know not wether Naturalists are acquainted with this curious circumstance neither have I read sufficiently to know what opinions they give of it if they are I firmly believe it is a different species from the night jar of the hawk tribe who like the owl is a nocturnal plunderer that hides in the day from the light and glaring of the sun—if you have read of any thing that resembles this bird I shall be glad to hear of it I think the noise cannot be unknown to curious observers in nature tho it lives at a time when the Naturalist and Poet are not expected to be on their rambles unless by accident which is very often the friend and cause to new discoverys for the time when its call is most often repeated is at the

dead of night between the hours of eleven and one   before and after
this it is but seldom heard—what a beautiful night picture are those
glow worms   I have wrapt them up in leaves and taken them home
to examine them by daylight but they was nothing then but a dead
shriveld insect   I never coud find how that illuminating principal
coud exist which hangs at one end like a drop of dew filld with a
sun beam that daylight had left behind it   there are several inscects
that have a shining quality in the dark and one often calld a
'gloworm' by night and the 'Forty leg'd worm' by day has this
property but different to the above   it is of a more silvery hue which
will cling to the object that is put to touch it as tho it was some
powder or substance adhering to the skin   this inscect is of a red
color by day with a great number of legs—touch wood is possesd of an
illuminating property in the dark in a great degree—but I must
stop   my sheet is always full

yours etc

John Clare

['I went to take my walk to day']

April 21

I went to take my walk to day and heard the Nightingale for the
first time this season in Royce wood° just at the town end   we may
now be assured that the summer is nigh at hand   you askced me a
long while back to procure you a Nightingales nest and eggs and I
have try'd every season since to find if the bird nesting boys have
ever taken one out but I have not been able to procure one—when
I was a boy I usd to be very curious to watch the nightingale to
find her nest and to observe her color and size for I had heard many
odd tales about her and I often observed her habits and found her nest
so I shall be able to give you a pretty faithful history—she is a plain
bird somthing like the hedge sparrow in shape and the female Firetail
or Redstart in color but more slender then the former and of a
redder brown or scorchd color then the latter   the breast of the male
or female is spotted like a young Robin and the feathers on the rump
and on parts of the wings are of a fox red or burnt umber hue   one
of them is of a darker brown then the other but I know not
wether it be the male or female   they generally seek the same

solitudes which they haunted last season and these are the black thorn clumps and thickets about the woods and spinneys   they sit in the water grains of oaks or on a twig of hazel and sing their varied songs with short intervals both in the night and day time and sing in one as common as the other   I have watchd them often at their song   their mouths is open very wide and their feathers are ruffled up and their wings trembling as if in extacy   the superstition of laying their throats on a sharp thorn is a foolish absurdity but it is not the only one ascribed to the nightingale   they make a large nest of the old oak leaves that strew the ground in woods and green moss and line it with hair and some times a little fine witherd grass or whool   it is a very deep nest and is generaly placed on the root or stulp of a black or white thorn somtimes a little height up the bush and often on the ground   they lay 5 eggs about the size of the wood-larks or larger and of a deep olive brown without spot or tinge of another color   their eggs have a very odd appearance and are un-like any other birds in the county   when they have young their song ceases and they make an odd burring noise as if calling their young to their food   they are very jealous of intrusions on their privacy when they have young and if one goes in their haunts at that time they make a great chirping and buring and will almost perch close to you noising and chirping as if to fright you away   at first one assails you and after it has been chirping about you a while the other approaches to join it but as soon as you get a little distance from their haunts they leave you and are still when if you return they resume their former chirping and continue fluttering about you among the branches till you leave them agen to their privacy   their nest[s] are very difficult to find   indeed it is a hopeless task to hunt for them as they are seldom found but by accident being hidden among the tall weeds that surround the roots and cover the woods undisturbed recesses   when I was a boy I found three nests one season and all were found by chance in crossing the woods hunting the nests of other birds—the Red breast frequently builds on the ground under the shelter of a knoll or stulp and its nest is often taken for that of the nightingales but it is easily distinguishd from it as the robins is built with dead grass and moss on the out side while the Nightingale never forgets her dead oak leaves and this is so peculiar to her taste that I never saw a nest of theirs with out them nor are they used by any other bird for their nests—

[*Letter to Messrs Taylor and Hessey*, II]

I forgot to say in my last that the Nightingale sung as common by day as night and as often tho its a fact that is not generaly known   your Londoners are very fond of talking about this bird and I believe fancy every bird they hear after sunset a Nightingale   I remember when I was there last while walking with a friend in the fields of Shacklwell° we saw a gentlman and lady listening very attentive by the side of a shrubbery and when we came up we heard them lavishing praises on the beautiful song of the nightingale which happend to be a thrush but it did for them and they listend and repeated their praise with heart felt satisfaction while the bird seemd to know the grand distinction that its song had gaind for it and strove exultingly to keep up the deception by attempting a varied and more louder song   the dews was ready to fall but the lady was heedless of the wet grass tho the setting sun as a traveller glad to rest was leaving his enlargd rim on the earth like a table of fire and lessening by degrees out of sight leaving night and a few gilt clouds behind him   such is the ignorance of nature in large Citys that are nothing less then over grown prisons that shut out the world and all its beautys

The nightingale as I said before is a shoy bird   if any one approaches too near her secret haunts its song ceases till they pass when it is resumd as loud as before but I must repeat your quotation from Chaucer to illustrate this

'The new abashed nightingale
'That stinteth first when she beginneth sing
'When that she heareth any herde's tale
'Or in the hedges any wight stirring
'And after siker doth her voice out ring'°

As soon as they have young their song ceases and is heard no more till the returning may   after they cease singing they make a sort of gurring guttural noise as if calling the young to their food   I know not what its for else but they make this noise continually and doubt-less before the young leave the nest   I have said all I can say about the Nightingale—In a thicket of black thorns near our village calld 'bushy close'° we have great numbers of them every year but not so many as we usd to have   like the Martins and Swallows and other birds of passage they seem to diminish but for what cause I know not.

As to the cuckoo I can give you no further tidings than what I have given in my last   Artis° has one in his collection of stuffd birds but I have not the sufficient scientific curosity about me to go and take the exact description of its head rump and wings the length of its tail and the breadth from the tips of the extended wings   these old bookish descriptions you may find in any natural history if they are of any gratification   for my part I love to look on nature with a poetic feeling which magnifys the pleasure   I love to see the nightingale in its hazel retreat and the cuckoo hiding in its solitudes of oaken foliage and not to examine their carcasses in glass cases yet naturalists and botanists seem to have no taste for this poetical feeling   they merely make collections of dryd specimens classing them after Leanius° into tribes and familys and there they delight to show them as a sort of ambitious fame   with them 'a bird in the hand is worth two in the bush'   well every one to his hobby I have none of this curosity about me   tho I feel as happy as they can in finding a new species of field flower or butter flye which I have not seen before yet I have no desire further to dry the plant or torture the Butterflye by sticking it on a cork board with a pin—I have no wish to do this if my feelings woud let me   I only crop the blossom of the flower or take the root from its solitudes if it woud grace my garden and wish the fluttering butterflye to settle till I can come up with it to examine the powderd colours on its wings and then it may dance off from fancyd dangers and welcome   I think your feelings are on the side of Poetry for I have no specimens to send you so be as it may you must be content with my descriptions and observations . . .

P.S. I can scarcly believe the account which you mention at the end of your letter respecting the mans 'puzzling himself with doubts about the Nightingales singing by day and about the expression of his notes wether they are grave or gay'—you may well exclaim 'what solemn trifling'   it betrays such ignorance that I can scarcely believe it—if the man does but go into any village solitude a few miles from London next may their varied music will soon put away his doubts of its singing by day—nay he may get rid of them now by asking any country clown the question for its such a common fact that all know of it—and as to the 'expression of its notes' if he has any knowledge of nature let him ask himself wether nature is in the habit of making such happy seeming songs for sorrow as that of the Nightingales —the poets indulgd in fancys but they did not wish that those matter of fact men the Naturalists shoud take them for facts upon their credit—What absurditys for a world that is said to get wiser and wiser every day—

yours etc

J. Clare

['*It has been often asserted that young frogs*']

It has been often asserted that young frogs and fish will fall from the clouds in storms and it has often [been] wrongly asserted when the phenomena has sprung from natural causes—I have seen thousands of young frogs crossing a common after a shower but I found that they had left their hiding places and pursued their journey after the shower began   early in the morning early risers may see swarms of young frogs leaveing their birth place and emegrating as fast as they can hop to new colonys and as soon as the sun gets strong they hide in the grass as well as they are able to wait the approach of night to be able to start again but if in the course of the day showers happen to fall they instantly seize the chance and proceed on their journey till the sun looks out and puts a stop to their travelling again   as to young fish I always found them in holes that were very near neeghbours to brooks and had held communications (tho not then) with them in wet weather when dykes were full—it has been asserted that eels fall with the rain in ponds   it has been so asserted because they did not know how to account for it any other way—once when I was a young man on staying late at a feast I cross[d] a meadow about midnight and saw to my supprise quantitys of small nimble things emigrating across it a long way from any water   I thought at first they were snakes but I found on a closer observation that the[y] were young eels making for a large pond call[d] the Islet pool which they journeyd to with as much knowledge as if they were acquainted with their way   I thought this a wonderfull discovery then but I have since observd the same thing in larger eels going from one pond to another in the day time and I caught two very large ones in the act of emigrating

[*'Blackbirds and Thrushes'*]

Blackbirds and Thrushes particularly the former feed in hard winters upon the shell snail horns by hunting them from the hedge bottoms and wood stulps and taking them to a stone where they brake them in a very dexterous manner—any curious observer of nature may see in hard frosts the shells of pootys thickly litterd round a stone in the lanes and if he waits a short time he will quickly see one of these birds coming with a snailhorn in his bill while he constantly taps on the stone till it is broken   he then extracts the snail and like a true sports man eagerly hastens to hunt them again in the hedges or woods where a frequent rustle of their little feet is heard among the dead leaves

[*'Swallows'*]

Swallows (but wether the chimney swallows I know not) build on the beam of a shed in Milton gardens° which support the roof by running from end to end of the building—they have a very odd appearance and are placed in the same manner as a saucer on a mantel piece or a bason on a shelf and look exactly as if put there

[*'The country people here distinguish'*]

The country people here distinguish the viper from the common snake by a seemingly just conclusion—if they see any of the serpent kind near water they conclude them to be the common snake and tho when irritated they will snap like the viper they are reckoned harmless and when one is found distant from water on heaths and in dry woods they instantly recognize it as the viper and shun it according   the little snake called the black viper here is easily known from its size and colour and considered more venom[ous] than the viper—I have seen two one in southey wood° where it lapt its nether end or tail round a bit of rotten stick as if to give it support and hissed and errected it self almost on an end and then made a snap with its fangs and tryed to escape among the dead leaves that litter woody ground— the other was found by a cat in a homstead and thought to have been

brought there in some furze faggots that came from Southey wood—
that [the] cat attackd and attempted to kill it and succeeded after a
long trial in doing so when she would have eaten it had it not been
taken away—but she had been used to eating live eels which were
thrown to her when caught out of the pond and this may account for
the matter

['When Woodpeckers are making or boring']

When Woodpeckers are making or boring their holes in the spring
they are so attentive over their labours that they are easily caught
by boys who watch them when they are half hid in the holes they are
making and climbing softly up the tree make them prisoners—a nest
thus left unfinished is never resumed by another   the male makes the
holes generally and when finished sets up a continued cry to invite a
companion that seldom fails to join him in seeking materials for lining
the nest—the pied woodpecker never bores holes in the body of the
tree but in the larger grains very high up and always on the
underneath side so that they are inaccesable to nest hunting boys—it
is easy to see where this tribe are making new nests by the litter they
make at the foot of the tree as if it where sawdust . . .

['When the young of the Nightingale']

When the young of the Nightingale leave the nest the old ones bring
them out of the woods into old hedgrows and bushy borders about the
fields—where they seem to be continualy hunting along the roots and
hedge bottoms for food   Their haunts here are easily known from
the plaintive noise of 'toot toot' that the old ones are constantly
making at passers bye where the path runing by a hedge side make
such intrusions frequent—the fire tail and the Robin make a similar
noise—the Nightingale often makes another noise of 'chur chur'
which on hearing I have seen the young one instantly hopping down
from the hedge into the bottom of the dyke and when she made the
noise of 'toot toot' they would in a moment be all as still as if nothing
was there but the old ones   I always took the 'chur chur' as a food
call and the tooting noise as a token of alarm

[*'I have often been amused with the manners'*]

I have often been amused with the manners and habits of Insects but
I am not acquainted with entemology to know the names they go
bye—when I was following my avocations of husbandry last summer
at weeding in a Beanfield while sitting at dinner I observed one of
those small green nimble beetles repeatingly running up to some
object and then retreating again   at last my curosity urged me to
examine what he coud be at when I found that he was attacking a
large moth and when ever the moth made a trial to escape (which
it coud not do for the weeds) and struggled it retreated back and as
soon as it was still it returnd to the attack again   at length the
moth became quite exausted and the beetle with the utmost dexterity
began to bite off his wings and when ever the moth made feint
struggles the beetle instantly fell to wounding him agen in the body
as if he had not sufficiently disabled him   then he returned to the
wings which he soon got off and as soon as he had accomplished it
he paused a while by the body as if to watch wether his object needed
any further butchering to dispatch him and on finding him laying
quite still he then took a wide circuit all round the body as if like a
murderer he was afraid of being seen and taken—the[n] he nimbled
off somwere as if he had accomplished his object and going about
his business and I wonderd what his object coud be in killing the
moth and then leaving him but before I had much time for reflection
the beetle again made his appearance with a companion   they went
round the moth without attempting to seize it and seemd in a consult-
ing posture for some seconds when both of them started agen in
contrary directions and bye and bye both returnd each leading in his
track a compannion and then one of them instantly started agen while
the other three took a circuit round the moth   presently the beetle
that went out returned with two more companions and the company
making 6 in all when they came up instantly began (as if the whole
family was now got together) to make their dinner on the moth   they
first turnd him over on his back and fed on his body 3 on each side
and when satisfied they all joind help in hand and dragd the remainder
of their prey home to a hole between the furrows and disappeard—I
was much astonished at the time and made up my mind that
Insects have a language to convey their Ideas to each other and it
always appears to me that they posses the faculty in a greater degree
[then] the large animals   if one of the red pissmires finds in his

rambles a spot were a shephcrd has spent his dinner hour and litterd some crumbs of bread he returnd to his hill and brought two or three of his companions who return agen and bring more till a multitude is collected and the prizes is cleard off—a whasp if it feeds unmolested for a while in a grocers shop will quickly bring a hundred comrades to share in the spoils

I have often amused myself in summer by lying in the grass to see the quantitys of different insects passing and repassing as if going to a market or fair some climbing up bents and rushes like so many church steeples and others getting out of the sun into the bosoms of flower[s]   the most common seen in these busy motions is the long legged shepherd the green beetle and red and yellow lady flyes

[*Signs of Spring*]

March

We are now meeting with the pleasing indications of spring   the birds have left the barn doors and are chirping about in the thickets as if making up their minds to chuse partners and prepare for building —the beast and young colts are running races round the straw yards and rubbing at the gates anxious to greet the sprouting grass and loathing their winter food   the chaffinch or pink (so calld from its note) is busy over its little pleasing note of 'pink pink' that speaks of summer weather and is a joyous prophecy of leaves and sunshine and flowers—it is one of the plainest of the Finch tribe   it builds a beautiful round nest   its outside is made of grey moss and lind with cow hair   it lays 5 eggs of a dark ash color blotchd at the large end with ruby colord spots   it is very fond of its young and if the nest be taken out and put in a fresh place it will still feed them and bring them up   the cock bird is not an unhansome bird   it is a tootling song of 2 or 3 notes which it sings to cheer its mate while hatching her young whom it assists and takes alternate sittings—the Bullfinch is a beautiful bird   the plumage is fine and its shape tho rather heavy is commanding and noble   it begins to build in may   its nest is an odd curious one nearly flat made in a negligent manner of small sticks and lined with morsels of fine twitch and roots   it generally builds in a thick clump of Briars or black thorn   its eggs are about as large as the hedgesparrows of a greenish or watery white freckled at the thick end with pale lilac and dark

brown spots not much unlike the green linnets   its song is rather
varied and pretty   it is a great destroyer of the buds of fruit trees
in winter like the black and blue Tit-mouse and its fine plumage
and pretty song cannot make any petition for its crime to the enraged
gardiner who shoots it with the others indiscriminatly—in winter it
frequents gardens and orchards and in spring it returns to its wild
solitudes of woods and commons were it can feed in saftey

The gold finch is well known   its song and beautiful plumage
like the fair face of womoan proves its enemey and is the cause of
making it a prisoner for life   it is among the most frequent and
commonest of cage birds   it builds its nest on the eldern or apple
tree and makes its outside of grey moss like the pinks which it greatly
resembles but its lining is different and instead of cowhair it prefers
thistle down   it lays 5 pale eggs thinly sprinkled with feint red
spots   in spring it pleasures the cottager with its song beside his
door in the eldern tree and apple by the orchard pails   it feeds in
summer on the groundsel seed and the broad leafd plantain   when
it has raisd its family they all live happily together parents and
childern till the next spring and may be seen in such companys in
winter tracing the common and the fallow fields were the thistles are
in plenty on the seed of which it feeds till summer returns with its
other food—it is not uncommon while walking down a green lane
in early spring to see it perched on the top of a thistle picking out the
seed or pulling the soft down for its nest and flying into the neighbouring hedge at the approach of a passerbye   The poet saw it in
this manner when he paid it one of the finest compliments that it
ever met with from poetry

> 'Up springs the Gold finch from the cowering grass
> 'And wings its way into the nearest bower
> 'And there it sits within the mass
> 'Of playful leaves were the blythe roseys cower
> 'Like fairey buds itself a featherd flower.'°

Bird catchers have a trap cage to decoy the old birds into it and when
they take a nest of young ones they hang it up were they take the
nest for the old birds to come and feed them which they will do till
they are ready to flye and then when they find there is no means for
their escape they bring some food that poisons them   this I have
heard asserted as a fact by more then one and the bird catchers
always contrive to take them away soon enough to prevent it

You asked me last summer wether we had a bird about us calld

the spider catcher   we have not but there is a scarse bird with
us calld the Fly catcher   it is not unlike the blue titmouse in its
colour and shape but larger   I think its a bird of passage and rather
a scarce one for I dont see a pair of them for 3 or 4 years together   they seem to feed on insects and may be seen squatting about
old walls and peeping into crevices and runing up trees like the
wood pecker   it builds in walls and old trees   two boys brought
me a nest last year which they found in the eaves of an old wheat
hovel   it was most curiously made of long straws and cobwebs wove
together on the out side and lind with finer materials of straw and
cobwebs within   it had 5 eggs of a dirty brown or brun color
somthing like the robins but more slender and of a deeper color   they
described the bird as being like the blue cap but larger

[*More Signs of Spring*]

Feb 7 [1825]

I always think that this month the prophet of spring brings many
beautys to the landscape tho a carless observer woud laugh at me for
saying so who believes that it brings nothing because he does not give
himself the trouble to seek them—I always admire the kindling freshness that the bark of the different sorts of trees and under wood
asume in the forest—the 'foulroyce' twigs kindle into a vivid color
at their tops as red as woodpiegons claws the ash with its grey bark
and black swelling buds the Birch with its 'paper rind' and the darker
mottled sorts of hazle black alder with the greener hues of
sallows willows and the bramble that still wears its leaves with the
privet of a purple hue while the straggling wood briar shines in a
brighter and more beautiful green even then leaves can boast   at
this season too odd forward branches in the new laid hedges of white
thorn begin to freshen into green before the arum dare peep out of
its hood or the primrose and violet shoot up a new leaf thro the
warm moss and ivy that shelter their spring dwellings   the furze
too on the common wear a fairer green and ere and there an odd
branch is coverd with golden flowers and the ling or heath nestling
among the long grass below (coverd with the witherd flowers of
last year) is sprouting up into fresh hopes of spring   the fairey rings
on the pasture are getting deeper dyes and the water weeds with long
silver green blades of grass are mantling the stagnant ponds in their

summer liverys   in fact I find more beautys in this month then I
can find room to talk about in a letter and particulary as you prefer the
living objects to the landscape—In this month the Mavis thrush
begins to build its nest   it is about as large as the field fare and
not much unlike it   its song is very stunt and unvaried and seems
like the song of a young bird while learning to sing but the season
at which it sings always makes it welcome and beautiful for it begins
very early and if its a open Winter it may be heard at the end of
December and beginning of January   it loves to frequent at this
season old orchards and hedge borders in home steads near the village
when it can get shelter and cover as if it loved to treat the village
with a song at such a dreary season   as the spring advances its song
ceases and it disappears to its more solitary haunts of woods and
forrests were it generaly builds its nest beside a large tree on the
twigs and water grains that shoot from the body   its nest is made
of the blades of dead grass moss and cow dung lined with warmer
materials of wool and a finer sort of grass intermixd   it often lays
six eggs much like the black birds but larger of a deeper blue green
dusted with brun colored spots   its nest has been often mistaken for
the black birds but it is easily distinguishd by the more curious
observer as the blackbird uses moss on the out side and lines the
inside with fine twitchy roots and hair while the mavis never forgets
her dead ramping grass for the out side covering and a plentiful
supply of wool within   the wool is what bird nesting boys know
it bye—the Thrush celebrated for its fine song is a small bird not
much larger then a ground lark   it does not begin its varied song till
May which is said by some to equal the nightingales which it very
much resembles tho it is not so various   it builds its nest about the
latter end of april and makes the out side of green moss and lines the
inside with touch wood from decayd trees and cowdung which it
plasters round in a very workman like manner and makes it as round
as the spoon of a Ladle that dryes as hard as brick after it is
finished   tho this may be thought to be a hard bed for its young
it uses no other lining   it lays 5 and some times six eggs smaller
then the black birds of a beautiful blue like the hedgesparrows but
thinly mottled at the large end with inky spots   it mostly nay I
might say always chuses the white thorn to build on and seeks the
most retired places of the wood seldom venturing to hazard its nest
in the hedge or near the side   I have often remarkd an odd
scircumstance respecting these birds in laying time which I never
coud account for which is the frequent desertion of their nests after

they were finished not only of one but of 19 out of twenty as if the birds had by a natural impulse joind their minds to leave their new made dwellings and migrate to other countys   this does not appear to be the case every season but when it is so it seems to be general   the year before last I found 12 nests in Oxey wood° all left in this manner as if they all left off at the same instant   it was before the cuckoo had made her appearance or I shoud have laid the blame to her   when this general desertion takes place the nests are always more numeros then at other times—but there are a many of natures riddles not yet resolved—The long taild Titmouse calld with us Bumbarrel and in yorkshire pudding bags and feather pokes is an early builder of its nest   it makes a very beautiful one in the shape of an egg leaving an entrance on one side like the wren   it forms the outside of grey moss and lines it with great quantitys of feathers   it lays a great number of small eggs   I have found them with 18   they are very small of a white color sprinkled with pink spots at the larger end   one might think that by the number of eggs these birds lay they woud multiply very fast but on the contrary they are not half so plentiful as other birds for the small hawks make a terrible havock among their young broods as soon as they leave their nests—its song is low and pretty   the young ones that escape the school boy and hawk live in familys and never forsake their parents till the next spring   they may be seen to the number of 20 in winter picking somthing off the twigs of the white thorn in the hedgerows

[*Letter to Messrs Taylor and Hessey*, III]

I believe that the habits of the land rail or landrake and the Quail are little known   in fact I know but little of them myself but that little is at your pleasure   Were is the school boy that has not heard that mysterious noise which comes with the spring in the grass and green corn   I have followd it for hours and all to no purpose   it seemd like a spirit that mockd my folly in running after it   the noise it makes is a low craking very much like that of a Drake from whence I suppose it got the name of Landrake   I never sturted it up when a boy but I have often seen it flye since   About two years ago while I was walking in a neighbours homstead we heard one of these landrails in his wheat   we hunted down the land and accidentily as it were we sturted it up   it seemd to flye very awkard and

its long legs hung down as if they were broken   it was just at dewfall
in the evening   it flew towards the street instead of the field and
popt into a chamber window that happend to be open when a cat
seizd and killd it   it was somthing like the quail but smaller and
very slender with no tail scarcly and rather long legs   it was of a
brown color   they lay like the quail and partridge upon the ground
in the corn and grass   they make no nest but scrat a hole in the
ground and lay a great number of eggs   My mother found a landrails
nest once while weeding wheat with seventeen eggs and they were not
sat on   they were short eggs made in the form of the partridges but
somthing smaller staind with large spots of a dark color not much
unlike the color of the plovers   I imagine the young run with 'the
shells on their heads' as they say by partridges and plovers for most
of these ground hatchd birds do—what time they leave this country
or wether they leave it at all I cannot say   they are known to remain
here very late in the year   the year before last I was helping to carry
yaumd beans which are shorn with a hook instead of being mown
with a scythe, and stoukd in shoves like wheat   as I was throwing
one of these shoves upon the waggon somthing ran from under it very
quick and squatted about the land   I mistook it at first for a rat
as it hastend bye me and struck at it with my fork but on percieving
my mistake I stoopd down to catch [it] when it awkardly took wing
and settld in a border of bush   I found it was a landrail by its
legs dangling down as it flew   I remember it was a very cold day
and near the beginning of november   I was supprisd at the discovery
and almost doubted wether they were birds of passage at all   The
quail is almost as much of a mystery in the summer landscape and
comes with the green corn like the landrail tho it is seen more often
and is more easily urgd to take wing   it makes an odd noise in
the grass as if it said 'wet my foot wet my foot' which Weeders and
Haymakers hearken to as a prophecy of rain and believe in it as an
infallable sign   they are less then the Partridge and rise not unlike
them when they take wing   they lay on the ground and seem to
prefer the meadow grass to the cornfields as their nests are oftenest
found in the meadows while the Landrakes taste seems the contrary   the quail like the other lays a great quantity of eggs   I
have found them with 16   they are smallish for the size of the bird
and very near the color of the More hens but not half so large being
about the size of the small thrus[h]es   I understand they grow very
bold while in the act of sitting   my father tells me while writing
this that he has often mown over them in hay time when the bird

woud not flye up but run about the swaths and squat down as if on
her nest several times erc shc took to wing—beautiful as these two
images are in the book of nature the poets have hardly mentiond
them . . .

['*The little Robin*']

March

The little Robin has begun his summer song in good earnest   he
was singing at my chamber window this morning almost before
daylight as he has done all the week and at night fall he comes regularly to his old plumb tree and starts it again—there is a plaintive
sweetness in the song of this bird that I am very fond of   it may
be calld an eternal song for it is heard at intervals all the year round
and in the Autumn when the leaves are all fled from the trees there
is a mellancholy sweetness in it that is very touching to my feelings—
the Robin is one of the most familiar birds that a village landscape
posseses and it is no less beloved for even childern leave its nest
unmolested but the Wren and the Martin are held in the like venera-
tion with a many people who will not suffer their nests to be
destroyed—the Robin seems to be fond of the company and haunts
of man   it builds its nest close to his cottage in the hovel or out
house thatch or behind the woodbine or sweet briar in the garden
wall   nor does it seem to care to make any secret of its dwelling
were its only enemy is the cat to whom its confidence of saftey often
falls a prey—and it seeks its food by his door on the dunghill or on
the garden beds   nay it will even settle on the gardeners spade when
he is at work to watch the worm that he throws up and unbears and
in winter it will venture into the house for food and become as tame
as a chicken—we had one that usd to come in at a broken pane in
the window three winters together   I always knew it to be our old
visitor by a white scar on one of the wings   it grew so tame that it
woud perch on ones finger and take the crumbs out of the hand   it
was very much startled at the cat at first but after a time it took little
notice of her further then always contriving to keep out of her way—
it woud never stay in the house at night tho it woud attempt to perch
on the chair spindles and clean its bill and ruffle its feathers and put
its head under its wing as if it had made up its mind to stay but
somthing or other always molested it when it suddenly sought its old

broken pane and departed when it was sure to be the first riser in the morning   what I observed most remarkable in its manner was that it never attempted to sing all the time it visited us   what became of it at last I never knew but I suppose some cat destroyd it—it has been a common notion among heedless observers that the robin frequents no were but in villages but this is an erronuous one for it is found in the deepest solitudes of woods and forrests were it lives on insects and builds its nest on the roots or stools of the underwood or under a hanging bank by a dyke side which is often mistook for that of the nightingales. I have often observed its fondness for man even here for in summer I scarcly cross a wood but a Robin suddenly falls in my path to court my acquaintance and pay me a visit were it hops and flutters about as if pleased to see me and in winter it is the woodmans companion for the whole day and the whole season who considers it as his neighbour and friend

It is not commonly known that the Robin is a very quarrelsome bird   it is not only at frequent warfare with its own species but attacks boldly every other small bird that comes in its way and is gennerally the conqu[e]ror   I have seen it chase the house sparrow which tho a very pert bird never ventures to fight it   hedge sparrows linnets and finches that crowd the barn doors in winter never stands against its authority but flyes from its interferences and acknowledge it the cock of the walk and he always seems to consider the right of the yard as his own

The Wren is another of these domestic birds that has found favour in the affections of man   the hardiest gunner will rarely attempt to shoot either of them and tho it loves to haunt the same places as the Robin it is not so tame and never ventures to seek the protection of man in the hardest winter blasts   it finds its food in stackyards and builds its nest mostly in the roof of hovels and under the eaves of sheds about the habitations of man tho it is often found in the cow-sheds in closes and sometimes aside the roots of under wood in the woods   its nest is made of green moss and lined with feathers   the entrance is a little hole in the side like a corkhole in a barrel   it lays as many as 15 or 16 white eggs very small and faintly spotted with pink spots   it is a pert bird among its fellows and always seems in a conscieted sort of happiness with its tail strunted up oer its back and its wings dripping down—its song is more loud then the Robins and very pleasant tho it is utterd in broken raptures by sudden starts and as sudden endings   it begins to sing in march and continues till the end of spring when it becomes moping and silent

The Hedge sparrow may be called one of these domestic birds for it is fond of frequenting gardens and homesteads near villages   it is a harmless peacable bird and not easily alarmed at the approach of man   its song is low and trifling   it builds its nest early in the Spring in hedges and close bushes about gardens and homsteads of green moss lined with fine whool and cow hair   it lays 5 eggs of a very fine blue   nay it may be calld a green blue   they are clear without spots   it feeds on insects and small seeds and is frequently robd of its eggs by the cuckoo who leaves one of her own in its stead which the hedge sparrow hatches and brings up with an unconsous fondness and if she lays any more eggs of her own after the cuckoo has deposited hers it is said that the young cuckoo has the instinct to thrust the young sparrows out of the nest to occupy it himself   wether this be true or not I cannot say for I have never witnessd it tho I have fo[u]nd a young cuckoo in the hedge sparrows nest and in the Wagtails also but in no other birds beside   these two seem to be the selected foster parents of its young   The hedge sparrow is very early at building its nest   I found one last year in a box tree with three eggs on the 3rd of February°   the birds had built in the same bush 3 years together—a sharp blast happend when the young was just hatched and perishd them and the[y] brought off another brood in the same nest

[*Letter to Messrs Taylor and Hessey*, IV]

I do not know how to class the venemous animals further then by the vulgar notion of putting toads common snakes black snakes calld by the Peasantry Vipers Newts (often calld eatherns) and a nimble scaly looking newt-like thing about the heaths calld Swifts by the furze kidders and cow keepers   all these we posses in troublsome quantitys all of which is reckond poisonous by the common people tho a many daring people has provd that the common snake is not for I have seen men with whom I have workd in the fields take them up and snatch them out of joint as they calld it in a moment so that when they was thrown down they coud not stir but lay and dyd   others will take them up in one hand and hold the other agen that double pointed fang which they put out in a threatning manner when pursued and which is erroniously calld their sting and when it touches the hand it appears utterly harmless and turns again as weak as an horse

hair   yet still they are calld poisonous and dreaded by many people
and I myself cannot divest my feelings of their first impressions tho
I have been convincd to the contrary   we have them about us in
great quantitys   they even come in the village and breed in the dunghills in farm yards and harbour in old walls   they are fond of lying
rolld up like a whipthong in the sun   they seem to be always
jealous of danger as they never lye far from their hiding places and
retreat in a moment at the least noise or sound of approaching
feet   they lay a great number of eggs white and large   the shell
is a skinny substance and full of glutiness matter like the white in
birds eggs   they hang together by hundreds as if strung on a
string   they lay them on the south side of old dunghills were the
heat of the sun and the dung together hatches them   when they first
leave the shells they are no thicker then a worsted needle or bod-
kin   they nimble about after the old snakes and if they are in danger
the old ones open their mouths and the young dissapear down their
throats in a moment till the danger is over and then they come out
and run about as usual   I have not seen this myself but I am as
certain of it as if I had because I have heard it told so often by those
that did   when I have been pilling bark in the woods in oaking time°
I have seen snakes creeping half errect by the sides of the fallen oaks
that were pilld putting their darting horse hair like tongue every now
and then to the tree and I was a long while ere I coud make out what
they were doing but I made it out at last in my mind that they were
catching flyes that were attracted there in great quantitys to the
moister of the sap just after the bark had been ripd off—this I have
observd many times and I think if it were examind they have a sticky
moister at the end of those double ended fangs that appears like a bit
of wailbone split at the end or a double horse hair which attaches to
the flye as soon as touchd like bird lime and I think this is the use for
which nature designd their mistaken stings   the motion was so quick
that the prey which it seizd coud not be percievd when taken but I
have not the least doubt that such was its object   people talk about
the Watersnake but I cannot believe otherwise then that the water and
land snake are one tho I have killd snakes by the water in meadows
of a different and more deep color then those I have found in the
fields   the water snake will swallow very large frogs   I have often
known them to be ripd out of their bellys by those who have skind the
snake to wear the skin round their hats which is reckond as a charm
against the headach and is often tryd but with what success I am not
able to say   some say that snakes are as wholsom as eels to eat and

when the french prisoners were at Norman cross Barracks° it was a
very common thing among the people of the villages round to go in the
fens a snake catching and carry home large sticks of them strung like
eels on osiers which the French men woud readily buy as an article of
very palatable food   I know this to be a fact but I rather doubt the
frenchmens good taste in cookery by eating such things—the fens
swarm with snakes   I have walkd by the brink of a large dyke among
the long grass in a morning when they have ran away from every step
I took and dropt into the water by scores   the Fenmen care nothing
about them no more then childern do for the common flye   when
we see any we kill them and think we get rid of a danger by so doing
but the fen people pass them without fear or notice   in fact if they
dreaded them they coud not stir out of their doors they are so
numerous there   The black snake or Viper a very small one about
a foot long and not often thicker then ones little finger is very scarce
here and venemous   I believe the fens have none   they seem to
inhabit high land   a place calld Southey wood° is a spot were they
are oftenest seen with us   a woodman got stung by one in worthorp
Groves° near Burghley some few years ago and his hand and arm
swelld very large   another man while cutting up furze on a place
calld the Lings at Casterton was stung over the leg by one and lay ill
a long time and when I was a boy I can remember a next door
neighbour named Landon° was stung with one of these vipers in
crossing a close of long grass   he describd the sensation as if a thorn
had prickd him just above his shoe top on the ancle and shoud have
believd it had been so had not his wife been following him who saw at
the moment somthing hustle qui[c]kly in the grass when she told him
and he turnd back and killd it with his stick   on coming up to some
gipseys they advisd him to take the dead viper home to boil it and
apply the broth to the wound which he did but it got worse and worse
and the doctors when they saw it expected it woud have mortified but
he got well—I have seen three of these black snakes   they are very
qui[c]k eyd looking things with a fang darting out like the common
ones   their heads are shorter and much flatter then the large snake
and their colors are more deep and bright   their backs are black
and their bellys bright yellow interspersd with scaly bars of blackish
hues—I have heard some people affirm that even these are not
venom[ous] and that people who suppose themselves bitten by them
mistake sudden yumours falling in their limbs for a bite   I believe
this is the Docters opinion with us—all I can say is that I never was
harmd by them—toads and knewts harbour in ruins and under large

stones   they will live either in the water or out of it—I believe the
knewts is calld the water Lizard by many—and the nimble one on
heaths is the land Lizard of a light brown coverd with small
scales—ugly as these things are they give the poet a delight to
mention them

The common snake is very fond of milk and it often makes its way
into a dairy by a mouse hole or some other entrance to sip the
cream—in the fens (were they are as numerous as flies) they will creep
up the milk pails that are set to cool at the door of an evening by 3
or four together—they have a very quick sense of hearing and retreat
in a moment at the approach of danger—this no doubt is the order of
providence for if the venomous serpant was as slow to retreat as the
toad what numbers woud be injured by falling in its way

Shakspear and Thompson both speaks of the common snake   I
cannot refer you to the place in eithers poems but I believe one of
them describes it as lying 'curld in the sun'   I think its
Thompson°

['*I took a walk*']°

March 25th 1825

I took a walk to day to botanize and found that the spring had taken
up her dwelling in good earnest   she has covered the woods with the
white anemonie which the childern call Lady smocks and the hare
bells are just venturing to unfold their blue drooping bells   the green
is covered with daiseys and the little Celadine   the hedge bottoms
are crowded with the green leaves of the arum were the boy is
peeping for pootys with eager anticipations and delight—the sallows
are cloathed in their golden palms were the bees are singing a busy
welcome to spring   they seem uncommonly fond of these flowers
and gather round them in swarms—I have often wonderd how these
little travellers found there homes agen from the woods and solitudes
were they journey for wax and honey   I have seen them to day at
least 3 miles from any village in Langley wood working at the palms
and some of them with their little thighs so loaded with the yellow dust
as to seem almost unable to flye   it is curious to see how they collect
their load   they keep wiping their legs over their faces to gather the

dust that settles there after creeping in the flowers till they have got a
sufficient load and then they flye homward to their hives—I have
heard that a man curious to know how far his bees travelld in a sumers
day got up early one morning and stood by one of the hives to powder
them as they came out with fine flour to know them agen and in the
course of an hour after wards he observed some of them at the
extremity of the Lordship and having to go to the market that day he
passd by a turnip field in full flower about 5 miles from home and to
his supprise he found some of his own in their white powderd coats
busily huming at their labour with the rest—the Ivy berrys too are
quite ripe and the wood pigeons are busily fluskering among the Ivied
dotterels on the skirts of the common   they are very fond of them—
and a little namless bird with a black head and olive green back and
wings—not known—it seems to peck the Ivy berries for its food and I
have remarked that it comes as soon as they are ripe to the Ivy
trees and dissapears from them when they are gone—I fancy it is
of the tribe of the Tit mice and I have often found a nest clinging
by the side of trees among the Ivy which I think belongs to it   I
know nothing further of its Life and habits—I think I had the good
luck today to hear the bird which you spoke of last March as singing
early in spring and which you so apropriatly named the mock
nightingale for some of its notes are exactly similar   I heard it singing in 'Open Wood'° and was startled at first to think it was the
nightingale and tryd to creep into the thicket to see if I coud discover
what bird it was but it seemd to be very shoy and got farther from
me as I approachd till I gave up the pursuit—I askd some Woodmen
who were planting under wood at the time wether they knew the bird
and its song seemd to be very familiar to them   they said it always
came with the first fine days of spring and assured me it was the wood
chat but they coud not agree with each others opinion for another
believd it to be the large black cap or black headed Titmouse so I
coud get nothing for fact but I shall keep a sharp look out when I
hear it again—you have often wished for a blue Anemonie the
Anemonie pulsitilis of botanists and I can now send you some for I
have found some in flower to day which is very early but it is a very
early spring   the heathen mythology is fond of indul[g]ing in the
metormorp[h]ing of the memory of lovers and heroes into the births of
flowers and I coud almost fancy that this blue anemonie sprang from
the blood or dust of the romans° for it haunts the roman bank in
this neighbourhood and is found no were else   it grows on the roman
bank agen swordy well° and did grow in great plenty but the plough

that destroyer of wild flowers has rooted it out of its long inherited dwelling   it grows also on the roman bank agen Burghley Park in Barnack Lordship°   it is a very fine flower and is easily cultivated by transporting some of its own soil with it   a heathy sandy soil seems to suit it best—you enquired last summer wether we had any plants indegenious to our neighbourhood   I think we have some but I dont know much of the new christning system of modern botany that has such a host of alphabetical arangments as woud fill a book to describe the Flora of a Village like the types of the chinese characters that fill a printing house to print one book with—we have a very fine fern of the maiden hair kind that grows large with a leaf very like the hemlock but of a much paler green and another very small one that grows on the old stools of sallows in damp hollows in the woods and by the sides of brooks and rivers   we have also the thorn pointed fern of lenius° that grows on one spot in a dyke by Harisons closes near a roman station and the harts tongue that grows on the brinks of the badger holes in Open wood   in fact we have a many ferns   there is a beautiful one which a friend of mine calls 'Lady fern' growing among the boggy spots on Whittlesea Mere° and a dwarf willow grows there about a foot high which it never exceeds   it is also a place very common for the cranberry that trails by the brink of the mere   there are several water weeds too with very beautiful or peculiar flowers that have not yet been honored with christ[n]ings from modern botany—we have a great variety of Orchises among which the Bee orchis and Spider Orchis are reckond the finest   both of them may [be found] in an old deserted quarry calld Ashton stone pits—but perhaps they are more common on Whittering heath° were grows the 'Cross leaved heath' and a fine tall yellow flower of the Mullein species which the villagers call Goldilocks   these are all the rare flowers of our neighbourhood that I am acquainted with and botanical [enthusiasts] will come miles to gather them which makes me fancy they are not common else-were   I will send you some dryd specimens in their successions of flowerings this season—have you never heard that cronking jaring noise in the woods at this early season   I heard it to day and went into the woods to examine what thing it was that caused the sound and I discoverd that it was the common green woodpecker busily employd at boreing his hole which he effected by twisting his bill round in the way that a carpenter twists his wimble   with this differ-ence that when he has got it to a certain extent he turns it back and then pecks awhile and then twists agen   his beak seems to serve all the purposes of a nail passer gough and wimble effectually   what endless new lessons may we learn from nature

I am yours sncr

J Clare

[*Hunting Pooty Shells*]

Feb^y

You ask me wether I have resumed my botanizing and naturalizing excursions and you will laugh at my comencement for I have been seriously and busily employd this last 3 weeks hunting Pooty shells and if you are not above them I must get you to assist me in the arangment or classification of them   I have been making some drawings of them for you but they are so miserable that I must send the shells with them

There is a pleasing assosiation attachd to these things   they remind me and I think every one of happy hours   who has not been a gatherer of them in his school boy days—how anxious I usd to creep among the black thorn thickets and down the hedge sides on my hands and knees seeking them as soon as the sun lookd warm on the hedges and banks and wakend the daisey to open its golden eye and the arum to throw up its fine green leaves   I cannot forget such times as these   we used to gather them to string on thread as birds eggs are strung and some times to play with them at what we calld 'cock fighting' by pressing the knibbs hard against each other till one broke —I think there is one shell peculiar to our neighbourhood and almost to one spot in it   it is a large one of a yellow green color with a black rim round the base   there is another yellow one very common which we calld when boys 'painted Ladys' but the one I imagine as a scarce one is very different from this—they are found in low places by brook sides   the snail is of a blackish yellow and appears to feed on a species of brooklime—there is another not very common   I have stiled it the yellow one banded   the others are common the red one banded the red self and the red many banded and yellow many banded and small many banded with a mottld sort calld badgers by school boys—there is many others but they all seem variations of the same kinds   the large mozzld garden snail is well know[n]—but I found many of them in a spot were it woud puzzle reason to

know how they got there   A person had been digging a dyke in the
old roman bank by the side of a fence and in some places it was 6 feet
deep and in the deepest places I found the most shells most of them
of the large garden kind which had been clarified as it were in the
sandy soil in which they were bedded   I suppose them to have lain
ever since the road was made and if it is so what a pigmy it makes
of the pride of man   Those centurions of their thousands and 10
thousands that comanded those soldiers to make these roads little
thought that the house of a poor simple snail horn woud out live
them and their proudest temples by centurys   it is almost a laughable gravity to reflect so profoundly over a snail horn but every trifle
owns the triumph of a lesson to humble the pride of man—every
trifle also has a lesson to bespeak the wisdom and forethought of the
Deity   I was struck to day with a new discovery   I stood looking
over the wall of a bridge at the brook rippling beneath me and
observd a large shell and on examining it I found it a sort of fresh
water Perewinkle of which there are several varietys in our brooks
but none that has the peculiar construction that this has which is a
sort of Lid that it opens or shuts at pleasure that fits as close as the lid
of a snuff box and keeps out the water when ever it chuses to be
weary of wandring or wants to be dry in its boat   its joint as it were
attaches and sticks under the chin and is of no more inconvenience
then a mans beard   when it is open it serves the double purpose of
clogs or shoes to keep the sharp gravely bottom of the brooks from
hurting its tender flesh which it might easily do if it was not thus
guarded

The instinct of the snail is very remarkable and worthy notice tho
such things are lookd over with a carless eye—it has such a knowledge of its own speed that it can get home to a moment to be save
from the sun as [a] moment too late woud be its death—as soon as the
sun has lost it[s] power to hurt in the evening it leaves its hiding place
in search of food which it is generally aware were to find   if it is a
good way off it makes no stoppages on the road but appears to be in
great haste and when it has divided its time to its utmost by travelling
to such a length as will occ[u]poy all the rest of its spare time to return
its instinct will suddenly stop and feed on what it finds there and if it
finds nothing it will go no further but return homwards and feed on
what it chances to meet with and after it gets home shoud the sun be
under a cloud it will potter about its door way to seek food but it
goes no further and is ready to hide when the sun looks out—when
they find any food that suits them they will feed on it till it lasts and

travel to the same spot as accuratly as if they knew g[e]ography
or was guided by a mariners compass—the power of Instinct in the
most trifling insect is very remarkable and displays the omnipotence of
its maker in an illustrous manner   nature is a fine preacher and her
sermons are always worth attention

[*Taste*]

Taste finds pleasure where the vulgar cannot ever find amusement   the man of taste feels excessive rapture in contemplating the
rich scenery of an autumn Landscape which the rude man passes
unnoticed—the rich colours of the forrest trees the wild hurry of the
autumn clouds never harmonize his feelings into raptures—he never
turns a look to the sky save in the dread of a coming shower—he
never gazes on the painted wilderness of woods and hedges unless
business leads his occupation thither and then his eye is dead and sees
no praise—he tramples thoughtlessly over the wooden brig that leads
him on his path and never so much as glances on the stream that
seems smoothening the little pebbles beneath him with its chafing
gurgles   he never heeds it or hears it but plods his way to the end of
his intentions with a mechanic impulse of uninterrupted selfishness
that occupys all his little mind—to the man of dissernment there is
happiness in contemplating the different shapes of leaves of the
various kinds of trees plants and herbs   there is happiness in
examining minutely into the wild flowers as we wander amongst them
to distinguish their characters and find out to what orders they belong
in the artificial and natural systems of botany   there is happiness in
lolling over the old shivered trunks and fragments of a ruined tree
destroyed some years since by lightening and moping and wasting
away into everlasting decay—to wander among the hills and hollows
of heaths which have been old stone quarrys roman excavations and
other matter of fact fancys that the mind delights to indulge in in
rambles—this is happiness—to lean on the rail of wooden brigs and
mark the crinkles of the stream below and the little dansing beetles
twharling and glancing their glossy coats to the summer sun—to bend
over the old woods mossy rails and list the call of the heavy bumble
bee playing with the coy flowers till he has lost his way—and anon
finds it by accident and sings out of the wood to the sunshine that leads
him to his mossy nest lapt up in the long grass of some quiet nook—

such is happiness—and to wander a pathless way thro the intricacys of woods for a long while and at last burst unlooked for into the light of an extensive prospect at its side and there lye and muse on the landscape to rest ones wanderings—this is real happiness—to stand and muse upon the bank of a meadow pool fringed with reed and bulrushes and silver clear in the middle on which the sun is reflected in spangles and there to listen the soulsoothing music of distant bells this is a luxury of happiness and felt even by the poor shepherd boy

[*Grammar*]

Those who have made grammar up into a system and cut it into classes and orders as the student does the animal or vegetable creation may be a recreation for schools but it becomes of no use towards making any one so far acquainted with it as to find it useful—it will only serve to puzzle and mislead to awe and intimidate instead of aiding and encouraging him   therefore it pays nothing for the study

A person may be very clever at cutting trees and animals on paper but he is nothing as an artist and a person may be very clever at detecting faults in composition and yet in the writing of it may be a mere cypher him self and one that can do nothing

And such a one as Cobbet° who has come boldly forward and not only assailed the outworks of such a pedantic garison but like a skilful general laid open its weakness to all deserves more praise for the use of his labour then all the rest of the castle building grammarians put together for he plainly comes to this conclusion—that what ever is intellig[i]b[l]e to others is grammer and what ever is commonsense is not far from correctness

A man who learns enough of grammer to write sufficiently plain so as to be understood by others as well as to understand his own consceptions himself and trys out the way to make his consceptions correct thinkings rather then the correct placing of particles and stops and other trifling with which every writer on grammar seems to be at loggerheads about with each other—such an attainment will get the possessor an enlightened and liberal mind and if he attain not with this broad principle an excellence in composition the niceties of intricate Lectures on grammer with its utmost perfection will not attain it for him

There has been more words used and study uselessly expended in the settlement of what is grammar and what should be grammer in the argument of opinions urged and in the explanation of opinions refuted then there has been arguments and refutations hustled up in the matters of politics or even in opinions of religion . . .

[*Life Peerages*]

They must not copy the french as far as to make the english nobility life annuals   if they do danger is apparent—the modern creations of modern parliments let them model as they please—ornament is not strength—modern decorations perhaps are often more accordant with difference of taste then union of perfection—and therefore in some instances the simplicity of the old building will rather be restored then injured—yet some of these moderns even are ancients and from merit deserve [to be preserved] and who but the brutish deeds of mobs would destroy the young plantations of their pedigree —let them beware if the building stands when the pillars are taken away   it stands by miracle and not by precedent and therefore destruction is more to be expected than preservation—let them draw conclusions from commonsense and not from modern extravagance and popular delusions

[*Knowledge*]

Knowledge gives a great number of lessons for nothing   like Socrates she is not confined to Halls or colledges or forum[s] but like him accompanys us in our walks in the fields and attends on us at our homes   in fact she is every where with us ready to instruct and assist our enquireys   we have only to feel a desire to come at the means of her acquaintance and she is instantly ready to instruct us how to meet with the matter

[*Letter to William Hone*]°

April 1825

Sir

I met tother day with a number of your 'Every-day-book' and as I
feel a great pleasure in any thing relating to the superstitions and
manners of former times I need not say how much entertainment I felt
in its perusal   The following miscellaneous superstitions and
shadows of customs almost worn out here are at your service to do as
you please with—I desire no acknowledgment of them in your
numbers as they are [not] worth that

On saint Marks Eve it is still a custom about us for young maids
who are sometimes joined by young men to make the 'dumb cake' a
mystical ceremony which has lost its origin and in some countys may
have ceasd altogether—the number of the partys is never to exceed
three   they meet in silence and at twelve oclock they eat it still silent
for if one speaks the spell is broken   when they have done they walk
up to bed backwards and those that are to be married see the likness
of their sweet hearts hurrying after them as if they wanted to catch
them before they get to bed but the maids being apprised of this
beforchand take care nearly to undress them selves before they start
and are ready to slip into bed before they are caught and if nothing
is seen the token is sure to be heard in a knocking at the doors or
rustling in the house as soon as they have left and to be convinced
that it comes from nothing else but the desired cause they take care
to turn out the cats and dogs on that night in particular   those that
are to dye unwed see nor hear nothing but have terrible dreams which
are sure to be of graves and rings that fit no finger and if they do
crumble into dust as soon as on—there is another dumb ceremony
of eating the yolk of an egg in silence and filling the shell with salt
when the sweetheart is sure to make his appearance in some way or
other before morning   on this same night too the more stout
hearted watch the church Poach   they go in the evening and lay a
branch of any tree or flower in the Poach and then return home and
wait till 12 o clock at night when two goes as far as the church gate
and one stays till the other fetches the bough   if they are to be
married they will see their own persons hanging on the arms of their
future husbands with the priest etc. as if going to be married and as
many couples of bride men and maidens as they shall see following
them so many months shall it be ere they are married and if they are to

dye unwed then the procession that passes them is a funeral   a coffin coverd with a white sheet appears to be born by shadows without heads and the number of carriers betokens the number of years that the partys are to live—this as terrible as it seems is a custom very often practiced—and an odd character who had no fear calld Ben Barr° a prophet usd to watch the porch every year and pretended to know the fates of every one in the villages round as who should be married or dye in the year but as a few pence generally predicted a good omen he seldom prophecied the deaths of his believers

On Whit sunday the youth of both sexes used to meet at a Fountain calld 'East well'° to drink s[p]ring water as a charm for good luck and a preventive of disease   this was undoubtly a roman catholic custom as some of the troughs remain still that betoken it to have been an holy well   the initials of names and crosses rudely cut with knives are still visible—a pond a league distant from this spring is still famous for cureing many diseases and people go often on spring mornings to drink it tho the custom of meeting at the spring on Whitsunday to drink sugar and water has been abolished ever since the inclosure

On Holy thursday they go round the fields opening the me[res] or land marks where they still keep up an ancient custom [of] scrambling in the mere holes for sugar plumbs and running races for cross skittles in which old and young often join—there is also a curious superstition which has forgotten the cause in which it origionated—young boys and girls the sons and daughters go on purpose to be placed on their heads in the mere or +°

On may day a multiplicity of sports and customs are still observed but some of them are so popular that they need no mention yet they differ in places—about us the first cow that is turnd upon the pasture gets the Garland and the last has the mawkin a large bunch of thorns tyd to her tail   the young men who wish to win the favour of their favourites wait on the green till a late hour and then drive out the cows of the maiden whom the[y] love who of course wins the garland and in the evening she is considerd the Queen of the May and the man wether her favourite or not claims her as his partner for the dance at night a custom that she dare not refuse to comply with as she woud loose her reputation and sweetheart into the bargain and grow into a byeword for a shrew and be shund accordingly

On Holy rood day it is faithfully and confidently believd by old and young that the Devil goes a nutting on that day—and I have heard a many people affirm that they once thought it a tale till they ventured to the woods on that day when they smelt such a strong smell of birmstone as nearly stifled them before they coud escape out again—and the cow boy to his great dissapointment finds that the devil will not even let his black berrys alone and he believes them after that day to be poisond by his touch

On St Tomases Eve it is a common custom for the young girls to lay a red peeld onion under their pillows to dream of their sweethearts—loves annals are overrun[n]ing with these old superstitions yet there is one on New Years Eve that I think you woud not have passd over in silence had you known of it   On the first moon in the new year young men and maids look through a silk hankerchief (that has been drawn through a ring) at the New moon and as many moons as each person sees through it as many years will they be ere they are married

The Morris Dance is very popular now with us   they begin to go round the week before christmass—it appears to have been a burlesque parody on some popular story at the time but it has been so mutilated by its different performers that I coud not make sense of it tho I tryd to transcribe from the mouths of 3 or four persons who had all been actors in it   there are 4 characters   2 of them the Kean and Young° of the piece are finely dressd   their hats are deckorated with carpenters dale shavings and cut paper and without side their cloaths they wear a white shirt hung with ribbons of different colors   a silk hankerchief serves them for a sash and another slung over their shoulders is a belt for their swords which are some times real and sometimes wooden ones   the third character is a sort of Buffoon grotesqu[e]ly dressd with a hunch back and a bell hung between his legs together with a tail trailing behind him   his face is blacked and he generaly carrys in his hand a hugh club   the 4th is a docter dressd as much in character as their taste or circumstances alows—the plot of the thing is some thing as follows—the Kean of the Drama steps in first and on speaking a sort of prologue discovers him self to be a no less personage then the king of Egypt   his errand appears to be to demand his lost son who seems to have married a lady not worthy the heir of Egypt or to be confined in prison for it is so destitute of common sense that you can not tell which and as they refuse his enquirys his champion prince George is calld in who after talking a great deal of his wonderful feats in slaying dragons and hacking his enemeys as small as flyes begins a dialogue with his majesty then the fool is introduced with his bell who gives a humerous description of himself and his abilitys when all three

joins in the dialogue and instantly a quarrel is created between the
Kean and Young from what cause I know not and they draw their
swords and fight   the fool gets between them to part them and pre-
tending to be wounded by the king falls down as dead when the other
confesses that the murderd man is the kings own son in disguise whose
rage is instantly turnd to sorrow and the docter is called in and a large
reward is offerd him if he can restore him to life who after
enumerating his vast powers in medical skill and knowledge declares
the person to be only in a trance and on the docters touching him
he rises and they all join hands and end the Drama with a dance
and song—

There used to be a common custom—when old men and women
and childern used to go stone gathering in the fields if one found a
stone with a hole in it to put a st[r]ing thro it and hang it at the masters
coat button behind where if he did not discover it in a certain time
they fell laughing and calling out 'riddy riddy wry rump' and
claimed the boon of a largess when the stone gathering was finished—
from what scourse could such a strange custom origionate—inclosure
came and destroyed it with hundreds of others—leaving in its place
nothing but a love for doing neighbours a mischief and public house
oratory that dwells upon mob law as absolute justice

I am sorry to bring a dirty reality so near your poetical description
of plough monday but I think a custom of half the northern countys
will not be unwelcome   on this day in our county (Northamptonshire)
and in the neighbouring ones of Rutland Lincoln Cambridge &c. it is
the custom for the plough boys (whose anxiety for the sport almost
wakens before the morning) to meet at the blacksmiths shop to
dress themselves and get ready not with white shirts and ribons but to
black their faces with a mixture of soot and greese and all that will not
under go this are reckond unworthy of the sport and excluded the
company—they get an old skeleton of a plough with out share or
colter and attach to it a waggon rope in which sticks are loopd and on
each side these sticks the boys take their station   they are calld
plough bullocks   the stoutest among them is selected for the holder
of the plough and thus equipd they pull it round the village from door
to door for what they can get   when they have gotten beer at the door
they run the 'wind up' as they call it to please their benefactors and
chusing the dirtiest place in the yard he that gets the most mauled and
complains of it the least is reckoned a brave fellow   in this wind up
they try to entangle the holder of the plough in the ropes who by
superior strength not only keeps from tumbling but contrives by

dextorusly man[oeuvring] and throwing the plough to get most of the
plough bullock[s] wound up in their own [   ]—to those
that will not give [to] them they let loose their mischief by pulling up
shoe scrapers at the door or gate posts and winding up the person in
the rope and as it is reckoned a lawless day the constable will rarely
interefere if calld upon—several of the boys of the neighbouring
villages used to meet at Milton Hall° to get beer were they had it
without stint when before the wind up commenced the different
villagers usd to bang each others ploughs together and pull against
them to try which was the strongest—which caused such confusion of
quarreling that it was abolished—the men grown servants 3 or 4 of
them go round the Village drest up in a grotesque manner   they are
calld the 'plough witches'   2 of them has their faces blackd and a
hunch back of straw stuffed into their smock frocks   their hats are
tyd up into a three cockd form and figured with chalk   in their hands
they carry a beesom and a spoon filld with soot and greese to sweep
the dirt on and black the faces of the servants maids they happen to
meet with who generally take care to keep out of the way   the 'she
witch' as he is calld is dressd up in a laughable joanish manner in
womans cloaths   he has no hunch back and his face is ruddled   they
carry a box with half pence in it which they shake [as] they come
to the door—at night the bullocks and witches meet together in a
sociable party and enjoy their supper cake and ale—this is the real
custom of plough monday which 'is known to this day'

NOTES

ABBREVIATIONS

Manuscript numbers preceded by a single capital letter refer to the Peterborough Museum collection. Those without a capital letter belong to Northampton Public Library. Manuscripts with the letters 'Pfz.' belong to the Carl and Lily Pforzheimer Library, New York.

Deacon George Deacon, *John Clare and the Folk Tradition* (London, 1983).
Knight W. F. Knight transcripts at Northampton Public Library.
RL J. Clare, *Poems Descriptive of Rural Life and Scenery* (1820).
RM J. Clare, *The Rural Muse* (1835).
VM J. Clare, *The Village Minstrel* (1821).

POETRY

1–13 These early poems from MS A3 were written between 1809 and 1819 and first printed in *RL*.

14–23 From MS 1, inscribed by Clare in imitation of the title-page of a book 'A Rustic's Pastime, in Leisure Hours' and dated 1814. Into it he copied those poems to date which he thought worthy of preservation.

18 *The Lamentations of Round-Oak Waters*. Dated by Clare 1818. Round Oak Waters is the stream fed by Round Oak Spring, a natural spring in the south-west corner of Royce Wood.

22 l. 141. 'O T—l. Richard Turnill, a childhood companion who died early of typhus.

24 *Noon*. l. 18. The quotation is from John Cunningham, 'Day', stanza xxv; but in D2, p. 8, Clare writes:

not my own alter the Couplet thus:

> Forcing from each vaunting spring
> Many a Curdling ring and* ring

> * or *in* as may suit best

27–59 The two manuscripts, B2 at Peterborough and 3 at Northampton, were at one time one and the same manuscript, a large quarto volume of neatly copied poems by Clare, many of which were first printed in *VM*. They should be reunited if possible, either at Northampton or Peterborough.

30 *Langley Bush*. Clare's Journal, Wednesday, 29 September 1824: '. . . but nothing is lasting in this world   last year Langley bush was destroyd an old whitethorn that had stood for more then a century full of fame   the Gipseys Shepherds and Herdmen all had their tales of its history and it will be long ere its memory is forgotten'

l. 7. Langley Bush was formerly the meeting-place of the old hundred court of Nassaburgh. It was a favourite spot for gipsies.

37 *The Woodman*. l. 187. A reference to *The Shipwreck* (London, 1762) by William Falconer (1732–69). Clare possessed *The Poetical Works* (1798).

38 l. 217. Revd Isaiah Knowles Holland, Congregational minister at Market Deeping, who befriended Clare between 1817 and 1820, when he moved to St Ives, Hunts.

Childish Recollections. Title followed by: 'Perhaps it is foolish to remark it but there are times and places when I am a child at those things' (H. Mackenzie, *Man of Feeling*, 1771).

47 *Song*. l. 2. Oxey Wood, another favourite spot of Clare's frequently mentioned in his Journal.

49 *The Village Minstrel*. The title poem of *VM* and Clare's longest poem to date was subjected to excisions and alterations by Taylor. The complete version will appear in our edition of Clare's poetry in the Oxford English Texts series.

50 l. 30. 'Barbara Allen', a famous traditional ballad. See Deacon, p. 29.

l. 52. See p. 191 for Clare's version of 'Peggy Bond'.

59 *My Mary*. Published in *RL*, but omitted from the third and fourth editions under pressure from some of Clare's patrons. It was not everybody's idea of a love poem and doubtless offended because of the crude vigour of its language, but it makes an interesting contrast with Cowper's sad lament in his 'My Mary', otherwise identical in stanza-form, rhythm, and refrain.

62 *Helpston Green*. Helpston Heath, an ancient common field in Clare's childhood.

64 *The Meeting*. Published in the Introduction to *RL*, set to music by Haydn Corri and sung in London by Madame Vestris. See Deacon, pp. 64–7.

66–91 The Pierpont Morgan manuscript is headed 'Village Scenes and Subjects on rural Occupations' and dated 'Helpstone August 21 1820'. We print six of the sixteen poems it contains.

67 *Rural Morning*. l. 11. A broadside reproduction of 'The Wantley Dragon' is published in Deacon, who tells us that, of the 3,000 ballad-titles in the stock of broadsides printed by Dicey, we have evidence of only about 100 actually being sung. Clare's evidence here shows that 'The Wantley Dragon' and 'The Magic Rose' were part of the oral tradition. 'The Magic Rose' remains unidentified, but it may have been related to the folk-tale, 'The Magic Rose Tree'.

80 *The Fate of Genius*. l. 2. Torpel in the parish of Ufford. Torpel Manor was the seat of one of the Norman barons of Peterborough Abbey and remains of his castle still survive.

93 *The Last of March, written at Lolham Brigs.* Lolham Bridge is on the Ermine Street, at the point where that road, running north from Castor, crosses the Welland. Half a dozen stone arches carry the Roman road (l. 94) called King Street over the flood meadows of the Welland.

98–124 Taken from MS A40, a large volume of poems neatly copied by Clare and covering various periods.

98 *The Parish.* This long satirical poem was never considered suitable for publication in Clare's lifetime and has received only fragmentary editing since. We intend to rectify this shortly. Useful comparisons may be made with William Cobbett's *Autobiography* and *Rural Rides*, but Clare's description is the most authentic and detailed portrait of village life and government surviving from the period.

In a prefatory note Clare wrote: 'This poem was begun and finished under the pressure of heavy distress with embittered feelings under a state of anxiety and oppression almost amounting to slavery—when the prosperity of one class was founded on the adversity and distress of the other—The haughty demand by the master to his labourer was work for the little I chuse to alow you and go to the parish for the rest—or starve—to decline working under such advantages was next to offending a magistrate and no oppertunity was lost in marking the insult by some unquallified oppression . . .'

99 l. 39. William Enfield's *The Speaker; or, Miscellaneous Pieces, Selected from the Best English Writers* (London, 1774) went into three more editions at least by 1790 and was a very popular anthology. Enfield, a Unitarian minister, had been a teacher at Warrington Academy and was a friend of Joseph Priestley.

100 l. 77. Demonstrates the eighteenth-century tradition of the Grand Tour.

108 *Bloomfield I* and *II*. Robert Bloomfield (1776–1823), author of *The Farmer's Boy*, which was published in 1800 and of which 26,000 copies are said to have been sold within three years. Clare owned many of his works and so admired his poetry that he had plans of writing a biography.

116 *Childhood.* l. 93. See reference to 'our wooden horse' in 'Childish Recollections', p. 39, l. 23.

134 *The Cottager.* l. 63. Clare's Journal, Monday, 22 November 1824: 'Lookd into Miltons Paradise lost   I once read it thro when I was a boy   at that time I liked the Death of Abel better   what odd judgments those of boys are   how they change as they ripen   when I think of the slender merits of the Death of Abel against such a giant as Milton I cannot help smiling at my young fancys in those days of happy ignorance'

The Death of Abel by Salomon Gessner (1730–88) in English translation (London, 1761) was popular for a time.

l. 65. Thomas Tusser (*c*.1520–*c*.1580), author of *A Hundreth Good Pointes of Husbandrie* (London, 1557), amplified to *Five Hundreth Points of Good Husbandry United to as Many of Good Huswiferie* (London, 1573). Clare's edition of this popular collection of verse instructions on gardening, farming, and housekeeping was *Five Hundred Points of Good Husbandry* (1812).

135 l. 81. A reference to the crowning victory of Admiral George Rodney over the French fleet under the Comte de Grasse on 12 April 1782 off Dominica. Lord Robert Manners, second son of the Marquis of Granby, was wounded in the action, which later resulted in his death from lockjaw.

The Shepherd's Calendar. Clare's first mature poem and an important social document, 'The Shepherd's Calendar' was written between 1823 and 1824, though not published till 1827. The delay was due to Taylor's procrastination. He complained of the 'unphilosophical' element and disliked the provincial words and cut and altered as he saw fit. For the restored text see *The Shepherd's Calendar*, eds. Eric Robinson and Geoffrey Summerfield (London, 1964).

147 [*The Lament of Swordy Well*]. Usually known as Swaddy Well, an ancient stone quarry used by the Romans, famed in Clare's childhood for wild flowers, white lizards, and a fine species of copper-hued butterfly. Five part-stanzas are omitted in our text.

157 *The Progress of Ryhme.* l. 190. The seat of the Marquis of Exeter, where Clare was employed as a gardener when a boy.

170–200 Clare tried to find a local publisher for 'The Midsummer Cushion/Or Cottage Poems' manuscript in 1832, but could not obtain the necessary number of subscribers. The contents consist of 360 neatly copied poems of his maturity and were finally published in *John Clare, The Midsummer Cushion*, eds. Anne Tibble and R. K. R. Thornton (Carcanet Press, 1979).

172 *Shadows of Taste.* l. 81. *Donns.* John Donne (1573–1631).

174 *St. Martins Eve:* 10 November.

178 l. 144. Cf. Thomas Gray's 'Ode on a Distant Prospect of Eton College', l. 99.

181 *Emmonsales Heath.* The ancient grazing land to the south of Helpston was variously known as Emmonsales Heath, Helpston Heath, or Ailsworth Heath (Ailsworth was the name of the next parish). It was here that Clare as a young child went in search of the horizon and the world's end.

191 *Peggy Band.* In a letter of 15 February 1821 replying to Taylor's enquiry whether 'Peggy Bond' or 'Peggy Band' is correct Clare writes: 'tho its not of much consequence I like to be particular as to trifles in such matters   the old song alluded to is "Peggy *Band*"   there is a song of modern date thats call'd "Peggy Bond" but tis nothing like the old one neither in words or music for the tune of the old one is Capital as my father used to sing it but I cannot say much for the words for you know

the best of our old English ballads thats preserved by the memorys of our rustics (what ever they might have been) are so mutilated that they scarcly rise to mediocrity while their melodys are beautiful and the more I hear them the more I wish Id skill enough in music to prick them down'. See Deacon, pp. 146–9.

193 *The Flood*. l. 1. *Lolham Brigs*. See note to p. 93, 'The Last of March'.

l. 14. Cf. Coleridge, 'The Ancient Mariner', Part III: 'The Night-Mare Life-in-Death was she.'

205–43 BIRD POEMS. These closely observed bird poems are among the most impressive achievements of Clare's maturity. He intended a separate volume in which birds and their nests would be described in short poems of varying stanzas, the whole collection being called 'Birds Nesting'.

205 *To the Snipe*. Whittlesey Mere was the habitat of snipes and other water birds. In Clare's day a watery wilderness of some 2,000 acres, it was drained in 1850 and turned into arable land.

212 *Emmonsails Heath in Winter*. See note to p. 181, 'Emmonsales Heath'.

244–9 ANIMAL POEMS. In these poems written between 1835 and 1837 at Northborough Clare is obsessed by man's cruelty to animals and they share an unusual starkness with other poems written at this time.

250–61 These three poems share the theme of lost childhood and are rooted in Clare's sadness at leaving native Helpston for his new cottage at Northborough in May 1832.

250 *The Flitting*. l. 24. Royce Wood was one of Clare's favourite haunts, the home of his beloved nightingales. It is usually given on the maps as Rice Wood, but it is claimed that Clare's spelling recalls the name of the farmer after whom the wood was named.

251 l. 48. See note to p. 30, 'Langley Bush'.

258 *Remembrances*. This map of Clare's boyhood brings together many of the favourite places that are mentioned elsewhere in his work, many of which can be located on enclosure and ordnance maps.

l. 6. See note to p. 30, 'Langley Bush'.

l. 11. See note to p. 484 (2).

259 l. 15. Lea Close Oak was one of many trees felled in the Enclosure. It was a favourite of Clare's. The carpenter who bought it made him two rulers from its wood.

l. 21. Crossberry Way passes through the yard of the Blue Bell Inn and was a favourite walk of Clare's. The footpath started on the edge of the moors and went along to Ufford skirting ancient Torpel.

l. 24. See note to p. 147, ['The Lament of Swordy Well'].

l. 25. Round Oak, above the ancient spring, was another favourite hollow tree cut down in the Enclosure. Clare remembered it again in a poem dated 19 June 1846 written in the Northampton Lunatic Asylum (see p. 367).

l. 44. These are three adjacent areas between the centre of Helpston and Woodcroft. Snip Green is at the junction of Heath Road and Woodcroft Road, while old Hilly Snow is now the Snow field.

260 l. 62. Clare's Journal, Wednesday, 26 January 1825: 'Fetchd some soil from Cowper green for my ferns and flowers . . .' He once saw some men unearth human remains here while they were digging stones and this incident later resulted in the poem 'On Seeing a Skull on Cowper Green' (*RM*, pp. 41–4). Another early poem is entitled 'Cowper Green' (*VM* i, pp. 109 20).

262 ['*The hoar frost lodges on every tree*']. l. 16. 'Jessey' is one of three songs by Robert Tannahill which Clare selects for special praise in his Journal for Thursday, 14 October 1824. Tannahill's *Poems and Songs, Chiefly in the Scotish Dialect* (1817) was one of the books in his library. See also note to p. 191, 'Peggy Band'.

272 [*The Puddock's Nest*]. l. 11. *the old ones*. Possibly Clare's slip of the pen for 'young'.

278 'The Water Lilies' and 'The Gipsy Camp' are two of twenty poems written at the High Beach Asylum in 1840 or early 1841 that Clare gave to Cyrus Redding when he was visited by him. They were all published in the *English Journal*, 'The Water Lilies' 15 May 1841, and 'The Gipsy Camp' 29 May 1841. No autograph exists for either of these poems.

279 *Child Harold*. Written during the spring and summer of 1841 at High Beach, continued at Northborough in the autumn, and possibly interrupted only by Clare's removal to Northampton, 29 December. For a discussion of the dating and the sequence of the parts of 'Child Harold' see the Introduction to *The Later Poems of John Clare*, eds. Eric Robinson and Geoffrey Summerfield (Manchester, 1964).

288 ll. 317–18. Cf. Coleridge's 'The Pains of Sleep': 'To be beloved is all I need, | And whom I love, I love indeed.'

318 *Don Juan A Poem*. Written at High Beach in 1841 and, apart from 'The Parish', Clare's only satire.

319 l. 32. Possibly an allusion to Thomas Holcroft's celebrated play *The Road to Ruin* (1792).

320 l. 76. A reference to the recent election of July 1841, in which the Whigs were defeated.

l. 80. To oil someone's wig = to make him drunk.

l. 84. The marriage of Lord John Russell to Lady Fanny Elliott, second daughter of the Earl and Countess of Minto, took place on 26 July 1841: it was announced in the *Northampton Mercury*, 12 June and 17 July 1841.

l. 86. Albert's first absence from England was in fact in March 1844. Until that date he had not been separated from the Queen since their marriage.

321 l. 113. Melbourne resigned as Prime Minister 28 August 1841.

l. 115. Victoria Adelaide, the Princess Royal, was born 21 November 1840.

l. 116. Ass milk is nearer to human milk than that of any other mammals and was often used for babies before proprietary baby foods were made. The Prince of Wales was born 9 November 1841.

322 l. 148. Ponders End is three miles to the west of High Beach, one mile from Enfield.

l. 152. Eliza Phillips is not yet identified, but Clare dedicates 'Don Juan' to her in a letter following the draft of the poem in MS 8.

325 l. 255. 11 July was a Sunday in 1841.

l. 262. Byron's birthday was 22 January—Clare himself was born on 13 July.

326 l. 276. 'The Isle of Palms', by 'Christopher North' [John Wilson] (London, 1812). Clare possessed *Poems* by John Wilson, 2 vols. (Edinburgh and London, 1825). Vol. i contains 'The Isle of Palms'.

['*Tis martinmass from rig to rig*']. Written at Northborough on 11 November 1841 after Clare's return home from Essex.

327 ['*Lord hear my prayer when trouble glooms*']. Written at Northborough in late 1841. Cf. Ps. 102: 1–17. Perhaps the best of the many biblical paraphrases that Clare wrote at this period, all of which are printed in our OET edition of Clare's later poetry.

328–36 From an octavo notebook of Clare's in Northampton, 1845.

329 *Spring.* ll. 31–6. This 'late summer' stanza seems out of place in a poem on spring.

334 ['*Look through the naked bramble and black thorn*']. l. 4. It seems that Clare intended the '-ing' in 'morning' to be carried over from the previous line.

336–8 From MSS 9 and 10 at Northampton in 1850.

337 ['*I'll come to thee at even tide*']. l. 29. One of the many women for whom and about whom Clare wrote poems.

338–427 We include here 102 poems from the two volumes of the Knight transcripts, which contain over 800 poems, some dated but the majority not, and are the chief source for Clare's poetry after 1841, the originals having nearly all disappeared. The Knight transcripts are published in full in our OET edition of Clare's later poetry. W. F. Knight was the house-steward at the Northampton Asylum between 1845 and 1850, and the work of transcribing was continued by other copyists. The poems were written between about 1842 and 1856 and appear in roughly chronological order, but exact dating is impossible. Facing a pencil sketch of Clare's cottage at Helpston Knight has written:

Poetry by John Clare
   written by him while an
     Inmate of the Northampton
      General Lunatic Asylum.

Copied from the Manuscripts as presented to me by Clare—and favoured with others by some Ladies and Gentlemen, that Clare had presented them to—the whole of them faithfully transcribed to the best of my knowledge from the pencil originals many of which were so obliterated that without refering [*sic*] to the Author I could not decipher, some pieces will be found unfinished, for Clare will seldom turn his attention to pieces he has been interrupted in, while writing—and in no instance has he ever rewritten a single line—whenever I have wished him to correct a single stanza he has ever shewn the greatest disinclination to take in hand what to him seems a great task.

'To the Lark', 'Song' ('A seaboy on the giddy mast'), 'Song' ('The daiseys golden eye'), 'Sleep of Spring', 'Song' ('Love lives beyond'), 'Song' ('The autumns come again') are printed in the order they appear in Knight, but as we have Clare autographs for them we do not follow the Knight text.

340   *Song: O wert thou in the storm.* This poem derives from Burns's 'Oh wert thou in the cauld blast'.

347   *Song* ('A seaboy on the giddy mast'). Cf. Shakespeare's *2 Henry IV*, III. i. 27: 'the wet sea-boy in an hour so rude.' 'The Sea Boy on the Giddy Mast' is the title of a song in *A Garland of New Songs*. See also A 50 (37) in the Harding Collection, Bodleian Library, where 'The Sea Boy' has the refrain line 'A sea boy on the high and giddy mast'.

359   *Evening.* l. 21. Cf. Pope's 'An Essay on Man: Epistle IV', l. 332: 'But looks thro' Nature, up to Nature's God.'

366   *My Early Home was This.* l. 14. In Spenser's *Faerie Queene*, Book II, Canto xii, the enchanted home of Acrasia, demolished by Sir Guyon.

367   *The Round Oak.* See note to p. 259, l. 25.

391   ['*Swift goes the sooty swallow o'er the heath*']. l. 1. Clare is referring here to the swift, not the swallow.

392   *The Wind.* l. 12. This line should perhaps read: 'From the smoke all around hiding meadow and farm'.

397   *Clifford Hill.* Clifford or Clifford's Hill is three miles east of the asylum and on the River Nene. It is a never-finished Norman earthwork castle and in Clare's day it was a favourite walk from Northampton.

401   *Little Trotty Wagtail.* The pied wagtail.

405   *The Peartree Lane.* One of Clare's favourite spots in Helpston.

408   *In Green Grassy Places.* l. 19. See H. Stevenson, *Birds of Norfolk* (London, 1866), ii. 131–2: 'Until the last 40 or 50 years, herons did not build exclusively in lofty trees, seeking the vicinity of man's dwellings,

and gathering together in colonies like rooks, but were scattered in pairs over the Fens and Broads, where the nests were placed, sometimes on a lofty alder in a carr, sometimes on the dwarf sallow or alder bushes in the Marsh, or were hidden, like those of the bittern, among the reeds and sedges.'

409 *Lines on 'Cowper'*. l. 9. Cf. Cowper's *The Task*, Book v, 'The Winter Morning Walk', ll. 1–57.

415 *The Winters Come*. l. 27. i.e. Robert Burton's *The Anatomy of Melancholy*.

427 We print two of the last six poems known to have been written by Clare. They are all in Clare's hand.

To John Clare. Dated 10 February 1860.

ll. 12–14. See ['Autobiographical Passages'], p. 429.

Birds Nests. Clare's last poem, written in the winter of 1863–4.

PROSE

429 [*Autobiographical Passages*]. [ii]. The last three lines of the late sonnet 'To John Clare' (see p. 427) recall Clare's reading habits of many years earlier.

430 [iii]. '*a little learning is a dangerous thing*'. Cf. Pope, *An Essay on Criticism*, l. 215.

Bonnycastles Mensuration ... John Bonnycastle, *An Introduction to Mensuration and Practical Geometry* (10th edn., London, 1807); Daniel Fenning, *The British Youth's Instructor; or, a ... Guide to Practical Arithmetic* (2nd edn., London, 1754), and *The Young Algebraist's Companion* (London, 1750).

432 [*Journey out of Essex*]. Clare's account of his journey is to be found in MSS 6 and 8 at Northampton. MS 8 contains preparatory drafts of part of the account and was carried by Clare on his journey. Immediately after writing it up in 6, Clare added the following letter:

To Mary Clare—Glinton

Northborough July 27 1841

My dear wife

I have written an account of my journey or rather escape from Essex for your amusement and hope it may divert your leisure hours—I would have told you before now that I got here to Northborough last friday night but not being able to see you or hear where you was I soon began to feel homeless at home and shall bye and bye feel nearly hopeless but not so lonely as I did in Essex—for here I can see Glinton Church and feeling that Mary is safe if not happy I am gratified though my home is no home to me my hopes are not entirely hopeless while even the memory of Mary lives so near me God bless you My dear

Mary—give my love to your dear and beautifull family and to your
Mother—and believe me as I ever have been and ever shall be
My dearest Mary
Your affectionate Husband
John Clare

'*The Labour in vain*'. We have no knowledge of a public house at Enfield
Highway called the Labour in Vain. Robson's Directory (1839) lists no
less than twelve public houses in Enfield Highway. Nine of these are
mentioned by name, but the remaining three are listed under the name of
the proprietor. Perhaps the Labour in Vain was one of the three
unnamed ones.

433 *the next village*. In a footnote Clare gives the name of the next village as
'Baldeck' (i.e. Baldock).

the 'Plough'. This public house has not yet been identified.

gave me no answer. Clare's footnote:

Note On searching my pockets after the above was written I found
part of a newspaper vide 'Morning Chronicle' on which the following
fragments were pencilled soon after I got the information from
labourers going to work or travellers journeying along to better their
condition as I was hoping to do mine in fact I believed I saw home in
every ones countenance which seemed so cheerfull in my own—
'There is no place like home' the following was written by the Road
side:—

1st Day—Tuesday Started from Enfield and slept at Stevenage on
some clover trusses—cold lodging

Wednesday—Jacks Hill is passed already consisting of a beer shop and
some houses on the hill appearing newly built—the last Mile stone 35
Miles from London got through Baldeck and sat under a dry hedge
and had a rest in lieu of breakfast

(Jack's Hill is about half-way between Stevenage and Baldock.)

434 *the 'Ram'*. Presently an old house, over a mile from Potton on the road to
Gamlingay Great Heath. It was a public house within living memory and
is still known locally as the Ram. First identified in *The Journal, Essays,
The Journey from Essex*, ed. Anne Tibble (Carcanet Press, 1980).

Tollgate. There was a Turnpike Gate at Temsford or Tamesford or
Tempsford, four miles and six furlongs south of St Neots.

435 *highland Mary*. 'Highland Mary' is by Burns. See *Poems and Songs*, ed.
James Kinsley (London, 1969), pp. 526–7. It was widely published as a
broadside during the nineteenth century and appears in many song-
books in the Harding Collection, Bodleian Library. Burns set the words
to an older air. However, Clare 'got the tune of "Highland Mary" from
Wisdom Smith a gipsey' (see Journal, Friday, 3 June 1825). See also
Deacon, p. 210.

I forget the name. Clare's footnote: 'It was St Neots'.

on a flint heap. MS 8, p. 25, contains the following note, written in a very disordered hand which was due in all probability to a conjunction of fatigue and emotional agitation:

> The man whose daughter is the queen of England is now sitting on a stone heap on the highway to bugden without a farthing in his pocket and without tasting a bit of food ever since yesterday morning—when he was offerd a bit of Bread and cheese at Enfield—he has not had any since but If I put a little fresh speed on hope too may speed tomorrow—O Mary mary If you knew how anxious I am to see you and dear Patty with the childern I think you would come and meet me

(This was presumably written late on Wednesday the 21st. Bugden was an accepted variant of Buckden.)

Shefford Church . . . by doing so. See F. W. Martin's *The Life of John Clare* (2nd edn., eds. Eric Robinson and Geoffrey Summerfield, London, 1964), p. 310: 'Clare's narrative, understandably, is not entirely consistent. For example, when he met the young gipsy woman about a mile and a half west of St Neots it would have been impossible for her to have pointed to Shefford Church, if by Shefford is intended the town midway between Bedford and Hitchin. The confusion may have been due to the fact that Shefford was the home of Thomas Inskip, Clare's friend, and it is symptomatic of Clare's sense of urgency that he did not make the short detour to Shefford where Inskip could have been counted on for help and shelter. Some of Clare's landmarks, however, are tolerably clear and agree with those described in Cary's *New Itinerary* (1815 edn.). His route corresponded for the most part to the recognized Coach Road and Waggon Way.'

436 *passing by me.* Clare's footnote: 'The Coach did pass me as I sat under some trees by a high wall and the lumps lasshed in my face and wakened me up from a doze when I knocked the gravel out of my shoes and started'.

to the right. i.e. at Norman Cross, $5\frac{3}{4}$ miles to Peterborough.

437 *the Beehive.* Whellan's Directory, 1849, mentions only the Cock, the Blue Bell, the Wheat Sheaf, and the Three Horse Shoes. The nearest 'Beehive' in the area was at Stamford and Clare may have been remembering this one.

Byron. The quotation is from 'Sonnet on Chillon', lines 13–14:

> . . . May none those marks efface!
> For they appeal from tyranny to God.

438 [*The Farmer and the Vicar*]. *Ralph Wormstall.* Probably a mythical character.

acorn time. In another version, at Pfz. Misc. 198-1/7, the Vicar declined the request for fear of being laughed at but 'the Clerk of the parish tryd his skill and accepted the prize which he instantly applaud[ed] and declared the clerk was wiser then his master . . .'. In this account the farmer is called 'Horse shoe Jack' and his real name is given as Job Thrifty.

the witch of Endor. 1 Sam. 28: 7–25.

Dame to the Fair. Pfz. Misc. 198-1/7, p. 4, adds 'nor ever takes a Gun but when he goes to shoot the sparrows when the grain ripens'.

439 ... *'Speed the Plough'.* A version of 'When this Old Hat was New' appears in G. Greig, *Folk Song of the North East* (Hatboro, Pennsylvania, 1963), Article 101, and also as a chapbook (A4, 43 in the Harding Collection, Bodleian Library) entitled *Luckidad's Garland or, When my Old Hat was New* ... Entered according to Order, 1799; 'Toby Fillpot' can be found in M. W. Disher, *Victorian Song* (London, 1955), p. 68; 'Speed the Plough' is a well-known country dance. Clare's interest in songs and ballads is well described in Deacon, and M. Grainger, *John Clare: Collector of Ballads* (Peterborough Museum Society Occasional Papers, No. 3). Clare himself collected both words and tunes. The Librarian, Peterborough Museum Society, gives the following details:

'Toby Fillpot' was written by Rev. F. Fawkes (1721–1777) ... He was a thirsty old soul who 'among jolly topers bore off the bell'. He died, whilst boozing in his arbour, 'full as big as a Dorchester butt'. His body turned to clay and from this a jug was made (hence 'Toby Jug').

> His body when long in the ground it had lain,
> And lime into clay had resolved it again,
> A potter found out in its covert so snug,
> And with part of fat Toby he formed this brown jug,
> Now sacred to friendship, to mirth and mild ale.
> So here's to my lovely sweet Nan of the Vale.

(He suggests that this is the source of Clare's 'Sweet patty of the Vale'.) In Pfz. Misc. 198 there are references to 'Dear Tom his brown jug', 'Old Toby Philpot', and 'Speed the Plough'.

440 *'laughing stock'.* The whole of this passage showing the change of fashion in household goods is interesting for the student of the Industrial Revolution. Glasses replace 'drinking horns'; china, perhaps Wedgwood's, takes the place of brown earthenware; tea-drinking has become a regular social occasion for farmers' wives and daughters. There are parallels with many passages in 'The Parish'.

G. M. Trevelyan, *English Social History* (London, 1978), p. 416: 'Not only Cobbett but everyone else, complained that farmers were "aping their betters", abandoning old homely ways, eating off Wedgwood instead of pewter, educating their girls and dashing about in gigs or riding to hounds.'

441 *Moll Huggings.* Possibly a mythical character.

442 *Mores Almanack.* Francis Moore, astrologer and quack physician, began an almanac forecasting the weather in 1699 to advertise his pills. Clare's Journal, Monday, 6 September 1824: '. . . all I have read today is Moores

Almanack for the account of the weather which speaks of rain tho its very hot and fine'.

'Whole duty of man'. The Whole Duty of Man, usually attributed to Richard Allestree, was first published in 1659 and became a popular theological work going through numerous editions. Clare's copy is dated 1815.

Elliots Husbandry. Jared Eliot, *Essays upon Field-Husbandry in New England, as it is or may be ordered* (Boston, 1760): given in *Bibliotheca Britannica* as Elliott, *Essays upon the Husbandry in New England* (London, 1764), 4to.

'George Barnwell'. George Lillo (1693–1739), *The London Merchant: or, The History of George Barnwell*, a play in prose, was first performed in 1731. It is a melodramatic morality concerning an apprentice who is led by a courtesan to commit murder, and who expiates his crime.

'. . . had been the plough'. The quotation is from Thomas Tusser, *Five Hundred Points of Good Husbandry*, 'The Author's Epistle', p. iv, line 7: 'My musick since hath been the plough' (Clare's copy).

Old Tussers Husbandry. See note to p. 134, l. 65.

443 *preserve them*. Pfz. Misc. 198-8:

> his Son got the name of 'ring Dick' from a circumstance of being taken in at a Fair by 'Black Legs' as the country folks call the London sharpers who pretend to pick up a bundle before him which on examining was found to contain rings and jewels which they declared was 'nothing but gold' and from offering him a share of the prize for a trifle they got him to purchase the whole which cost him the price of a couple of Cows which the old Farmer had sent him to sell—and all believed he had got double the worth of the cows when he got home but the old man who stuck to it that they were nothing but 'Black Legs' and he never trusted him to sell stock afterwards.

'. . . in that important hour'. This couplet is so far unidentified.

'great July flood'. This was probably July of 1816. *Northampton Mercury*, 3 August 1816: 'The general accounts of the continued fall of rain, which has caused rivers to be flooded and land to be deluged, are distressing. In Staffordshire, the damage is estimated at £5,000; a labourer . . . was drowned, in endeavouring to save some hay from going down the river on Sunday night. The town of Stone and its vicinity suffered severely: a small house was washed away by the flood: but its inmates escaped unhurt. . . .'

'hot Wednesday'. 13 July 1808. *Northampton Mercury*, 16 July 1808: 'The heat of the weather on Tuesday and Wednesday was most intense. At one o'clock in the afternoon of Wednesday, the thermometer in the shade, and exposed to a current of air, stood at 84 degrees; partially exposed to the sun it rose to 104; and when fully exposed in a south aspect in the afternoon, its range was from 111 to 116 . . .

From the intenseness of the heat on the above days, many persons in this town and neighbourhood were so completely overpowered as to require being carried from their work in the fields. Horses and cattle were likewise equally affected, and we are informed that several around this place died in consequence.'

444 *as her husband.* Pfz. Misc. 198-6/7:

> ... The Vicar was an odd sort of man and the only thing he seemd to prize most on this side the grave was a curious walking stick that was his constant companion and he was continually repeating its History to the company from the first hour he had [it] when a scholar at Cambridge thro all its hair breadth escapes from being lost and stolen up to the hour he was holding it in his hand which was a tale of 50 years old   he would repeat with a proud sort of [   ] the prizes he had been offered for it by Lord such a one and Dean so and so and tho it was often repeated being the only story he made use of for all companys yet he personified it in such close connection with his own feelings and history calling it his 'old friend in need' and his 'old horse that carried him thro all weathers' that it never failed to entertain and as much from the simplicity of the subject as the love he seemed to feel in relating it ...

445–7 [*Apology for the Poor*]. The dating of this passage from internal evidence is not so simple as it at first appears. The Corn Law of 1815, which artificially raised the price of bread, benefited the farmer but proved disastrous for the poor. Vansittart halved the leather duty in 1822 and Goulburn abolished the remainder in 1830. In 1825 there was a reduction in the spirits duty from 11s. $8\frac{1}{4}d.$ to 7s. per gallon. Brougham attacked the excise on malt in 1822. In 1823 the 'Intermediate Beer' Act was passed. A further Act of 1824 lowered licence rates for brewers at the lowest scale of production. In 1828 Estcourt's Comprehensive Licensing Bill was passed. There was a considerable debate about the malt and beer tax in 1826. See the *Edinburgh Review*, Sept. 1826. The passage may derive from 1829–30.

448 ['*Every farmer ... an orator*']. Cf. passages in 'The Parish' and Clare's letter to Darley, 1830: 'How the times have altered the opinions and views of the people even here we have our villages mustering into parliments and our farmers puffing themselves up into orators and there is scarcley a clown in the village but what has the asumption to act the politician'.

450 [*The Poor man* Versus *the Rich Man*]. '*to be poor*'. An uncharacteristic Old Testament sentiment. The nearest reference seems to be Prov. 14: 20. The quotation also occurs in *The Pleasing Art of Money-Catching and the Way to Thrive by Turning a Penny to advantage ; with a new Method of Regulating Daily Expenses* (Printed for the Booksellers, Falkirk, 1840).

'*Life of the race horse*'. Unidentified.

452 [*Nature Notes*]. *hilly wood* was a favourite spot for Clare's botanizing and there are several references in his Journal.

Milton gardens. See note to p. 487.

453–79 [*Letters to Messrs Taylor and Hessey*]. Clare's Journal, Monday, 18 April 1825: 'Resumed my letters on Natural History in good earnest and intend to get them finished with this year if I can get out into the fields for I will insert nothing but what comes or has come under my notice'. Clare's Journal and the Natural History letters were written between 1824 and 1825 and we have noted a number of parallels.

453 [*Letter* I]. *Emmingsales*. Emmonsales Heath. See note to p. 181, 'Emmonsales Heath'.

Artis. Edmund Tyrell Artis, friend of Clare's, house steward at Milton Hall, archaeologist, discoverer of the Roman site at Castor.

D' Skrimshire. Dr Fenwick Skrimshire, who in 1841 signed the certificate of insanity that admitted Clare to the Northampton General Lunatic Asylum.

Henderson. Joseph Henderson, friend of Clare's, head gardener at Milton Hall, enthusiastic botanist.

Sonnets. Charlotte Smith (1749–1806) was born in London of a wealthy family and at 16 married Benjamin Smith. She wrote novels, poems, letters, children's books, and did translations in order to support her ten children. Sir Walter Scott admired her novels and wrote a critique of them. Her popular *Elegiac Sonnets, and Other Essays* appeared in 1784.

454 *Pattys Lodge*. Walkherd Lodge, three miles north of Stamford, was the home of Patty, whose father was a smallholder there.

455 ['*I went to take my walk to day*']. *Royce wood*. See note to p. 250, l. 24.

457 [*Letter* II]. *Shacklwell*. Shacklewell was in the former borough of Hackney, Middlesex.

'. . . *her voice out ring*'. The quotation is from 'Troilus and Criseyde', Book III, lines 1233–7.

'*bushy close*'. Another favourite haunt of Clare's and referred to in the Journal.

458 *Artis*. See note to p. 453 (2).

Leanius. Linnaeus (1707–78), the founder of modern botany.

460 ['*Swallows*']. *Milton gardens*. See note to p. 487.

['*The country people here distinguish*']. *southey wood*. Clare's Journal, Thursday, 29 December 1824: 'Went with neighbour Billings to Southey Wood . . . to hunt ferns . . .' A favourite spot of Clare's.

464 [*Signs of Spring*]. '. . . *a featherd flower*'. The quotation is from *The Garden of Florence and Other Poems* (1821) by John Hamilton Reynolds (1796–1852). See Journal entry for 3 October 1824 for Clare's comments.

467 [*More Signs of Spring*]. *Oxey wood*. See note to p. 47, l. 2.

471 [*'The little Robin'*]. *February*. Clare's Journal, Friday, 4 February 1825: 'on the third of this month I found an hedge-sparrows nest in Billings Boxtrees before the window with three eggs in it   I lookd again in March and found two young ones pen-featherd starved to death—she laid again in the same nest and brought off a fledgd brood in April'.

472 [*Letter* IV]. *oaking time*. The oak trees had been peeled of their bark, which was used in tanning in the local leather industries.

473 *Norman cross Barracks*. French prisoners were housed in the Norman Cross Barracks during the Napoleonic Wars. See T. J. Walker, *The Depot for Prisoners of War at Norman Cross, Huntingdonshire, 1796 to 1816* (London, 1913).

Southey wood. See note to p. 460 (2).

worthorp Groves. Wothorp Groves, adjoining the parish of Wothorp, near Burghley.

Landon. Probably Thomas Landon, who was married at Helpston 2 July 1792. The christening of his son Thomas, 29 September 1793, is the next entry in the Helpston parish register to Clare's own.

474 *Thompson*. Clare may have had in mind either *Titus Andronicus*, II. iii. 13: 'The snakes lie rolled in the cheerful sun', or 'While from the flowery brake the serpent rolled | His fairer spires, and played his pointless tongue', lines which appeared in all editions of 'Spring' from the first (in 1728) to that of 1738, following lines 271–97.

[*'I took a walk'*]. See note to p. 30, 'Langley Bush'.

475 *'Open Wood'*. Usually known as Open Copy Wood. Clare's Journal, Saturday, 20 November 1824: 'Went out to hunt the harts tongue species of fern . . . I have found it growing about the badger holes in Open Copy wood . . .'

of the romans. The whole of the area between Stamford and Peterborough, and around Castor, is thick with material from the Roman period and from the Civil War. Clare shared antiquarian interests with Artis and Henderson, two of Earl Fitzwilliam's house-servants.

swordy well. See note to p. 147, ['The Lament of Swordy Well']

476 *Burnack Lordship*. See note to p. 157, l. 190.

lenius. Linnaeus (1707–78), the founder of modern botany. Harrison's grounds, near Oxey Wood. Clare's Journal, Wednesday, 15 December 1824: 'Went to Milton   saw a fine Edition of Lenniuses Botany with beautiful plates and find that my fern which I found in Harrisons close dyke by the wood lane is the "thorn-pointed fern" . . .'

Whittlesea Mere. Clare's Journal, Friday, 19 November 1824: 'Had a visit from my friend Henderson . . . he had pleasing News to deliver me having discoverd a new species of Fern a few days back growing among the bogs on Whittlesea Mere . . .' See also note to p. 205, 'To the Snipe'.

Whittering heath. Wittering, five miles west of Helpston.

481 [*Grammar*]. *Cobbet*. The full title of William Cobbett's popular grammar was *A Grammar of the English Language in a Series of Letters Intended for the Use of Schools and of Young Persons in general: but, more especially for the Use of Soldiers, Sailors, Apprentices, and Plough-boys* (London, 1819).

483 [*Letter to William Hone*]. William Hone (1780–1842), miscellaneous English writer and bookseller, whose obscure antiquarian interests were reflected in such works as *Apocryphal New Testament* (1820), *Every-Day Book* (1826–7), and *Table-book* (1827–8). There is a copy of the *Every-Day Book* in Clare's library.

484 *Ben Barr*. The character Ben Barr whom Clare mentions in connection with the custom of porch watching does not appear in either the available parish records or in the militia list for 1762, which listed all the males in the parish between the ages of eighteen and forty-five. However, in her book *Clare's Village*, Bessie Garfoot-Gardiner gives an account of his activities in the village which explain his non-appearance in parish records. From her account it would appear that Barr only stayed in the village for a short time before moving on to escape the wrath of villagers. Mrs Garfoot-Gardiner does mention the passage in *The Every-Day Book* which describes Barr's role as seer and 'porch watcher', but she appears to have been unaware that its author was none other than John Clare. (We are indebted for this note to George Deacon, *John Clare and the Folk Tradition*, p. 288.)

'*East well*'. In his Autobiography Clare writes about going to 'Eastwell on a Sunday to drink sugar and water at the springhead but enclosure came'. Eastwell Spring never went dry and supplied the whole village in dry times. It had another purpose as the waters were said to have medicinal value, especially for eye troubles. At the different seasons the villagers came to drink the waters and hold some kind of seasonal festival there. They sweetened the water with honey and the place of foregathering became known as Golden Drop after the pale gold tint of the sweetener. Cf. 'eastwells boiling spring' in 'Remembrances', line 11, p. 258.

mere or +. The cross sign presumably refers to a continuation of this passage which has not so far been traced. The use of such signs is common practice in Clare MSS.

485 *Kean and Young*. Edmund Kean (*c*.1789–1833) and Charles Mayne Young (1775–1856), rival English actors who played opposite each other in Shakespeare at Drury Lane two or three years previous to the date of this letter. Clare saw Kean on the stage on one of his visits to London.

487 *Milton Hall*. Milton Park, the seat of Earl Fitzwilliam, was a favourite resort of Clare's and excellent for bird-watching. Earl Fitzwilliam was one of Clare's benefactors and it was he who was responsible for obtaining for Clare the cottage at Northborough.

FURTHER READING

MAJOR EDITIONS

The Poems of John Clare, ed. J. W. Tibble, 2 vols., London, 1935.
Selected Poems of John Clare, ed. G. Grigson, London, 1949.
The Later Poems of John Clare, eds. E. Robinson and G. Summerfield, Manchester, 1964.
John Clare: The Shepherd's Calendar, eds. E. Robinson and G. Summerfield, Oxford, 1964.
Selected Poems and Prose of John Clare, eds. E. Robinson and G. Summerfield, Oxford, 1966.
John Clare: The Midsummer Cushion, eds. A. Tibble and R. Thornton, Manchester, 1979.
John Clare: The Rural Muse, ed. R. K. R. Thornton, Ashington, 1982.
The Later Poems of John Clare, 1837–1864, eds. E. Robinson and D. Powell, 2 vols., Oxford, 1984.

BIOGRAPHY, CRITICISM, AND BIBLIOGRAPHY

The best bibliography to date is in G. Crossan, *A Relish for Eternity*, Salzburg, 1976.

Biography

E. Blunden (ed.), *Sketches in the Life of John Clare*, London, 1931.
—— *Keats's Publisher: A Memoir of John Taylor*, London, 1936.
E. Robinson and G. Summerfield (eds.), *Frederick Martin: Life of John Clare*, London, 1964.
J. W. and A. Tibble, *John Clare: A Life*, London, 1932.

Criticism

J. Barrell, *The Idea of Landscape and the Sense of Place, 1730–1840*, Cambridge, 1972.
T. Brownlow, *John Clare and Picturesque Landscape*, Oxford, 1983.
G. Deacon, *John Clare and the Folk Tradition*, London, 1983.
I. Jack, *English Literature, 1815–1832*, Oxford, 1963.

Prose

M. Grainger, *The Natural History Prose Writings of John Clare, 1793–1864*, Oxford, 1983.

GLOSSARY

Flowers and birds in this glossary have been referred to in accordance with *English Names of Wild Flowers: A List Recommended by the Botanical Society of the British Isles*, by John G. Dony, Franklyn Perring, and Catherine M. Rob (Butterworths, for The Botanical Society of the British Isles, 1974), and *Check-list of the Birds of Great Britain and Ireland* (British Ornithologists' Union, 1952). References to Baker are to A. E. Baker, *Glossary of Northamptonshire Words and Phrases* (2 vols., 1854).

a' litter *comb.*, cover the ground

addle *v.*, earn

again, agen *prep.*, against, near, beside

agen *adv.*, again

agrimony *n.*, *Agrimonia eupatoria*, found on waste places and roadsides

air-bell *n.*, harebell, *Campanula rotundifolia*

a(i)riff *n.*, var. of hairif; goosegrass, *Galium aparine*

al'as, al'ays *adv.*, always

amain *adv.*, (1) at once, in all haste; (2) loudly

anker *v.*, hanker

ariff *n.*, *see* airiff

arum *n.*, cuckoopint, *Arum maculatum*

ater *prep.*, *adv.*, after

awe *n.*, haw

awk *n.*, hawk

awthorn *n.*, hawthorn

ayont *prep.*, beyond

badger *n.*, merchant, hawker

bairn *n.*, child

balk, baulk, bawk *n.*, narrow strip of grass dividing two ploughed fields

ball *n.*, Ball, traditional name for an ox

bandy *n.*, knobbed stick used to strike the ball in games such as hockey. *See* clink

bang *v.*, rush violently

bashing *adj.*, bashful

bate *v.*, harass, teaze, worry

battled *adj.*, bespattered with mud, splashed

baulk, bawk *n.*, *see* balk

beatle *n.*, var. of beetle; heavy hammer or mallet

beaver *n.*, hat, originally of beaver fur

beavering, booning (hour) *adj.*, time of refreshment, used especially of harvesting and haymaking

beck *adv.*, back

beesom *n.*, besom; applied dialectically to heath and broom, plants used for besoms or brushes

beetle *v.*, beat (of a storm)

bents *n. pl.*, (1) coarse or wiry grass; (2) seed stalk of grass, especially when old and dry

benty *adj.*, (1) long, coarse (of grass); (2) made of dried grass stalks (of a nest)

besprent *v.*, besprinkle, besprinkled

Bess in her bravery *n.*, probably the double-flowered garden daisy with a mass of crimson-tipped white petals, but we have not encountered the phrase elsewhere

bicker *v.*, brawl (of a stream, rain, etc.)

bield *n.*, protection, shelter, cover

big *v.*, build

billet *n.*, thick piece of firewood

bin *p.p.*, been

birdboy *n.*, boy who frightens birds from the corn

birmstone *n.*, brimstone

bitter sweet *n.*, woody nightshade, *Solanum dulcamara*

blackcap *n.*, (1) Clare's March Nightingale, one of our earliest warbler migrants, *Sylvia atricapilla*; (2) As in Clare's sonnet 'The Blackcap', great tit, *Parus major*

blackthorn *n.*, sloe, *Prunus spinosa*

blea *adj.*, bleak, exposed, wild

blealy *adv.*, coldly, bleakly

bleb *n.*, drop or bubble

blind eggs *n.*, blind champ, a boy's game, consisting of champing or breaking birds' eggs blindfold. The eggs are placed on the ground, and the player, who is blindfolded, takes a certain number of steps in the direction of the eggs; he then slaps the ground with a stick thrice, in the hope of breaking the eggs

blink v., look

blow n., v., bloom, blossom

blue skippers n. pl., variety of butterfly

bluecap n., (1) blue cornflower, *Centaurea cyanus*; (2) blue tit, *Parus caeruleus*

blunt n., money

blushy adj., red, blushing

bodge v., repair clumsily, patch

bolt v., appear or move suddenly

bookman n., travelling pedlar

boon v., grant

booning adj., see beavering

booted hogs n. pl., 'A long form is placed in the kitchen, upon which the boys who have worked well sit, as a terror and disgrace to the rest, in a bent posture, with their hands laid on each other's backs, forming a bridge for the hogs (as the truant boys are called) to pass over; while a strong chap stands on each side, with a boot legging, soundly strapping them as they scuffle over the bridge, which is done as fast as their ingenuity can carry them' (Clare's description in *The Village Minstrel*, 1821)

bottle n., bundle of hay, reeds, sticks, etc.

bottle v., tie into bundles

bottle tit n., long-tailed tit, *Aegithalos caudatus*

bounce v., move hastily, swoop

bove prep., above

bow n., var. of bough

bowl n., var. of bole

brake n., fern, bracken

brake v., break

brakes n. pl., bundles of brushwood

brawl v., murmur, sound

breath v., Clare's usual spelling of breathe

brere n., briar

brig n., bridge

brink n., brim of a hat

brouze v., browse

brun adj., nut-brown or freckled with brown

brunt n., blow, buffet, shock

brush v., rush

brustle v., (1) brush, rustle; (2) bustle about, make a great fuss or stir

bum v., hum, buzz

bumbarrel n., long-tailed tit, *Aegithalos caudatus*

bumper n., brim-full glass of wine

bumping adj., brim-full

burr v., var. of birr; purr, hum

burred adj., haloed (of the moon)

canna v., cannot

canophy n., var. of canopy

car(r)lock n., charlock, *Sinapis arvensis*

cawdymawdy n., (1) herring gull, *Larus argentatus*; (2) lesser black-backed gull, *L. fuscus*, (3) black-headed gull, *L. ridibundus*

chat n., (1) wheatear, *Oenanthe oenanthe*; (2) spotted flycatcher, *Muscicapa striata*

checkering part., creating a pattern like that of a chequer or chessboard

chelp v., (1) chatter, gossip, (2) chirp

chickering adj., chirping (of a cricket or grasshopper)

childern n. pl., children

chimble v., nibble, chew

chimley n., var. of chimney

chink n., ready money, loose coins

chitter v., chirp, twitter

choak v., var. of choke

chock n., game of marbles played by chocking or pitching marbles into a hole instead of shooting at a ring

chuff adj., fat, chubby

chuffd p.p., swollen, puffed

churn n., churn owl (or fern owl), nightjar, *Caprimulgus europaeus*

churring part., whirring (of a nightjar)

cirging part., surging

clack n., chatter, gossip

clammed p.p., parched with thirst or exhausted for lack of food

clamper v., tread heavily

clane v., var. of clean

clap v., set (dogs) on

claum n., clamm, clamp, device for holding something fast

claum v., seize, clutch

clench v., rivet nails

clink n., as in 'clink and bandy chock': 'clink' may be onomatopoeic, expressive of the contact of marble; alternatively, it may signify 'clench', in which case 'clink and bandy chock' may

denote marbles played by first 'clenching' the thumb and then allowing it, on
release, to strike the marble as the
bandy or hockey-stick strikes the ball

clipping pink (or posey) *n.*, flowers presented to sheep-shearers

clock a clay *n.*, lady-bird

clodhopper, clothopper *n.*, (1) wheatear,
Oenanthe oenanthe; (2) whinchat,
Saxicola rubetra

clohs *n. pl.*, clothes

clomb *p.p.*, climbed

close *n.*, enclosed field, usually for pastur-
ing cattle

closen *n. pl.*, small fields

clout *v.*, clothe

clouted *adj.*, clothed, patched

clouts *n. pl.*, clothes

clown *n.*, rustic

clum(b) *p.p.*, climbed

clumping *adj.*, growing in clumps

coat *n.*, var. of cote

cock *n.*, pooty, landsnail, *Capaea*, particularly the shell of *C. nemoralis.*
Baker, i. 133: 'It is a common boyish
pastime to hold one of these shells
between the last joints of the bent
fingers, and forcibly press the apex
against another held in a similar
manner by an opponent, until one of
them, by dint of persevering pressure,
forces its way into the other; and the
one which in these contests has gained
the most victories is termed the con-
queror, and is highly valued by its
juvenile owner'

cock *v.*, smoke (nineteenth-century slang)

coil *n.*, stir, bustle, movement

cole *n.*, var. of coal

conceit *v.*, imagine, persuade oneself,
think extravagantly

copple *n.*, crest of a bird

coppled *adj.*, crested

copt *p.p.*, (of hay) put into heaps or cocks

cot(t) *n.*, cottage

cotter *n.*, farm tenant, cottager

cowslap *n.*, var. of cowslip

cozie *adj.*, cosy, snug

crab *n.*, crab apple

crack *n.*, boast or jest

craik, crake *v.*, croak

crane *n.*, as in 'long neckt sheet crane': 'A
man holds in his hand a long stick, with

another tied at the top in the form of an
L reversed, which represents the long
neck and beak of the crane. This, with
himself, is entirely covered with a large
sheet. He mostly makes excellent sport,
as he puts the whole company to the
rout, picking out the young girls, and
pecking at the bald heads of the old
men ...' (Clare's description in the
Introduction to *The Village Minstrel*,
1821)

crank *v.*, (1) turn, twist; (2) croak

crank *adj.*, croaky

crankle *v.*, turn, twist

crap *n.*, var. of crop

crawk *n.*, croak

creasing *adj.*, increasing

cree *v.*, cry, caw

creep up (a sleeve) *v.*, get into favour
with, ingratiate

creeper *n.*, tree-creeper, *Certhia familiaris*

crim con *n.*, criminal conversation, a legal
term for adultery

crimp(le) *v.*, ripple, ruffle, wrinkle

crizzle *v.*, crisp, roughen, as of water
when it begins to freeze

cronk *v.*, croak

croo *v.*, make a noise like a dove or pigeon

croodle *v.*, crouch, shrink from cold

crook *n., v.*, bend, curve

croppings *n. pl.*, crops

crumble *n.*, crumb

crump *v.*, (1) make a crunching sound, as
frozen snow when trodden on; (2)
crunch with the teeth

cucka ball *n.*, ball of flowers for throwing
in May games

cuckoo, cuckoo flower *n.*, applied by
Clare to varieties of *Orchidaceae*, particularly early-purple orchis, *Orchis
mascula*

cum mull *n.*, common call for cows to
come for milking

cumber ground *n. pl.*, useless things
(originally 'trees'), dregs. 'Cut it down,
why cumbereth it the ground'

curdle *n.*, bubbling up of disturbed water

curdle *v.*, make circular ripples in water

curnel *n.*, var. of kernel

cushion *n.*, the cushion dance is described
in Baker, ii. 437–9: 'The Cushion
Dance is still continued, with some
variations, by the humbler classes in

this county . . . and generally closes the evening's amusements'

dab *v.*, strike
dabble *v.*, make or become wet or muddy
dale *n.*, deal wood
dare *v.*, venture
daw *n.*, jackdaw
dead *n.*, death
dimp *v.*, dimple
dimute *adj.*, var. of diminute; diminished
distrain *v.*, seize
dither *v.*, shiver with cold
dizen *v.*, dress showily, adorn
doll *n.*, Doll, traditional name for a milkmaid
dotterel *n.*, pollard tree
dowie *adj.*, dull, dreary, dowdy
drabble *v.*, trail along in the mud
drabbled *adj.*, dirtied or splashed with walking in the mud
drebble *v.*, var. of dribble
dripple *v.*, fall in drops
dropple *n.*, drop
drove *v.*, drive
drowk(ing) *adj.*, drooping from drought
duck(s) and drake(s) *n*, game of skimming flat pieces of stone across the surface of still water
ducking stone *n.*, 'ducks' is a boy's game, played with three stones, surmounted by a fourth, which the player tries to dislodge by throwing at it from a short distance
dusty miller *n.*, kind of rude farce performed at the harvest supper and described by Clare in the Introduction to *The Village Minstrel*, 1821

edding *n.*, var. of heading; grass at the end of a ploughed field
eddish *n.*, aftermath, second crop of grass
een *n. pl.*, eyes
eke *v.*, stretch out, lengthen, increase, add to
eking *adj.*, stretching, spinning out
eldern *n.*, elder tree, *Sambucus nigra*
elting *adj.*, moist, damp (of soil newploughed)
empherion *adj.*, ephemeral, short-lived. Cf. ephemeron *n.*, an insect living only a day

enarmourd *adj.*, enamoured
erst *adv.*, formerly, of old

fairing *n.*, present bought at a fair
farden, farding *n.*, farthing
fei(g)n *v.*, Clare's spelling of fain
fern owl *n.*, nightjar, *Caprimulgus europaeus*
fetch *n.*, vetch
fin weed *n.*, restharrow, *Ononis repens*
firdale *n.*, fir tree
firetail *n.*, redstart, *Phoenicurus phoenicurus*
firey *adj.*, fiery, red
firey parrot *n.*, 'A candle lighted is placed on the mantle-piece or elsewhere, and on the far side of the house stands a tub full of water, with a sheet over the top, on each side of which, on the edge of the tub, sits a girl, while a young fellow is selected out to sit between them . . . who, as he drops down, rise in an instant, while the loosed sheet gives way, and often lets him in over head and ears . . .' (Clare's description in the Introduction to *The Village Minstrel*, 1821)
flags *n. pl.*, reeds, rushes
flaze *n.*, smoky flame, blaze, flare
flirt *v.*, flit, flutter
flitting *n.*, removal from one house to another
flusker *v.*, flutter, fly with sudden motion
flycatch *n.*, flycatcher
fob *v.*, pocket
fold *v.*, place sheep in the fold
footbrig *n.*, footbridge
footpad *n.*, footpath
fother *v.*, fodder, feed
fotherer *n.*, one who brings fodder
foulroyce *n.*, foul-rush, the dogwood or spindle-tree, i.e. either *Cornus sanguinea* or *Euonymus europaeus*, used for making musical instruments
fox and hounds *n.*, boy's game, in which the hounds chase the fox
frae *prep.*, from
frail *n.*, flail
freak *n.*, odd notion, fancy
freck(le) *v.*, mark with spots, dapple
freshing *adj.*, refreshing
frit *v.*, frighten, frightened

frumitory, frumity *n.*, frumenty, a dish made of hulled wheat boiled in milk and seasoned

furlong *n.*, originally the length of furrow in a common field

furze kidder *n.*, person who collects and makes up bundles of furze, or furze-kids

fuss *v.*, make a fuss of, fondle

gad *n.*, gad-fly

gadder *n.*, beast being tormented by gad-flies and running about wildly

gadding *part.*, moving in a restless, excited fashion

gale *n.* breeze

gamble *v.*, var. of gambol

gang *v.*, go

gant *adj.*, gaunt

gathering cream *comb.*, Clare's note in *The Village Minstrel* glossary: 'This alludes to the cream gathering round the bucket as the milk-maid journeys home, which often betrays the loitering with a sweetheart'

gauling *part.*, galling

gaup, gawp *v.*, gape

gen *v.*, gave

gen *prep.*, against

gerk *v.*, var. of jerk

gi(e) *v.*, give

gighouse *n.*, shed for storing a gig, a light two-wheeled one-horse carriage

gin *v.*, begin

ginnet *n.*, jinnet or gennet, a type of apple

gis *v.*, give

gleg *v.*, glance, look

glib(bed) *adj.*, smooth, slippery (of ice)

glidder *v.*, glitter

glower *v.*, look angrily at, stare rudely

goats beard *n.*, goat's-beard, *Tragopogon pratensis*

goody *n.*, familiar name for an old woman

goss *n.*, gorse, *Ulex europaeus*

gough *n.*, gouge

grain *n.*, larger branch of a tree, bough

green sickness *n.*, anaemic disease mostly affecting young women about the age of puberty and giving a pale or greenish tinge to the complexion, chlorosis

gris *n.*, var. of grist; corn for grinding

ground *n.*, enclosed piece of land, usually meadow-land

groundlark *n.*, meadow pipit, *Anthus pratensis*

group *v.*, var. of grope

grubbed *p.p.*, uprooted; the grub-axe was part axe and part hoe

grubble *v.*, var. of grub; dig, uproot

grunsel *n.*, groundsel

grunter *n.*, pig

guggle *n.*, *v.*, gurgle

gull(e)d *p.p.*, of a hole or rut washed out by water

gulphy *adj.*, gulping

gulsh *v.*, (1) splash; (2) tear up with force

gun *v.*, began

hant *n.*, var. of haunt

hap *v.*, cover

harts tongue *n.*, hart's tongue, *Phyllitis scolopendrium*

hartsomely *adj.*, cheerfully

hawl close to *v.*, sleep with

hay chat *n.*, lesser whitethroat, *Sylvia curruca*

haynish *adj.*, wretched, awkward

headache *n.*, common poppy, *Papaver rhoeas*

heaves *n. pl.*, eaves

heir long *n.*, heirloom

hen and chickens *n.*, described in Alice B. Gomme's *Traditional Games of England, Scotland and Ireland* (1894), i. 201: 'The game is played in the usual manner of "Fox and Goose" games. One is chosen to be the Hen, and one to be the Fox. The rest are the Chickens'

hep *n.*, var. of hip

hermit bee *n.*, female bee which separates itself from the hive and lays eggs in an old post

heronshaw, herrinshaw *n.*, heron, *Ardea cinerea*

hickerthrifts *n.*, Tom Hickathrift, the popular hero of a pamphlet carried by hawkers

hiloes *n. pl.*, high-lows, boots covering the ankles

hind *n.*, farm servant

hind *prep.*, behind

hing *v.*, hang

hirkle *v.*, cower, crouch, shrink so as to keep warm

hirple *v.*, (1) crouch (as from cold); (2)

walk lame, limp, move unevenly (as a hare)

hodge n., typical English agricultural labourer

Holyrood day n., 14 September, a day set aside by the Church for commemoration of the finding by St Helena of the cross believed to have been the one on which Christ had been crucified. It became a school holiday when boys went a-nutting in the woods

horn n., (1) drinking-vessel; (2) barley horn, keck horn

horse blob n., marsh-marigold, *Caltha palustris*

hovel n., animal shed in a field

howp v., var. of hoop

huff v., wuff, bark in a suppressed manner

hugh adj., Clare's spelling of huge

humble bee n., bumble-bee

hurd v., hoard

hurkle v., crouch

hussle v., var. of hustle

huzzing adj., tumultuous, clamorous, rushing

ic'el, 'icle n., icicle

in times adv., betimes, early

interscet v., intersect

invest v., infest

Jack by the hedge n., garlic mustard, *Alliaria petiolata*

jelt v., throw, fling

jobble v., move unevenly

Joe Millar n., old joke. Cf. *Joe Miller's Jests*, 1739

joll n., lurch

joll v., lurch, walk lumberingly along

keck n., dried stalk of umbellifers such as cow parsley and hogweed, and often used of the plant itself

ken v., know

key n., seed vessel of the ash tree

kid n., bundle of dry thorns, small faggot for firewood

kingcup n., marsh-marigold, *Caltha palustris*

kirchip n., noise of partridges calling to each other

knap v., snap with the teeth, bite, nibble

knarl v., gnaw, nibble

knarl(c)d adj., gnarled

knewt n., newt

knowl n., knoll

knowley adj., knolly, bumpy

ladslove n., southernwood, *Artemisia abrotanum*

lady smock n., cuckooflower, *Cardamine pratensis*

lambtoe n., common bird's-foot-trefoil, *Lotus corniculatus*

lammas tide n., 1 August, formerly observed as harvest festival

land n., arable division of a furlong in an open field

landrail, landrake n., corncrake

lanthorn n., lantern

lap v., wrap, fold

lare n., lair, rest, bed

lare v., rest in a shelter

lark n., meadow pipit, *Anthus pratensis*

lated adj., belated, overtaken by darkness

lauter n., var. of laughter, a sitting of eggs

lawn n., greensward open space, small pasture

lawrence wages bids comb., to be lazy, invite to idleness. St Lawrence is the genius of idleness

licken n., lichen

light v., lighten

ling n., heath; heather, *Calluna vulgaris*

lither adj., lazy, idle

loath adj., Clare's spelling of loth

lock pen n., lock-chamber

long legged shepherd n., crane-fly

looby n., silly fellow

loose v., Clare's spelling of lose

lothe v., Clare's spelling of loathe

lotted p.p., allotted

love grass n., floating sweet-grass, *Glyceria fluitans*

lown n., var. of loon; scamp, peasant

lucifer n., friction match

lud n., lord

lump v., thump, beat, thresh

lunge v., lurch, hide, skulk

lunnon, lunun n., London

lurch (on the) n., lurking in order to surprise

lurch v., lurk

mag *n.*, magpie

mare blob *n.*, marsh-marigold, *Caltha palustris*

martinmass *n.*, St Martin's Day, 11 November

matty *adj.*, matted, twisted, interwoven

maul *v.*, drag along wearily

mawkin *n.*, scarecrow

max *n.*, gin

meadow sweet *n.*, meadowsweet, *Filipendula ulmaria*

meal(e)y *adj.*, pale yellowish-white, dappled

mere *n.*, boundary

mere hole *n.*, hole caused by the removal of a stone boundary mark

mete *v.*, measure

mete *adj.*, meet, suitable, fit

mickle *adj.*, much

midgen *n. pl.*, gnats

mizardly *adv.*, miserly

mizled *adj.*, wet with mizzle or drizzle

moil *v.*, toil, labour

moiler *n.*, labourer

moister *n.*, var. of moisture

mooze *v.*, doze, moon about

moping *adj.*, dreamy, vacant

more *n.*, var. of moor

mort *n.*, lot, large number

mouldiwarp, mouldywharp *n.*, mole

mozzld, mozzling *adj.*, of rubbed indistinct pattern, mottled, of various colours

mulldering *part.*, decaying to dust, mouldering

mun *v.*, must

nail passer *n.*, corruption of nail-piercer, i.e. auger or gimlet

nap *v.*, bite, nibble

nap(py) *n.*, strong ale

nauntle *v.*, elevate, hold oneself erect, raise

neak *n.*, see nook

near *adv.*, Clare's spelling of ne'er

netterd *n.*, neatherd, cowherd

neuk *n.*, see nook

nick *n.*, familiar name for the devil

nighted *adj.*, benighted

nimble *v.*, move quickly, dart

noahs ark *n.*, streaks of cloud in the shape of a boat, supposed to portend floods

nook, neak, neuk *n.*, angular corner of a field

odlin, oddling, *adj.*, (1) one different from the rest of a family, brood, or litter; generally applied to the smallest, or to one with a peculiarity; (2) solitary

old mans beard *n.*, traveller's-joy, *Clematis vitalba*

ony *adj.*, any

orison *n.*, var. of horizon

outherod *v.*, outdo Herod (represented in the old Mystery Plays as a blustering tyrant)

pad *n.*, var. of path

padded *adj.*, well-trodden

paigle *n.*, cowslip, *Primula veris*

pail *n.*, var. of pale

pailing *n.*, paling

pale *n.*, enclosed land

palm *n.*, goat willow, sallow, *Salix caprea*

palm grass *n.*, reed meadow-grass, *Poa aquatica*

pat *n.*, quick succession of small sounds or taps

pattin *n.*, var. of patten; overshoe with wooden sole on iron ring for raising wearer's shoes out of the mud

paul *v.*, pall, satiate

pawl *n.*, pall, mantle

peace-plenty, peace and plenty *n.*, harvest toast

peep, pip *n.*, single blossom of flowers growing in a cluster

peg morris *n.*, nine-peg morris; game played with wooden pegs and stones, moved as in draughts, on squares cut in turf

pend *v.*, depend

pettichap *n.*, (1) chiffchaff, *Phylloscopus collybita*; (2) willow-warbler, *P. trochilus*

pie *n.*, magpie

piegon *n.*, Clare's usual spelling of pigeon

pilewort *n.*, lesser celandine, *Ranunculus ficaria*

pill *v.*, peel, strip off

pindar, pinder *n.*, person employed to impound strayed cattle

pinderd *adj.*, shut in, impounded

pin-feathers *n.*, incipient feathers before the birds are fully fledged

pingle *n.*, (1) close, small meadow; (2) small spinney

pink *n.*, chaffinch, *Fringilla coelebs*; occasionally Clare may mean the yellowhammer

pinsor *v.*, snip, pincer

pip *n.*, *see* peep

pis(s)mire *n.*, ant

plash *n.*, *v.*, splash

plashy *adj.*, splashy, wet

plat(t) *n.*, flat stretch of ground

plate *v.*, var. of plait

pleachy *adj.*, sun dried, bleached

plough monday *n.*, first Monday after Epiphany, on which the commencement of the ploughing season used to be celebrated. From a religious occasion, it became just another day for riotous merrymaking

poach *n.*, var. of porch

poddle *v.*, toddle

poesy *n.*, (1) poetry; (2) posy

pointings, points *n.*, the removal of which is necessary in preparing the grain for the mill

poot(e)y *n.*, landsnail, *Capaea*, particularly the shell of *C. nemoralis*

popple *n.*, poplar

pound *n.*, pen for stray animals

prank *v.*, adorn, decorate

pranking *adj.*, frolicsome, flitting about

praxis *n.*, practice

pregon *n.*, var. of piegon (Clare's spelling of pigeon)

presevere *v.*, var. of persevere

prevade *v.*, var. of pervade

prime, primp *v.*, trim, preen (of a bird's feathers)

princess feather *n.*, prince's feather, i.e. the lilac, *Syringa vulgaris*

prog(g), proggle *v.*, prod, poke, stir up

prospect *n.*, aspect, respect

protentious *adj.*, var. of portentous

prune *v.*, preen (of a bird's feathers)

pudding bag *n.*, (of a nest), so described from its being in the form of a long pudding-bag, with a hole in the middle

puddock *n.*, kite, *Milvus milvus*, but also used by Clare of the buzzard

pudge *n.*, puddle

pudgy *adj.*, muddy, full of puddles

puther *v.*, reek, puff (of smoke or dust)

putter *v.*, patter

pye *n.*, magpie

quake, quawk *v.*, squawk, caw

quere *adj.*, var. of queer

querk, quirk *v.*, search or dart about

rabble *v.*, act in a disorderly manner

rack *n.*, thin cloud

ramp *v.*, romp, rampage, grow luxuriantly

ramping *adj.*, coarse, tall, growing luxuriantly

rath *adj.*, var. of rathe; early blooming

rauk, rawk *n.*, mist, fog

rawky *adj.*, misty, foggy

receipt, reciept *n.*, recipe

red water *n.*, disease in cattle and sheep characterized by the presence of free haemoglobin in the urine

redcap *n.*, goldfinch, *Carduelis carduelis*

reign *n.*, Clare's spelling of rein

restharrow *n.*, field shrub with tough roots, *Ononis repens*

riddle *v.*, var. of ruddle; mark with red ochre

ride, riding *n.*, open space or greensward road in a wood

rig *n.*, (1) joke, trick; (2) ridge (of a building or land)

risp *v.*, make a grating sound

rispy *adj.*, rasping, grating

rock *n.*, var. of rack; thin cloud

rock *v.*, sway, walk unsteadily

roil *v.*, climb, tumble

roll *n.*, large, heavy wooden roller for breaking clods

roozing *adj.*, rousing, blazing (of a fire)

rotten *n.*, rotten wood

rougery *n.*, var. of roguery

rout *n.*, Clare uses the same word for 'route' and 'rout' and it seems to share something of both senses wherever it occurs

rowl *v.*, var. of roll

rucking *n.*, heap or stack of hay

ruff *v.*, ruffle

ruff *adj.*, rough

runnel *n.*, stream, brook, rill

rushcap *n.*, bonnet, cap made of rushes

russeting *n.*, russet apple

ryhme *n.*, Clare's spelling of rime

safforn *adj.*, var. of saffron

saint Marks Eve *n.*, 24 April: the St Mark's Day practice was known as 'Making the Dumb Cake'

St Tomases Eve *n.*, 20 December

sawn *v.*, saunter, loiter, dally

scoop *n.*, depression, hollow

scotch pedlars *n. pl.*, kind of rude farce performed at the harvest supper and described by Clare in the Introduction to *The Village Minstrel*, 1821

scourse *n.*, var. of source

scrat *v.*, var. of scratch

scrawl *v.*, sprawl, crawl

screed *n.*, (1) shred or fragment; (2) narrow strip, edge

scrowed *adj.*, marked or scratched in lines

sear, seer *adj.*, var. of sere

sedge bird *n.*, sedge warbler *Acrocephalus schoenobaenus*

seer *adj.*, *see* sear

seethe *v.*, soak, steep

selfheal *n.*, *Prunella vulgaris*; kinds of plants supposed to enable people to do without a doctor, regarded as a cure for quinsy

sell, sen *n.*, self

shagged *adj.*, shaggy, rough-haired

shanny *adj.*, shy

shepherds purse *n.*, common cruciferous weed, *Capsella bursa-pastoris*

shield *n.*, shelter

shill *adj.*, shrill

shoaf *n.*, var. of sheaf

shoffle *v.*, var. of shuffle

shool *v.*, (1) saunter lazily, stroll; (2) saunter around with

shoon *n. pl.*, shoes

shoves *n. pl.*, sheaves

shoy *adj.*, shy

shoyley *adv.*, shyly

shut *n.*, close (of eve)

sich *adj.*, such

side *prep.*, beside

sidle *v.*, saunter, meander

sile *v.*, glide, fleet past

sin *conj.*, since

sink *n.*, pool or pit formed in the ground for the receipt of waste water, sewage etc.; cesspool

sinkfoil *n.*, cinquefoil, *Potentilla reptans*

sinkfoin *n.*, sainfoin, *Onobrychis viciifolia*, rather than cinquefoil

skirting *n.*, lower part or skirt of a garment

skreek *v.*, shriek, scream

skreeker *n.*, wooden rattle

slidder *v.*, slide, slither

slighty *adj.*, slight

slive *v.*, slide, slip

sloomy, *adj.*, slow, dreamy

slop frock *n.*, labourer's smock-frock

sloven *adj.*, untidy, slovenly, slipshod

slow *n.*, (1) sloe, *Prunus spinosa*; (2) slough, swamp

sluther *v.*, slide, slither

snagg *n.*, rough protuberance on a tree

snob *n.*, colloquialism for shoemaker

snub *adj.*, cut short, stumpy

snudge *v.*, be snug and quiet, nestle

snuff, snuft *v.*, snuffle, sniff

soak *n.*, hard drinker

sock *n.*, wet land not properly drained, boggy ground

soodle *v.*, linger, dawdle, saunter

sosh *v.*, dip as in flight, swoop

spank *adj.*, spanking, smart

spavin *n.*, disease of horse's hock-joint resulting in lameness

speed *v.*, thrive

sphinx *n.*, hawk-moth

spider catcher *n.*, spotted flycatcher, *Muscicapa striata*

spindle *n.*, shoot or stem of plant

spindle *v.*, shoot up (as of plants)

spir(e)y *adj.*, pointing and tapering like a spire

sprent *v.*, sprinkle

sprent *adj.*, sprinkled

sprotes *n. pl.*, small twigs for firewood

sprunt *v.*, spread out suddenly

squab *v.*, splash about

squash *v.*, splash

squashy *adj.*, splashy

squirk *v.*, squeak

squirt *v.*, move swiftly or quickly, dart, frisk

stall *v.*, stick fast in a muddy road

starnel *n.*, starling

statute *n.*, Michaelmas fair for hiring agricultural workers

steal *n.*, var. of steel

stibble *n.*, var. of stubble

sticker *n.*, wood-gatherer

sticking *adj.*, gathering wood or sticks

stive *v.*, stuff, cram

stock *n.*, livestock, cattle

stool *n.*, stump of tree in the ground, especially one from which young shoots spring; cluster of stems arising from the same root, as in hazel stools

stouk *n., v.*, var. of stook; shock of wheat or barley; arrange corn in sheaves

stoven *n.*, stump of a tree

stowk *n.*, var. of stook; shock of wheat or barley

streak, streck *v.*, stretch

strinkle *v.*, sprinkle

stript *adj.*, striped

strown *p.p.*, strewn

struggle *n.*, var. of strag or straggle; thin growing straggly crop

strunted (up) *adj.*, cut short, up-turned (of a bird's tail)

struttle *n.*, any small freshwater fish, stickleback

stubbs *n. pl.*, stubble

stulp *n.*, stump of a tree

stump *n.*, leg

stunt *v.*, curtail, reduce

stunt *adj.*, stunted

stuntly *adv.*, abruptly

sturt(le) *v.*, startle, move suddenly

sue *v.*, sigh, rustle, whistle (of the wind)

suff *v.*, var. of sue or sugh, make a rustling sound

sut *n.*, soot

sutheing *adj.*, soothing

suther, suthy *v.*, sigh heavily, make a rushing noise, whistle (as the wind among trees); also used of birds in flight

suthering *n.*, noise of the wind through trees

sutty *adj.*, sooty

swab(b) *v.*, sway about

swad *v.*, var. of swaddle; twist about, swing, sway

swail *n.*, shade

swail(e)y *adj.*, shady

swaliest *adj.*, shadiest

swarm *v.*, climb

swa(r)th *n.*, range or row of cut grass or corn, as it falls from the scythe

swea, swee *v.*, sway, swing

swee *n.*, swing

swee swaw *n.*, see-saw

swift *n.*, common newt or eft

swiver *v.*, sweep round, hover, flutter

swoof *n.*, var. of sough; sigh, grief

swop *v.*, swoop, pounce

taen *p.p.*, taken

tarbottle, *n.*, tar mark

taw *n.*, marble

team *v.*, empty, pour out

teaze *v.*, (1) irritate; (2) play, flutter

teazel, teazle *n.*, var. of teasel, *Dipsacus fullonum*

ted *v.*, spread about new mown grass

tent *v.*, watch, attend

thack *n.*, thatch

thacker *n.*, thatcher

then *conj.*, Clare's usual spelling of than

thorow *adv.*, through

threat *v.*, threaten

thrum *v.*, twang

Thumb *n.*, Tom Thumb

thurrow *n.*, furrow

tight *adj.*, neat, tidy

tillage *n.*, cultivated soil

timely *adv.*, early

tink *n.*, tinkle

tittle *v.*, tickle

tolter *v.*, hobble, move clumsily

tootle *v.*, chirp, whistle

tother *pron.*, the other

totter grass *n.*, quaking-grass, *Briza media*

town *n.*, used by Clare for village

toze *v.*, pluck, snatch

trace *v.*, walk

tramper *n.*, tramp, vagrant

trawling *adj.*, combination of trailing and brawling

tray *n.*, (1) hurdle; (2) feeding-trough

troubles by *v.*, is disturbed as the wind passes through

truding *adj.*, intruding

tuff *adj.*, tough, severe

tutle *v.*, var. of tootle; chirp, whistle

twank *v.*, sound sharply

twharl *v.*, twirl, whirl

twit *v.*, chirp, twitter

twitch *n.*, common couch grass, *Agropyron caninum*

twitch(e)y *adj.*, made of couch grass

uggling *part.*, gurgling

unbrunt *adj.*, unharmed

unfold *v.*, release sheep from the fold

ushering *adj.*, summoning, calling
usuage *n.*, var. of usage

vill *n.*, village

waffle *v.*, yap, bark
waggon-see *n.*, waggon-seat
wain *v.*, var. of wane
waken *adj.*, awake
wallet *n.*, bag
warp *v.*, entwine, weave
watchet *adj.*, light blue
water blob *n.*, marsh-marigold, *Caltha palustris*
weal *n.*, stripe, blow
weal *v.*, raise marks on the skin with a whip
wear *v.*, (1) travel quietly or slowly; (2) persevere in
weigle *v.*, inveigle
were *adv.*, Clare's almost consistent spelling of where
wetting *part.*, whetting
whelm *v.*, overwhelm, engulf
whelp *n.*, bad-mannered child
whemble *v.*, turn over, turn upside down
where *v.*, Clare's occasional spelling of were
whew *n.*, *v.*, cry of a bird; make the noise
whew *v.*, whirl, rush through the air
while *conj.*, until
whilom *conj.*, whilst
whimble *n.*, twisting and turning
w(h)imper *v.*, ripple, meander
whimsey *n.*, whim
whipe away *v.*, clear away, put aside, remove
whirp *v.*, wharp or warp, bend or turn
w(h)opstraw *n.*, countryman, country bumpkin (term of contempt)
wift *n.*, whift or whiff; a puff of smoke as from a pipe
wight *n.*, creature, fellow
wilder(e)d *adj.*, pathless, wild
wild(l)ing *n.*, wild flower, wild rose, wild apple, i.e. crab-apple
wimble *n.*, auger or gimlet
wimmy *adj.*, full of whims and fancies, changeable
wimper *v.*, *see* whimper
winner, winnow *v.*, beat the air (cf. winnowing wheat)
wip *n.*, whip

wipe by, wipe aside *v.*, clear away, put aside, remove
wis *comb.*, with his
wisker *v.*, whisk
witching *adj.*, bewitching
witchingly *adv.*, bewitchingly
wood chat *n.*, either the garden warbler, *Sylvia borin*, or wood warbler, *Phylloscopus sibilatrix*
wood sear *n.*, var. of wood seer; cuckoo-spit. 'Insects that lie in little white knots of spittle on the backs of leaves and flowers. How they come I don't know, but they are always seen plentiful in moist weather, and are one of the shepherd's weather-glasses. When the head of the insect is seen turned upward, it is said to betoken fine weather; when downward, on the contrary, wet may be expected. I think they turn to grasshoppers, and am almost certain, for I have watched them minutely' (Clare's note in the glossary to *The Village Minstrel*, 1821)
woodlark *n.*, tree pipit, *Anthus trivialis*
woolpack *n.*, the rack or high clouds
wop *v.*, thrash, beat
wopstraw *n.*, see whopstraw
wornt *v.*, won't
wrack *n.*, var. of rack; thin cloud
wrecky *adj.*, composed of wreckage, fragments, etc.
writing lark *n.*, yellowhammer, *Emberiza citrinella*; derived from the irregular black, zig-zag lines upon the eggs, resembling writing

yah *pron.*, you
yaum *n.*, length of dampened straw for thatching
yaumd *adj.*, (of beans) cut carefully and gathered into a manageable sheaf of about the same size and shape as a thatcher's yealm
yed *comb.*, you would
yer(e) *pron.*, your
yere *comb.*, you are
yeve *comb.*, you have
yoe *n.*, ewe
younker *n.*, youngster
yule *n.*, weevil
yumour, *n.*, var. of humour; water, fluid

zemblance *n.*, resemblance

INDEX OF TITLES AND FIRST LINES

Each of the sonnets in a sonnet group and the first lines of the songs and ballads in 'Child Harold' and 'Don Juan' are indexed separately. An index of titles of prose passages follows the index of poems.

A Bean field full in blossom smells as sweet 388
['*A hugh old tree all wasted to a shell*'] 269
A little slender bird of reddish brown 235
A maiden head the virgins trouble 18
A seaboy on the giddy mast 347
All how silent and how still, 24
Among the meadow hay cocks 339
Among the stubbles when the fields grow grey 232
Among the taller wood with ivy hung 248
And looked about and started none to find 265
['*And often from the rustling sound*'] 237
And what is Life? An hour-glass on the run 26
And wheres there a scene more delightfully seeming 47
['*And yonder by the circling stack*'] 241
Angling 196
Angling has pleasures that are much enjoyed 196
As boys where playing in their schools dislike 270
Autumn ('Autumn comes laden with her ripened load') 131
Autumn ('I love the fitfull gusts that shakes') 382
Autumn ('Syren of sullen moods and fading hues') 161
Autumn ('The autumn day it fades away,') 348
Autumn ('The thistle down's flying Though the winds are all still') 405
[*Autumn Birds*] 267
Autumn comes laden with her ripened load 131
[*Autumn Evening*] 241
Autumn I love thy latter end to view 44
[*Autumn Morning*] 266
Autumn Robin, The 225
Autumn Wind, The 372

[*Badger, The*] 246
Ballad ('I love thee sweet mary but love thee in fear') 40
Ballad ('We'll walk among the tedded hay,') 357
Ballad ('Where the dark ivy the thorn tree is mounting') 91
Ballad ('Winter winds cold and blea') 29
Bean Field, The 388
Beautiful mortals of the glowing earth 353
Beside a runnel build my shed 27
Bird of the morn 344
[*Birds in Alarm*] 242
Birds Nests ('How fresh the air the birds how busy now') 207
Birds Nests ('Tis Spring warm glows the South') 427, 496 n.
Birds: Why are ye Silent? 415
Black grows the southern clouds betokening rain 102

Blackbird, The   365
Blackcap, The   232
[Bloomfield I]   108, 490 n.
[Bloomfield II]   108
Born upon an Angels Breast   425
Boys and Spring   387
But little lingerers old esteem detains   209
But they who hunt the fields for rotten meat   248

Careless Rambles   103
Child Harold   279, 493 n.
Childhood ('O dear to us ever the scenes of our childhood')   394
Childhood ('The past it is a magic word')   113, 490 n.
Childish Recollections   38, 489 n.
Chiming Bells, The   423
Clifford Hill   397, 495 n.
Clock a Clay   391
Close where the milking maidens pass   273
Cock Robin he got a neat tippet at spring   403
Cocks wake the early morn wi' many a Crow   12
Come luscious spring come with thy mossy roots   223
[Copse in Winter, A]   28
Corn Craiks Rispy Song, The   404
Cottager, The   133, 490 n.
Cowper the Poet of the field   409
[Crane's Nest, The]   276
Crow, The   376
[Crow Sat on the Willow, The]   406
[Crows in Spring]   222

Day burnishes the distant hills   109
Decay A Ballad   256
Deckt out in ribbons gay and papers cut   269
Delicious is a leisure hour   200
Did I know where to meet thee   295
Don Juan A Poem   318, 493 n.
Draws up his scarlet snout and cools to grey   273
Droneing Bee, The   343
Dying gales of sweet even   292
[Dyke Side]   275

Each scene of youth to mes a pleasing toy   38
Eliza now the summer tells   322
Emmonsails Heath in Winter   212, 492 n.
Emmonsales Heath   181, 491 n.
Enough of misery keeps my heart alive   345
Epigram   9
Eternity of Nature, The   165
Evening ('How beautiful the eve comes in')   383
Evening ('It is the silent hour when they who roam,')   358, 495 n.
Evening ('Now grey ey'd hazy eve's begun')   6
Evening Bells   31

Fair was thy bloom when first I met 180
Far from the life of market towns was seen 80
Far spread the moorey ground a level scene 167
[*Farmer's Boy*] 267
Fate of Genius, The 80, 489 n.
[*Fen, The*] 265
Fens, The 238
Fern Owls Nest, The 209
Field Cricket 236
Firetails Nest, The 212
First Love 398
Fixed in a white thorn bush its summer guest 221
Flitting, The 250, 492 n.
Flood, The 193, 492 n.
Flow on Winding River 426
Flow on winding river in silence for ever 426
For fools that would wish to seem learned and wise 9
[*Fox, The*] 245
Fragment 427
From huddling nights embrace how chill 83

Gardeners Bonny Daughter, The 402
Gipseys Camp, The 48
Gipsies Evening Blaze, The 9
Gipsy Camp, The 278, 493 n.
[*'God looks on nature with a glorious eye'*] 336
[*Green Woodpecker's Nest, The*] 271
[*Groundlark, The*] 273

Hail gentle winds I love your murmuring sounds 65
Hail humble Helpstone where thy valies spread 1
Hail scenes of Desolation and despair 11
Happy Bird, The 211
Hares at Play 244
Harvest Morning, The 12
Hay Making 132
Haymaking 339
He loved the brook's soft sound 408
He scampered [to] the bushes far away 245
He turns about to face the loud uproar 247
He waits all day beside his little flock 267
Heath, The 145
Hedge Sparrow 233
[*Hedgehog, The*] 248
Helpston Green 62, 489 n.
Helpstone 1
Her cheeks are like roses 302
Here sparrows built upon the trees 366
Here we meet too soon to part 64
Heres a health unto thee bonny lassie O 301
Heres where Mary loved to be 282
Hesperus 367
Hesperus the day is gone 367

['*High overhead that silent throne*']   241
Home Pictures in May   102
How beautiful is Spring! the sun gleams gold,   356
How beautiful the eve comes in   383
How beautiful the white thorn shews its leaves   382
How fond the rustics ear at leisure dwells   76
How fresh the air the birds how busy now   207
['*How hot the sun rushes*']   379
How oft on Sundays when Id time to tramp   48
How peaceable it seems for lonely men   376
How peaceful sound the chiming bells   423
How pleasing simplest recollections seem   46
How sweet and pleasant grows the way   233
How sweet the wood shades the hot summer hours   109
How sweet when weary dropping on a bank   27
Humble Bee, The   399

'*I Am*' ('I am—yet what I am, none cares or knows;')   361
'*I Am*' ('I feel I am;—I only know I am,')   361
I am—yet what I am, none cares or knows;   361
I' crime and enmity they lie   425
I do not love thee   377
I envy e'en the fly its gleams of joy   422
I feel I am;—I only know I am,   361
I fly from all I prize the most   370
I found a ball of grass among the hay   263
I hid my love when young while I   411
I lost the love, of heaven above;   343
I love it well oercanopied in leaves   183
I love the fitfull gusts that shakes   382
['*I love the little pond to mark at spring*']   334
I love the rath primroses pale brimstone primroses   417
['*I love thee nature with a boundless love*']   378
I love thee sweet mary but love thee in fear   40
I love to hear the evening crows go bye   241
I love to peep out on a summers morn   45
I love to see the old heaths withered brake   212
I love to wander at my idle will   103
I ne'er was struck before that hour   398
I often pause to seek thee when I pass   237
I peeled bits o straws and I got switches too   413
I saw her in my springs young choice   316
I sleep with thee, and wake with thee,   342
I talk to the birds as they sing i' the morn   419
I think of thee at early day   304
I wandered out one rainy day   268
I went my Sunday mornings rounds   393
I wish I was where I would be   411
I would not be a wither'd leaf   374
Idle Hour, An   193
['*I'll come to thee at even tide*']   336, 494 n.
Impulses of Spring   109
In autumn time how oft hes stood to mark   49

In every step we tread appears fresh spring 419
In Green Grassy Places 408, 495 n.
In the cowslips peeps I lye 391
['*In the hedge I pass a little nest*'] 242
In the white thorn hedges the blackbird sings 408
In this cold world without a home 306
In thy wild garb of other times 181
Insects 189
Invitation, The 354
Invite to Eternity, An 351
It is the evening hour, 341
It is the silent hour when they who roam, 358
Ive left my own old home of homes 250
Ive often on a sabbath day 190
['*Ive ran the furlongs to thy door*'] 261
I've wandered many a weary mile 281

[*Joys of Youth*] 46
June 135
Just as the even bell rung we set out 41
Just by the wooden brig a bird flew up 230

['*Know God is every where*'] 410

Labours Leisure 194
Lady Flye, The 130
Ladybird, The 404
Ladybird ladybird where art thou gone E're the daisy was open or the rose it was
    spread 404
Lament, A 346
[*Lament of Swordy Well, The*] 147, 491 n.
Lamentations of Round-Oak Waters, The 18, 488 n.
Landrail, The 233
Langley Bush 30, 488 n.
Larks and Spring 371
Last of March, The 93, 490 n.
Leaves from eternity are simple things 165
Let us go in the fields love and see the green tree 354
Lines on 'Cowper' 409, 496 n.
Little Trotty Wagtail 401, 495 n.
Little trotty wagtail he went in the rain 401
Lone occupiers of a naked sky 208
['*Look through the naked bramble and black thorn*'] 334, 494 n.
['*Lord hear my prayer when trouble glooms*'] 327, 494 n.
Love and Memory 187
Love lives beyond 363
Love meet me in the green glen 418
Lovely Mary when we parted 288
Lover of swamps 205
Love's Pains 338
Loves Story 377

Maiden-haid, A
Many are poets—though they use no pen   18
Maple Tree, The   279
March Nightingale, The   423
[Marten, The]   210
Mary   244
Mary Helen from the Hill   341
Maytime is in the meadows coming in   424
Meadow Grass, The   120
Meet Me in the Green Glen   200
Meeting, The   418
Mist in the Meadows   64, 489 n.
Moorehens Nest, The   195
Mores, The   219
Morning   167
[Morris Dancers]   352
[Mouse's Nest, The]   269
Muse of the Fields oft have I said farewell   263
My Early Home was This   104
My Mary   366, 495 n.
                                                                   59, 489 n.

Nightingale, The   355
Nightingales Nest, The   213
No single hour can stand for nought   293
None but true anglers feel that gush of joy   197
Noon   24, 488 n.
[Noon]   65
November ('Sybil of months and worshiper of winds')   130
[November] ('The shepherds almost wonder where they dwell')   266
November ('The village sleeps in mist from morn till noon')   139
Now evening comes and from the new laid hedge   132
Now grey ey'd hazy eve's begun   6
Now sallow catkins once all downy white   210
Now sport the waterflyes with tiny wings   198
Now summer is in flower and natures hum   135
Now swathy summer by rude health embrownd   124
Now that the year grows wearisome with age   174
Now with the rivers brink he winds his way   197
[Nuthatch, The]   276
Nutting   131

['O could I be as I have been']   396
O dear to us ever the scenes of our childhood   394
O for a pleasant book to cheat the sway   198
O for that sweet untroubled rest   362
O for the feelings and the carless health   194
O I love the dear wild and the outstretching heath   145
O it was a lorn and a dismal night   191
O Langley bush the shepherds sacred shade   30
O Love is so decieving   338
O Mary dear three springs have been   297
O Mary sing thy songs to me   288
O poesy is on the waine   256

O poesys power thou overpowering sweet   219
O soul enchanting poesy   153
O wert thou in the storm   340
Old Elm that murmured in our chimney top   96
Old stone pits all with ivy overhung   169
Old Willow, The   113
On Lolham Brigs in wild and lonely mood   193
On Seeing Two Swallows Late in October   208
On sunday mornings freed from hard employ   74
[On Taste]   45
On[e] almost sees the hermit from the wood   200
One day accross the fields I chancd to pass   276
One day when all the woods where bare and blea   268
One gloomy eve I roamd about   47
Oppress'd wi' grief a double share   18
Out of Door Pleasures   349

Pale sun beams gleam   334
Parish, The   98, 490 n.
[Partridge, The]   276
Partridge Coveys   232
[Partridge's Nest, The]   277
Pasture, The   203
[Pally]   66
Peartree Lane, The   405, 495 n.
Peasant Poet, The   408
Peggy Band   191, 491 n.
Perplexities   419
Pe[ti]tioners are full of prayers   147
Pettichaps Nest, The   229
Pleasant Places   169
'Poets are born'—and so are whores—the trade is   318
Pretty Swallow once again   401
Primroses   417
Progress of Ryhme, The   153, 491 n.
Proposals for Building a Cottage   27
[Puddock's Nest, The]   272, 493 n.

[Quail's Nest]   268

Ravens Nest, The   218
Rawk o' the Autumn, The   421
Reccolections after a Ramble   52
Recolections of Home   386
Recollections after an Evening Walk   41
Red Robin, The   403
Reed Bird, The   235
Remembrances   258, 492 n.
Right cautious now his strongest line to take   197
Right happy bird so full of mirth   216
Robins Nest, The   223
[Rook's Nest]   274
Round Oak, The   367, 495 n.

Rural Evening 70
Rural Morning 66, 489 n.
Rustic Fishing 74

Sabbath Bells 190
St Martins Eve 174, 491 n.
Sand Martin 208
Sauntering at ease I often love to lean 193
Say What Is Love—To Live In Vain 309
Scene, A 11
Second Adress to the Rose Bud in Humble Life 43
Sedge Birds Nest 221
Setting Sun, The 6
Shades tho yere leafless save the bramble spear 28
Shadows of Taste 170, 491 n.
She tied up her few things 412
[*Sheep in Winter*] 263
Shepherd Boy, The 390
Shepherd's Calendar, The: June 135, 491 n.
Shepherd's Calendar, The: November 139
[*Showers*] 200
Signs of Winter 195
Silent Love 376
Simple enchantress, wreathd in summer blooms 92
Sky Lark, The 215
Sky Lark Leaving Her Nest, The 216
Sleep of Spring 362
Snow Storm 199
So moping flat and low our valleys lie 146
Some Days Before the Spring 364
Some keep a baited badger tame as hog 247
Song ('A seaboy on the giddy mast') 347, 495 n.
Song ('And wheres there a scene more delightfully seeming') 47
Song ('I fly from all I prize the most') 370
Song ('I hid my love when young while I') 411
Song ('I peeled bits o straws and I got switches too') 413
Song ('I went my Sunday mornings rounds') 393
Song ('I wish I was where I would be') 411
Song ('I would not be a wither'd leaf') 374
Song ('Love lives beyond') 363
Song ('O Love is so decieving') 338
Song ('O wert thou in the storm') 340, 495 n.
Song ('One gloomy eve I roamd about') 47, 489 n.
Song ('She tied up her few things') 412
Song ('Swamps of wild rush beds and sloughs squashy traces') 46
Song ('The autumns come again') 385
Song ('The bird cherrys white in the dews o' the morning') 332
Song ('The daiseys golden eye') 347
Song ('The rain is come in misty showers') 381
Song ('Tis evening the sky is one broad dim of gray') 380
Song Last Day 330
Songs Eternity 122
Sonnet ('Enough of misery keeps my heart alive') 345

Sonnet ('How beautiful the white thorn shews its leaves')   382
Sonnet ('The flag top quivers in the breeze,')   349
Sonnet ('The silver mist more lowly swims')   352
Sonnet: 'I Am'   361
Sonnet: The Crow   376
Sonnet: The Nightingale   355
Sonnet: Wood Anemonie   375
Soon as the twilight thro the distant mist   66
Sport in the Meadows   120
Spring ('How beautiful is Spring! the sun gleams gold,')   356
Spring ('In every step we tread appears fresh spring')   419
Spring ('Pale sun beams gleam')   334
Spring ('The sweet spring now is come'ng')   328, 494 n.
['Spring comes and it is may—white as are sheets']   337
Spring Wind   388
[Squirrel's Nest, The]   268
Stanzas   359
[Stone Pit]   270
[Storm in the Fens]   264
Sudden Shower   102
[Summer]   27
[Summer Evening]   14
Summer Images   124
['Summer is on the earth and in the sky']   331
[Summer Morning]   45
Summer morning is risen   279
Summer pleasures they are gone like to visions every one   258
Summer Shower, The   183
Sunday Walks   76
Swallow, The   401
Swamps of wild rush beds and sloughs squashy traces   46
Sweet chesnuts brown, like soleing leather turn,   414
Sweet days while God your blessings send   290
Sweet little Bird in russet coat   225
Sweet little minstrel of the sunny summer   236
Sweet the merry bells ring round   31
Sweet twilight, nurse of dews   368
Sweet unasuming Minstrel not to thee   108
Sweet uncultivated blossom   10
['Swift goes the sooty swallow o'er the heath']   391, 495 n.
Sybil of months and worshiper of winds   130
Syren of sullen moods and fading hues   161

Taste is from heaven   45
Taste with as many hues doth hearts engage   170
Tennant of leaves and flowers and glossy stalks   130
That good old fame the farmers earnd of yore   98
That summer bird its oft repeated note   213
The Apple top't oak in the old narrow lane   367
The autumn day it fades away,   348
The Autumn wind on suthering wings   372
The autumns come again   385
The badger grunting on his woodland track   246

The beating snow clad bell wi sounding dead   32
The bird cherrys white in the dews o' the morning   332
The birds are gone to bed the cows are still   244
The Blackbird Has Built In The Pasture Agen   312
The blackbird is a bonny bird   365
The cat runs races with her tail—the dog   196
The chaffinch in the hedge row sings In the brown naked thorn   402
The corncraik rispt her summer call Just as the sun went down   404
The crib stock fothered—horses suppered up   199
The crow sat on the willow tree   406
The crow will tumble up and down   222
The daiseys golden eye   347
The day is all round me the woods and the fields   349
['The dew drops on every blade of grass']   413
The dew it trembles on the thorn   376
The dreary fen a waste of water goes   265
The droneing bee has wakened up,   343
The Elm tree's heavy foliage meets the eye   427
['The Even comes and the Crow flies low']   410
The evening oer the meadow seems to stoop   195
The fire tail tells the boys when nests are nigh   242
The fitful weather changes every hour   200
The flag top quivers in the breeze,   349
The f[l]aggy forrest beat the billows breast   264
The flaggy wheat is in the ear   424
The floods come oer the meadow leas   303
The fly or beetle on their track   390
The frighted women takes the boys away   247
The frog croaks loud and maidens dare not pass   275
The frolicksome wind through the trees and the bushes   392
The green woodpecker flying up and down   271
The happy white throat on the sweeing bough   211
The heavens are wrath—the thunders rattling peal   285
The hedgehog hides beneath the rotten hedge   248
['The hoar frost lodges on every tree']   262, 493 n.
The idle turkey gobbling half the day   274
The juicey wheat now spindles into ear   113
The landscapes stretching view that opens wide   11
The Maple with its tassell flowers of green   423
The martin cat long shaged of courage good   244
The martin hurrys through the woodland gaps   245
The mid day hour of twelve the clock counts oer   65
The mist lies on the weeds but clears away   266
The morn is still and balmy all that moves   196
The morning comes—the drops of dew   352
The mower tramples on the wild bees nest   264
['The old pond full of flags and fenced around']   275
The partridge makes no nest but on the ground   277
The passer bye oft stops his horse to look   276
The passing traveller with wonder sees   270
The past it is a magic word   113
The pewet is come to the green   203
The rain is come in misty showers   381

The rawk o' the Autumn hangs over the woodlands 421
['*The red bagged bee on never weary wing*'] 331
The river rambles like a snake 397
The rolls and harrows lies at rest beside 215
The rooks begin to build and pleasant looks 274
The Rose Of The World Was Dear Mary To Me 313
The rosey day was sweet and young 52
The sailing puddock sweeps about for prey 272
['*The schoolboys in the morning soon as drest*'] 271
['*The seeding done the fields are still at morn*'] 263
The sheep get up and make their many tracks 263
The shepherd musing oer his summer dreams 108
The shepherd on his journey heard when nigh 245
The shepherds almost wonder where they dwell 266
The silver mist more lowly swims 352
The sinken sun is takin leave 14
The small wind wispers thro the leafless hedge 96
The snow falls deep; the Forest lies alone: 278
The spring is come forth, but no spring is for me, 359
The spring may forget that he reigns in the sky 293
The sun had stooped his westward clouds to win 131
The sun has gone down with a veil on his brow 280
The sun looks from a cloudy sky, 346
The sun now sinks behind the woodland green 70
The sunny end of March is nigh 371
The sunshine bathes in clouds of many hues 102
The sweet spring now is come'ng 328
The tame hedge sparrow in its russet dress 233
The thistle down's flying Though the winds are all still 405
['*The thunder mutters louder and more loud*'] 333
The turkeys wade the close to catch the bees 273
The village sleeps in mist from morn till noon 139
The Water Lilies, white and yellow flowers, 278
The weary woodman rocking home beneath 209
The wild duck startles like a sudden thought 267
['*The wind blows happily on every thing*'] 335
The wind blows the trees about 388
The winter comes I walk alone 374
The wood anemonie through dead oak leaves 375
The woodlark rises from the coppice tree 235
['*There is a charm in Solitude that cheers*'] 390
There is a day a dreadfull day 330
There is a small woodpecker red and grey 272
There's a gladness of heart in the first days of Spring 364
There's places in our village streets 405
These childern of the sun which summer brings 121
They near read the heart 294
This is the month, the Nightingale, clod-brown, 355
This love, I canna' bear it, 338
This scene how beautious to the musing mind 6
Thou art gone the dark journey 187
Thou hermit haunter of the lonely glen 208
Thou lowly cot where first my breath I drew 43

Thou tiney loiterer on the barleys beard   189
Though o'er the darksome northern hill   93
Thourt dearest to my bosom   305
Thrushes Nest, The   210
Tis autumn now and natures scenes   298
Tis evening the sky is one broad dim of gray   380
Tis hay-time and the red complexioned sun   132
['*Tis martinmass from rig to rig*']   326, 494 n.
Tis Spring warm glows the South   427
Tis winter plain the images around   195
To a Fallen Elm   96
To a Rose Bud in Humble Life   10
To a Winter Scene   11
To John Clare   427, 496 n.
To Mary   342
To me, how wildly pleasing is that scene   9
To my Cottage   43
To P * * * *   180
To see the Arum early shoot   387
To the Lark   344
To the Rural Muse ('Muse of the Fields oft have I said farewell')   104
To the Rural Muse ('Simple enchantress, wreathd in summer blooms')   92
To the Snipe   205, 492 n.
To the Winds   65
True as the church clock hand the hour pursues   133
[*Turkeys*]   273
Tweet pipes the robin as the cat creeps bye   212
Twilight   368

Under the twigs the blackcap hangs in vain   232
Up this green woodland ride lets softly rove   213
Upon an edding in a quiet nook   231
Upon the collar of an hugh old oak   218

Village Minstrel, The   49, 489 n.
Vision, A   343
[*Vixen, The*]   248

Wandering by the rivers edge   238
Water Lilies, The   278, 493 n.
Waves trough—rebound—and fury boil again   194
We'll walk among the tedded hay,   357
Well honest John how fare you now at home   427
Well in my many walks I rarely found   229
What is Life?   26
What is songs eternity   122
What time the wheat field tinges rusty brown   103
Wheat Ripening, The   103
When lifes tempests blow high   399
When midnight comes a host of dogs and men   246
When shall I see the white thorn leaves agen   417
When we stray far away from the old pleasant village   386
Where the dark ivy the thorn tree is mounting   91

Who lives where Beggars rarley speed?   59
Whose wrecky stains dart on the floods away   194
Why are ye silent   415
Why is the cuckoos melody preferred   211
Wild Bees   121
[*Wild Bees' Nest*]   264
Wild delight of fairest feature   43
[*Wild Duck's Nest*]   270
Wild Flowers   353
Wilt thou go with me sweet maid   351
Wind, The   392, 495 n.
Winter ('From huddling nights embrace how chill')   83
Winter ('The small wind wispers thro the leafless hedge')   96
Winter Evening   199
Winter Fields   198
[*Winter in the Fens*]   146
Winter is come in earnest and the snow   199
Winter winds cold and blea   29
Winters Come, The   414, 496 n.
Winters Spring, The   374
['*With hook tucked neath his arm that now and then*']   267
Within a thick and spreading awthorn bush   210
Woman had we Never Met   421
Wood Anemonie   375
[*Woodland Thoughts*]   109
Woodlarks Nest, The   235
Woodman, The ('Now evening comes and from the new laid hedge')   132
Woodman, The ('The beating snow clad bell wi sounding dead')   32, 489 n.
[*Woodpecker's Nest*]   272
Wren, The   211
Written in November   44
Written in Prison   422
Wrynecks Nest, The   213

Ye injur'd fields ere while so gay   62
Ye swampy falls of pasture ground,   66
Yellow Wagtails Nest, The   231
Yellowhammer, The   417
Yellowhammers Nest, The   230
Yet chance will somtimes prove a faithless guest   236

PROSE

[*Apology for the Poor*]   445, 501 n.
[*Autobiographical Passages*]   429, 496 n.
['*Blackbirds and Thrushes*']   460
['*Every farmer is growing into an orator*']   448, 501 n.
[*Farmer and the Vicar, The*]   438, 498 n.
[*Grammar*]   481, 504 n.
[*Hunting Pooty Shells*]   477
['. . . *I fear these tory radicals*']   450
['*I have often been amused with the manners*']   462
['*I never meddle with politics*']   448

['I say what good has been yet done']   449
['I took a walk']   474, 503 n.
['I went to take my walk to day']   455, 502 n.
['If the nessesitys of the poor']   447
['It has been often asserted that young frogs']   459
[Journey out of Essex]   432, 496 n.
[Knowledge]   482
[Letter to Messrs Taylor and Hessey]   453, 502 n.; 457, 502 n.; 467; 471, 503 n.
[Letter to William Hone]   483, 504 n.
[Life Peerages]   482
['long speeches']   449
[More Signs of Spring]   465, 502 n.
[Nature Notes]   452, 502 n.
[Poor Man Versus the Rich Man, The]   450, 501 n.
[Signs of Spring]   463, 502 n.
['Swallows']   460, 502 n.
[Taste]   479
['The country people here distinguish']   460, 502 n.
['The little Robin']   469, 503 n.
['These out of place patriots']   449
['When the young of the Nightingale']   461
['When woodpeckers are making or boring']   461